Children's
Literature
Review

Guide to Gale Literary Criticism Series

For criticism on	Consult these Gale series
Authors now living or who died after December 31, 1999	*CONTEMPORARY LITERARY CRITICISM (CLC)*
Authors who died between 1900 and 1999	*TWENTIETH-CENTURY LITERARY CRITICISM (TCLC)*
Authors who died between 1800 and 1899	*NINETEENTH-CENTURY LITERATURE CRITICISM (NCLC)*
Authors who died between 1400 and 1799	*LITERATURE CRITICISM FROM 1400 TO 1800 (LC)* *SHAKESPEAREAN CRITICISM (SC)*
Authors who died before 1400	*CLASSICAL AND MEDIEVAL LITERATURE CRITICISM (CMLC)*
Authors of books for children and young adults	*CHILDREN'S LITERATURE REVIEW (CLR)*
Dramatists	*DRAMA CRITICISM (DC)*
Poets	*POETRY CRITICISM (PC)*
Short story writers	*SHORT STORY CRITICISM (SSC)*
Black writers of the past two hundred years	*BLACK LITERATURE CRITICISM (BLC)* *BLACK LITERATURE CRITICISM SUPPLEMENT (BLCS)*
Hispanic writers of the late nineteenth and twentieth centuries	*HISPANIC LITERATURE CRITICISM (HLC)* *HISPANIC LITERATURE CRITICISM SUPPLEMENT (HLCS)*
Native North American writers and orators of the eighteenth, nineteenth, and twentieth centuries	*NATIVE NORTH AMERICAN LITERATURE (NNAL)*
Major authors from the Renaissance to the present	*WORLD LITERATURE CRITICISM, 1500 TO THE PRESENT (WLC)* *WORLD LITERATURE CRITICISM SUPPLEMENT (WLCS)*

ISSN 0362-4145

volume 65

Children's Literature Review

Excerpts from Reviews,
Criticism, and Commentary
on Books for Children
and Young People

Jennifer Baise
Editor

GALE GROUP

Detroit
New York
San Francisco
London
Boston
Woodbridge, CT

STAFF

Lynn M. Spampinato, Janet Witalec, *Managing Editors, Literature Product*
Kathy D. Darrow, *Product Liaison*
Jennifer Baise, *Editor*
Mark W. Scott, *Publisher, Literature Product*

Thomas Ligotti, *Associate Editor*
Patti A. Tippett, *Technical Training Specialist*
Deborah J. Morad, Kathleen Lopez Nolan, *Managing Editors*
Susan M. Trosky, *Director, Literature Content*

Maria L. Franklin, *Permissions Manager*
Edna Hedblad, *Permissions Associate*
Julie Juengling, *Permissions Assistant*

Victoria B. Cariappa, *Research Manager*
Tracie A. Richardson, *Project Coordinator*
Tamara C. Nott, *Research Associate*
Sarah Genik, Timothy Lehnerer, Ron Morelli, *Research Assistants*

Dorothy Maki, *Manufacturing Manager*
Stacy L. Melson, *Buyer*

Mary Beth Trimper, *Manager, Composition and Electronic Prepress*
Carolyn Fischer, *Composition Specialist*

Michael Logusz, *Graphic Artist*
Randy Bassett, *Imaging Supervisor*
Robert Duncan, Dan Newell, *Imaging Specialists*
Pamela A. Reed, *Imaging Coordinator*
Kelly A. Quin, *Editor, Image and Multimedia Content*

Library of Congress Catalog Card Number 76-643301
ISBN 0-7876-4571-0
ISSN 0362-4145
Printed in the United States of America

10 9 8 7 6 5 4 3 2 1

Contents

Preface vii

Acknowledgments xi

Preface

Literature for children and young adults has evolved into both a respected branch of creative writing and a successful industry. Currently, books for young readers are considered among the most popular segments of publishing. Criticism of juvenile literature is instrumental in recording the literary or artistic development of the creators of children's books as well as the trends and controversies that result from changing values or attitudes about young people and their literature. Designed to provide a permanent, accessible record of this ongoing scholarship, *Children's Literature Review* (*CLR*) presents parents, teachers, and librarians—those responsible for bringing children and books together—with the opportunity to make informed choices when selecting reading materials for the young. In addition, *CLR* provides researchers of children's literature with easy access to a wide variety of critical information from English-language sources in the field. Users will find balanced overviews of the careers of the authors and illustrators of the books that children and young adults are reading; these entries, which contain excerpts from published criticism in books and periodicals, assist users by sparking ideas for papers and assignments and suggesting supplementary and classroom reading. Ann L. Kalkhoff, president and editor of *Children's Book Review Service Inc.,* writes that "*CLR* has filled a gap in the field of children's books, and it is one series that will never lose its validity or importance."

Scope of the Series

Each volume of *CLR* profiles the careers of a selection of authors and illustrators of books for children and young adults from preschool through high school. Author lists in each volume reflect:

- an international scope

- representation of authors of all eras

- the variety of genres covered by children's and/or YA literature: picture books, fiction, nonfiction, poetry, folklore, and drama

Although the focus of the series is on authors new to *CLR,* entries will be updated as the need arises.

Organization of the Book

A *CLR* entry consists of the following elements:

- The **Author Heading** consists of the author's name followed by birth and death dates. The portion of the name outside the parentheses denotes the form under which the author is most frequently published. If the author wrote consistently under a pseudonym, the pseudonym will be listed in the author heading and the author's actual name given in parentheses on the first line of the biographical and critical information. Also located here are any name variations under which an author wrote, including transliterated forms for authors whose native languages use non-roman alphabets. Uncertain birth or death dates are indicated by question marks.

- A **Portrait of the Author** is included when available.

- The **Author Introduction** contains information designed to introduce an author to *CLR* users by presenting an overview of the author's themes and styles, biographical facts that relate to the author's literary career or critical responses to the author's works, and information about major awards and prizes the author has received. The introduction begins by identifying the nationality of the author and by listing genres in which s/he has written for children and young adults. Introductions also list a group of representative titles for which the author or illustrator being profiled is best known; this section, which begins with the words "major works include," follows the genre line of the introduction. For seminal figures, a listing of major works about the author follows when appropriate, highlighting important biographies about the author or illustrator that are not excerpted in the entry. The centered heading "Introduction" announces the body of the text.

- **Criticism** is located in three sections: **Author Commentary** (when available), **General Commentary** (when available), and **Title Commentary** (commentary on specific titles).

  The **Author Commentary** presents background material written by the author or by an interviewer. This commentary may cover a specific work or several works. Author commentary on more than one work appears after the author introduction, while commentary on an individual book follows the title entry heading.

  The **General Commentary** consists of critical excerpts that consider more than one work by the author or illustrator being profiled. General commentary is preceded by the critic's name in boldface type or, in the case of unsigned criticism, by the title of the journal. *CLR* also features entries that emphasize general criticism on the oeuvre of an author or illustrator. When appropriate, a selection of reviews is included to supplement the general commentary.

  The **Title Commentary** begins with the title entry headings, which precede the criticism on a title and cite publication information on the work being reviewed. Title headings list the title of the work as it appeared in its first English-language edition. The first English-language publication date of each work (unless otherwise noted) is listed in parentheses following the title. Differing U.S. and British titles follow the publication date within parentheses. When a work is written by an individual other than the one being profiled, as is the case when illustrators are featured, the parenthetical material following the title cites the author of the work before listing its publication date.

  Entries in each title commentary section consist of critical excerpts on the author's individual works, arranged chronologically by publication date. The entries generally contain two to seven reviews per title, depending on the stature of the book and the amount of criticism it has generated. The editors select titles that reflect the entire scope of the author's literary contribution, covering each genre and subject. An effort is made to reprint criticism that represents the full range of each title's reception, from the year of its initial publication to current assessments. Thus, the reader is provided with a record of the author's critical history. Publication information (such as publisher names and book prices) and parenthetical numerical references (such as footnotes or page and line references to specific editions of works) have been deleted at the discretion of the editors to provide smoother reading of the text.

- A complete **Bibliographical Citation** of the original essay or book precedes each piece of criticism.

- Selected excerpts are preceded by brief **Annotations,** which provide information on the critic or work of criticism to enhance the reader's understanding of the excerpt.

- Numerous **Illustrations** are featured in *CLR*. For entries on illustrators, an effort has been made to include illustrations that reflect the characteristics discussed in the criticism. Entries on authors who do not illustrate their own works may include photographs and other illustrative material pertinent to their careers.

Special Features: Entries on Illustrators

Entries on authors who are also illustrators will occasionally feature commentary on selected works illustrated but not written by the author being profiled. These works are strongly associated with the illustrator and have received critical acclaim for their art. By including critical comment on works of this type, the editors wish to provide a more complete representation of the artist's career. Criticism on these works has been chosen to stress artistic, rather than literary, contributions. Title entry headings for works illustrated by the author being profiled are arranged chronologically within the entry by date of publication and include notes identifying the author of the illustrated work. In order to provide easier access for users, all titles illustrated by the subject of the entry are boldfaced.

CLR also includes entries on prominent illustrators who have contributed to the field of children's literature. These entries are designed to represent the development of the illustrator as an artist rather than as a literary stylist. The illustrator's section is organized like that of an author, with two exceptions: the introduction presents an overview of the illustrator's styles and techniques rather than outlining his or her literary background, and the commentary written by the illustrator on his or her works is called "Illustrator's Commentary" rather than "Author's Commentary." All titles of books containing illustrations by the artist being profiled are highlighted in boldface type.

Indexes

A **Cumulative Author Index** lists all of the authors who have appeared in *CLR* with cross-references to the biographical, autobiographical, and literary criticism series published by the Gale Group. A complete list of these sources is found facing the first page of the Author Index. The index also includes birth and death dates and cross-references between pseudonyms and actual names.

A **Cumulative Nationality Index** lists all authors featured in *CLR* by nationality, followed by the number of the *CLR* volume in which their entry appears.

A **Cumulative Title Index** lists all author titles covered in *CLR*. Each title is followed by the author's name and corresponding volume and page numbers where commentary on the work is located.

Citing *Children's Literature Review*

When writing papers, students who quote directly from any volume in the Literary Criticism Series may use the following general format to footnote reprinted criticism. The first example pertains to material drawn from periodicals, the second to material reprinted from books.

Cynthia Zarin, "It's Easy Being Green," *The New York Times Book Review* (November 14, 1993): 48; excerpted and reprinted in *Children's Literature Review,* vol. 58, ed. Deborah J. Morad (Farmington Hills, Mich: The Gale Group, 2000), 57.

Paul Walker, *Speaking of Science Fiction: The Paul Walker Interviews,* (Luna Publications, 1978), 108-20; excerpted and reprinted in *Children's Literature Review,* vol. 58, ed. Deborah J. Morad (Farmington Hills, Mich: The Gale Group, 2000), 3-8.

Suggestions are Welcome

In response to various suggestions, several features have been added to *CLR* since the beginning of the series, including author entries on retellers of traditional literature as well as those who have been the first to record oral tales and other folklore; entries on prominent illustrators featuring commentary on their styles and techniques; entries on authors whose works are considered controversial; occasional entries devoted to criticism on a single work or a series of works; sections in author introductions that list major works by and about the author or illustrator being profiled; explanatory notes that provide information on the critic or work of criticism to enhance the usefulness of the excerpt; more extensive illustrative material, such as holographs of manuscript pages and photographs of people and places pertinent to the careers of the authors and artists; a cumulative nationality index for easy access to authors by nationality; and occasional guest essays written specifically for *CLR* by prominent critics on subjects of their choice.

Readers who wish to suggest new features, topics, or authors to appear in future volumes, or who have other suggestions or comments are cordially invited to call, write, or fax the Managing Editor:

Managing Editor, Literary Criticism Series
The Gale Group
27500 Drake Road
Farmington Hills, MI 48331-3535
1-800-347-4253 (GALE)
Fax: 248-699-8054

Acknowledgments

The editors wish to thank the copyright holders of the excerpted criticism included in this volume and the permissions managers of many book and magazine publishing companies for assisting us in securing reproduction rights. We are also grateful to the staffs of the Detroit Public Library, the Library of Congress, the University of Detroit Mercy Library, Wayne State University Purdy/Kresge Library Complex, and the University of Michigan Libraries for making their resources available to us. Following is a list of the copyright holders who have granted us permission to reproduce material in this volume of *CLR*. Every effort has been made to trace copyright, but if omissions have been made, please let us know.

COPYRIGHTED EXCERPTS IN *CLR*, VOLUME 65, WERE REPRODUCED FROM THE FOLLOWING PERIODICALS:

ALAN Review, v. 11, Spring, 1994. Reproduced by permission.—*The American Spectator,* v. 28, July, 1995. Copyright © The American Spectator 1995. Reproduced by permission of the publisher.—*Black American Literature Forum,* v. 18, Summer, 1984. Copyright © 1984 by the author. Reproduced by permission of the publisher and the author.—*The Black Scholar,* April, 1986. Copyright 1986 by *The Black Scholar.* Reproduced by permission.—*The Book Report,* v. 11, September, 1992. © copyright 1992 by Linworth Publishing, Inc., Worthington, Ohio. Reproduced by permission.—*Bookbird,* v. 5, 1967. Reproduced by permission.—*Booklist,* v. 72, February 15, 1976; v. 72, June 1, 1976; v. 75, September 1, 1978; v. 75, April 1, 1979; v. 79, February 15, 1983; v. 82, January 15, 1986; v. 83, February 1, 1987; v. 83, August, 1987; v. 84, October 15, 1987; v. 84, April 15, 1988; v. 84, June 15, 1988; v. 85, October 15, 1988; v. 85, May 1, 1989; v. 86, March 15, 1990; v. 87, November 15, 1990; v. 87, June 1, 1991; v. 88, March 15, 1992; v. 88, June 15, 1992; v. 89, November 1, 1992; v. 89, April 15, 1993; v. 90, September 15, 1993; v. 90, November 15, 1993; v. 90, March 1, 1994; v. 91, April 15, 1995; v. 92, September 1, 1995; v. 92, January 1, 1996; v. 92, April 15, 1996; v. 92, May 1, 1996; v. 92, June 1, 1996; v. 93, October 1, 1996; v. 93, February 15, 1997; v. 94, April, 1998; v. 95, September 1, 1998; v. 95, November 1, 1998; v. 95, November 15, 1998; v. 95, January 1, 1999. Copyright 1976, 1978, 1979, 1983, 1986, 1987, 1988, 1989, 1990, 1991, 1992, 1993, 1994, 1995, 1996, 1997, 1998, 1999 by American Library Association. All reproduced by permission.—*Books for Keeps,* n. 58, September, 1989; n. 75, July, 1992; n. 85, March, 1994; n. 86, May, 1994; n. 96, January, 1996; n. 103, March, 1997; n. 104, May, 1997; n. 106, September, 1997; n. 110, May, 1998; n. 112, September, 1998. © School Bookshop Association 1989, 1992, 1994, 1996, 1997, 1998. All reproduced by permission.—*Books for Your Children,* v. 11, Spring, 1976; v. 13, Winter, 1977; v. 14, Autumn, 1979; v. 17, Summer, 1982; v. 20, Spring, 1985; v. 23, Summer, 1988; v. 24, Autumn-Winter, 1989; v. 28, Autumn-Winter, 1993; v. 30, Spring, 1995. © *Books For Your Children* 1976, 1977, 1979, 1982, 1985, 1988, 1989, 1993, 1995. All reproduced by permission.—*Books Magazine,* v. 11, July 8, 1997. Reproduced by permission.—*The Bulletin of the Center for Children's Books,* v. 29, May, 1976; v. 29, June, 1976; v. 32, April, 1979; v. 34, October, 1980; v. 38, January, 1985; v.38, September, 1985. v. 41, January, 1988; v. 41, May, 1988; v. 43, October, 1989. Copyright © 1976, 1979, 1980, 1985, 1988, 1989 by The University of Chicago. All reproduced by permission./ v. 45, June, 1992; v. 46, February, 1993; v. 46, May, 1993; v. 50, December, 1996; v. 50, June, 1997. Copyright © 1992, 1993, 1996, 1997 by The Board of Trustees of the University of Illinois. All reproduced by permission.—*Callaloo,* v. 20, 1987. © 1987 Charles H. Rowell. Reproduced by permission of the John Hopkins University Press.—*Children's Book Review,* v. VI, October, 1976. © 1976 Five Owls Press Ltd. All rights reserved. Reproduced by permission.—*Children's Book Review Service Inc.,* v. 8, August, 1980; v. 20, Spring, 1992. Copyright © 1980, 1992 Children's Book Review Service Inc. Both reproduced by permission.—*Children's Literature Association Quarterly,* v. 13, Winter, 1988. © 1988 Children's Literature Association. Reproduced by permission.—*Children's literature in education,* v. 13, Winter, 1982 for "Kim" by Rosemary Sutcliff. Copyright © Agathon Press, Inc. Reproduced by permission of Plenum Publishing Corporation and the author.—*The Christian Science Monitor,* v. 68, July 1, 1976; v. 80, December 3, 1987; v. 80, May 6, 1988. © 1976, 1987, 1988 The Christian Science Publishing Society. All rights reserved. Reproduced by permission from *The Christian Science Monitor.*—*Encounter,* v. VIII, April, 1957. © 1957 by Encounter Ltd. Reproduced by permission.—*English Journal,* v. 77, April, 1988 for a review of "Dawn" by Elizabeth A. Belden and Judith M. Beckman. Copyright © 1988 by the National Council of Teachers of English. Reproduced by permission of the publisher and the authors—*Extrapolation,* v. 23, Spring, 1982. Copyright © 1982 by The Kent State University Press. Reproduced by permission.—*Fantasy & Science Fiction,* v. 58, February, 1980; v. 67, August, 1984. Copyright © 1979, 1984 by Mercury Press, Inc. All rights reserved. Both reproduced by permission.—*Growing Point,* v. 6, November, 1967 for a review of "The Wish Cat" by Margery Fisher; v. 14, November, 1975 for a review of "Tell Me a Tale" by Margery Fisher; v. 11, December, 1975 for a review of "The Island Sunrise" by Margery Fisher; v. 15, September, 1976 for a review of "Unleaving" by Margery Fisher; v. 15, April, 1977 for a review of "Tell Me Another Tale" by Margery Fisher; v. 16, November, 1977 for a

COPYRIGHTED EXCERPTS IN *CLR*, VOLUME 65, WERE REPRODUCED FROM THE FOLLOWING BOOKS:

PHOTOGRAPHS APPEARING IN *CLR*, VOLUME 65, WERE RECEIVED FROM THE FOLLOWING SOURCES:

Octavia E. Butler
1947-

(Full name Octavia Estelle Butler) American novelist.

Major works include *Patternmaster* (1976), *Kindred* (1979), *Bloodchild* (1984), *Dawn: Xenogenesis* (1987), and *Parable of the Sower* (1993).

INTRODUCTION

Butler is a science fiction writer whose forays into imaginary, interplanetary universes often touch on social issues in American life. The six novels in her "Patternist" series and the "Xenogenesis" trilogy feature protagonists who are black and female—two rare qualities in a genre dominated by white males. While critics hail the advancement of racial and gender issues in her work, they also praise her abilities as a storyteller and as an architect of alternative, believable universes. Butler's writings appeal to adults and young adults equipped to deal with questions of reproduction and personal identity.

BIOGRAPHICAL INFORMATION

Butler was born and has spent most of her life in southern California. Her father died when she was still a baby, and she grew up in the household of her mother, who worked as a maid, and her grandmother. "I believed I was ugly and stupid, clumsy, and socially hopeless," she once told *Essence* magazine, and much of her youth was spent reading and making up stories. Butler was educated at Pasadena City College, California State, and the University of California at Los Angeles, where she took evening creative writing classes. To support herself, she worked in a variety of jobs including dishwasher and telephone solicitor, experiences that would later evolve into a fictional portrayal in *Kindred* and other of her novels. In 1970, the prolific and influential writer Harlan Ellison introduced Butler to a six-week Clarion Science Fiction Writer's Workshop. She sold her first two stories, and thus began a groundbreaking career that would lead to numerous awards in the genre and a MacArthur Foundation Genius Grant in 1995.

MAJOR WORKS

By 1975, writing was Butler's full-time job, and her first novel, *Patternmaster* emerged from the stories she had written as a girl. In this and the other novels in the Patternist series, a 4,000-year-old Nubian spirit occupies a succession of human bodies and generates offspring with telepathic abilities. These are the Patternists, and they exist alongside two other groups of beings: the Clayarks are humans who have been mutated by a galactic disease; the Missionaries of Humanity are a religious group opposed to mutation. *Survivor*, the third novel in the series, adds two more warring tribes, the Gharkohn and Tehkohn. Kohns can change their color, but they nonetheless identify one another by their true or original colors, which determine social status. The narrative travels back and forth in history to relate the saga of these factions, and the differences between them are often interpreted as commentary on issues of race and gender in modern American society.

Kindred, a dark, time-travel fantasy, emerged from Butler's ambition "to write a novel that would make others feel the history: the fear and pain that black people have had to live through in order to endure." The novel's protagonist is a young black woman, Dana, newly married and living in modern day Los Angeles, who is repeatedly thrust back to the Antebellum South whenever the life of a man named Rufus is in jeopardy. Rufus, a cruel and villainous slave owner, is revealed to be Dana's ancestor, and with each successive rescue she comes to question her role as "a black to watch over him in a society that considered blacks subhuman, a woman to watch over him in a society that considered women perennial children." The book's conclusion is a metaphorical indictment of the racism and sexism that continue to afflict society.

The Xenogenesis Trilogy starts with a premise familiar to readers of the science fiction genre: most of the earth's population has been destroyed in a nuclear war, and the survivors must merge with an alien race in order to go on living. In the first installment it is a character named Lilith who must make this difficult decision. Her half-human, half-alien son Akin is the hero of the second book. Jodahs, the hero of the third book, *Imago,* belongs to a "third sex." One reviewer described him as "bizarrely talented, miraculous, deeply alien, yet human as well, both repellent and fascinating—even seductive. The same terms serve to describe *Imago.*"

Butler's novelette *Bloodchild* was first published in *Isaac Asimov's Science Fiction Magazine* in June 1984. The work depicts the conflict between species of different planets as a way of reimagining racial problems in America. A race of human males must bear the children of an alien race. This work earned the most enthusiastic reviews of the author's career, as well as three of the top awards in science fiction, the Nebula, the Hugo, and the Locus.

Butler's later novels, *Parable of the Sower* and *Parable of the Talents,* feature Lauren Olamina and her daughter Larkin as they struggle for personal and political freedoms amidst global conflict in the near future. Recognition of Butler's contribution to the science fiction genre has approximately coincided with her crossover onto the general fiction best-seller list. Her work has been compared to that of Alex Haley and Toni Morrison. It is within the genre, however, that she is most appreciated. Her works are viewed

as part of a tradition that includes the works of her mentor Harlan Ellison, Arthur C. Clarke's *Childhood's End,* and the works of Samuel R. Delany. Like Delany, who is also black, Butler has attracted a readership that extends beyond aficionados of science fiction.

AWARDS

In addition to the Nebula, Hugo, and Locus awards that Butler won for *Bloodchild,* she has received the YWCA Achievement Award for the Creative Arts. In 1995 she became one of the very few science fiction writers to receive a MacArthur Foundation fellowship.

AUTHOR COMMENTARY

Octavia Butler with Frances M. Beal

SOURCE: An interview in *The Black Scholar,* April, 1986, pp. 14-18.

SCHOLAR: Why did you decide to turn your writing skills to the science fiction genre?

BUTLER: I didn't decide to become a science fiction writer. It just happened. I was writing when I was 10 years old. I was writing my own little stories and when I was 12 I was watching a bad science fiction movie and decided that I could write a better story than that. And I turned off the TV and proceeded to try and I've been writing science fiction ever since.

What interested you about science fiction?

The freedom of it; it's potentially the freest genre in existence. It tends to be limited by what people think should be done with it and by what editors think should be done with it, although less now than in the past. In the past, there were editors who didn't really think that sex or women should be mentioned or at least not used other than as rewards for the hero or terrible villainesses.

Blacks were not mentioned without there being any particular reason. Sex was kept out because science fiction began in this country as a genre for young boys. They were either at their girl-hating stage or they had broken out in pimples and had wonderful brains and terrible bodies so they were not wildly beset by the opposite sex.

Some science fiction writers focus on futuristic technological advances and interplanetary plots. Your works, however, often appear to look at the problems of the current society by projecting an alternative ideal society.

I've actually never projected an ideal society. I don't write utopian science fiction because I don't believe that imperfect humans can form a perfect society. I don't really worry about sub-genres or genre really. I write what I have to write and when I finish, I send it off to my publisher and they worry about what genre it falls into.

Now with *Kindred* that was quite a problem. I sent it off to a number of different publishers because it obviously was not science fiction. There's absolutely no science in it. It was the kind of fantasy that nobody had really thought of as fantasy because after all, it doesn't fall into the sword and sorcery or pseudo-medieval and fantasy that everyone expects with a lot of magic being practiced.

One editor thought that it might possibly be converted into a historical romance type of novel. I got all sorts of reaction to it such as, "Well this is awfully good but we don't know what to do with it." So I wound up going back to Doubleday but not to their science fiction section. I wound up going to their general fiction, their mainstream fiction department and being published by them that way. Unfortunately not with as much publicity as I had expected, but at least I was published by them.

Could you briefly explain the plot and conception of your best seller book, **Kindred?**

Kindred is the story of a black woman who is pulled back in time to the antebellum South. She is a woman from the present era who is pulled back and enslaved. She has a long association with a pair of her ancestors—one black and one white.

I wrote this book because I grew up during the sixties—that was the period of my adolescence—and I was involved with the black consciousness raising that was taking place at the time. And I was involved with some people who had gone off the deep end with the generation gap. They would say things like, "I would like to get rid of that older generation that betrayed us. I'm not going to do anything because to start, I would have to kill my parents."

My attitude was what the older generations, not just my mother who had gone through enough for heavens sake, but my grandmother on back had suffered a lot from oppression. They endured experiences that would kill me and would probably kill that guy. He didn't know what he was talking about and there were a great many people who sounded the way he did.

I wanted to deal with my own feelings. My mother was a maid and sometimes she took me to work with her when I was very small and she had no one to stay with me. I used to see her going in back doors, being talked about while she was standing right there and basically being treated like a non-person; something beneath notice, and what was worse, I saw all this.

My mother had almost no education. She was taken out of school at age ten and put to work. Not only that, she had only been in school for a year or two. She was born on a sugar plantation in Louisiana and her mother had no school to send her to. Her mother taught her to read and write, not as well as the school would have but she did the best she could.

So my mother had very little to fall back on. And I could see her later as I grew up. I could see her absorbing more of what she was hearing from the whites than I think even she would have wanted to absorb. I can see from watching her why, for instance, that guy might have thought, "Oh they betrayed us." Without knowing what they had gone through and what it had cost them, some people were making rash judgments.

What are some of the philosophical points that **Kindred** *ends up making?*

Oh I think you would have to read it for yourself. I remember going to a conference in San Diego and having someone read a paper about my work and misinterpreting it badly. I got up and said so. I have the feeling now though that what people get out of my work is worth something even if it wasn't what I intended.

Maybe I should rephrase the question. What were you trying to express?

Various kinds of courage. For instance, there is a woman in the novel who was never called mammy but perhaps she could have been. At a certain point, my character becomes angry at her because she is pushing the other slaves to work. My character says, "Well, they're not getting paid; they are going to get knocked around; why should they work hard?" And the woman says, "Well, do you want to do it? Someone will be made to do it. Do you want to do it? It should be shared if we have to do it." . . . [This woman has] absorbed a lot of the garbage but she is still her own person and she's still doing what she can. She has her own forms of resistance but my character really doesn't see this at first and gradually does come to see this. There's a point in the book when she goes back and forth between the two time periods involuntarily.

Whenever her white ancestor is endangered—and he is a very self-destructive person—she pulls back physically and especially when he's a child, she willingly saves him. Because after all, a child drowning or about to burn to death, you would naturally save the child no matter what color it was.

And later when he's a man and a much less savory person, she saves him because her ancestor has not been born yet. She's not quite sure how these things work, but she is a little afraid. She understands that there is a paradox here. How could everything depend on her. But anyway, she goes on saving him. I've had people come up and ask me why doesn't she just kill him as soon as the ancestor is born.

My attitude when I wrote the book was that TV and movies advertise killing as a very easy thing—how simple to blow somebody away. If it is that easy it shouldn't be, and I didn't want my character to be someone who felt the need to murder somebody. Most of us will never be confronted with that need and the few of us who will be, will generally be confronted by something that demands an immediate decision. He's going to kill you or you are going to kill him. You won't have time to think about it which can be a terrible thing under any circumstances.

Why is science fiction a literary form that black and female writers have not sufficiently explored?

I think part of the reason, as I mentioned earlier, is that science fiction began as a boy's genre. So it was white, it was adolescent and it involved a particular kind of adolescent best described as a nerd. So this did not make it popular with blacks or adults or women for quite a long time.

Later, I think the movies helped advertise it to the kids and helped turn the adults off. For instance, you go to the movies and there are monsters running around. This is science fiction, suitable for someone that is twelve, not to be taken seriously as a literary form.

But slowly people are being drawn in. Some of the bestsellers, I think, have helped to draw people in

who otherwise would never touch science fiction. A lot of the science fiction writers have gotten older, a little bit better accepted and some of them still write very well, and their books bring people in. Science fiction writers come from science fiction readers. I think that as more and more blacks begin to read science fiction, then more blacks will take up writing science fiction, and this is already happening to a certain degree.

Why has there been such an expansion of women writers of science fiction in recent years?

I think that was part of the women's movement. Women were finally asserting their right to write it and define themselves. I think they were sick to death of princesses and witches, which is the kind of role women played in the science fiction I remember when I began.

I came into science fiction when things were opening up for women, when it was okay to notice the fact that the universe wasn't just white or male. So I could write about black women, black heroines and not get anybody upset. I got readers who wrote me letters wondering why there always seemed to be a black person in my work, but most people seemed to either accept it or shut up about it.

Do you think that women find that female writers have brought a different type of perspective to the genre?

I think that they have done a lot for characterization in science fiction. But you can't really talk about "women's science fiction" because there are women writing all kinds of science fiction, from the sword and sorcery to the medieval to hard science fiction to soft science fiction. There is no women's genre in science fiction.

A science fiction writer has the freedom to do absolutely anything. The limits are the imagination of the writer. There are always blacks in the novels I write and whites. In *Quasar* there is a Japanese man and a Mexican woman. In the one I'm working on now there is a Chinese man and a lot of different people are lumped together.

Could you talk a little bit about the work you have in progress now?

I'm working on a trilogy at the present time and the novel that I'm finishing is called *The Training Boar.* It is a story, post Holocaust, of human beings being changed from one generation to another—not entirely human any longer—but human beings who have survived the Holocaust.

They are captured by aliens and this is why they lasted so long as a species. They don't become over-specialized by some conditions. In a way maybe a form of specialization is killing us off now and we don't generally think of it that way. But size may have been a problem with the dinosaurs and we may be about to be killed off by our greatest advantage. My characters are told that human beings have two characteristics that are fine and conducive to the species survival individually, but are a lethal combination.

The first of those characteristics is intelligence and the other is something that can be projected through history—something that keeps showing up in us that has been doing a great deal of harm: It's hierarchical structure/behavior. The combination, because intelligence tends to serve the hierarchical behavior, is what may eventually wipe us out.

Do you think that hierarchical behavior is inborn?

Absolutely. It's not a matter of thinking about it really. I mean look at our closest animal relatives. Look at everything on earth right down to the algae. Two clones of algae are slowly covering Iraq. Eventually only one clone of algae will survive. I mean it's part of life on this planet. So hierarchical behavior is definitely inborn and intelligence is something new that we've come up with and like I said, I happen to think that the combination is lethal.

I think that it doesn't have to be lethal if we deal with it. But unfortunately, the ways in which we tried to deal with it in the past have not really acknowledged the problem. Too often when people start talking about inborn characteristics, they start talking about who shall we eliminate, who has the negative characteristics. And we get to decide what's negative and we get into the eugenics and the real nasty stuff where people use something that could be and is in fact part of behavior science as a reason to put somebody else down to get rid of your enemies, using science for hierarchical purposes.

Do you believe that black writers and their works will become popular to the point where they will be read by everyone and not primarily by blacks?

I'm not read primarily by blacks now strangely enough. Most of my readers are science fiction readers. I don't know. It depends. In this country being black tends to bring out a lot of negative emotions that don't necessarily have anything to do with us.

It's sort of like being Jewish in Nazi Germany. I don't really know if that is the case. It sounds as though it might be. People who are willing to look at all sorts of materials regarding the Holocaust get very upset when they hear anything about what's happened here either during slavery or much more recently during the civil rights movement.

For instance, I think most people don't know or don't realize that at least 10 million blacks were killed just on the way to this country, just during the middle passage. People have a hard enough time believing that. They don't really want to hear it partly because it makes whites feel guilty.

Something that I would like to relate illustrates this. Just an anecdote. Another writer during the first *Star Wars* movie had done a review of the movie, a three-page review of it. He praised it very highly and said very nice things about it. Near the last paragraph, he said that one thing about this movie was that it shows every kind of alien, but there is only one kind or human—white ones; no black people were shown. There are no non-whites at all and where are they. He says that he got three pounds of hate mail.

A lot of the mail said that blacks make us feel uncomfortable. We want to see movies with no blacks in them. And this goes back to something that I heard at a science fiction convention. I was sitting next to the editor of a magazine that no longer exists and he was also doing some science fiction writing. He said that he didn't think that blacks should be included in science fiction stories because they changed the character of the stories; that if you put in a black, all of a sudden the focus is on this person. He stated that if you were going to write about some sort of racial problem, that would be absolutely the only reason he could see for including a black.

He went on to say that well, perhaps you could use an alien instead and get rid of all this messiness and all those people that we don't want to deal with. It reflected his view of black people as being other. There's another anecdote that points up this problem. Several years ago I was trying to put together an anthology of science fiction by and about black people. In the first place nobody would buy it. Most of the stories that we got (I was working with another man) were about racism, as though that was the sum total of our lives. Especially, and I hate to say it, all the stories we got from white people were about racism because that was all they apparently thought that we dealt with.

How did you finally succeed in actually becoming a professional writer?

I had my first short stories published in 1970 when I was 23. I sold my first novel in 1975 but it wasn't published until 1976. That was **Patternmaster.** While **Patternmaster** was out with the publisher, I wrote **Mind of My Mind** and sent it out to another publisher. And while those two novels were both out, I began revising an old novel that I had begun writing while in my teens called **Survivor.**

And while I was working on **Survivor,** I got a rejection from the publisher that I had sent **Mind of My Mind** to and an acceptance from the publisher that I had sent **Patternmaster** to.

I was able to find the time for that kind of output during that time because I had been laid off my job and I had unemployment compensation and I was desperate. I was 27 and I felt that nothing was happening in regards to my writing. I was afraid that maybe nothing was going to happen and that perhaps my relatives were right and that I should go and get a civil service job.

I was really grabbing at straws. I don't think that I could have quit writing, but it would have been very bad for me if I had gone on and written those three novels and had no success. It would have been deadly.

Octavia Butler with Charles H. Rowell

SOURCE: An interview in *Callaloo,* Vol. 20, No. 1, Winter, 1987, pp. 47-66.

[This interview was conducted by telephone on January 31, 1997, between Charlottesville, Virginia, and Los Angeles, where Ms. Butler lives.]

ROWELL: At the end of your interview with fiction writer Randall Kenan (published in Callaloo, *Vol. 14.2, Spring 1991), you said, "I don't feel that I have any particular literary talent at all. It [writing] was what I wanted to do, and I followed what I wanted to do, as opposed to getting a job doing something that would make more money . . . it would make me miserable." As I think of the number of books of fiction you have created and the many awards you have received (including a MacArthur Foundation Fellowship) for your work, I begin to wonder, what did Octavia mean when she made that statement to Randall?*

BUTLER: It's a problem that I have quite often encountered with would-be writers—and I'm sorry to say especially black would-be writers. So many of these would-be writers are afraid they don't have the talent. And I actually wrote about this in an essay in **Bloodchild and Other Stories** (1995). But what I mean, I guess, is that I had to learn my craft. And I mean I had to learn it, bit by bit, by doing things wrong, and by collecting years and years of rejection slips. But I kept writing because I liked doing it. The quote that you read is a bit condensed from the original. I did have lots of jobs. I worked at all sorts of things. Anyone who has read my novel **Kindred** (1979) can find a number of the kinds of jobs that I had, from blue collar to low grade white collar, clerk typist, that kind of thing. And I did these jobs because I had to live, but always while I was doing them and between jobs I wrote, because it was the only thing I actually cared about doing. All the other jobs were just work to keep a roof over my head and food on the table. I felt like an animal, just living in order to live, just surviving. But as long as I wrote, I felt that I was living in order to do something more, something I actually cared about.

What is it then that you're talking about if it's not talent you have as a writer?

I'm talking about learning your craft. And practicing it, and learning as you practice it, even though it often hurts to be told that you're doing something that doesn't work in your writing. Writing is very personal, and it does hurt sometimes to be told that something is wrong with some work you really love and feel is perfect. Your writing is an expression of your inner feelings and thoughts and beliefs and self. One of the reasons it is difficult to learn to write professionally is that that kind of thing is so painful; rejection is so painful. It sounds as though you are personally being rejected, and in a sense you are—no matter how much somebody tells you not to worry, "It's not you; it's just the work." But the work is you; so it hurts. You need to go through that, and you never really stop going through that, even though you've learned to write professionally; you go on learning. If you don't go on learning, then your writing becomes stale, and you do the same thing over and over again.

Now sad to say, doing the same thing over and over can be lucrative for some people. But most often it's just a form of death, literary death. In that essay that I mentioned—it's called **"Furor Scribendi"** and it's in **Bloodchild and Other Stories**—I talk about the ways in which you gather and train your writing skills. Of course I talk about reading, I talk about writing every day, and I talk about having a schedule, about keeping that writing schedule. Even if you can write only one hour a day, to actually do that writing is very important. To do your reading is also important. You use your reading not only to learn about the mechanics of writing but also to learn how other people have written to gather information that has nothing to do with your writing because everything goes into the well. And when you begin to write, it's surprising what you suddenly find coming out. The things that come out of your writing are often things that you are on friendly terms with, even though you perhaps never intended to write about them. Say a year ago you read a very intricate book about the geology of California. You read it because there was an earthquake and you were curious, and then later you find yourself doing something that relates to the geology of California or geology in general. But you did not read that book so you could write about geology. You read the book for amusement and information, but eventually it does come out. Anything that happens that makes you emotional is almost certain to come out in your writing. I say to students, anything that doesn't dismember or kill you will probably come out in your writing. You go on learning to write for as long as you live and write. If you don't do this, if you're not willing to do this, you might want to *be* a writer, but you don't really want to write.

I think there are many people who want to be writers because they think that it is a good thing to be, that it is important or whatever. But they don't actually want to get down and do the work. So they wind up talking about how they're going to write the great American novel someday. There's so much you can do that will contribute to the writing. One thing, for instance, is to keep a journal. I mentioned how important I emotionally felt experience is. If you keep a journal and let yourself overflow with the things that affect you, the things that make you joyous, the things that make you furious, the things that make you jealous; if you can be honest with your journal and not write about what you had for breakfast or what load of washing you did (nobody's going to care about that ever), but what you felt and what you care about, you will discover that these are things other people feel and care about. It's difficult sometimes I think, especially for men, because they feel that they are revealing themselves in public, and they might feel uncomfortable about that. But it's one of the exercises that I like to give students when I'm teaching a writers' workshop. I want the students to delve into their emotional experiences. Since emotional experiences tend to be personal. I want my students then to fictionalize an emotional experience with the same emo-

tion. It does not have to deal with the same emotional experience. It just has to deal with the same emotion, which I then ask the student to turn into a story. It's just practice for writing honestly, writing what you feel and what's important to you.

I have no doubt that the established writer and the literary critic understand what you mean when you say, "Learn your craft." But I am not certain that the beginning or developing writer and the general reader understand what you mean. Will you say more about what you mean when you talk about learning one's craft?

First of all, if you're in school you should take writing classes. The great thing about writing classes is not only that the teacher might provide you with information that will help you improve your writing, but that the other students in the class are an audience. So often new authors will argue that they didn't really mean what everybody thinks they meant, that they meant something else altogether. That's when, if they're really going to be writers, they learn to say what they meant and stop arguing about what other people are seeing in their work. That's one of the major difficulties in communication. Sometimes we writers tend to be alone too much, and we write for ourselves. We can't help doing that. But later we discover that we haven't really communicated what we think we communicated. That means that the writing needs to be fixed. Fixing it doesn't mean that you won't be misinterpreted. Inevitably you will be. It just means that people need to work harder to do it. Another kind of exercise that I have students go through is to look at their trouble spots. For instance, if they have difficulty with beginnings—they have wonderful stories to tell but don't know where to begin or how to begin—I have them look at work that they enjoy reading, novels or short-stories—it doesn't matter. I then ask them to copy half a dozen beginnings; I ask them to copy them directly, word for word. It's difficult to say how much to copy, anything from the first couple of paragraphs to the first page. It's just a matter of finding out how each writer gets into the story that the writer is telling. And in this case it's taking those half dozen or so beginnings (more is okay, but fewer is not a good idea) and figuring out what each writer has done in order to begin. They find dialogue beginnings, they find action beginnings, and they find the kind of beginning that gets you immediately into a mystery. They also find descriptive beginnings. Learning what other people have done by way of beginnings helps them to understand what's possible. This is not about imitating someone else's beginnings; that's why I want at least a half a dozen. This is about learning what is possible. One of the big problems we have as writers is that we either know too much or not enough. Sometimes we manage to know both at the same time. We know that there is an ocean of possibilities out there, and we're overwhelmed. And we don't know how to take from that ocean just what we need. Sometimes focusing on what other people have done (not just beginnings, but transitions, descriptions of important characters, for instance, those elements of fiction writing that give people trouble, in general) may help beginning writers. I like my students to go through their own favorite works—not something I pick, but something they actually like—and copy down what the writers have done and figure out why it works. This is something that I have used on any number of problems, and in fact it's something that I am using right now on a problem that I'm having.

Could you share that writing problem?

[*Laughter.*] Maybe later.

Okay. Two elements of your background fascinate me: your family background and your formal, higher education. I would like to begin first by talking about your family background. Like many African-American writers and scholars of our generation, you come from a working-class family, one whose roots are in Louisiana, where you never lived, of course. Your mother was a domestic, in California, where you've lived all of your life. Has that working-class background, as far as you can tell, contributed in any way to your work as a fiction writer? One can probably say, on a superficial level, that you used Louisiana—that is to say, 19th-century Louisiana—as a setting in **Wild Seed** *(1980).*

Yes, for part of **Wild Seed.** I don't know enough about Louisiana to talk about it knowledgeably. I did some research to use it as a background for **Wild Seed.** My mother's life and my grandmother's life and the little bit I know of her ancestors' lives were very hard and very terrible. These were not lives that I would have wanted to live. I mean the reason my mother did domestic work was not only that she was black, but because she was the oldest daughter. This meant that after only three years of education, she was pulled out of school and put to work. The oldest son, who was a couple of years older than she, got a chance to go to school. But as the daughter she was the one that was kind of sacrificed, I guess you would say, and sent off to work. She never really got back into education.

She was born in 1914, so she was a child quite a long time ago. Her mother chopped sugar cane, and she also did the family laundry, not just her own family but the white family for whom they worked. She washed clothes in the big iron pots with paddles and all that. That was hard, physical labor. It's no wonder she died at fifty-nine, after having a lot of children and working her life away. This is the kind of life that she had no choice but to live. The reason I mention the place is that there was no school in that area—no school for black children, and racial segregation was very rigid in those days. There was no integrated schooling in that part of Louisiana. My grandmother and grandfather moved to a more urban area to get the kids into school. My mother was already about seven or eight years old. Because she was big, and obviously not a kindergartner from appearance, they put her in the third grade, which meant that she was suddenly confronted with concepts she knew nothing about. To the end of her life, she felt that she was stupid and couldn't learn, because she was presented with all these concepts that other kids had been taught early on and that she had never been confronted with at all. She really learned quite a lot, but she felt inferior. She was physically courageous, willing to take on whatever came. But emotionally, intellectually, she felt that she was inferior, and she always kind of, figuratively, ducked her head when it came to anything requiring intellectual competence. I used to try to talk to her about that, but I think it was something so ingrained that it was something she was never able to get away from.

Her big dream for me was that I should get a job as a secretary and be able to sit down when I worked. My big dream was never to be a secretary in my life. I mean, it just seemed such an appallingly servile job, and it turned out to be in a lot of ways. I can remember watching television, which is something, of course, that my mother as a child never had access to, and seeing secretaries on television rushing to do their bosses' bidding and feeling the whole thing to be really kind of humiliating. I was occasionally taken to work with my mother and made to sit in the car all day, because I wasn't really welcome inside, of course. Sometimes, I was able to go inside and hear people talk about or to my mother in ways that were obviously disrespectful. As a child I did not blame them for their disgusting behavior, but I blamed my mother for taking it. I didn't really understand. This is something I carried with me for quite a while, as she entered back doors, and as she went deaf at appropriate times. If she had heard more, she would have had to react to it, you know. The usual. And as I got older I realized that this is what kept me fed, and this is what kept a roof over my head. This is when I started to pay attention to what my mother and even more my grandmother and my poor great-grandmother, who died as a very young woman giving birth to my grandmother, what they all went through.

When I got into college, Pasadena City College, the black nationalist movement, the Black Power Movement, was really underway with the young people, and I heard some remarks from a young man who was the same age I was but who had apparently never made the connection with what his parents did to keep him alive. He was still blaming them for their humility and their acceptance of disgusting behavior on the part of employers and other people. He said, "I'd like to kill all these old people who have been holding us back for so long. But I can't because I'd have to start with my own parents." When he said *us* he meant black people, and when he said *old people* he meant older black people. That was actually the germ of the idea for *Kindred* (1979). I've carried that comment with me for thirty years. He felt so strongly ashamed of what the older generation had to do, without really putting it into the context of being necessary for not only their lives but his as well.

I wanted to take a character, when I did *Kindred,* back in time to some of the things that our ancestors had to go through, and see if that character survived so very well with the knowledge of the present in her head. Actually, I began with a man as main character, but I couldn't go on using the male main character, because I couldn't realistically keep him alive. So many things that he did would have been likely to get him killed. He wouldn't even have time to learn the rules—the rules of submission, I guess you could call them—before he was killed for not knowing them because he would be perceived as dangerous. The female main character, who might be equally dangerous, would not be perceived so. She might be beaten, she might be abused, but she probably wouldn't be killed and that's the way I wrote it. She was beaten and abused, but she was not killed. That sexism, in a sense, worked in her favor. Although if you could take the character and give her life and ask her if she thought she had been favored, it would be likely that she wouldn't think so, because of what she suffered. But, anyway, that's long-winded answer. And that's how I came to write *Kindred.*

You have referred to yourself as growing up as "an out kid." Did you read a lot? What did you read as a child? What do you mean when you said you were "an out kid"?

I was not an out kid because of my reading or writing, at least not at first. I was an out kid because, as

an only child, I never really learned to be part of a group. At first it didn't matter. When you are four years old in preschool, kids tended to play by themselves anyway. I was like most of the kids. You know, the kids talked together, but they didn't exactly play together. Later on, I really knew more about being around adults than I knew about being around other kids. This made me very awkward and strange around kids, and, unfortunately, children have a pecking order and it was very much in effect. If you're pecked and you don't peck back, then you'll go on being pecked. If you're a little chicken, you die of it, but if you're a little kid, you only want to die of it. I spent a lot of time getting hit and kicked and not really knowing what to do about it, because if you're most of the time around adults and they hit you and you hit them back, it's definitely not a good idea, especially black southern adults of that day. So it took me awhile to learn to hit back. It was strange for awhile because I was bigger than most kids my age. That meant, by the way, that I was originally being bothered by kids who were older than I. The ones my own age pretty much left me alone, but the older ones saw me as a marvelous target. Later, when I realized that I could fight back, I discovered that I was a lot stronger than I had thought. I hurt people by accident. I had a lot of empathy, and hurting somebody really bothered me. So I found that I was hesitant to hurt them for those reasons. That was just elementary school. Elementary school is very physical for kids. Later there are fewer fights because, after all, fights are more dangerous as you get older; you could really do damage. So later I had few fights, but a lot more social ostracism.

By the time I was ten I was writing, and I carried a big notebook around so that whenever I had some time I could write in it. That way, I didn't have to be lonely. I usually had very few friends, and I was lonely. But when I wrote I wasn't, which was probably a good reason for my continuing to write as a young kid. I read a lot also, for the same reasons. I discovered the library back in kindergarten, I guess. We didn't have a library at the school, but we were not that far from the main city library in Pasadena. The teachers would have us join hands and walk down to the library together. There we would sit, and someone would tell us—or read us—a story. Someone would also talk to us about how to use the library. When I was six and was finally given books to read in school, I found them incredibly dull; they were Dick and Jane books. I asked my mother for a library card. I remember the surprised look on her face. She looked surprised and happy. She immediately took me to the library. She had been taking me home, but now she immediately took me to the library and got me a card. From then on the library was my second home. In a way, reading and writing helped me not to be lonely, but in another way they permitted me to go on being an oddball as far as other kids were concerned. So reading and writing both helped and, I suppose in some ways, hindered.

I often wonder what kind of person I would have been if my brothers had lived. I had four older brothers. My mother had difficulty carrying a child to term. And she lost them all, either at birth or before they should have been born. I wonder what kind of person I would have been if they had lived and if I had had more of the society of kids when I was a kid. But, anyway, since I didn't have that, I made my own society in the books and in the stories that I told myself. I began telling myself stories at four. I can recall the specific time when I began doing that. I couldn't go out and play when I was being punished. I saw other kids having a good time. I lived near some of my cousins at that point, and it was less than a year that we were living there. It was sort of fun, for that little period, having them nearby.

You also asked me about TV and film. That's interesting, because I think my first strong influence was radio. Not because I'm so terribly old—although I guess to some people I might seem so—but because at first we didn't have a television. There were still radio dramas on. I was introduced, for instance, to characters like Superman and the Shadow by way of the radio. The Whistler and Johnny Dollar, "My True Story," and other programs. Radio was fun; it has been called theater of the mind, and it really is. As a young child, you have no idea what the adults mean when they say a lot of different things, and you imagine all sorts of things. For instance, I was a small child during the McCarthy era, when we finally got television. There was a program on television called "I Led Three Lives." It was supposed to be the story of an American who was a double agent pretending to be a communist, but actually working for the FBI. A wonderful fellow, yes. Anyway, every now and then during this program he would talk about someone having been "liquidated." You can just imagine a little kid sitting there wondering what "liquidated" means and imagining them being dissolved in a mixing bowl or something. Everything was theater for the mind at that point for me because I had no idea what most things meant.

Movies didn't play a big part in my life because my mother felt that movies were sinful. We didn't go. Then we did go when I was about seven, because my stepfather would take us to the movies. My father died when I was a toddler, almost a baby, and I really don't have any strong memory of him. When I was about seven, my mother thought she might marry again. My potential stepfather would take us to the movies. My mother would go because it was someplace she could take me along, too, and she didn't have to pay for a baby-sitter. I got to see, for instance, "Invasion from Mars." This ridiculous movie—and I think they've done a remake of it—is about a little boy who sees a flying saucer land, and the flying saucer people are turning everybody into them, by doing something to the backs of their heads. They finally grab his parents and do it to them, and then the whole thing turns out to be a dream. That gave me nightmares. I, by the way, enjoyed my nightmares. I had wonderful fun with my nightmares. Some of them really scared me to death, but they were all so much fun. They were like movies that scared me to death on television. When movies came on television, they, in the eyes of my mother, were somehow not evil—or at least she did not say they were. I was smart enough never to question this, but it did occur to me. It also occurred to me to shut up. So I did watch movies on television. I could watch over and over again. I think they were the ones that caught my attention and held it. There was something called Channel 9 Movie Theater back when there were RKO stations. Channel 9 was an RKO station. You could watch the same movie every night for a week and twice on Sundays or something like that. It's been a long time, so I don't really recall. Some were science fiction movies, and some were Fred Astaire dancing along. I think those movies that I had the chance to watch over and over were the ones more likely to have the greatest effect on me—not so much those that I only saw once. The television, once we got one, was a great friend to me; I spent a lot of time with it.

Will you say more about what you were viewing and reading—how, for example, radio, television and books might have helped to shape you as a writer? You mentioned seeing science fiction movies—for example, "Invasion from Mars."

It almost had to be defined as science fiction, if Mars was somewhere in it. Actually, it wasn't "Invasion from Mars" that mattered. It was just a movie that I described. The movie that got me writing science fiction was "Devil Girl from Mars." That was just one of the old sub-genre of science fiction movies that talked about how the people of some other world have used up all men. So this beautiful, gorgeous, Martian woman has come to Earth to get some more men. The men, of course, don't want to go to Mars, a planet full of man-hungry women; the men, they want desperately to stay here. It was a silly movie, although it wasn't as bad as I make it sound. I watched it as a kid, and it seemed a silly movie to me, so I turned it off and I began writing. My idea was, gee, I can write a better story than that. And since the story that I had seen was supposed to be science fiction, I began writing science fiction as I thought of it then, even though I didn't know much in the way of science. What I had already discovered was that I liked science documentaries, whether they were television movies or the kind of films that teachers showed at school. I was probably one of the few who really liked those films. They tended to be rather preachy and dull. But, quite often, they gave me something to think about, taught me something that I didn't know about before. I got my first notions of astronomy and geology from those little films. I guess I was interested enough in astronomy to learn more because the second book I ever bought new was a book about the stars; I bought it to learn more. I knew that what I was writing was completely imaginary because I didn't know anything about Mars or anyplace else out there in space. I wanted to know more, so that's when I went and bought the book about the stars.

When was that?

I was twelve then. Before that, I had bought a book about horses because, when I was ten, I was crazy over horses, even though I had no contact at all with them. I bought a book about the different breeds of horses, and I was writing a kind of—I guess in a way you could call it—either part of a novel or a long soap opera about a marvelous, magical wild horse. And it couldn't end because then what would I do? So I just wrote on and on and on about this marvelous, magical wild horse in number two pencil in a notebook. After a while you couldn't read most of the pages, because they were so smudged. Anyway, that was some of my early writing.

I went on writing science fiction because I enjoyed it. I enjoyed reading and hearing about science. I enjoyed finding out what was real, or at least what everybody assumed was real then and what wasn't. I enjoyed trying to understand how the universe worked. I think if you're going to write something like science fiction, you do need that basic interest in science and not just a desire to write about spectacular things that you know nothing about. I can remember a young man who sat next to me on a bus. I like to talk to people on buses, since I write them all the time. Sometimes people are interesting. But this

young man didn't make conversation, and he said, "Oh, science fiction. I've always wanted to write science fiction, about creatures from other galaxies." I said, "Why do they have to be from another galaxy?" And we talked a bit, and I realized he didn't know what a galaxy was. It was just something he had heard. And this was a young man in college. To him a galaxy and the solar system were pretty much the same thing. And I realized that there probably are people who want to write science fiction and who might be good at it, but who have the wrong idea of it. They've gotten their idea from television or movies. And they think science fiction is anything weird that they choose to write. That is not what science fiction is. If you are interested in science fiction, I hope you are also interested in science. Or you just might want to call what you're writing fantasy. Fantasy has totally different rules from those in science fiction.

What are some of the elements or characteristics that distinguish science fiction from fantasy and other related forms of prose fiction? Then there is also speculative writing. There are also horror stories.

Science fiction uses science, extrapolates from science as we know it to science as it might be to technology as it might be. A science fiction story must have internal consistency and science. Fantasy can make do with internal consistency. Speculative fiction means anything odd at all. Sounds nice though. Labels tend to be marketing devices. All too often, they mean anything, and thus nothing.

You can make an easy division—science fiction and fantasy. Obviously they both have a tendency to be fantastical, but science fiction basically uses science, and uses it accurately up to a point. It extrapolates from sciences. Fantasy goes where it likes. All that is required of fantasy is that it remains internally consistent. You can be comic the way *The Hitchhiker's Guide to the Galaxy* is comic. But you have to be careful about the kind of science fiction that gets to be called science fiction on television and sometimes in movies. That kind of stuff would not be considered science fiction if you were trying to publish it in a magazine or as a book with a publisher.

You and many other writers usually recommend to other writers that they should read if they want to become writers. You've already done so in this interview. I find myself telling developing writers the same. What do you really intend to convey to them when you tell them to read? How does the practice of reading, as you view it, contribute to a writer's development? Now, I, of course, assume you're recommending that they read the best writing.

Not at all.

I am appalled sometimes when I meet some young poets, for example, and they tell me that they've been reading certain poets who are very bad writers. Some of these young writers have never heard of the work of people like Rita Dove, Jay Wright, or Robert Hayden, for example.

I hope they'll read a little of everything. I am alarmed by adults who say to little children, "Oh, my God, I don't want my children reading comic books," "I don't want my children reading the Goosebumps series," or "I want them only to read enlightened literature," which bores the crap out of kids. Understandably, it wasn't written for them. I recommend anything that gets them into reading. When they're older, when they're in high school, when they're in college, even then a little junk food for the mind won't hurt, as long as that's not all they read. I can remember a science fiction writing teacher telling me most young would-be science fiction writers read too much science fiction. I didn't really understand what he meant at the time. I thought if you were going to write science fiction, you should read it, which is, of course, true. But if it's all you read, then you just wind up reproducing what someone else has done.

I have to be careful what I say to younger people, because every now and then someone will come up to me and say—"Oh, this touches on reading, but is not just reading." "What should I major in at college to become a writer?" I have to stop myself from saying that it's not so much what you major in at college or even that you go to college. It's that you read. I'm more likely to say, "What you should major in is something like history. Maybe you should take a good look at psychology and anthropology and sociology. Learn about people. Learn about different people. When I say history, I don't mean to tell you just to study the kings and queens and generals and wars. Learn how people live and learn the kinds of things that motivate people. Learn the kinds of things that we unfortunate human beings do over and over again. We don't really learn from history, because from one generation to the next we do tend to reproduce our errors. There are cycles in history. Even look into things like evolutionary biology; that goes back further, for instance, than history, further back than cultural anthropology would go. Learn all you can about the way we work, the way we tick.

Read all kinds of fiction. In school you're going to be assigned to read classics, and that's good, that's

useful. A lot of it is good writing and will help you with your writing. But a lot of it is archaic good writing that won't necessarily help you with what you are doing now. So read the current best sellers; read something that is maybe going to spark a new interest in you."

I used to, and I still do this every now and then when I am between projects. I'll go to the library and do what I call "grazing," which means that I'll wander through some department in some place that I can't ever recall having been before and just browse the titles until something catches my attention. Then I'll build into something that I know nothing about. Sometimes it's something that interests me a lot. Sometimes it's something that after a few pages bores me. I was just at the library about a week ago, and I had this big load of books and tapes, audio tapes. And I said to the library clerk who checked out my books, "I'm starting a new project, and I really don't know what I'm doing, so naturally I have to get a lot of books." If you know what you're after, a few books will do it. But if you have no idea, you've got get this big mountain of books.

I love audio tapes. I'm a bit dyslexic and I read very slowly. I've taken speed reading classes, but they don't really help. I have to read slowly enough to hear what I'm reading with my mind's ear. I find it delightful. I learn much, much more and better if I hear tapes. I can recall when I was a very little girl being read to by my mother. Even though she was doing the domestic work that I talked about, she would, during my very early years, read to me at night. And I loved it. It was, again, theater for the mind. As a matter of fact, I think anybody who has children couldn't go wrong by reading to those children at night just as the kids are falling asleep. I love the tapes now, possibly going back to that memory but also because I happen to learn things better by hearing them than I do by reading. I had book tapes and I had books, and I brought them home and started "grazing."

What are the books that are still important to you today that you've been reading? I mean, Octavia Butler, the writer. And what are some books that you return to, probably return to ever so often, not just merely for enjoyment, but for form or language or character development? Are there such books that you go back to from time to time?

There is a book that was recommended to me when I was a student; it's called *The Art of Dramatic Writing* by Lajos Egri. This is a book that I go back to when I get into writing trouble, and it helps sometimes. It's old. If you haven't read Ibsen, it might mystify you a bit. The way Egri teaches in this book has been very effective for me. I often recommend it to students. He's very clear in what he's saying. Sometimes writers writing books about writing aren't. They assume that you know perhaps more than you do, but Egri doesn't. He just tells you without being condescending; it's very basic, but it's also complex and very clear somehow. He's done a very good job in that book. As for novels that I like, they're not classics for the most part. They're novels that took me someplace that I'd never been. For instance, one of my favorite books—and I emphasize the word book here because I'm not talking about the movie—is *The Godfather*, because that book took me to another world—not necessarily a real world, but it did make good guys of some rather unpleasant people. It did take me to another world. Oh, yes, a book like *Shogun*. *Dune* is one of my favorite science fiction novels. There are just any number of favorite science fiction novels. Those are a few. I don't know what kind of list you are looking for here, but those are a few.

I love specialized dictionaries and encyclopedias—these are usually one or two volume encyclopedias. For instance, *The Oxford Companion to Medicine* is sitting here right next to my knee. It's something that I have to be careful with, because it has British spellings and some things that surprise me still. I have dozens and dozens of specialized dictionaries covering everything from geography to anthropology to psychiatry to religion. I've got a two volume set about religion in America and about ancient Egypt. You name it, and I've probably got a specialized dictionary that touches on it. I use them for more than just looking up things. If that's all they were for, I would suppose that a regular encyclopedia would do it. To whet my appetite when I am shopping for ideas, to just find things—that's another reason I use them; it's another form of grazing. I find things that I perhaps wouldn't have thought of before and maybe wouldn't want to read a long article on. Just going through and finding something in, for instance, the American Medical Association's *Encyclopedia of Medicine* would be useful, or discovering some animal or something in my dictionary of land animals really has managed to surprise me. Or finding something in my encyclopedia on invertebrates. That one is really good for science fiction, because some of the invertebrates seem so other-worldly. It has all sorts of things. As I said, you name the subject, and I'll probably go to a specialized dictionary or encyclopedia that touches on it.

What do you mean when you say "shopping for ideas"? I like that.

When I'm "shopping for ideas," I'm just looking for something that catches my attention and that evokes or provokes an emotional response from me. For example, I have a book about animals without backbones. I also have a particular aversion to some invertebrates, really a phobia. I ran across one, a picture of one that made me drop the book. The thing is something like maybe an inch long and utterly harmless and doesn't even exist in my part of the country, I'm happy to say. It is a revolting little creature, and I'm really glad it's not bigger. I would end up using part of its appearance to create the alien characters in my Xenogenesis books, ***Adulthood Rites*** (1988) and ***Imago*** (1989). Every now and then there's something that's made a big impression. Some things make small impressions. I was wandering through a book about guns awhile back and hadn't thought about using the information I was finding at all until I wrote a book called ***Clay's Ark*** (1984). Then I realized I had to go back and find that book and use some of that information about guns. Again, I had to use it in ***Parable of the Sower*** (1993). Reading fills the well. Reading fills the well of your imagination. You can return to the well and draw the water that you've put in there. You can also think of it as a bank. You can go back and take out that intellectual money that you've put away. If you don't read and your bank account goes down to nothing, you can't really go to it to take anything out. So your writing is going to be pretty impoverished. It's going to be totally confined to things that you somehow have learned without reading, which means that you might be a one-book writer, if you're a writer at all.

Your formal education is for me a study in itself. That is, you graduated from Pasadena City College, a two-year college, and you attended but did not graduate from California State. But you later took creative writing classes at UCLA at different periods.

I took writing courses wherever I could find them. If somebody said "writing course" and "free" in the same sentence, I was probably there. Later when I was earning a little bit more money at the horrible little jobs I mentioned, I was able to go and take classes at UCLA. As a matter of fact, I sold my first novel while I was taking the class from Theodore Sturgeon at UCLA. It was the novel I had sent away before I got into the class, of course, but I got the very, very conditional acceptance while I was taking his course. I remember it, because I took the acceptance letter to Sturgeon. Sturgeon, by the way, is a very well-known science fiction writer. He's dead now, but he was a very well-known writer. I liked his work because he was such a good craftsman. Sometimes science fiction writers were more pulp writers than they had to be because they didn't bother to learn. I'm talking about the old-time science fiction writers now, the ones who were more concerned with the wonderful machine than with the people who were supposed to be having something to do with the machine. They didn't characterize very well. Their women characters in particular were stick people, puppets, and Sturgeon, even though he was easily old enough to be my father, didn't write that way, and a few others didn't write that way. I especially paid attention to their writings. And when I had this chance to take a class from Sturgeon, I grabbed it.

This was an interesting sort of class. It taught me something about writers. By the way, I don't believe that Sturgeon ever graduated from high school. He made a comment when he was teaching the class, an extension course: he said probably America is the only country where a man who never graduated from high school can teach at college. He might have had a point. I don't think that writing is something you have to go to a university to learn, although education of any kind helps. *Writing is something that you're going to teach yourself, no matter how many classes you go to.* The classes, as I said, are audiences, and they help you to correct the obvious problems.

One of my problems, when I took my first college writing class, was that I punctuated by instinct. I had no strong idea of punctuation, and my spelling was horrible. I don't think I had ever heard the word dyslexic. I had done something about my vocabulary—this goes back to when I was twelve. I may have been younger than twelve, but back when Kennedy was running against Nixon. My family was all for Kennedy, and nobody liked Nixon. We were Californians, and we'd seen a bit too much of him. I wanted to find out more about Kennedy, because everybody seemed to like him so much. And I would tune in on television and get the news and hear Kennedy talking. I couldn't understand half of what he was saying. At twelve years old, you know, and it never occurred to me that some of this might have been deliberate. I didn't know about politicians in those days, but not understanding him devastated me really. I felt so depressed, because I realized that I was even more ignorant than I thought. I wanted to learn more words; I wanted to understand better what people were saying, especially people that I thought of as being important, you know, people who went on television and said things. That pushed me to read

things that were perhaps a little bit more difficult than what I had been reading. It also pushed me into non-fiction. It made me pay more attention to English teachers who recommended things that I might not otherwise have paid any attention to. I had learned early on that often I couldn't finish a book if it was assigned for me to read. I read too slowly, so I learned to scan, but scan is the wrong word. I learned to kind of read in summary. You know, the beginning, the end, and a little bit of the middle, and I could usually fake it pretty well. My grades weren't that bad, but I started paying closer attention. I started to try to write in what I thought of as more sophisticated English, which meant my writing became stilted and strange and just exactly what you would expect from a kid who was trying to pretend to be older than she was. I don't know whether I mentioned it, but I started sending things out, submitting things for publication when I was thirteen. So this meant that some editors were getting the most awful garbage from me, but the writing helped me to go on learning more about the way English is used.

I was working while I was going to Pasadena City College, so I took three years to get through two years of college. And the last year and the last semester was in 1968, which was very strange, because we had assassinations for midterm and finals. Very, very bad. Martin Luther King and Robert F. Kennedy. PCC had its first black lit class in 1968—its very first—and it was a night class, which was a good thing, because I was working full time then. A professor, a marvelous black woman, came over from California State at Los Angeles. I'm sorry to say that I can't remember her name at this moment; it's been awhile now since that course. But I really liked her, because she challenged us. I couldn't get through all the books, although I think I did a pretty decent job faking it. I always loved essay tests, because they allowed me to show off, and she gave all essay tests. You know, you can show off pretty well if you've read part of the book. She introduced me to writers I'd never heard of and to a literature I knew almost nothing about and to words I'd never heard before. She would deliberately use them. If we looked mystified, she would define them in context, and I could see her doing it, but I wasn't offended by it. She was that good. And I'd never had a teacher like her before. If I am ever going to say that a teacher was inspiring, she definitely was. I had a few others who were, but she was one of the last. That's why I remember her. I wish I could think of her name. That's odd because I can recall the names of all of my elementary school teachers, most of my junior high teachers, but after that they kind of blur.

Let's imagine that today you were commissioned to write a book on what one calls "the writing life." What would be the first thing you'd say about it? You know, a lot of people have called it solitary.

Well, I've already talked a lot of the reading and the writing on an everyday schedule. I've also talked about keeping a journal and taking classes. One of the most important things you must do to be a writer is that you have to find your own way. I mentioned earlier using models from published writing—that is, copying down half a dozen beginnings or transitions or endings or character descriptions or whatever. You might also look at the lives of a half dozen writers to see what they do. That doesn't mean that you'll do what any of them do, but what you'll learn from what they do is that they have felt their ways. They have found out what works for them. For instance, I get up between three or four o'clock in the morning, because that's my best writing time. I found this out by accident, because back when I used to work for other people I didn't have time to write during the day. I did physical work, mostly hard physical work, so I was too tired when I came in at night. I was also too full of other people. I found that I couldn't work very well after spending a lot of time with other people. I had to have some sleep between the time that I spent with other people and the time that I did the writing, so I would get up early in the morning. I generally would get up around two o'clock in the morning, which was really very much too early. But I was ambitious, and I would write until I had to get ready to go to work. Then I would go off to work, and I'd be sleepy and grumpy all day. It's a good thing that my mother was a nice Baptist lady who taught me not to cuss. I learned to cuss later, but I also learned that I could put a sock in it when I had to, because I generally felt so bad while I was working that I would have been happy to cuss most people out when they said anything to me. Fortunately, I had enough control not to do that. I learned that I really liked the early morning hours before it got to be light, when I'd had some sleep and it was still dark out. That's one of the reasons I like the long nights of winter best. I think the other reason I like winter best is I live in southern California, where winter means occasional rains. I love writing while it's raining.

Will you allow me to enter the privacy of your writing space and stand over your shoulder while you're working and observe the process while you work? Let's say now you're creating **"Bloodchild"** *or* **"The Evening and the Morning and the Night,"** short narratives.

Well, it's sort of hard to do that. It's hard because I'm not watching myself write. I realize that most of the time people would think that I wasn't working at all, because maybe I'm just sitting here. Maybe I've got some music on the radio—not so much the radio, but a tape or a CD in the stereo. For instance, when I was working on *Parable of the Sower,* I had a lot of ecological audio tapes. I can't watch television while I'm actually doing the original work. I can watch television if I have to rewrite something, but I can't watch television while doing original work, because I do tend to watch it. But I can have anything on the tape recorder or whatever, and I had tapes of Nova and other programs that I had taped—books as well—about ecological problems, because those play a big part in *Parable of the Sower.* The ecology, especially global warming, is almost a character in *Parable of the Sower.* So I had a lot of those tapes on, and you can imagine my having them on over and over again. I don't think anyone else could stand it. I've heard other writers say this, too. I don't have a family living here with me, so I'm not annoying other people. But I've heard other writers say they had to write with headphones, because they played the same piece of music or the same whatever over and over again.

This goes back to what kind of habits writers should establish. Whatever works for you, as long as it isn't physically detrimental. I mean, I don't really recommend that you go and have a drink. I don't think your writing is going to be improved by it. And, for the sake of your health, don't sit there with a cigarette; it's probably not going to help you either. Do anything that helps you. For instance, some people, like me, need to be in a certain location, at a certain time of day. Maybe they have clothes that they like to write in. I have a friend who writes in the nude. He just shuts the door and goes to it. Whatever works for you. I remember a kind of paraphrase, a quote from Maya Angelou; I don't recall the exact words, but paraphrased it kind of goes like this: if you have to hang by your feet and smear honey on your legs to get yourself writing, then do it. You know whatever works.

That goes back to how do you get into the writing life. Well, you get into the writing life by finding out what works for you and then doing it. The best way to find out is by seeing what other people do and usually rejecting it. By the way, one of ways I get ideas is to look through books of quotations. I'm bound to find in the book of quotations—the longer the better—something with which I violently disagree. Once I've done that, then I have to think about what I really think, what I really believe, and why and how to support it. It's no good to just say, "Oh, that guy's an idiot." I mean it's a matter of having actually to think about things. One of the nice things writing does for you is to make you think about things, think of other people's lives, think about what other people might believe, for instance, other people's religions, which fascinate me. Anything that isn't what you're familiar with.

One of the problems I had at school was that I was already into looking at things from a lot of points of view. This is junior high school, especially when people are incredibly rigid, because they've gone to the trouble of learning something and it's got to be the one and only true way. You remember how that goes in junior high. Even in high school you could get laughed at by possessing a different opinion or doing something that the group didn't know about and therefore didn't approve of. For me though it was always fascinating to find out what else there was—what's out there that I don't know about, what's out there that I've never even thought of. If something out there grabbed my attention to read more about, I'd go to the library and find out something else.

In your interview with Randall Kenan, you said that "the wall next to my desk is covered with signs and maps." Why are they there? I hope that question is not too personal.

That's not particularly personal. At the moment they're not there because I'm beginning something. But by the time I'm half way through this project, the wall will be covered again. I like maps. When I was writing *Parable of the Sower,* I had maps of the areas that my characters were traveling through. I went to the map store and spent a lot of money buying detailed copies of maps of different parts of California, going up to and over the Oregon border because I wasn't quite sure where my characters were going to stop. But once I realized they were going to stop in Humbolt County, which is one county south of Oregon, I got a nice big detailed map of Humbolt County, and hung it on the wall so that I would understand where they were and what kind of terrain they were in. Aside from the map, I also had vocabulary lists filled with words that I habitually misspell or words that are specific to this story that I've never used otherwise. They were reminders of what story this particular book is telling, what story this particular chapter is telling. I also had character lists. I guess you could call them cast lists. In *Parable of the Sower* I had a number of families, a fairly sizable community in the first part of the book, and in order to keep people straight I had to make lists of the families—

for instance, who was in what family. Actually I never even used most of those people. They got mentioned occasionally—some of them did—but most of them never showed up on-stage except as part of a crowd. But it was necessary that I knew who they were and where they lived and how they related to my character—what she thought of the family. This family was crazy and this family was really super-dependable. You know the kind everybody went to if they had a problem. This family was a little odd because the old lady snooped. This family was weird because there was this guy who was really kind of a snitch. If he could find something bad about you and spread it around, he'd love to do that; and when my character's parents had problems with the police, he was the one who went to them and threw suspicion in their direction, in secret of course. There were all these people who were doing all these things, and I had to know about them even if they never personally stepped on-stage. So that was up there as part of the wallpaper, you might say, and almost anything that was giving me trouble was up there. The reminder. I was not only writing in the first person but in journal form, which made it very difficult to foreshadow anything. If my character couldn't know what was coming, then I had to arrange for her not to know—but still to be the intelligent woman I was writing her as. Had she been a fool, it would have been easier. But she was not a fool. So I had to let people see what was coming without necessarily having her see it as clearly as the readers did. And she did see, to some degree, what was coming; but, when it came, it was worse then she could have foreseen. So I had notes with regard to foreshadowing future trouble, and I also had notes about religion, because she sort of forms her own religion. I had to do research; I looked into a number of different religions. I put what I discovered up there on the wall, if it at all related to the book. Sometimes it got so awful that I had to take things down because there were notes on top of notes and notes hanging from notes. It looked like a hodgepodge; it was. My office usually looks like a tornado blew through. No other room in the house looks like that, but my office seems inevitably to be a total wreck.

What were you trying to do in the Patternmaster *saga?*

I was trying to tell a good story about a strange community of people. I find myself doing that over and over again. That's not all I was trying to do. In each book, I was trying to do something a little different. But overall to gather these people and start this community that didn't work very well, if you noticed. There are people who think that they've won, so everything's fine. But they were really not very nice, the Patternists. When you get to *Patternmaster,* you'll see that. Really they were pretty awful. You wouldn't want to live in that society. And why were they so awful? Well, they were so awful because they had, shall we say, a bad teacher. And it didn't really occur to me until I had been working on the series for awhile that I might have been making some comment on Black America. Once the thought came to me, I realized that I probably was commenting on Black America. Then I had to ask myself how I felt about that—that I was perhaps making a comment on learning the wrong thing from one's teachers. I realized that maybe it was something that I needed to think about and maybe it was something that I needed to say, so I certainly wasn't going to stop saying it or deny having said it.

You, Samuel Delany, Steve Barnes, and Charles Sanders (he lives in Canada) are our only science fiction writers. That makes you different from other African-American writers.

Well, there seem to be more coming around now. But they're mainly fantasy and horror writers. There is Jewelle Gomez who wrote *The Gilder Stories,* a story about a black lesbian vampire. Winston A. Howlett and Juanita Nesbitt—both black—have also written novels: *Allegience* and *The Long Hunt.* They write together. Howlett has also written with a white writer named Jean Lorrah. Tananarive Due has two novels, *The Between* and *My Soul to Keep.* HarperCollins is her publisher. Her second book is not out yet, but will be soon. There are other black science fiction writers out there. Unfortunately, they have not achieved prominence, but they're out there writing.

Will you talk about what it was like for you in the early days, as opposed to present times—you a black woman writing science fiction?

When I first started with my writing, I guess people didn't think I looked like a writer. I don't look like what people think a writer is. I have difficulty just conveying the idea that I write for a living—conveying it in person I mean. Somebody would ask, "What do you do?" And I would answer, "I'm a writer." I learned to say I write for a living, although even that didn't penetrate sometimes, and usually their comment would be, "Oh how nice. Maybe someday you'll sell something." That was bad enough, but there were also those people who, when I said I'm a writer, went on to talk about other things. Later they said, "Well, what do you do for a living?" In one case, at a party, I actually said to a woman, "Well, what did you think I meant when I said I was a

writer?" She said, "I thought you were talking about your hobby." I can understand what she meant, because here in Los Angeles everybody is a writer. Everybody is going to write that wonderful book someday, or they've got that wonderful book in their bottom drawer, but the publishers are so small-minded and can't see how wonderful it is. Someday they're going to self-publish it. Actually one of the Los Angeles TV stations several years ago did a person-on-the-street interview, in which a journalist would walk up to people walking on the street, and ask, "How's your screenplay?" Nine out of ten people talked about the screenplay they either had written or were writing. In this area there are so many people who call themselves writers, and either don't write at all or who write to the bottom drawer or who are crazy. There are so many odd things going on that it is not easy to get through to people that you are a writer. After so many times of telling people that I write for a living and after hearing them tell me, maybe someday you'll sell something, I started to say, "Wait a moment. I just told you I write for a living. I did not tell you that I'm independently wealthy. I told you I write for a living." At that point, from the tone of my voice, they figured that they better change the subject.

As far as being a black science fiction writer here, my early isolation helped me. On one level, I was aware that there was only one other black science fiction writer that I knew of—and that was [Samuel] "Chip" Delany. I was aware of him because he was one of my teachers at Clarion. Before that I'd seen his work, but I didn't know he was black. Harlan Ellison was one of my teachers with the Screen Writers Guild of America, West's free classes. As I said earlier, when anyone said free and writing classes in the same sentence, I was there. So that's how I ended up in these classes learning screen writing which I don't like at all. Harlan mentioned the Clarion science fiction writers workshop and asked me if I was interested. I think the first question I asked him after what Clarion was, was this: Are there going to be any other black people there? You see, it was going to be held in a little tiny town in the hills of Pennsylvania. He said, Chip will be there. That was the first time I knew Samuel R. Delany was black. He was the only black science fiction writer I knew about.

I remember my first science fiction convention. I went to that while I was at Clarion. A group of us was going to go down to Pittsburgh to a science fiction convention that was run annually there. It was called Phlange. I didn't know what it was about, but other students gave me the idea that it was fun, so I went along. One girl had a van, and we all piled in,

14 or 15 people in one van. That was in 1970. We went down to Phlange, and I was totally out of my element. I didn't have a clue as to what was going on. I wandered about and saw one black guy in the whole place. I walked up to him, and said, "Are you a writer?" He said, "No. Are you a writer?" I had no confidence, so I said, "No." I wasn't a published writer. We wandered off in different directions to find more important people to talk to. It wasn't a matter of anyone coming and saying you can't come in here, it's all white. It was just a matter of my not really knowing socially how to get in. I would just show up at these things, and, since nobody would throw me out, eventually I learned my way around a little bit. I never was very social; that's sort of a carryover from my childhood. Some science fiction writers are extremely social. Harlan certainly is. And then there are some of us that are practically reclusive. We barely get out of the house, and that's me more than it should be, I suppose.

Being found by other black writers was interesting, too. I was not known as a black writer, not because I was being ignored but because I have never liked the picture that was taken of me. I suppose I really look like that, and there's nothing I can do about that. I guess always I hope I'll look better or something. I've never allowed a picture on the back of any of my books. Black writers did not know I was black, but a couple of experiences helped that. I was asked by the *Washington Post* to review two books: one was Claudia Tate's *Black Women Writers at Work,* a book of interviews, and the other one was *Confirmation,* a huge anthology of black women writers edited by Amina and Amiri Baraka. After I went through the two books, I woundered why I was not in them. Then I thought, "I'm not in here because nobody knows about me." I had been in *Essence,* but apparently it hadn't reached anybody. One of the editors at Doubleday—her name is Veronica Mixon—did an article on me for *Essence* Magazine, but it didn't attract any particular attention. At any rate, I reviewed those two books. Then I went to a gathering of black writers here. I also attended a gathering of black women of the Diaspora writers at Michigan State University. I think that's when people began to realize, "Oh, she's black." There I was surrounded by other people who had maybe read my stuff, because I write with black characters. Suddenly these people discovered that I am black. So I guess that's when I began to be known. The little bit I did in *Essence* Magazine helped. Another writer, Sherley Anne Williams, did an article about me in *Ms.* Magazine—back when *Ms.* was more commercial. I guess the more exposure I got, the more people realized, "Oh, yeah,

she's black." I began hearing from people who were interested in me because I am a black writer as well as people who were interested in me because I write science fiction or because I am female.

I always try to convince my publishers that I have these three specific audiences for all my work—and occasionally another audience. For instance, I tried to push the idea that a New Age audience would be interested in *Parable of the Sower,* but I was never able to get it over with the publishers. They tend to think that you're going to appeal to one audience, and for most of my career it's been the science fiction audience. I was kind of confined there. I got another letter from another writer who asked whether she should worry about being put into this kind of category, the horror category or the science fiction category or whatever. I said, as long as your publisher doesn't put you there, it's fine. If your publisher won't advertise you to anybody but to one very small community, then you're in trouble. I know because I've been in that kind of trouble. I was in it for a long time. Some of them wouldn't advertise me at all. And none of them would send me out on tour until I got to this very small publishing company that was originally called Four Walls, Eight Windows. My editor, Dan Simon, did see that it might be possible to send me out on tour, and he did do that. No one else had. Dan's new publishing company is Seven Stories Press. Before that I had only gone out speaking when I was invited. Someone else paid for the travel because I wasn't making much money.

What was the response of your white readers who did not know that you are black?

By the time I went out on the tour that Dan sent me on, I was pretty much known, because my face had shown up quite a few places. There was a book called *Faces of Science Fiction,* and I was in that. I was also in some of the science fiction reference books—like encyclopedias or guides. I had attended conventions. So I don't think I shocked anybody in particular, except for some British people who came over here and asked if I would come and be interviewed for their television program. The man told me afterward that he hadn't heard that I was black, but he didn't seem to have a problem with it. He just didn't know. By the time I went out on tour, I was pretty much known.

Octavia Butler with Lisa See

SOURCE: "Octavia E. Butler," in *Publishers Weekly,* Vol. 240, No. 50, December 18, 1993, pp. 50-1.

Octavia E. Butler has made a reputation for herself as the only African American woman in the science fiction field. She has won back-to-back Hugos and a Nebula, science fiction's most prestigious prizes, and so far has published 10 books, including the highly successful *Patternmaster* and *Xenogenesis* series. Feeling, however, that the conventional labels attached to her name—African American, woman, feminist, SF writer—have been a hindrance as well as a blessing, she decided to place her latest book, **The Parable of the Sower,** with Four Walls Eight Windows with the express purpose of reaching a broad general audience. In its marketing materials, the publishing company and Butler's editor Dan Simon have tried to position Butler differently, comparing **The Parable of the Sower** to the "speculative fiction" of Toni Morrison's *Beloved* and Toni Cade Bambara's *The Salt Eaters.*

Butler lives in Pasadena, close to where she grew up, in an old-fashioned California court. On the day *PW* comes to visit, a brush fire is raging in the hills behind her bungalow. Perhaps for this reason, Butler has the shades drawn in the small living room where books and magazines stand in floor-to-ceiling shelves, in piles, in boxes. In what might have been a breakfast nook, Butler has her work area: a typewriter, notes jammed up on the wall, and more piles of books and papers.

At six feet tall, Butler cuts an imposing presence. She speaks with a deep, strong voice. "I'm black. I'm solitary. I've always been an outsider," she says. Like many writers, Butler daydreamed as a child, as a way to escape real life: her father died when she was a baby, her mother worked as a maid. Reading became a solace as she worked her way through the children's section of the Pasadena Library. When she found she had to be 14 to gain admittance to the adult section, she discovered science fiction magazines and fell in love with the genre. At age 12, inspired by the movie *Devil Girl from Mars,* Butler began writing what would become the first version of her *Patternmaster* series. The following year, she began submitting stories to magazines.

During her first semester at Pasadena City College, Butler won a short-story contest, but then there was a long dry spell before she received any other recognition for her work. She moved on to Cal State-L.A. where she "took everything but nursing classes. I'm a little bit dyslexic and worried about killing people," she says. (For this reason, Butler doesn't drive a car.)

In 1969, Butler was admitted to the Open Door Program of the Screen Writers' Guild, where she took a class from Harlan Ellison. He suggested she enroll in the Clarion Science Fiction Writers' Workshop, a "science fiction boot camp," which was then held in Pennsylvania. Butler's mother loaned her the money, and the 23-year-old Butler spent six weeks immersed in science fiction. At Clarion she found "another 25 outsiders. The first thing I did was hide and sleep in my room. The woman next door did the same thing. But then we emerged. We were all social retards, but we seemed to get along with each other."

She pauses. "I can't *think* how *that* will go over," she says, then lets out a big, deep, rolling laugh. "But to write science fiction you do have to be kind of a loner, live in your head, and, at the same time, have a love for talking. Clarion was a good place for that."

As luck would have it, Butler sold her first two pieces while she was still at the workshop: one to the Clarion anthology, the other to a projected Ellison collection that was never published. Then she didn't sell a word for the next five years.

To support herself, she took menial jobs: washing dishes, sweeping floors, doing warehouse inventory, sorting potato chips, all the while getting up at two or three in the morning to write. When she was laid off from a telephone solicitation job two weeks before Christmas, 1974, she decided it was time to fish or cut bait.

Earlier attempts to write a novel had been frustrated because Butler had been intimidated by the length. Determined now to look at each chapter as a short story, and finding inspiration in her earliest stories, she was able to produce **Patternmaster** in a matter of months. The book chronicles a future where humanity is divided into "Patternists," the ruling class who are joined together through telepathy, mute humans who serve the Patternists and "Clayarks," mutant human/griffin creatures who've been contaminated by a disease brought back from outer space.

With information gleaned from *Writer's Market,* Butler mailed her manuscript to Doubleday. By return mail, Doubleday editor Sharon Jarvis voiced her interest in buying the novel, albeit with the changes she outlined in a three-page, single-spaced letter. Elated, Butler complied, and she continued writing; by the end of the year, she had written **Mind of My Mind** and more than half of **Survivor.** Beginning in 1976, Doubleday began releasing the first four books in the *Patternmaster* series. (In 1984, St. Martin's published a fifth, **Clay's Ark.**)

Midway through the series, Butler realized she had the need to write another kind of book. It was **Kin-**

dred, in which an African American woman is transported from Southern California back through time to the antebellum South and the plantation of the man who is her ancestor. Doubleday published it as mainstream fiction in 1979; Butler herself calls it "a grim fantasy."

"I had this generation gap with my mother. She was a maid and I wished she wasn't. I didn't like seeing her go through back doors. . . . I also had this friend who could recite history but didn't feel it. One day he said, 'I wish I could kill all these old black people who are holding us back, but I'd have to start with my own parents.' He hadn't sorted out yet what the older generation had gone through. He thought they should have fought back. Well, it's easy to fight back when it's not your neck on the line."

Butler, on the other hand, had already made her peace with the past and what African Americans—including her own mother—had done in order to survive. "If my mother hadn't put up with those humiliations, I wouldn't have eaten very well or lived very comfortably," she explains. "So I wanted to write a novel that would make others feel the history: the pain and fear that black people had to live through in order to endure."

Since Butler had already been pigeon-holed as a science fiction writer, *Kindred* was, in many ways, a break-out novel. Later, it was the first of Butler's many titles to be reissued (by Beacon Press as part of its Black Women Writer Series) and is now often used in African American Studies classes. Still, the SF label stuck. Coming off the SF awards, Butler's agent, Merrilee Heifetz, negotiated a three-book deal with Warner Books for the *Xenogenesis* series, for which Butler drew heavily from the world around her.

"I'm a news junkie," Butler has explained in her author bio. "Science fiction fascinates me. Mythology interests me. Medicine sends my imagination all sorts of places. Whatever doesn't interest me today may very well interest me tomorrow." In person, she elaborates, "I started the series at a time when Reagan was saying we could have winnable nuclear wars and how we'd all be safer if we had more nuclear weapons. I thought if people believed this, then there must be something wrong with us as human beings."

These thoughts, combined with other news about captive breeding projects, prompted Butler to pursue a theory in which human intelligence is put at the service of hierarchical behavior. Through the mid-

'80s, Butler buried herself in the story of a post-nuclear earth and the aliens who offer salvation to the handful of human survivors by altering their negative genetic structure through interbreeding with the anemone-like aliens. The result: *Dawn* (1987), *Adulthood Rites* (1988) and *Imago* (1989).

What followed was what Butler calls on good days a "literary metamorphosis" and on bad days a "literary menopause," more commonly known as writer's block. "I knew that I wanted my next book to be about a woman who starts a religion, but everything I wrote seemed like garbage," she says. Over four years, Butler composed the first 75 pages several times. Reflecting back, she sees the problems as being threefold: "I was bored with what I was doing. I was trying to rewrite *Xenogenesis.* I also had this deep-seated feeling that wanting power, seeking power, was evil."

Poetry finally broke the block. "I'm the kind of person who looks for a complex way to say something," she explains. "Poetry simplifies it. When I started to write poetry, I was forced to pay attention word by word, line by line." (Poetry appears in *The Parable of the Sower* in the form of excerpts from "Earthseed: The Books of the Living," the holy works written by the protagonist, Lauren Oya Olamina.)

Butler still faced the problems of creating a religion she herself could believe in. "I didn't want to make fun of religion. Lauren's father, a Baptist minister, is neither a fool nor a hypocrite. He's a decent man who can't cope with the situation he's in. Lauren feels about religion the way I feel about writing. For her it's a positive obsession, even while she realizes it's ridiculous and impossible."

Lauren's "Earthseed" religion is centered around the idea that God is change. "I think one of our worst problems as human beings is our lack of foresight and our denial. Educated people behave this way so they can keep their jobs. Uneducated people do it by doing drugs and taking too much alcohol. I used to think that we'd all die from nuclear war. Now I see that we're not going to do that, but it wouldn't be much different than drinking ourselves to death. So for the book I looked around for a force that nothing could escape. One of the first poems I wrote sounded like a nursery rhyme. It begins: God is power, and goes on to: God is malleable. This concept gave me what I needed."

In her writing Butler has probed science fiction's three premises: what if, if only and if this goes on. In *The Parable of the Sower* she pursues the and-if-this-goes-on category, once again drawing from the news—smart pills, gangs, global warming, drought, sociopathic behavior, the swallowing up of American companies by foreign conglomerates—to create a story that takes place in a desperately dry 21st-century Southern California, a place of walled enclaves and drugged-out arsonists, where people murder for water, food and jobs. Lauren is a "sharer," one who suffers from a congenital trait: her mother took a "smart" drug while pregnant, and Lauren feels other people's physical pain as well as her own. "This is a rough disability for her time," Butler concedes. "Lauren's ability is perceived as a problem, not a power."

Most of Butler's female characters, including Lauren, appear almost incidentally to be black. "The fact that they're black is not the most important thing on my mind," she says. "I'm just interested in telling a story, hopefully a good one." Nevertheless, she concedes that she offers a unique voice in a field dominated by white men. "I'm the only black woman writing science fiction today *because* I'm the only black woman writing science fiction," she explains. "I don't mean to be facetious, but it's true."

White women have already prospered in the genre, of course, and Butler herself has been influenced by many of them. At the Clarion workshop, she was encouraged by Joanna Russ to stop using her initials, a then-common practice for women who wanted to write science fiction. In addition to Ursula Le Guin and Kate Wilhelm, Butler has also been inspired by Marion Zimmer Bradley and Zena Henderson. "But for me the greatest influences were the early pulp magazine writers. I loved the story by Ray Bradbury and Leigh Brackett [she was one of the best-known early women science fiction writers] called 'Lorelei of the Red Mist.' Its central idea was having a private eye on Venus instead of on Main Street."

As time goes on, Butler hopes to shuck off all her labels. "I write about things that interest me, and I'm not the most unique person on earth," she concludes. "So I figure what will interest me will interest other people."

GENERAL COMMENTARY

Frances Smith Foster

SOURCE: "Octavia Butler's Black Female Future Fiction," in *Extrapolation,* Vol. 23, No. 1, Spring, 1982, pp. 37-49.

The mythology that Octavia Butler creates in her first three books, *Patternmaster* (1976), *Mind of My Mind* (1977), and *Survivor* (1978),[1] has elements of familiarity. She writes about a future society wherein a network of telepaths control the Earth and occasionally get out of control themselves. She writes of colonists who settle on an alien planet and battle hostile, furry creatures. She writes of strange, microorganisms brought to Earth by astronauts that threaten the existence of human civilization. She writes of genetic evolution and selective breeding. Like most contemporary women authors, she writes of women in nontraditional roles.

From the start, her work has been labeled "fine, old fashioned sf." Reviewers consider her "a vigorous, nimble storyteller," "erratic and gifted," and an author who "may give us something really first rate one of these days." Her characters are judged "surprisingly adaptive." Her ideas have "intrinsic energy."[2] In short, reviewers consider her a speculative fiction writer who is adequate, potentially outstanding, but at present neither particularly innovative nor interesting. However, Octavia Butler is not just another woman science fiction writer. Her major characters are black women, and through her characters and through the structure of her imagined social order, Butler consciously explores the impact of race and sex upon future society.

Ironically, many speculative fiction scholars have been lamenting the neglect of those very areas with which Butler has been dealing. Marilyn Hacker, for example, has declared it a "serious drawback" that speculative fiction has devoted so little attention to "the vast area of human experience" which includes "family structures, child-rearing, and child-bearing, sexual relations—and relations between sexes (*not,* as some men would have it, the same topic at all)."[3] Ursula Le Guin is one who has decried the fact that "in general, American sf has assumed a permanent hierarchy of superiors and inferiors, with rich, ambitious, aggressive males at the top, then a great gap, and then at the bottom the poor, the uneducated, the faceless masses, and all the women."[4] And Pamela Sargent has mentioned, what most of us know, that "the number of black sf writers can be counted on the fingers of one hand."[5] Since Octavia Butler is a black woman who writes speculative fiction which is primarily concerned with social relationships, where rulers include women and nonwhites, the neglect of her work is startling.

Octavia Butler consciously chose to introduce the *isms* of race and sex into the genre and obviously did not set out to write "fine, old fashioned sf." She stated: "When I began reading science fiction, I was disappointed at how little . . . creativity and freedom was used to portray the many racial, ethnic, and class variations. Also, I could not help noticing how few significant woman characters there were in science fiction. Fortunately, all this has been changing over the past few years. I intend my writing to contribute to the change."[6] A brief summary of her mythos and an analysis of her female characters will show the significant changes that Octavia Butler is making.

She posits a society of mentally superior persons created by the selective breeding of those with special sensitivities, mentally linked to each other in a hierarchical pattern. Our space exploration will cause a cataclysmic event which compels these persons to manifest themselves and to take a more direct role in governing human society in order to insure its survival. The humans of ordinary abilities, with the consensus of this ruling class, will try to preserve the "American way of life." The story goes like this: one day not too long from now, our first starship will return to Earth. Contaminated by a space virus, our heretofore disciplined and loyal astronauts will evade their quarantine, return to their communities, and spread a disease which will eventually kill one-half of the world's population and mutate the children of any afflicted who survive. It is characteristic of Clayark disease, as it will be called, that those infected will be compelled to spread their contagion; thus, "Clayarks" will become the common enemy of every healthy human being on Earth.

At this time, the Patternists, persons whose psychic proclivities had been developed secretly through several centuries of breeding, will reveal themselves. Doro, a genetic mutant whose ability to consume the vitality and assume the body of any human allowed him to live for thousands of years, had bred these people partially to insure himself a continuous resource for his own revitalization and partially to satisfy his intellectual curiosity. Individually, these telepaths have influenced people for years, but it was not until the mid-twentieth century that their appetites for power and their mutual antagonisms were controlled enough to allow them to organize. A Patternist society developed when Doro's daughter, Mary, during her transition from latent to active telepath, created a mental connection between herself and the most advanced actives. Mary, as the nucleus, became their ruler, for not only was she the strongest, but through the pattern, Mary was able to neutralize the inherent hostilities of actives, to discern satisfying outlets for their special skills, and to relieve the suffering of la-

tent telepaths by facilitating their transition and thus ridding society of much of its violence and crime.

The Patternist society is a total hierarchy, from Patternmaster, as Mary's position came to be known, to Housemaster, to journeymen and apprentices of various rank, down to mutes, or those with no telepathic powers at all. Because of their limited mental capacities, until the revelation precipitated by the Clayark crisis, the mutes will have no idea that their actions and thoughts are not their own. Programmed to supreme loyalty to Patternists, they freely perform such mundane activities as producing and selling goods, providing governmental services, and rearing children (both their own and those of the Patternists). Though subjugated, mutes will continue to operate within their own class with relative autonomy. Their activities, values, and prejudices will remain essentially those of twentieth-century America, but violence and crime will be obviated by removal of troubled latents, by the mutes' recognition of the higher authority of the Patternists, and by the Patternists' programming of mutes for docility.

The Clayark crisis will not only cause the Patternists to reveal themselves but will necessitate their dividing Earth into sectors protected and ruled by Housemasters. This will create new governing units, new loyalties, and new cultures, for so insidious will be the Clayark micro-organism that the survivors of sectors decimated by Clayarks will not be admitted into other Households, but will become wild humans who spend their lives hunting and being hunted. The new elite will be determined not by color, sex, or national origin, but by extrasensory powers. Having no special mental powers, the mutes cling within their own group to their notions of superiority based on physical appearance. Since Clayark disease changes the human form to that of a four-legged beast, some mutes will develop cults that worship the form. Patternists will sometimes reward faithful mutes by allowing groups of them a one-way trip to search for new planets upon which they might be able to continue their race.

One such group, the Missionaries of Humanity, will find a "second earth," but it is inhabited by Kohn, furry creatures of various hues from rare blue to most common yellow. The Kohn have a humanlike form, but because their fur, color, and culture are different, the Missionaries will consider them primitive, inferior, and tractable. This ethnocentricity will allow one of the tribes, the Garkohn, to enslave the Missionaries as easily and unobtrusively as the Patternists had, thus giving a clue that it is not entirely their lack of extrasensory abilities as much as their limited concept of humanity that jeopardizes the survival of most of the human race. These colonists will receive another chance to continue Earth's culture when Alanna, a wild child saved from execution and adopted by a Missionary couple who dared defy custom, liberates the colonists from the Garkohn. However, given their history, it is by no means certain that the Missionaries will be able to develop the necessary tolerance of and respect for differences in appearance and culture that would insure their survival.

Butler indicates a future influenced by continued development of our current scientific inquiry, but one which is also determined by chance, nature, or destiny. For example, Doro is a genetic mutant who comes to terms with his unique powers. He combines self-preservation and intellectual curiosity to explore the possibilities of an existing phenomenon. Mary is his creation, but the pattern that develops around her is inexplicable. The Clayark disease is a mysterious ailment brought to Earth as a result of investigations in space, but starships are also the means of possible salvation. Humans will not control nature, but they will be able to develop knowledge of and influence over natural occurrences in both positive and negative ways.

About social relations, Butler is more explicit, though here, too, she appears to conform to a recognized hypothesis. A race of mental giants will dominate society. Laws and customs will become more rigid and authoritarian as major power struggles are limited to those of a select group. Though the extremes of rebellion and abuse will be eliminated, both telepaths and mutes will continue to have the usual emotional and physical needs, desires, and weaknesses.

The story line is interesting but not provocative. Having no particular technological ideology and inventing no special devices, presenting a hierarchical society with no extraordinary personality developments, Octavia Butler does seem a mite old-fashioned. But her story has striking differences from other literature of the genre, and it is because of her particular mythos that she can assiduously develop the implications of these differences without sacrificing the pleasure of her tales. First, the elite in Butler's new world includes women. White males are proportionately represented in the lower classes not because they are male, but because as a sex they possess no unusual quantity of special gifts and a usual quantity of foibles. And, most significantly, Butler's major characters are black women. Not only does her work present a possible answer to Joanna Russ's ques-

tions,—"What can a heroine do?"[7]—but it goes further as it represents a place where Afro-American literature with no unnecessary or significant loss of identity may legitimately mingle with the so-called mainstream literature even as that "mainstream" is accommodating the tributary of women.

One of Butler's major concerns is the possibility of a society in which males and females "are honestly considered equal."[8] This idea is developed by her manipulation of three major characters; however, it is important that she also creates several secondary female characters who are not identified by race. The reader can then assume that these characters are not necessarily black and therefore generalize about the position of all women in future society even as the levels of racial integration that Butler assumes are recognized.

In *Patternmaster,* Jansee, the lead wife of Patternmaster Rayal, is an excellent example of Butler's use of minor female characters to suggest the ambiance within which the major characters exist. Jansee is the only sibling that Rayal did not kill during his struggle to gain the Pattern. Jansee, the "strongest sister," had chosen not to compete with him, not through fear, but through a strong reverence for life. She chose instead to be Rayal's conscience. As such she risks his wrath continually, steadfastly lecturing Rayal about his duties to his subjects and goading him into critical analyses of power. Rayal's reply to a taunt by Jansee, that perhaps he would prefer her to worship him as did many of his people, shows that he recognizes her value and strength. "Not that you would," he says, " . . . but it doesn't matter. There are times when I need someone around me who isn't afraid of me." Jansee's knowledge of her own worth is clear when she replies, "Lest your own conceit destroy you" (p. 10).

Another example of a minor character who gives insight into the possible roles of women is Gehl in *Survivor.* Gehl is a Garkohn huntress with whom Alanna, the protagonist, has exchanged language lessons and friendship. Like so many of the Butler women, Gehl is ambitious but realistic. "I'm going to challenge the Third Hunter," she tells Alanna. "I can beat him. I know I can. . . . Natahk [the First Hunter] . . . says my ambition will kill me. He knows that if I beat the Third Hunter, I will take on the Second." But Gehl has no intention of sacrificing her life in pursuit of ultimate power. She does not, for example, plan to challenge Natahk, for, as she says, "I only challenge where there is a chance for me to win" (pp. 17-18). Gehl does become Second Hunter in the tribe and the mistress of Natahk, thus forming a union with power. Of course, their relationship is not without problems. Natahk covets Alanna, and this contributes to, but is not the sole cause of, a rupture in the friendship between the two women.

Among the ideas garnered from secondary characters is the possibility that society will eventually allow open access to jobs and positions of authority; that while some women will be defeated by their ambitions and jealousies, many will exhibit an unusual resistance to self-destructive power quests; and that one way women will compensate for their physical limitations is by forming liaisons with persons of power. While such alliances may be sexual, Butler makes it clear that these women, powerful and purposeful in their own right, need not rely upon eroticism to gain their ends.

A brief analysis of the evolution of her three major women characters facilitates further understanding of Butler's speculations on the future. The first book, *Patternmaster,* gives us Amber as a significant and complex individual who functions as a symbol, a catalyst, and a mentor. The plot, however, centers around the struggle between an older brother, Coransee, and his younger brother, Teray, for the inheritance of the Pattern. Amber discerns in Teray a power to heal as well as to kill, and in teaching him to develop his humane tendencies, she teaches him the skills he needs to ultimately defeat his brother.

In *Mind of My Mind,* Mary gradually emerges as the protagonist; however, a central issue in this work concerns the effect of extraordinary mental powers upon individuals and their social relationships. Mary is the most developed of Doro's several children who people this book. She comes into her own when she overthrows her father; but Doro, his experiment, and his use of power are as much a focus of this work as Mary, who defines the limits of and represents an alternative to Doro's power.

It is not until the third novel, *Survivor,* that Butler presents a heroine. From beginning to end, *Survivor* is Alanna's story. Unlike Mary and Amber, Alanna has no extrasensory powers. Alanna (the etymological meaning of this word is "My Child," and it is a term of endearment) is an archetype, the kind of human who can survive in the future. Her attempts to overcome her weaknesses, to know and protect that which is vital, and to accept necessary changes inform our sensibilities concerning the potential of ordinary human beings and constitute the plot.

Each of these women is black. This is given as a fact, and it does, at times, affect their attitudes and influence their social situations; however, racial conflict or even racial tension is not the primary focus of the novels. Butler explains that she feels no particular need to champion black women, but that she writes from her own experience and sensitivities:

> The Black women I write about aren't struggling to make ends meet, but they are the descendants of generations of those who did. Mothers are likely to teach their daughters about survival as they have been taught, and daughters are likely to learn, even subconsciously. I usually put my characters into positions that show us how well they've learned.[9]

With this statement she affirms her place in Afro-American literary history without excluding her work from a larger context. Butler is theorizing upon the same questions that Ursula Le Guin, for example, has raised: "What about the cultural and the racial Other?" Like Butler, Le Guin affirms the inextricability of humankind:

> If you deny any affinity with another person or kind of person, if you declare it to be wholly different from yourself—as men have done to women, and class has done to class, and nation has done to nation—you may hate it, or deify it; but in either case you have denied its spiritual equality, and its human reality. You have made it into a thing, to which the only possible relationship is a power relationship. And thus, you have fatally impoverished your own reality. You have, in fact, alienated yourself.[10]

Butler explores the future implications of racism and sexism by focusing upon relationships between powerful persons who are various kinds of Other.

In *Patternmaster,* Amber, "a golden brown woman with hair that was a cap of small, tight black curls," is not only a healer of special skill, but also "a terrifyingly efficient killer" (p. 56). As a child, she had been victimized by her schoolmaster. Knowing that he was not mentally strong enough to keep her as his lover once she entered transition, the schoolmaster manipulated a situation wherein Amber had to kill a Housemaster. Though it was clearly in self-defense, her crime was exacerbated by the shame of the other Housemasters that a child, not yet in full possession of her powers, could be strong enough to kill one of their number. The heroic efforts of Kai, a female Housemaster, save Amber from death, and Amber subsequently lives as an Independent, welcome in any House because of her superior healing skills but refusing to join any Household permanently.

When Amber chooses to become Teray's mentor, she is choosing to join her power with his. She chooses further to become his lover, and finally, without consulting him, she conceives their child. But she will not marry him. Consider this exchange:

> [Teray] "Stay with me, Amber. Be my wife—lead wife, once I have my House." She shook her head. "No. I warned you. I love you. . . . But no. . . . Because I want the same thing you want. My House. Mine. . . . I could have given my life for you. . . . But I could never give my life *to* you."

"I'm not asking for your life," he said angrily. "As my lead wife you'd have authority, freedom . . . ."

"How interested would you be in becoming my lead husband?" she asks. (pp. 108-9)

Not only does Butler introduce a rarity in science fiction, a major character who is an independent and competent woman, but she makes this woman bisexual. Teray questions her, "Which do you prefer, Amber, really?" Amber, comfortable with her sexuality, explains, "When I meet a woman who attracts me, I prefer women. . . . And when I meet a man who attracts me, I prefer men." Butler implies that bisexuality will not be the taboo in the future that it is today, for Teray, after brief thought, decides, "If that's the way you are, I don't mind" (p. 108); and thereafter, sexual preference is not an issue between them.

Some members of the *Patternmaster* society may be more sexually tolerant, but women are still sex objects and even Amber can be sexually exploited. For instance, the lust of her schoolmaster, Coransee, complicates her life. When Amber and Teray become his prisoners, Coransee uses her to strike at Teray. He orders Teray to send Amber to his bed. When informed of this, Amber replies, "I'm sorry Teray. . . . Sorry to be of use to him against you. . . . He doesn't give a damn about me now except to break me. He's doing this to humiliate you" (p. 128).

The relationship between Amber and Teray shows how males and females may relate to each other in the future, but it is secondary to the inevitable confrontation between Teray and Coransee. Amber has taught Teray to use his killing powers and to discover his healing strength as well. She, as mentor, made him ready for the confrontation, and she, as lover, becomes the catalyst for the fight. Teray decides he can help Amber, free her from Coransee, only by winning the Pattern. The central conflict of the novel, the rivalry between the brothers, is symbolized by their attitudes toward this woman: Coransee desires to subjugate her and to benefit from her skills through ownership. Teray wants her to be free and hopes she will freely work with him.

In *Patternmaster,* the major woman character complements the male hero. Teray has defeated Coransee, Amber nurses his wounds. "You saved me," he tells her. "Healed you," she corrects (p. 153). Teray has won the Pattern and Amber agrees to set up her House in Forsythe to be near him. Together they represent a good power. Rayal, in dying words, tells Teray that Amber will "always be a better healer. You won't ever surpass her in healing skill. And she won't ever surpass you in strength. . . . You have the right combination of abilities" (p. 160). In Butler's second book, Mary is the mother of the Pattern and thus has preceded Amber by many years. Perhaps it is for this reason that race is a more obvious concern. Amber, though consistently described as black, attributes no particular significance to her ancestry. Mary, on the other hand, must reconcile a number of racial issues in order to establish the First Family.

Although the question of power is central to *Mind of My Mind,* and once again we have a serious confrontation between conflicting manifestations of that power, the resolution of basic questions concerning race is vital to the overall theme. Mary's "light coffee" skin color and her "traffic light green" eyes are unwelcome reminders to her that she was conceived when Doro was wearing a white man's body. Though her respect and love for Doro do not cease when he is white, she likes him best when he is a black man. Since he can assume any physical appearance, Mary finds it essential to determine what race Doro really is. "Who were your people?" she asks him. He answers, "They had another name then, but you would call them Nubians." "Black people," Mary says. Doro affirms this, but states, "It doesn't matter." To this Mary replies, "You mean you don't want to admit you have anything in common with us. But if you were born black, you *are* black. Still black, no matter what color you take on" (pp. 60-61).

When she discovers that her prescribed husband is white, Mary is enraged. Karl, her prospective mate, is not happy with the arrangement either, but race is not his primary objection. He tells Mary, "You shouldn't get the idea that I dislike you because you're black. . . . I wouldn't want you here no matter what color you were" (p. 20). Karl values his autonomy and wants no interference. In spite of their animosity, Karl and Mary, being two of the most highly developed telepaths, realize that unless they can cooperate, the Pattern is doomed. As they work toward the common goal, they realize that they have "something that is working" and that they have become "a unit." Recognizing that they have come to respect, trust, and even love each other, Mary and

Karl decide to create a child to "give some validity" (p. 143) to their union.

Mary is neither of the two basic black female characters which Daryl Dance so aptly describes in her essay, "Black Eve or Madonna: A Study of the Antithetical Views of the Mother in Black American Literature."[11] Mary does, certainly, exhibit Madonna characteristics. She is "a figure of courage, strength, and endurance." As mother of the Pattern, she does give "birth and sustenance to positive growth and advancement among her people." But her people, Mary decides, are of every race. Nor is she a stereotypical Madonna in other ways. As a child she would steal anything that caught her fancy, particularly books, for she declared, "If I didn't have anything to read, I'd go really crazy" (p. 2). She is violent. When a man tries to force his way into her house, nineteen-year-old Mary breaks his head open with a cast-iron skillet and calmly walks out of the house, leaving him for dead. Throughout her life, Mary is impetuous and often fights those who offend her, including Doro, her father, and Karl, her husband. Though she becomes more disciplined as she matures, her pugnacity remains. Yet, Mary is not an Eve, the sin symbol of sex and seduction. Though she succumbed "to the tempting allures and wiles" of her father and became one of his lovers, Mary does not share his casually murderous attitude, and she, in fact, has the social conscience that Doro lacks. It is Doro, not Mary, who "gives birth to the sins of the world which destroy." It is Mary who destroys Doro for the good of society.

Mary is a tough-talking, hard-fighting woman who can be physically over-powered but not defeated. Her competitiveness and aggression are tempered by a fine compassion. When she discovers her ability to create a means through which pain-crazed people can gain peace, she fervently incorporates them into the Pattern. At the same time, she recognizes that her desire to succor is intertwined with her desire to control, and she accepts this:

> Why did I want to see as many latents as possible brought through transition? So I could be an empress? I wouldn't even say that out loud. It sounded so stupid. But, whatever I called myself, I was definitely going to wind up with a lot of people taking orders from me, and that really didn't sound like such a bad thing.... Altruism, ambition—what else is there? Need? (pp. 104-5)

Mary discovers that her strength is insured by her power to tap the energy of others. Though she believes herself a parasite, she is well aware that she

also brings peace, unity, and purpose to the Patternists and to the society which they control.

Mary and, to a lesser extent, Amber are women of special mental abilities and purpose. They are complex and independent women, combinations not only of Eve and Madonna, but also of God and Satan, and as such they represent a new kind of female character in both science fiction and Afro-American literature. The men with which these women associate are also powerful. Their relationships provide occasion for Butler to explore closely the various forms and combinations of power available to persons of unusual ability. Through them, she is able to speculate about new human values which recognize differences in physical appearance, sexual preferences, and personal skills and which are ultimately concerned with insuring the survival of human beings by developing the best uses of power. Mary represents the best use of a superior mentality. Before his defeat Doro realizes this:

> Mary. She was like a living creature of fire. Not human.... He saw her now as she really was, and she might have been his twin.

But, no, she was not his twin. She was a small, much younger being. A complete version of him.... She was a symbiant, a being living in partnership with her people. She gave them unity, they fed her, and both thrived.... And though she had great power, she was not naturally, instinctively a killer. He was. (p. 165)

Unlike Mary and Amber, Alanna, in *Survivor,* has no extrasensory powers. She is a human of the future, one the Patternists would call a mute. Alanna neither supports her chosen man nor battles her father for power. Alanna is a survivor. Her parents died in a Clayark attack when she was eight years old. She existed as a wild child. When she was fifteen, a Missionary guard shot her for stealing food. Jules Verrick rescued her from execution. Alanna lived as the Verricks' alien foster child and was taken with them to colonize another planet. She was among a group captured by Tehkohn raiders and was the only prisoner to endure. After two years, she returned to the colony and was able through her skills, intelligence, and alliances to save the Missionary colony from complete subjugation by the Garkohns.

Alanna is Afro-Asian, but she is treated by the Missionaries as a black. Physically, she is a perfect balance of the two races, created from a loving and apparently equal relationship, for of her parents we are told that "they protected each other, these two, and together, they protected the child they had created. Even in the end when the Clayarks came to loot and kill, the man and woman held them off long enough for the child to escape" (p. 27). She is thus an outsider to the colony, both racially and culturally. She is self-sufficient, meets people and events with intelligence and courage, and assumes the risks involved in equal relationships. Though she is able to understand and to accept the Missionaries, they are never able to accept her; and they feel no need to understand her or any other non-Missionary. It is the absence of ethnocentricity that insures Alanna's survival. She is the only one who will bother to learn the Garkohn language and customs. When captured by Tehkohn, she wins their approval, because though she is "clearly secure in her private belief that [they] were the ones malformed and ugly," she evidences not only personal strength of character but a profound respect for their being. Alanna's tolerance, we understand, was acquired because she learned to distinguish between what is truly valid for humans and what is merely surface. And because she accepts herself as she is.

Alanna's strangeness and assurance intrigues Duit, the big, blue Hao, supreme leader of the Tehkohn. When Duit sees this captive knock out a hunter who needlessly provoked her and fearlessly stand off his two defenders, Duit determines to take her as his consort. Alanna has no choice but to enter the relationship, but Duit finds her unconquerable. He describes their early days thus: "When she behaved foolishly and I beat her, she fought back. No Tehkohn would have done that. . . . She behaved like another Hao, this furless one. She thought she was blue. And though that made me angry sometimes, it also pleased me" (pp. 110-11).

Theirs is such a tempestuous association that Alanna wears a knife to compensate for her lesser physical strength. Eventually, she finds Duit's size and strength, his sensitivity and adaptability more impressive than his strange blue fur. The turning point comes on a hunting trip when Alanna's carelessness results in her being attacked by a Jehruk. Weaponless, Duit risks his life for her by fighting the enormous beast. Alanna, in turn, saves Duit's life by making a spectacular kill with her bow and arrow. After this, Duit relates: "I did not beat her again. Not once. And most of the time, she obeyed. When she did not, we talked—sometimes very loudly. But in spite of our disagreements, our nights together became good again. I lay with her contentedly and her knife remained in its sheath" (p. 114).

Butler's females are usually healers, teachers, artists, mothers. Yet, they are not the traditional literary Earth Mothers or Culture Bearers. They exercise direct authority. They excel in a variety of careers (motherhood is rarely their major occupation), and they do, when necessary, kill brutally, efficiently, and even joyfully. Note the description of Mary's defeat of Doro: "Doro fought desperately, uselessly. He could feel Mary's amusement now. He had nearly killed her, had been about to kill the man she had attached herself to so firmly. Now she took her revenge. She consumed him slowly drinking in his terror and his life, drawing out her own pleasure, and laughing through his soundless screams."

The women represent a future, perfect use of power, but this does not suggest a future female monopoly nor a world of strong women alone. Mary killed Doro to solidify her position as sole ruler of the Pattern and to protect the Patternists; however, the needed thrust, her final surge of strength came when Doro started to kill the one individual with whom she had intimately allied herself. Each of Octavia Butler's major women characters choose to form intimate attachments with strong, humane males. If, like Amber, they refuse marriage because they want to head their own Houses, they, like Amber, also compromise, cooperate, and often, as Duit terms it, "obey" their male consorts.

The best summary of Butler's speculations on race can be seen through the relationship of Duit, the gigantic Hao, and Alanna, our archetypal human, biological child of an Asian woman and an African man, foster child of the European-Americans, Jules and Neila Verrick. Alanna tries to explain her marriage to her Missionary-of-Humanity foster parents and to gain their blessing for the union: "'I'm a wild human,' said Alanna quietly. 'That's what I've always been. . . . I haven't lost myself. Not to anyone. . . . In time, I'll also be a Tehkohn judge. I want to be. And I'm Duit's wife and your daughter'" (p. 168). The Verricks cannot accept this. Alanna's relationship with the furry blue alien is beyond their tolerance. With tears in her eyes, Alanna accepts their limitations and says, "For a while, I was your daughter. Thank you for that anyway" (p. 185). The Verricks represent those for whom racism may prove to be inextricable. For them the future is uncertain. We leave them following their cartload of possessions, searching for a place where they may live as they have historically. Alanna, able to reconcile the reality of her heritage with the demands of the present, survives.

The Earth people's failure to be humane is contrasted to the behavior of the Kohn at the naming ceremony of Alanna and Duit's daughter, Tien. Tien is a thickly furred, deep-green little girl who to the Kohn is "strangely shaded" and has "wrong hands and feet." But in their ritual, they accept her, saying, "We are an ancient people. The Kohn empire was the handiwork of our ancestors. . . . We are a new people. . . . In each child we welcome, we are reborn" (p. 180).

For the feminist critic, Octavia Butler may present problems. Her female characters are undeniably strong and independent; but whether, as Joanna Russ insists is crucial, "the assumptions underlying the entire narrative are feminist," is uncertain, for "who wins and who loses"[12] is less clear than that a compromise has been made which unifies the best of each woman and man. For Afro-American literary critics, Butler can present problems as well, for their attention has been focused upon the assumptions and depictions about the black experience of the past and the present; yet the implications of Butler's vision should be a significant challenge. For the science fiction critics, Butler's work offers numerous areas of inquiry, but there should exist no doubt that in her contribution this writer has already given us "something really first rate."

Notes

1. *Patternmaster* (1976; rpt. New York: Avon Books, 1979); *Mind of My Mind* (New York: Doubleday, 1977); *Survivor* (New York: Doubleday, 1978). References are to these editions and are noted in the text.

2. Reviews quoted are *Kirkus Review,* 15 May 1976; *Kirkus Review,* 15 Jan. 1978; *Kirkus Review,* 15 Apr. 1977; and *Library Journal,* 1 Apr. 1978. They are typical. In no review have I found any recognition concerning the implications of the sex and race of Butler's characters.

3. Marilyn Hacker, "Science Fiction and Feminism: The Work of Joanna Russ," *Chrysalis,* 4 (Spring 1977), 70.

4. Ursula Le Guin, "American SF and the Other," *Science Fiction Studies,* 2 (Nov. 1975), 210.

5. Pamela Sargent, "Introduction: Women in Science Fiction," *Women of Wonder* (New York: Vintage Books, 1975), p. xv.

6. Quoted in *Contemporary Authors,* vols. 73-76 (Detroit: Gale Research Company, 1978), p. 104.

7. Joanna Russ, "What Can a Heroine Do? or Why Women Can't Write," in *Images of Women in Fiction,* ed. Susan Koppelman Carnillar (Bowling Green, Ohio: Bowling Green Univ. Popular Press, 1972), pp. 3-20.

8. Quoted in Veronica Nixon, "Futurist Woman: Octavia Butler," *Essence,* 15 Apr. 1979, p. 12.

9. Nixon, p. 1.

10. Le Guin, pp. 209-10.

11. Daryl Dance, "Black Eve or Madonna: A Study of the Antithetical Views of the Mother in Black American Literature," in Roseann P. Bell et al., eds., *Sturdy Black Bridges* (New York: Anchor Press, 1979), pp. 123-32. Quotations which characterize the Eve and the Madonna are from this source unless otherwise noted.

12. "Reflections on Science Fiction: An Interview with Joanna Russ," *Quest,* 2 (Summer 1975), 43-44.

Ruth Salvaggio

SOURCE: "Octavia Butler and the Black Science-Fiction Heroine," in *Black American Literature Forum,* Vol. 18, No. 2, Summer, 1984, pp. 78-81.

A traditional complaint about science fiction is that it is a male genre, dominated by male authors who create male heroes who control distinctly masculine worlds. In the last decade, however, a number of women writers have been changing that typical scenario. Their feminine and feminist perspectives give us a different kind of science fiction, perhaps best described by Pamela Sargent's term "Women of Wonder."[1] In a sense, Octavia Butler's science fiction is a part of that new scenario, featuring strong female protagonists who shape the course of social events. Yet in another sense, what Butler has to offer is something very different. Her heroines are black women who inhabit racially mixed societies. Inevitably, the situations these women confront involve the dynamic interplay of race and sex in futuristic worlds. How a feminist science-fiction character responds to a male-dominated world is one thing; how Butler's black heroines respond to racist and sexist worlds is quite another.

Butler's concern with racism and sexism is a conscious part of her vision. As she herself explains, a particularly "insidious problem" with science fiction is that it "has always been nearly all white, just as until recently, it's been nearly all male."[2] Confronting this "problem" head-on, Butler places her heroines in worlds filled with racial and sexual obstacles, forcing her characters to survive and eventually overcome these societal barriers to their independence. Sometimes her black heroines are paired with white men who challenge their abilities; sometimes they are paired with powerful black men who threaten their very autonomy and existence. And, always, the society in which they live constantly reminds them of barriers to their independence. Tracing the plight of each heroine is like following different variations on a single theme, the yearning for independence and autonomy. That Butler's women, despite all odds, achieve that autonomy makes her science fiction a fresh and different contribution to the genre, and makes Butler herself an exciting new voice in the traditional domains of science fiction, feminism, and black literature.

This article is intended to introduce Octavia Butler through her science-fiction heroines—beginning with the defiant Amber in *Patternmaster* (1976), then moving to the confused but powerful Mary in *Mind of My Mind* (1977) and the compromising Alanna in *Survivor* (1978.)[3] The heroine I leave until last is one we encounter as the old woman Emma, hovering in the background of *Mind of My Mind.* She later appears as Anyanwu in Butler's most recent science-fiction novel, *Wild Seed* (1980). In Anyanwu we discover the inspiring force for all of Butler's heroines. And in *Wild Seed* we discover dimensions of Butler's fictive world—not the typical feminist utopia, but a flawed world in which racially and sexually oppressed individuals negotiate their way through a variety of personal and societal barriers.

Germain Greer's term "obstacle race" seems particularly appropriate when discussing Butler and her fiction, largely because the women discussed in both situations confront peculiarly social obstacles. Just as women artists, according to Greer, should be seen "as members of a group having much in common, tormented by the same conflicts of motivation and the same practical difficulties, the obstacles both external and surmountable, internal and insurmountable of the race for achievement,"[4] so Butler's heroines share in this social and personal struggle for assertion and understanding.

Their particular struggle, however, is accentuated by the extraordinary mental facilities they possess: Each of Butler's four science-fiction novels is built around a society of telepaths linked to each other through a mental "pattern." Thus when Anyanwu, the African woman in *Wild Seed,* is transported on a slave ship to colonial America, she senses the horror of slavery

well before she actually witnesses its real-life horrors. Or when Mary, in *Mind of My Mind,* ultimately confronts her oppressive father, she kills him through the machinations of a gruesome mental war game. The violence that accompanies such racial and sexual conflict rarely centers on women in the way that it does in Butler's novels. Here we have females who must take the kind of action normally reserved for white, male protagonists. White males, curiously, play an important role in Butler's fiction—sometimes as enemies, sometimes as foils to the women. We might begin with a discussion of them in Butler's first novel, *Patternmaster.* There they dominate the plot until, as one female science-fiction writer describes in a different context, "a woman appeared."[5] Let us begin, then, with the traditional science-fiction plot, and the sudden intrusion of a woman.

It should not be surprising that *Patternmaster,* Butler's first novel, revolves around that typical science-fiction plot: It employs two of the most traditional mythic structures—the inheritance of sons and the journey motif. Rayal, the Patternmaster, is dying; his two sons, Coransee and Teray, vie for control of the Pattern. This rivalry of sons for possession of the father's empire follows the outlines of an archetypal literary construct: Coransee, the stronger and more obvious heir, is defeated by the young and inconspicuous Teray, who ultimately proves himself—despite all outward appearances—to be the righteous heir. Ostensibly, then, *Patternmaster* is a novel which presents us with a "good-son" hero. We are glad when the honest Teray defeats his sinister sibling; we are glad that this decent young man has overcome the corruption and power lust of the older brother.

But all this is not really what *Patternmaster* is about. Before the adventures of our hero begin to unfold, our heroine appears—Amber. The circumstances of her appearance are just as curious as she is. Teray, captive in his brother's household, calls for a "healer" to treat a woman who has been beaten by a man. Enter Amber—a Patternist with extraordinary mental abilities to mend the human body. Immediately, her strong-minded, judgmental character emerges, and before long she and Teray, both captives in Coransee's household, plot to escape.

The story of their escape, their quest for freedom, now begins to change the typical "quest" motif that defines so much science fiction. For one thing, Teray soon realizes that he cannot physically survive their journey without Amber's healing powers—she may, in fact, be more physically powerful than Teray himself. For another, the fascinating relationship between hero and heroine overthrows all of our expectations about conventional romantic and/or sexual love. Because Teray is white and Amber black, their relationship continually reminds us of racial distinctions. And because Amber is a woman who refuses to act out traditional female roles (she will not be any man's wife, she is sexually androgynous, she is stronger and more independent than most men), their relationship continually highlights sexual and feminist issues.

Racism and sexism, then, are matters fundamental to an understanding of both plot and character. Coransee's household, for instance, is hierarchically structured so that those who possess power necessarily abuse those who are powerless: "Housemasters" control "Outsiders" who control "Mutes." In this futuristic mental society in which people have the ability to comprehend each other's thoughts, mental understanding gives way to mind control and ultimately mental oppression. The great "Pattern" itself—holding forth the promise of a mentally-unified culture which might use its combined intellectual powers for human advancement—instead has become the prize for Machiavellian power seekers. No wonder Butler continually uses the term "slavery" to describe the "mental leashes" which keep this society in its state of oppression.

Though Teray, the good son destined to inherit the Pattern, is the figure in whom we must place our trust and hope, it is Amber who most dramatically personifies independence, autonomy, and liberation. Forced, as a captive in Coransee's household, to be one of his "women," she nonetheless boasts, "'But I'm not one of his wives. . . . I'm an independent'" (ch. 3).[6] Asked by Teray, whom she truly does come to love, to be his wife, she refuses, "'Because I want the same thing you want. My House. Mine'" (ch. 6). Discussing with Teray her former sexual relationship with another woman, she explains, "'When I meet a woman who attracts me, I prefer women. . . . And when I meet a man who attracts me, I prefer men'" (ch. 6). This is clearly not your typical romance heroine. This is certainly not your typical science-fiction heroine. Ironically, *Patternmaster* makes Amber out to be the perfect prize for two rival brothers. Instead, this "golden brown woman with hair that was a cap of small, tight black curls" (ch. 3) turns out to be a model of independence and autonomy.

All ends well in *Patternmaster*. Teray and Amber, with their combined powers, defeat Coransee. And Teray, as the good son, will inherit the Pattern. But it is Amber who somehow stands out as having tran-

scended this political war of wits. In a final exchange between Amber and Teray, she reminds him of how easily she can tip the scales of power. Teray's response is filled with respect, but tinged with fear: "Not for the first time, he realized what a really dangerous woman she could be. If he could not make her his wife, he would be wise to make her at least an ally" (ch. 9).

All of Butler's heroines are dangerous women. Perhaps the most conspicuously dangerous is Mary who, in *Mind of My Mind,* has a tremendous potential for destruction. Perhaps the least conspicuously dangerous is Alanna who, in *Survivor,* exerts a subtle but radical influence on a foreign society which she and her parents have colonized. Mary and Alanna, both young black women, sport two very different types of feminism: Mary, a confused and disoriented child raised in the slums of twentieth-century Los Angeles, eventually becomes the leader of a mental empire; Alanna, an orphan in a futuristic Earth society, becomes a unifying force on a foreign planet inhabited by warring tribes. Mary must fight with and ultimately kill her father to achieve "freedom"; Alanna must reject the Christian beliefs of her parents to bring peace and respectability to her new culture. Mary is forced to marry a white man in order to establish and control her mental empire; Alanna chooses to marry the leader of a non-human tribe in order to survive and establish a home on a new planet. Whereas Mary learns to control and dominate, Alanna learns to compromise and survive. In these two women, we discover that the source of female strength can foster very different kinds of feminist power—and very different kinds of human response.

Mary's appeal derives from her brute force. Even as a child, she becomes conditioned to life in a sexist and violent world. The novel opens with threats of male aggression:

> I was in my bedroom reading a novel when somebody came banging on the door really loud, like the police. I thought it was the police until I got up, looking out the window, and saw one of Rina's johns standing there. I wouldn't have bothered to answer, but the fool was kicking at the door like he wanted to break it in. I went to the kitchen and got one of our small cast-iron skillets—the size just big enough to hold two eggs. Then I went to the door. The stupid bastard was drunk.

This same young girl who almost kills one of her mother's "johns" will end up killing her father, a man who forced her to have sex with him and who tries to control her mental powers. Not surprisingly, Mary's opinion of men is filled with bitterness. When her father forces her to marry Karl Larkin, a white man, she can only smirk and reflect how much "Karl looked like one of the bright, ambitious, bookish white guys from high school" (ch. 2). When she later questions Karl about their racial difference, her suspicions about his character prove correct: "'How do you feel about black people?'" she asks him, only to hear him reply, "'You've seen my cook'" (ch. 2).

Such racial differences call attention to other forms of enslavement in *Mind of My Mind.* When Doro, Mary's father, tries to explain the nature of "Mutes" to the old woman Emma, she snaps back: "'I know what you mean, Doro. I knew the first time I heard Mary use it. It means nigger!'" (ch. 9). Unlike her father, however, Mary comes to sympathize with the people under her mental control. When she kills Doro, patriarchical domination becomes maternal caring. Having the potential for destructive power thrust upon her, Mary learns to control that power, to use it wisely and cautiously. She is Butler's study in brute feminist force.

Alanna's appeal derives from her steadfast character, from intense psychological control and determination. Unlike Mary, Alanna possesses no extraordinary mental abilities. She is Butler's study in the power of human endurance. Instead of combating violence with violence, Alanna accepts the social obstacles which a foreign society imposes on her. Her object is to learn to survive among these obstacles, to accommodate to a culture that is far from perfect.

The most potent of these obstacles is the addictive drug meklah, a drug so powerful that withdrawal from it almost always proves fatal. Forced into addiction, Alanna not only survives withdrawal but also survives as a prisoner taken by one of the warring tribes. Living among this "Tehkohn" group, she confronts and learns to deal with even more obstacles: She proves herself to be a strong huntress (a mark of distinction in Tehkohn culture) and a loyal follower of Tehkohn customs. Ultimately, she marries the leader of the tribe and has their child.

Marriage is often a feminist issue in Butler's novels. Amber in *Patternmaster* refuses marriage; Mary in *Mind of My Mind* is forced to marry. Alanna's marriage to a non-human creature ironically turns out to be the most successful and respectable of all these marriage situations. Her joining with the Tehkohn leader at once liberates her from the enslaving Chris-

tianity of her missionary parents and the enslavement of the meklah drug. Moreover, it offers her the promise of establishing a home with people she has come to respect and love. Perhaps the most bitter irony of the novel is that the Christian earthlings, who call their new home "Canaan," cannot accept the marriage of their daughter into a tribe that will offer them their only hope of peaceful existence.

The Christian religion is depicted as notably racist in *Survivor.* As a young, wild black girl, Alanna is adopted by white parents and grows up in a world in which her color is always suspect. On one occasion, a Missionary suggests that Alanna would surely "'be happier with her own kind'" since, after all, "'the girl isn't white'" (ch. 3). When Alanna later asks her mother about this incident, she learns "for the first time how important some Missionaries believed their own coloring to be" (ch. 3). Color, in fact, turns out to be one of the major motifs in the novel. The Kohn creatures display a variety of colors as their moods and emotions change: They are gray in sobriety, white in amusement, bright yellow in anger. Their color also indicates hierarchical structure. Only a few of them, for instance, possess the blue, a sign of honor and power. Yet these colorful, non-human creatures show none of the racial bigotry associated with the Christian Missionaries. Ironically, Alanna's parents can laughingly dismiss the fear that their "black" daughter might mix with "whites," but are repulsed when that same daughter marries the honorable "blue" Tehkohn leader.

As a strong-minded black woman, Alanna submits to a surprising number of social restraints: first to the Christian Missionary code, then to the meklah drug, and finally to imprisonment by the Tehkohn tribe. But in her submission she discovers a source of strength. She learns, as Mary had learned, about herself—and about the different roles she has had to play in order to survive. We see in her an amazing capacity to compromise. Alanna's flexibility allows her to meander around some obstacles, and make other apparent obstacles into real avenues of liberation.

This ability to compromise and survive is what characterizes Butler's most fully-developed and intriguing heroine—Anyanwu in *Wild Seed.* Though all of Butler's protagonists are black, only Anyanwu is born in Africa. Both her African origin and her feminist determination give us every reason to think of her as the ancestress of Amber, Mary, Alanna, and the host of other prominent black women in Butler's fiction. Just as *Wild Seed,* by tracing the origins of Patternist society back to seventeenth-century Africa, provides a foundation for all four of the Patternist science-fiction novels, so does Anyanwu help to explain the yearning for independence and autonomy sought by Amber, Mary, and Alanna.

Before discussing Anyanwu as the character central to Butler's fiction, let me outline briefly the structure and plot of *Wild Seed* to show just how encompassing the novel is—in terms of both the time and space its characters inhabit.

The story spans two continents and nearly two centuries. Meeting in Africa in 1690, Anyanwu and Doro—female and male who have the potential to live forever—travel via slave ship to colonial New England. There Doro, a patriarchal dictator who aspires to breed a race of superhumans such as himself, exploits Anyanwu's abilities as a healer to propagate and maintain his small but growing empire. At first taken in by Doro's mystique, Anyanwu soon comes to realize that she is principally to serve as his breeder and slave. Forced to marry one of Doro's sons, she not only must partake in his animalistic breeding experiments, but must painfully endure their often tragic consequences. After her husband's death, she escapes from the New England colony. In 1840, Doro finds her on a plantation in Louisiana. There, in very real slave territory, Anyanwu has established her own free household only to have it invaded and controlled by Doro. After several of Anyanwu's children meet their deaths because of Doro's intrusion, Anyanwu decides that her only possible escape from his oppression is her own death. When she vows to commit suicide, however, Doro realizes how much the loss of Anyanwu would mean to him. Deprived of his only immortal compatriot, he would be doomed to face eternity alone. But more than that, he would lose the only effective humanizing force in his life. Their reconciliation at the end of the novel brings to a tenuous resolution over a hundred years of intense personal conflict. The ending of this novel, however, is actually the beginning of Butler's three previous novels, since in it we discover the origins of Patternist society.

We might best understand Anyanwu by appreciating the fundamental opposition between her and Doro. Both characters, for instance, are potentially immortal, but their means for achieving this immortality are strikingly different. Doro is a vampire-like figure who must continually kill people and assume their bodies in order to live. Anyanwu is a healer; instead of killing others, she rejuvenates herself. In this sense, she is the direct prototype of Amber in *Pattern-*

master. Just as Teray, in that futuristic novel, could not possibly survive without Amber's healing abilities, so the superhuman Doro immediately recognizes in Anyanwu's talents a means to secure his super-race. For all Doro's control over his life and the lives of others, he is necessarily restricted in the physical forms he can assume. True, he may invade other bodies, but the constraints of those bodies are a given. Anyanwu's powers allow far more flexibility and agility: In changing the physical construct of her own body, she can transform herself into various kinds of creatures—both human and non-human. On the slave ship, for instance, when one of Doro's sons tries to rape her, Anyanwu fantastically transforms herself into a leopard and mauls her assilant to his violent death. She also possesses the ability to change from youth to old age back to youth. She may even change her sex, and on one particular occasion when she does so, Anyanwu once again becomes a prototype of Amber—this time by virtue of her androgyny.

The very physical characteristics of Anyanwu, then, highlight her distinguishing qualities. She is flexible and dexterous, compared to Doro's stiffness and dominance. She uses prowess rather than direct, confrontational power. She heals rather than kills, and kills only by assuming a different form and only when she or her children are assaulted. In Anyanwu, we find a woman who—despite her imprisonment by a patriarchal tyrant—learns to use her abilities to survive. In this sense, she is most obviously the prototype of another of Butler's heroines—Alanna in *Survivor.*

The marriage motif in Butler's novels, which I have commented on earlier, is also crystallized in Anyanwu—not only through her willingness to accept husbands forced upon her by Doro, but ultimately through her final reconciliation with Doro himself. Like both Amber and Mary, Anyanwu has a defiant attitude about marriage, and particularly like Mary in *Mind of My Mind,* she initially refuses to marry a white man whom Doro has chosen for her. Defiance, however, soon gives way to acceptance—and it is here, once again, that Anyanwu closely resembles Alanna, accepting the constraints of her world and trying to make something decent and productive out of the indecent situation in which she finds herself. Left on her own, without Doro's scheming intrusions, Anyanwu is able to produce and raise children possessed of both superior powers and tremendous human warmth. Her aim is to have children who may live with her, not die after a normal life span and leave her to her loneliness. Doro's paternal concerns revolve around his mechanical breeding experiments: He does not create children, but Frankenstein monsters. Anyanwu's maternity, however, is the main source of her being, the principal reason for her existence. As she explains, "'I could have husbands and wives and lovers into the next century and never have a child. Why should I have so many except that I want them and love them?'" (ch. 13).

It is this kind of maternal generosity that will finally save Doro. Anyanwu, repulsed by Doro's inhumanity and his enslavement of the very superrace he has fathered, can all too easily kill herself. She can at least escape oppression through death. When Doro asks her why she has decided to die, Anyanwu explains her dilemma: "'It's the only way I can leave you. . . . Everything is temporary but you and me. You are all I have, perhaps all I would ever have.' She shook her head slowly. 'And you are an obscenity'" (ch. 14).

It is tempting to think that Doro pleads for Anyanwu to live not out of selfishness but out of love. We want to believe that, confronted with the possibility of her death, he comes to understand the most important aspect of life—human companionship. Perhaps this is so. Perhaps, however, Anyanwu decides to live not because she is suddenly convinced of Doro's humanity but because she at least sees some hope for a more humane future with him. If Anyanwu lives, she at least has the chance to save their children from Doro's oppression and save the two of them from eternal loneliness. It is the promise of human companionship that finally touches her. When Anyanwu chooses life, in spite of all the horrors which her relationship with Doro has produced and may still continue to produce, she is acting out of generosity both for their children and for him. Her decision reflects the courage and generosity that is in all of Butler's heroines.

Anyanwu is the great African ancestress. She encompasses and epitomizes defiance, acceptance, compromise, determination, and courage. Her personal goal is freedom, but given the obstacles that constantly prevent her from achieving that goal, she learns to make advancements through concessions. By finding her way through that great obstacle course, she is able to bring her best qualities—healing and loving—to a world that would otherwise be intolerable.

Butler's heroines, as I have been trying to show, can tell us much about her science fiction precisely because they are the very core of that fiction. These novels are about survival and power, about black women who must face tremendous societal constraints. We might very well expect them to be rebellious. We might expect them to reverse the typical male science-fiction stereotype and replace male tyranny with female tyranny. This does not happen. Though Butler's heroines are dangerous and powerful women, their goal is not power. They are heroines not because they conquer the world, but because they conquer the very notion of tyranny.

They are, as well, portraits of a different kind of feminism. Amber has the chance to marry the great Patternmaster; instead, she prefers her independence. Mary can easily become an awesome tyrant; instead, she matures into a caring mother. And Alanna, who possesses no extraordinary Patternist powers, learns to survive through accommodation rather than conflict. That very willingness to accommodate and compromise is what allows Anyanwu to endure over a century of oppressive patriarchy. At the end of each novel, we somehow get the impression that the victory of these women, though far from attained, is somehow pending. White men control the war, while black women fight a very different battle.

Notes

1. Sargent has edited several volumes of this new fiction, initiated by her collection *Women of Wonder: Science Fiction Stories by Women about Women* (New York: Vintage, 1975). Two recent critical studies of female/feminist science fiction are Marleen S. Barr, ed., *Future Females: A Critical Anthology* (Bowling Green, OH: Bowling Green State Univ. Popular Press, 1981), and Tom Staicar, ed., *The Feminine Eye: Science Fiction and the Women Who Write It* (New York: Frederick Ungar, 1982). Barr's anthology contains a checklist, compiled by Roger Schlobin, of women science-fiction writers.

2. "Lost Races of Science Fiction," *Transmission*, Summer 1980, pp. 17-18.

3. For a good introduction to Butler's first three science-fiction novels, see Frances Smith Foster, "Octavia Butler's Black Female Future Fiction," *Extrapolation,* 23 (1982), 37-49. My own study guide to Butler, focusing on her four science-fiction novels and *Kindred,* a mainstream/fantasy novel, is forthcoming this year in *The Reader's Guide to Charnas, Butler, and Vinge,* co-authored with Marleen S. Barr and Richard Law (Starmont House).

4. *The Obstacle Race: The Fortunes of Women Painters and Their Work* (New York: Farrar, Straus & Giroux, 1979), p. 6.

5. The term was used by Suzy McKee Charnas in her essay of that title, published in *Future Females,* pp. 103-108.

6. Butler's four science-fiction novels to date were originally published by Doubleday, but have since appeared in paperback editions. For convenience, I refer to chapter numbers rather than page numbers when quoting from the texts.

Thelma J. Shinn

SOURCE: "The Wise Witches: Black Women Mentors in the Fiction of Octavia E. Butler," in *Conjuring: Black Women, Fiction, and Literary Tradition,* edited by Marjorie Pryse and Hortense J. Spillers, Indiana University Press, 1985, pp. 203-15.

Being born black and female in contemporary urban America has taught Octavia Butler much about the uses—and abuses—of power. "To comprehend a nectar / Requires sorest need," Emily Dickinson has written, and Butler's understanding of social power certainly fits that definition. On the other hand, her recognition of personal power—survival power—comes from more direct experience. "The Black women I write about aren't struggling to make ends meet," Butler explains, "but they are the descendants of generations of those who did. Mothers are likely to teach their daughters about survival as they have been taught, and daughters are likely to learn, even subconsciously."[1] Not only have her black women learned "about survival," but also they transform that personal power into social power by teaching others.

Exploring what "mothers are likely to teach their daughters" brings Butler's fiction inevitably into comparison with the novels of other women. Annis Pratt has defined archetypal patterns, common to three centuries of women's fiction, which preserve female knowledge within the enclosure of patriarchal society as follows:

> It gradually became clear that women's fiction could be read as a mutually illuminative or inter-related field of texts reflecting a preliterary repository of feminine archetypes, including three particularly important archetypal systems—the Demeter/Kore and Ishtar/Tammuz rebirth myths, Arthurian grail narratives, and the Craft of the Wise, or witchcraft.[2]

Each of these patterns can be found in Butler's fiction, providing a framework for the transfer of knowledge, although one pattern governs each of the novels. Her first work, *Patternmaster* (1976), carefully follows the grail quest, leading the quester Teray to Forsyth, California, where he must accept the role of Patternmaster from his dying father, Rayal. "The Quest," Pratt quotes Jean Markale, "is an attempt to

re-establish a disciplined sovereignty, usurped by the masculine violence of the despoiling knight, while the kingdom rots and the king, the head of the family . . . is impotent." The quester must be compassionate, even "androgynous," and must "restore a kingdom punished for violating women." The grail itself, "as container of beneficence, feeder of the tribe, and locus of rebirth," symbolizes feminine power: "As 'mother pot,' 'magic cauldron' (with which Persephone can regenerate the dead heroes and heal the sick), golden bowl of healing, etc., this archetype expresses women's generative and regenerative powers."[3] In *Patternmaster,* Teray's older brother Coransee is the "despoiling Knight," violating Teray's prospective wife Iray, demanding his Housemaster's right to sexual favors from the independent healer Amber who accompanies Teray on his journey and allowing the mistreatment of those under his care, as Teray discovers when the beaten and abused Suliana comes to him for help. Rayal, suffering from Clayark's disease (a "gift" from the first returning starship which decimated the population of Earth and left mutants in its wake), is impotent to stop the stronger Coransee, who is also his son by his lead wife and sister Jansee. Teray is recognizable as the appropriate successor by his "androgynous" qualities: his protection of Suliana and others like her; his willingness to recognize the humanity in the feared and hated mutants the Clayarks; his unwillingness to kill except for survival. Yet Teray is young, lacking the necessary knowledge and skills to succeed in his quest. For these he must turn to the first of Butler's black women mentors, Amber. Amber's knowledge has literally been transferred to her and her healing skill has been brought through transition to a useful tool by her friend and lesbian lover, the Housemaster Kai, suggesting an archetypal Demeter/Kore pattern of "uniting the feminine generations."[4] She seems to symbolize the grail in herself, literally regenerating Teray's body after his final fight with Coransee.

Butler's next two novels, *Mind of My Mind* (1977) and *Survivor* (1978), follow the pattern of rebirth and transformation myths. *Mind of My Mind* can be seen as what Pratt calls a "novel of development," and young Mary struggles against much of the poverty and violence common to "the multiple alienation of sex, class, and race" which "intensifies physical and psychological suffering for the young Black woman."[5] She grows up in a California ghetto with a prostitute mother and finds it necessary at times to protect herself from unwanted men by wielding a cast-iron skillet. But Mary is exceptional; her "transition" from adolescence to selfhood leaves her an active telepath, controlling minds of others like her through a Pattern. In giving birth to the Pattern, Mary gives birth to a new society in which she is the most powerful figure and gives rebirth to thousands of "latent" telepaths who have been suffering from their uncontrollable reception of human pain from everyone around them. However reluctantly, Mary has learned survival from her female heritage—from her mother Rina and her ancestress Emma (whose name means grandmother)—and she is ready to become another black woman mentor, leading "her people" to constructive utilizations of their individual skills.

Although Frances Smith Foster argues that Mary, despite her name, cannot fit the stereotype of the Black Madonna as defined in Daryl Dance's essay "Black Eve or Madonna: A Study of the Antithetical Views of the Mother in Black American Literature," she must admit later that Mary combines the traits "not only of Eve and Madonna, but also of God and Satan" into "a new kind of female character in both science fiction and Afro-American literature."[6] That new character has been defined by Phyllis J. Day as follows:

> The new women of science fiction, then, whether witch or Earthmother, are real people, strong people, and they are integral to and often protectresses of Earth and ecology. Moreover, they are part of an organic whole, a return to our premechanistic past, and they represent a force against man in his assumption of the right to dominate either women or Earth/Nature.[7]

Much of this applies to Mary, daughter of the godlike Doro and descendant of Emma (whose African name Anyanwu means "sun," as does Doro), combining the male and female principles represented by these two and ending the domination of Doro by absorbing his life into her Pattern, allowing herself to offer rebirth to those dependent on her: "Karl lived. The family lived. . . . Now we were free to grow again—we, his children."[8] In her new role, Mary is the archetypal female defined by Pratt: "the mothers and daughters in women's fiction seem also to be enacting the various aspects of the triple goddess, who was virgin, maternal figure, and old woman at one and the same time. The third figure of the triad, who has often been gynophobically perceived as 'devouring mother' or 'crone,' represents the wise older mother's knowledge of the best moment to fledge or let go of her children, a moment that, if precipitous or delayed, can lead the maternal element to become destructive."[9] So it is with Mary. Her third aspect becomes apparent when she draws strength from her people through the Pattern. If she lets go too late, she kills them. But unlike Doro, whose power depended

upon killing his victims, Mary discovers that she doesn't have to destroy: "I'm not the vampire he is. I give in return for my taking" (p. 210). Doro finally recognizes that Mary is whole, "a complete version of him":

> She was a symbiont, a being living in partnership with her people. She gave them unity, they fed her, and both thrived. She was not a parasite, though he had encouraged her to think of herself as one. And though she had great power, she was not naturally, instinctively, a killer. He was. (p. 217)

As such, Mary fits Day's description of witch, as do the other "wise witches" of Butler's fiction:

> These capable women with power are most often called witches and considered deviant from their society. They are usually feared and hated by other tamed women, as well as by men. They are healers, wise women, religious leaders, or focal points for natural or preternatural powers. Their power is usually antimachine, though not always anti-technology—that is, they may use technologies but in a nondeterministic manner in which nature is enhanced rather than destroyed.[10]

In her role as Patternmaster, Mary will enhance what Doro has neglected by bringing the latent telepaths through transition, by providing unity for all Patternists, and by teaching individuals how to use their powers for the betterment of the community. Although Mary is hated at first, Butler reminds us that "people who must violate their long-held beliefs are rarely pleasant. I don't write about heroes; I write about people who survive and sometimes prevail."[11] Mary must kill Doro, but she does survive and she does prevail—teaching others to make the most of what they have and giving rebirth to the rejects of the society into which she was born. Through her, Butler can transmute her Afro-American heritage into archetypal human heritage and achieve her aim by bringing "together multi-racial groups of men and women who must cope with one another's differences as well as with new, not necessarily controllable, abilities within themselves."[12]

Alanna's rebirth in *Survivor* (1978) is personal rather than communal, following the structure Pratt provides for woman's spiritual quest into the self:

> Phase I: Splitting off from family, husbands, lovers
> Phase II: The green-world guide or token Phase III: The green-world lover Phase IV: Confrontation with parental figures Phase V: The plunge into the unconscious[13]

Butler's only novel set on another planet, *Survivor* offers alternatives to today's prejudices for those who do not fit into the Pattern she has created, to the non-telepathic "mutes." Unfortunately, the mutes have carried their prejudices with them. As Missionaries of Humanity, they have fought the Clayark threat by deifying the human image. Consequently, they are blind to humanity in any other guise—to the humanity of the native Kohn, furlike creatures of various hues who live in tune with their environment. Except for a few, their prejudice extends as well to Alanna, an Afro-Asian who had survived as a "wild human" after her parents had died protecting her from a Clayark attack. Alanna had been adopted by the leader of the colony, Jules Verrick, and his wife, Neila, despite the prejudices that would allow these religious people to kill wild humans as if they were animals and would further lead them to suggest that Alanna at least be put with a black family. Clearly, hers is at best an uneasy relationship with her society, making her a perfect candidate for a quest or rebirth journey which, Pratt asserts, can "create transformed, androgynous, and powerful human personalities out of socially devalued beings."[14]

Phase I is accomplished for Alanna when she is kidnapped with some other Missionaries and some of the Garkohn natives with whom they peacefully coexisted. The kidnappers are the Tehkohn, a native group bluer in color than the predominately green-furred Garkohn. Phase II is realized by something taken from rather than given to Alanna, as is the usual pattern. This "ordinary phenomenon that suddenly takes on extraordinary portent"[15] is the meklah fruit, which has become the staple diet of the Missionaries as it is for the Garkohn. Meklah, however, is addictive; withdrawal from it is so difficult that only Alanna, owing probably to her wild human brushes with starvation and her incredible will to survive, is alive when the five-day "cleansing period" ends.

Alanna has learned that not all is good in the green world—Nature can offer poison as well as life. She needs to discover Phase III, "an ideal, nonpatriarchal lover who sometimes appears as an initiatory guide and often aids at difficult points in the quest."[16] Her lover turns out to be the leader of the Tehkohn, their Hao Diut. Diut rules because he is the darkest blue; before him, the Hao Tahheh, a female, had ruled. However, though Diut can offer her knowledge of and participation in a society which lives in tune with its environment—constructing dwellings which "mimicked the mountains around it in its interior as well as its exterior,"[17] fighting without weapons, even recognizing the animal jehruk "as their wild relative and they took pride in its ferocity" (p. 110)—he must also learn from her the limits he must put on his

power before they can have a relationship "where differences existed, but were ignored" (p. 114). "We're not children squabbling in the inner corridors," she tells him. "You need not prove your strength or your coloring to me. We can talk to each other. Or we can go away from each other!" (p. 114)

Drawing on her memories of survival on Earth, Alanna is able to fit into this alien society much better than she could with the Missionaries. The shared knowledge of the green world, of working with rather than against nature, is lost on the Missionaries, whose walled settlement mars the natural landscape and who see all Kohn as animals. But Alanna is "rescued" from her new home, and in the process the life she has created there—a daughter Tien—is destroyed. She is forced into Phase IV, and her confrontation with her foster parents is bittersweet. While Neila could accept the changes in her daughter, Jules cannot condone the blasphemy of mating with "animals." Alanna must come to terms with her parents by doing all she can to enable them to survive, but then she must be rejected by them.

This rejection initiates the final phase, the plunge into the unconscious where Alanna must face her own actions and define her self. "I'm a wild human," she tells her foster parents. "That's what I've always been."

> She glanced at Jules. "I haven't lost my self. Not to anyone." And again to Neila. "In time, I'll also be a Tehkohn judge. I want to be. And I'm Diut's wife and your daughter. If . . . you can still accept me as your daughter." (p. 170)

Alanna has completed the quest for self and chosen that self above any social identity that would limit or enclose her, transforming even Diut through her personal integrity. Unfortunately, she is not able to share her survival skills with the Missionaries. While she is willing to teach, risking her life for them, they are not willing to learn. Their prejudices limit their humanity and their possibilities for survival.

Butler's next novel, *Kindred* (1979), is a departure from the science fiction mode which has enabled her to fantasize societies accepting of her strong and independent black women. If the feminine archetypes provided a framework for her own mythos, that mythopoeic vision was allowed room to expand by the possibilities inherent in the contemporary mythological form. Patricia Warrick has identified three ways in which science fiction offers this expansion. First,

> The radical element in all the myths is their setting in the future. They describe a future time that

will be different from the present in at least one significant way. In contrast, traditional myths typically are set outside time; they reflect all that is conceived to be eternal and unchanging in the universe.

Second,

It seems safe to assume that in previous myths both the teller and the listener believed the story to be true. In contrast, the participants in a science fiction myth are very conscious that the story is not true; however, they do believe that in the future it just might be true.

And third,

These earlier myths tend to be very clear in their meanings and their concepts of good and evil. . . . But science fiction myths have a quality of ambiguity about them. They are much less certain of what man's relationship to the natural world around him and to the cosmos is. Good and evil can no longer be easily labeled.[18]

Besides the acceptance of change and ambiguity in a probable future, science fiction also provides Butler with the one aspect her heritage neither as a black nor as a woman seemed to provide—freedom. This concept, central to everything she has written, drew her to the literary form where, as she explains,

I was free to imagine new ways of thinking about people and power, free to maneuver my characters into situations that don't exist. For example, where is there a society in which men and women are honestly considered equal? What would it be like to live in such a society? Where do people not despise each other because of race or religion, class or ethnic origin?[19]

Patternist society fits this description, but such a change is not without ambiguous results. The timelessness of the feminine archetypes and the experiences of the black woman have penetrated even Butler's fantasies to show that human beings will find new categories of prejudice—assigning subhuman status to mutes and Clayarks—and new abuses for power unless it is limited. Her communal solutions remain dependent on the humanity of its individual members: the compassion of the Patternmaster, the determination of others to preserve their freedom even if they must kill or die to accomplish this, and the willingness of all members of the society to overcome prejudice and accept differences. Only Tehkohn society seems potentially utopian, although the power hierarchy and stress on fighting separate it from most utopias.

Borrowing the vehicle of time travel from her science fiction, Butler turns in *Kindred* to apply her new understanding of power to the Afro-American experience today and yesterday. Dana, her contemporary black woman, finds herself mentor and healer to her own white slave holder ancestor Rufus when he pulls her back through time over and over again to save him. Certainly feminine archetypes again underlie Butler's fiction, as Dana "controls death and rebirth," not only that of Rufus but her own as his descendant. This rebirth myth most closely relates to Pratt's Ishtar/Tammuz pattern, as "the hero can be released from death only through feminine power."[20] That feminine power can also be used to destroy, and is so used when Rufus has concluded the rape through which Dana's ancestress is conceived and furthermore has ignored the limits set on his power. "I'm not property, Kevin," Dana had assured her contemporary white husband. "I'm not a horse or a sack of wheat. If I have to seem to be property, if I have to accept limits on my freedom for Rufus's sake, then he also has to accept limits—on his behavior toward me. He has to leave me enough control of my own life to make living look better to me than killing and dying."[21] So too had Alanna set limits on Diut in *Survivor:*

"And I have your bow and your arrows." She looked at me for a long time, her face already bruised and swollen, her eyes narrowed, the knife steady in her hand. "Then use them to kill me," she said. "I will not be beaten again." (p. 113)

Diut accepts and both survive; Rufus tests his limits once too often. The first time, he hits Dana when she objects to his selling a field hand out of jealousy: "And it was a mistake. It was the breaking of an unspoken agreement between us—a very basic agreement—and he knew it" (p. 239). In retaliation, Dana cuts her wrists, and the threat to her life returns her to the present. The next betrayal, attempted rape, forces her to overcome her compassion finally: "I could accept him as my ancestor, my younger brother, my friend, but not as my master, and not as my lover. He had understood that once" (p. 260). At the cost of her left arm, she kills him.

Dana is not a victim, as Beverly Friend concludes when she compares *Kindred* with novels by Eisenstein and Millhiser. Butler recognizes some truth in Friend's other conclusion "that contemporary woman is not educated to survive, that she is as helpless, perhaps even more helpless, than her predecessors,"[22] at least inasmuch as Dana accepts "that educated didn't mean smart. He had a point. Nothing in my education or knowledge of the future had helped me to escape" (p. 215). But Dana has learned to heed women's knowledge; as Kai had fed Amber all she knew in *Patternmaster,* Dana seeks out the cook-house because

> sometimes old people and children lounged there, or house servants or even field hands stealing a few moments of leisure. I liked to listen to them talk sometimes and fight my way through their accents to find out more about how they survived lives of slavery. Without knowing it, they pre-pared me to survive. (p. 94)

And, although Dana suffers a share of what her an-cestors had endured in slavery and loses her arm in saving her life, she never becomes an object; she maintains control of her life and acts out of a sense of responsibility even while she recognizes the irony of her position as Rufus's mentor:

> I was the worst possible guardian for him—a black to watch over him in a society that consid-ered blacks subhuman, a woman to watch over him in a society that considered women perennial children. I would have all I could do to look after myself. But I would help him as best I could. And I would try to keep friendship with him, maybe plant a few ideas in his mind that would help both me and the people who would be his slaves in the years to come. (p. 68)

Dana may, as Friend submits, be as much a slave as the heroines of the other two novels, but she does have heritage on her side—black women have sur-vived slavery before.

Kindred shows that Butler's wise witches, her com-passionate teachers armed with knives and cast-iron skillets, have survived and will survive, whether or not they are accepted by their society. Her conscious-ness of "the adaptations women with power must make in a patriarchal society,"[23] however, adds an African archetype to her mythology in her most re-cent novel, *Wild Seed* (1980). In *Mind of My Mind,* where we first met Emma/Anyanwu, Doro had told Mary that "Emma was an Ibo woman" (p. 95); so it seems particularly fitting that Sir James G. Frazer has specifically attributed the belief in shape shifting to her kinspeople: "They think that man's spirit can quit his body for a time during life and take up its abode in an animal. This is called *ishi anu,* 'to turn animal.'"[24] Anyanwu, a wild seed growing free in nature—not, until the beginning of this novel, under the control of Doro—has learned through an inner quest how to change her body, aging and becoming young again, hunting as a leopard or swimming as a dolphin. Symbolizing the adaptions she had made for

survival in a patriarchy headed by Doro, four-thousand-year-old patriarch of what would become the Patternists, Anyanwu's shape shifting is the pro-totype for Alanna's chameleon ability, which she draws on in *Survivor* to save the Missionaries: "But deception is the only real weapon we have. We face physical chameleons. To survive, we must be mental chameleons" (p. 118). Alanna accurately labels this awareness "survival philosophy."

Shape shifting is also the source of the healing power that Anyanwu will hand down to the Patternists, ulti-mately to Amber and Teray of *Patternmaster.* An-yanwu heals herself by turning inward and changing the shape of the injured or diseased part until it is again healthy. The archetypal witch most reflective of its designation by Pratt as "Craft of the Wise," An-yanwu is clearly the female principle of life itself. This Great Mother has already been living three hun-dred years when Doro tracks her down and coerces her into his selective breeding program by threaten-ing to use her children if she refuses. Typical of the black women who will follow her, however, she stays not out of fear of Doro or acceptance of slavery but out of compassion. In time she comes to recognize the truth in what her husband and Doro's son Isaac tells her: "I'm afraid the time will come when he [Doro] won't feel anything. If it does . . . there's no end to the harm he could do. . . . You, though, you could live to see it—or live to prevent it. You could stay with him, keep him at least as human as he is now."[25] When Anyanwu comes to feel that Doro is past learning from her, past feeling, she is ready to let herself die rather than be used by him. As Dana has challenged Rufus, as Alanna has challenged Diut, Anyanwu challenges Doro with the one thing beyond his control—her own life. Doro can destroy her, but he cannot make her live if she chooses not to. It is only when he sincerely recognizes and admits his need for her and his feeling for her that she decides to stay with him.

As much as Anyanwu offers her daughters as the Great Mother, she is not limited as this figure usually is. A living woman (*Wild Seed* begins in 1690, which puts her birth around 1390), she still fits Aldous Hux-ley's definition of "the principle of life, of fecundity, of fertility, of kindness and nourishing compassion; but at the same time she is the principle of death and destruction."[26] She, however, prefers not to kill and feels great remorse when she finds it necessary to do so. Nor is she an irrational force. Even science fic-tion, usually more open to ambiguity and change, has stereotyped men and women, as Scott Sanders ob-serves:

In much of the genre, women and nature bear the same features: both are mysterious, irrational, instinctive; both are fertile and mindless; both inspire wonder and dread in the hero; both are objects of male conquest. . . . Men belong to the realm of mind; women and nature, to no-mind. Women are the bearers of life; men are life's interpreters and masters.[27]

Yet Anyanwu, not the male principle Doro,[28] is the source of "logic, reason, the analytical workings of the mind" in *Wild Seed.* She has achieved her shape-shifting knowledge by careful, systematic inner quests, where she has studied herself down to the atoms. She learns what nature can provide—what foods are beneficial, which are poisonous—by ingesting small quantities and watching her bodily reactions. She can "clone" an animal or fish only after she has eaten some of it and studied within her its genetic makeup. She is both the scientist and the laboratory. Even then, she must consciously decide to shift her shape, and the process is painstaking as each part of her is absorbed or transformed.

Doro, on the other hand, is as much a life and death source as Anyanwu. He can be compared to the Nuban myth recounted by Frazer of the taboo person:

> The divine person who epitomizes the corporate life of his group is a source of danger as well as blessing; he must not only be guarded, he must be guarded against. . . . Accordingly the isolation of the man-god is quite as necessary for the safety of others as for his own. His magical virtue is in the strictest sense contagious; his divinity is a fire which, under proper restraints, confers endless blessings, but, if rashly touched or allowed to break bounds, burns and destroys what it touches.[29]

Doro is described as "a small sun" and seeks people who are "good prey," who will satisfy his appetite when he devours their life and assumes their body. He can exercise some control over his appetite if he has fed recently; otherwise his action is instinctual, irrational. He occupies the nearest body. Even his seemingly scientific quest for the right people for his selective breeding program is determined by his appetite for them—latent telepaths and people with other potential mental talents are "good prey." In fact, he began his breeding program originally as one would raise cattle—for food. He still uses his settlements for this, and the followers who love and fear him have come to accept the human sacrifices his appetite demands. Doro provides a frightening version of patriarchy; only the matriarchal balance which An-

yanwu, whom he calls Sun Woman, chooses to provide him keeps Doro human in any way, as Isaac had predicted. It is from these roots that Mary eventually evolves, encompassing the ambiguities of both principles in herself and thereby giving birth to a society in which men and women can be equal.

Butler's archetypal frameworks allow us to see how seemingly insurmountable differences can be recognized as artificial polarizations of human qualities. By combining Afro-American, female, and science fiction patterns, she can reveal the past, the present, and a probable future in which differences can be seen as challenging and enriching rather than threatening and denigrating and in which power can be seen as an interdependence between the leader and those accepting that leadership, each accepting those limits on freedom that still allow for survival of the self. Within the archetypes, embodying them, are wise witches, black women willing to share their survival skills out of compassion and a sense of responsibility with those of us who are still willing to learn.

Notes

1. Quoted by Veronica Mixon in "Futurist Woman: Octavia Butler," *Essence* 15 (April 1979), p. 13.

2. Annis Pratt with Barbara White, Andrea Loewenstein, and Mary Wyer, *Archetypal Patterns in Women's Fiction* (Bloomington: Indiana University Press, 1981), p. 170.

3. Pratt, p. 173-74.

4. Pratt, p. 170.

5. Pratt, p. 33.

6. Frances Smith Foster, "Octavia Butler's Black Female Future Fiction," *Extrapolation,* 23: 1 (Spring 1982), p. 37.

7. Phyllis J. Day, "Earthmother/Witchmother: Feminism and Ecology Renewed," *Extrapolation,* 23: 1 (Spring 1982), p. 14.

8. *Mind of My Mind* (New York: Avon, 1977), pp. 220-21. Subsequent references are to this edition and will appear as page numbers in the text.

9. Pratt, p. 172.

10. Day, p. 14.

11. Quoted by Mixon, p. 12.

12. Quoted by Curtis C. Smith (ed.), *Twentieth Century Science-Fiction Writers* (New York: St. Martin's Press, 1981), p. 93.

13. Pratt, pp. 139-41.

14. Pratt, p. 142.

15. Pratt, p. 139.

16. Pratt, p. 140.

17. *Survivor* (rpt. 1978; New York: New American Library, 1979), p. 53. Subsequent references are to this edition and will appear as page numbers in the text.

18. "Science Fiction Myths and their Ambiguity," in *Science Fiction: Contemporary Mythology,* ed. by Patricia Warrick, Martin H. Greenberg, and Joseph Olander (New York: Harper & Row, 1978), pp. 6-7.

19. Quoted by Mixon, p. 12.

20. Pratt, p. 172.

21. *Kindred* (Garden City: Doubleday & Co., Inc., 1979), p. 246.

22. Beverly Friend, "Time Travel as a Feminist Didactic in Works by Phyllis Eisenstein, Marlys Millhiser, and Octavia Butler," *Extrapolation* 23:1 (Spring 1982), p. 55.

23. Day, p. 14.

24. Frazer, *The New Golden Bough,* edited by Dr. Theodor H. Gaster (New York: Criterion Books, 1959), p. 601.

25. *Wild Seed* (rpt. 1980; New York: Pocket Books, 1981), p. 120. Subsequent references are to this edition and will appear as page numbers in the text.

26. Aldous Huxley, *The Human Situation,* ed. Piero Ferruci (New York: Harper & Row, 1977), p. 200.

27. Scott Sanders, "Woman as Nature in Science Fiction," in *Future Females: A Critical Anthology,* ed. by Marleen S. Barr (Bowling Green, O.: State University Popular Press, 1981), p. 42.

28. Sanders, p. 53.

29. Frazer, p. 165.

Sherley Anne Williams

SOURCE: "Sherley Anne Williams on Octavia E. Butler," in *Ms. Magazine* Vol. XIV, No. 9, March, 1986, pp. 70-2.

Octavia E. Butler, winner of the 1985 Nebula award and twice winner (1984 and 1985) of the Hugo award, science fiction's two most prestigious honors, describes herself as "a pessimist, if I'm not careful; a black, a feminist, a quiet egoist, and a former Baptist"—certainly an atypical profile for a science-fiction writer. Butler is the lone woman among a handful of black writers publishing in the field, but part of a larger wave of women writers—Doris Lessing, Marge Piercy, and Toni Cade Bambara, among others—who began in the 1970s and 1980s using some of the conventions of science fiction to explore a range of feminist ideas. In Butler's own ***Bloodchild*** (originally in *Isaac Asimov* science-fiction magazine), the eerie novella that won both the Hugo and the Nebula (and which Butler gleefully describes as her "pregnant man story"), human males born on an alien planet must incubate in their own bodies the progeny of the native race. The story explores the paradoxes of power and inequality, and starkly portrays the experience of a class who, like women throughout most of history, are valued chiefly for their reproductive capacities.

A tall, striking woman in her late thirties, with skin the dark, lustrous brown of espresso beans and a rich, mellifluous voice, Butler often uses the term "speculative fiction" rather than "science fiction" as a description of her work, and resents the genre's reputation as "weird." "Science fiction, extrasensory perception, and black people," she says wryly," are judged by the worst elements they produce."

While science fiction has been notorious for the almost total absence of black characters, Butler's fictional world is racially diverse—and in this sense, at least, more like the "real world" than the work of most other science-fiction writers. Since her main characters are almost always black women, it's no surprise that Butler, the author of six novels published over the past decade, has enjoyed cult status among many black women readers. Butler's work, though absent from contemporary anthologies of black literature, has excited a good deal of attention from literary scholars and other science-fiction writers, as well as devotees of the genre. (The Hugo is awarded by readers of science fiction, and the Nebula by science-fiction writers.) She also makes frequent guest appearances at science-fiction conferences and writers' workshops. Clearly, Butler's work has a scope that commands a wide audience.

Five of Butler's novels unfold a lively futurescape, loosely chronicling the division of humanity into "Patternists," members of a mental network or "Pattern" that joins together people with psionic powers such as telepathy and telekinesis; "mute" humans without psionic powers, whom the Patternists control by telepathic command; and "Clayarks," mutant human quadrupeds, spawn of humans who have been contaminated by an extraterrestrial disease brought back to earth by one man in Clay's Ark, the first—and last—spaceship to return from the stars. Butler may be a pessimist, but her fiction is neither grim nor depressing. The Clay's Ark plague, the epidemic that is a backdrop in her Patternist novels, is, to be sure, a worldwide catastrophe, but one that assumes that we somehow manage to avoid World War III. Butler's is a literature of survival, and her assumption that black people survive the present and participate in shaping the future is one of her work's most affirmative aspects.

Butler's 1979 novel, *Kindred,* however, stands apart from the others: published by Doubleday on its regular trade fiction list, rather than as a science-fiction book, it uses the plot device of time travel to launch a startling and engrossing commentary on the complex actuality and continuing heritage of American slavery. Dana, a contemporary black woman, is involuntarily pulled back in time to the antebellum slave South to save the life of Rufus, the abusive and fatally obsessed slaveholder who is destined to be her ancestor. In the guise of Rufus's slave, she protects him until he has fathered the "black" daughter who will be Dana's many times great-grandmother. Ironically, when Dana returns to the present with wounds from the overseer's whip, her cousin accuses Dana's husband, a caring and considerate man who is white, of abusing her. Thus, Dana's relationship with Rufus is a brutal reversal of her marriage in her own time.

While Butler doesn't avoid the political implications of a multiracial society featuring strong women characters, her stories aren't overwhelmed by politics, nor are her characters overwhelmed by racism and sexism. Invariably, the characters who triumph are those who see and act upon possibilities beyond the human experiences they know to affirm consciously chosen community.

Butler herself grew up in relative isolation on a chicken farm on the edge of the California desert with her Louisiana-born grandmother. A childhood fascination with horses, she says, led her to write, at the age of 10, "a lot of magic horse and flying horse stories." She turned to writing science fiction "simply because I liked to read it" and wrote the first version of her first published novel, *Patternmaster,* when she was 12. At 13, she began submitting her work to science-fiction magazines. She went on to attend college for a time, continued writing, and like Dana, the writer/heroine of *Kindred,* Butler supported herself through a series of temporary jobs. Her first story was published in *Clarion,* an anthology from the Clarion Science Fiction Writers' Workshop that Butler attended in 1970. "I was lucky," she admits. "Women were just getting into science fiction then. We had two women teachers, Joanna Russ and Kate Wilhelm, and neither of them was interested in work turned in under initials or male pseudonyms. Several of us were writing under initials, and we stopped."

Writing since then under her own name, Butler is now able to work full-time at writing. She lives comfortably in a modest bungalow in Los Angeles, but still recalls a particularly low period before her first publication: "I got laid off a really terrible telephone solicitation job in 1974, just about two weeks before Christmas." Driven by the twin goads of ambition ("I said to myself, 'This is it; either I'm going to make it, or I'm not'") and fear (having little money and no job prospects), she wrote at a desperate pace. By the end of 1975, she had written three novels, all of which were eventually published. Doubleday first accepted *Patternmaster* on the condition that Butler make certain revisions, and she had no problem with their request: "It's always been easy for me to revise when someone was waving money."

Butler is now at work on a trilogy she calls *Xenogenesis.* Set on a postnuclear holocaust earth that has been saved by alien beings who are undifferentiated by gender, the books of the trilogy will be narrated in turn from the point of view of a woman, a man, and a genetically engineered, human "third sex" created with the aliens' help. This work gives Butler ample room to explore at length how a nonhierarchical understanding of difference might expand our possibilities. "One of the things my aliens say is, 'You people'—meaning all humanity—'have two things that simply don't work together. You are intelligent and you are hierarchical. The combination is explosive no matter what the species. You were inevitably doomed to destroy yourselves.'" *The Training Floor,* volume one of *Xenogenesis,* will be published by Warner Books sometime next winter.

Sandra Y. Govan

SOURCE: "Homage to Tradition: Octavia Butler Renovates the Historical Novel," in *MELUS*, Vol. 13, Nos. 1 and 2, Spring-Summer, 1986, pp. 79-96.

Despite the fact that her novels are sometimes difficult to find, Octavia Butler has nonetheless firmly established herself as a major new voice in science fiction. The five published novels of her Patternist saga, depicting over a vast time span both the genesis and evolution of Homo Superior (psionically enhanced human beings) and his mutated bestial counterpart; the one novel, *Kindred,* outside the serial story; and the short stories, all speak exceptionally well for Butler's artistry and growth.[1]

Through the interviews she has given, the articles she's written, the pieces published about her, and of course, her novels, Octavia Butler emerges as a forthright and honest author. She is a writer very conscious of the power of art to affect social perceptions and behavior and a writer unafraid to admit that, when appropriate, she borrows from tradition, that she takes and reshapes African and Afro-American cultural values, that she has heuristic and didactic impulses which she transforms into art. With *Wild Seed* and *Kindred,* for instance, Butler seizes the possibilities inherent in the historical novel and the Black tradition in autobiography. She adapts these forms to produce extrapolative fiction which, for its impetus, looks to an historically grounded African-American past rather than to a completely speculative future. On the surface, this seems indeed a curious connection, this linkage of future fiction to the past. Regardless of the surface appearance, the format itself, extrapolating or projecting from social structures of the past to those possible in the future, is not new (Isaac Asimov's *Foundation* series is a model precursor). What *is* new and distinctive is Butler's handling of the format or frame, her particular choice of past cultures to extrapolate from. She has chosen to link science fiction not only to anthropology and history, via the historical novel, but directly to the Black American slavery experiences via the slave narrative. This is a fundamental departure for science fiction as genre. *Wild Seed* and *Kindred* demonstrate this new configuration aptly. However, before engaging in an immediate discussion of these two novels, it seems appropriate to delay the discussion momentarily in order to better frame it with some critical definitions.

Most of us probably have seen the historical novel as a continuation of the realistic social novel; we associate it with Sir Walter Scott or Charles Dickens, or perhaps with Margaret Mitchell or Margaret Walker. We know that its setting and characters are established in a particular historic context—the age of chivalry or the French Revolution or the antebellum American South. Casual readers of the European or Western historical novel are usually content to forgo the kind of rigorous economic, philosophic, political analysis that Georg Lukács, in *The Historical Novel,* brings to his discussion of the form's origins. Lukács argues, for instance, that of prime importance to the historical novel's development "is the increasing historical awareness of the decisive role played in human progress by the struggle of classes in history." In his analysis, knowledge of "the rise of modern bourgeois society" from "the class struggles between nobility and bourgeoisie, . . . class struggles which raged throughout the entire 'idyllic Middle Ages' and whose last decisive stage was the great French Revolution," is crucial to the historical novel (27-28).

Using Sir Walter Scott as his archetypal model, Lukács outlines Scott's principal contributions to the form: "the broad delineation of manners and circumstances attendant upon events, the dramatic character of action and, in close connection with this, the new and important role of dialog in the novel" (31). For my immediate purposes however, Lukács' remarks are most germane when he says the authentic historical novel is "specifically historical," that its history is not "mere costumery," and that it presents an "artistically faithful image of a concrete historical epoch" (19).

Slave narratives, the first Black autobiographies, have a great deal in common with our understanding of the attributes of the historical novel. Each narrative is "specifically historical" (Marion Starling has traced narratives as far back as 1703 and followed them forward to 1944; their peak period was 1836-1860).[2] The historical circumstances of each text are so far removed from "mere costumery" that extensive, often intrusive, documentation of the ex-slave's veracity is quite frequently an established feature of the text, part of what Robert Stepto refers to as the "authenticating" strategy of the narrative voice (35). And without question, slave narrators strove to produce a powerful yet "faithful image of a concrete historical epoch." Perhaps only a handful of the six thousand extant narratives became artistic successes, works with the strength and quality of Frederick Douglass' *The Narrative of the Life of Frederick Douglass* or Harriet Jacobs' *Incidents in the Life of a Slave Girl* or the dramatic tale of William and Ellen Craft's *Running a Thousand Miles for Freedom.*[3] But successful literary works or not, most slave narratives depicted faithfully and graphically the brutal reality of slave life and each showed the direct impact of slavery, that peculiar institution, not only on the narrator's own life and that of his/her family but also the debilitating and corrupting effects of such an institution on those who held power within it, slaveholders.

Because the slave narrative and the historical novel, especially the historical novel which concerns itself with life in the antebellum South, share some common characteristics, a clear relationship between them may be easily established. For instance, Harriet Beecher Stowe's *Uncle Tom's Cabin* is unquestionably indebted to the life story of Josiah Henson, fugitive slave. But of more importance than demonstrating a relationship between the historical novel and the slave narrative is our understanding of the specific function slave narratives served. Unlike the novel, whose primary purpose was entertainment, the primary function of the slave narrative was to educate and politicize in no uncertain terms. At the height of their popularity, slave narratives, called "those literary nigritudes—little tadpoles of the press which run to editions of hundreds of thousands,"[4] were highly influential tools used by abolitionist societies here and abroad to mold public opinion, to bend the public mind toward the task of eliminating slavery. As a group, slave narratives exhibited these characteristics traits: they focused on the special experience of racial oppression; they were intended to be records of resistance; they employed a variety of literary/rhetorical devices including concrete imagery and diction, understatement, polemical voice, and satire to describe vividly the actual conditions of slavery; they looked at the self outside the typical western perspective of the individual and chose instead to recognize or represent the self in relationship to the oppressed group with ties and responsibilities to group members.[5] Slave narrators were conscious of their own cultural schizophrenia, their burden of blackness in white America, or, as W. E. B. DuBois said in his seminal *The Souls of Black Folk,* their "double consciousness," their two "warring selves in one dark skin."

Slave narrators were conscious, too, that they were presenting objective fact through the filter of their own subjective experience. Taken collectively, their narratives frequently show recurrent patterns. There is a loss of innocence wherein the slave, usually as a child, recollects his or her first awareness of the personal impact of slavery. There are detailed descriptions of various phases of bondage as the slave witnesses them and then experiences them. There is the punishment factor, the resistance motif, the glimpse

of life-in-the-quarters. There is also the slave's quest for education, the slave's encounter with abusive sexual misconduct and immoral behavior, the slave's recognition of religious hypocrisy and the adulterated Christianity practiced by "Christian" slave holders, the slave's escape attempts, and, finally, the slave's successful escape. Of course, this pattern varied from narrative to narrative and oftentimes, what was stressed depended upon the discretion and sensibilities of the narrator or, sometimes, on the concerns or dictates of an editor or an amanuensis.

Butler's *Wild Seed* and *Kindred* are rich texts which neatly define the junction where the historical novel, the slave narrative, and science fiction meet. The two novels build upon tenets clearly identified with the expected conventions or norms of the genres she employs. Then, because Butler's forte is extrapolative fiction, we can easily see the melding as each novel moves us through the recreated, historically plausible, viable, yet totally speculative alternative reality which is the realm of science fiction—as distinct from the codified expectations we have of fiction which operates from the realistic or naturalistic realm. To phrase it succinctly, Octavia Butler's work stands on the foundation of traditional form and proceeds to renovate that form.

Wild Seed is not about Arthurian England or the French Revolution. Instead, it is about alienation and loneliness; about needs, dreams, ambitions, and power. It is also about love. Africa provides the cultural backdrop for the initial interaction between plot and character. Although the opening setting of *Wild Seed* is 17th-century west Africa, specifically the Niger river region of eastern Nigeria, the setting shifts through the course of the novel and we follow the lives of Butler's two immortal central characters, Doro, a four thousand year old Nubian, and Anyanwu, a three hundred year old Onitsha priestess, through the Middle Passage voyage to life in a colonial New England village, to life on an antebellum Louisiana plantation, to California just after the Civil War. In the course of two hundred years of movement we are privy to a broad and vivid historical canvas. Again, however, Butler's use of history and cultural anthropology do more than simply illuminate the text or serve as mere coloration. Both disciplines are intrinsic to our understanding of character, theme, and action. Their use also permits Butler to employ a more original approach to the old theme of the trials of immortality, the theme of the spiritual disintegration of the man who cannot die.

The specifically African segment of *Wild Seed* only occupies four chapters of the text but an African ethos dominates the whole book. The novel opens in 1690. Doro has returned to Africa to look for one of his "seed villages," one of several communities he has carefully nurtured, composed of people with nascent or lateral mutant abilities. They know things or hear things or see things others cannot and so in their home communities, they are misfits or outcasts or "witches" because of their abilities. In his autonomous villages wherein he collects and breeds these people, Doro is their protector; his motives, however, are far from altruistic for he needs his people in a very real way. He "enjoys their company and sadly, they provide his most satisfying kills."[6] Doro's mutant power is the ability to transfer his psychic essence to any human host; thus, he kills to live. And, as he kills, he literally "feeds" off the spirit of the host body. But whenever Doro kills or "takes" his own kind, he gains more sustenance from their heightened psychic energy than he derives from the "taking" of ordinary non-mutant human beings.

The village Doro returns to has been destroyed by slave hunters and as he contemplates the carnage and thinks about tracking and regrouping the captured survivors, his gift of attraction to other mutants, an innate tracking sense or "telescent" subtly makes him conscious of the distant Anyanwu. He finds himself pulled toward her. Butler's narration here adeptly conveys both character and place.

> He wandered southwest toward the forest, leaving as he had arrived—alone, unarmed, without supplies, accepting the savanna and later the forest as easily as he accepted any terrain. He was killed several times—by disease, by animals, by hostile people. This was a harsh land. Yet he continued to move southwest, unthinkingly veering away from the section of the coast where his ship awaited him. After a while, he realized it was no longer his anger at the loss of his seed village that drove him. It was something new—an impulse, a feeling, a kind of mental undertow pulling at him. (9)

It is a subtle awareness of Anyanwu which attracts Doro and pulls him to a country he has not visited in three hundred years. When he finally meets and talks with her, Doro suspects immediately that they are distant kin, that she is "wild seed," the fruit of [his] peoples' passing by [hers] during one of Africa's many periods of flux. Ironically, Anyanwu herself supports this idea when she recalls a half remembered and whispered rumor that she was not father's child but had been begotten by a passing stranger. Originally, Doro's people were the Kush, an ancient people part of the vast Ethiopian Empire (Williams, 92). Anyanwu's people are the Igbo or Onitsha Ibo

people of eastern Nigeria. Traditional Onitsha society, explains ethnologist Richard Henderson, was a "community strongly concerned with maintaining oral accounts of the past." Henderson tells us that "Onitsha lacked an elaborate mythology as its cultural charter, and instead emphasized a quasi-historical 'ideology' based on stories tracing the founding of its villages to prehistoric migrations and political fusions" (31). We see an example of this quasi-history when Doro questions Anyanwu, trying to place her in his long personal history. "'Your people have crossed the Niger'—he hesitated, frowning, then gave the river its proper name—'the Orumili. When I saw them last, they lived on the other side in Benin'" (14). At this point Butler deliberately employs the omniscient narrative voice in conjunction with Doro's to signal the embedded signs of heritage and culture she wants her audience to note. Anyanwu's near poetic reply compresses years of African history, years of tribal warfare and tribal development, years of gradual adaptation to change. "We crossed long ago. . . . Children born in that time have grown old and died. We were Ado and Idu, subject to Benin before the crossing. Then we fought Benin and crossed the river to Onitsha to become free people, our own masters" (14).

Butler's Anyanwu is partly based on a legendary Ibo heroine, Atagbusi, a village protector and a magical "shape shifter." Henderson, whom Butler acknowledges as a source,[7] says that Atagbusi "is said to have been a daughter of the tiny clan called Okposi-eke, a descent group renowned for its native doctors and responsible for magical protection of the northwestern bush outskirts of the town. She was believed capable, as are other persons of Okposi-eke, of transforming herself into various large and dangerous animals, and it is believed that she concocted the medicine that protects the community on its western front" (311).

Like the legendary Atagbusi, Butler's Anyanwu is also a shape-shifter, a woman capable of physical metamorphosis. She can become a leopard, a python, an eagle, a dolphin, a dog, or a man. For self-protection, most of Anyanwu's powers are hidden from the villagers. And to reduce fear of the inexplicable, Anyanwu alters her body gradually so that she seemingly ages at the same rate as the various husbands she has married over the years, the same rate as the people around her. But whenever she chooses Anyanwu can regain her natural body, that of a sturdy, beautiful, twenty-year-old woman. Anyanwu is the village healer, a doctor for her people. She grows traditional herbs to make the customary medicines even though her power to heal does not always require the use of herbs. A respected and powerful person in the village hierarchy, Anyanwu's place is well defined.

> She served her people by giving them relief from pain and sickness. Also, she enriched them by allowing them to spread word of her abilities to neighboring people. She was an oracle. A woman through whom a god spoke. Strangers paid heavily for her services. They paid her people, then they paid her. That was as it should have been. Her people could see that they benefited from her presence, and that they had reason to fear her abilities. Thus she was protected from them—and they from her—most of the time. (10)

Anyanwu's sense of protection, her maternal instinct of care and concern for her people, is part of the African ethos which pervades the text. Of paramount importance to Anyanwu is the well being and safety of her kin—her children and her grandchildren. This is entirely in keeping with African tradition which holds "children are worth." Henderson affirms this with the observation that the Onitsha are "rooted firmly in notions of filiation and descent. When Onitsha people assess the career of a person, their primary criterion is the number of children he has raised to support and survive him. Children are extolled in proverbs above any other good, even above the accumulation of wealth; 'children first, wealth follows' is a proverb affirming the route to success" (106).

After three hundred years, ten husbands and forty-seven children, Anyanwu's descendants people the land. Their security is the lever Doro uses to pry Anyanwu away from her homeland. He appeals first to her innate sense of isolation and loneliness, proclaiming her place is among her own kind, then he appeals to her maternal spirit, promising children with genetic traits like their mother. "A mother," he tells her," should not have to watch her children grow old and die. If you live, they should live. It is the fault of their fathers that they die. Let me give you children who will live!" (26) Reluctantly and somewhat apprehensively, Anyanwu agrees to leave the village with Doro. But, when Doro speculates that her children, although they manifest no sign of her mutant ability, are also his peoples' children and that perhaps they should accompany them to the new world, Anyanwu becomes adamant—"you will not touch my children"—and remains so until Doro pledges he will not harm her children.

Unwittingly, Anyanwu's resolute stand in protection of her children gives Doro yet another lever to use against her. Totally devoid of scruples, and possess-

ing a keen insight into her psychological makeup, quite early in their journey to the coast Doro plots the strategy he will use to bind Anyanwu to him. It is a time-encrusted masculine ploy. He will get her pregnant; then, with a new child,

> her independence would vanish without a struggle. She would do whatever he asked then to keep the child safe. She was too valuable to kill, and if he abducted any of her descendants, she would no doubt goad him into killing her. But once she was isolated in America with an infant to care for, she would learn submissiveness. (30)

Doro's power play, his perception of the most immediate method he can use to control Anyanwu reflects his understanding of cultural ties, of the "appropriate manners and customs" which are part of Anyanwu's historical legacy. Though a powerful woman on her own turf, essentially Anyanwu leaves her tribal homeland to protect her kin.

Of course, Anyanwu never does learn submissiveness. Although she and Doro share a link forged in a bygone age, his name means "the east—the direction from which the sun comes" and hers means "the sun," they are not alike. Anyanwu is distinct from any woman Doro has encountered in thirty-seven hundred years. She is his female counterpart with one important distinction—she is not a predator. Her powers have long made her independent not withstanding her emergence from a culture where wives are considered the property of husbands. In one sense, however, Doro assesses Anyanwu correctly; she remains in his compound for years, she even marries as he directs (primarily out of fear and a strong survival instinct); but, she remains, too, for the sake of the children she bears and out of her concern for the strange, sometimes pitiable, sometimes warped or dangerous children who are the products of Doro's mutant communities. Much of *Wild Seed*'s tension is controlled by Doro's efforts to break Anyanwu, to use and then destroy her. She resists and fights back with the resources she has—her own strength of will. Again, however, the struggle is not solely for her sake but also for the safety of the children, the kin she forever shields.

African kinship networks seem to be the major structural device Butler uses to build dramatic complexity in this novel. When the principal characters first meet, the question of identity is crucial. Following the customary "who are you?" comes the equally important "who are your people?" The latter question springs from the African sense of connectedness to a specific place, a specific people, or a specific heritage. As indicated above, Doro traces his origins to the ancient Kush, one of the three great sub-Saharan societies. Anyanwu ties the history of her people, through wars and unification, to the powerful kingdom of Benin.

The importance of kinship is demonstrated repeatedly. When Anyanwu embarks on an attenuated version of the slave trade's Middle Passage, she happens upon two captured slaves she can actually help. Fortunately, they have been sold to Doro. It is their good fortune in this sense: Okoye is the son of Anyanwu's youngest daughter. Udenkwo, a young mother stolen from her village and separated from her five-year-old son, is a more distant relative. Anyanwu tells Udenkwo to trace her lineage through her clan and her male ancestry, a process which suggests subtly the value Africans attached to collective identity, familial bonding, and communal history. It happens that one of Udenkwo's ancestors was Anyanwu's eighth son, another, Anyanwu's third husband. (Here Butler slips in a quick feminist thrust: although Udenkwo traces her patrilineage, it is her matrilineal descent, her connection to Anyanwu, literally an earth mother, which saves her.) Because both Okoye and Udenkwo are Anyanwu's descendants, they will be spared the more brutal aspects of slavery. They will not be separated or sold again to some terrifying white plantation master. They will not be assaulted or beaten by Doro or his people. And although they are kinsmen, they will be permitted to marry despite the idea of "abomination" such an act connotes for Anyanwu. The marriage will permit them to offer each other comfort in their new and strange surroundings for as Doro says of his seed people, "our kind have a special need to be either with our kinsmen or others who are like us" (61).

The initial contact with the new world is not quite as traumatic for Anyanwu as it was for true slaves but still, she must cope with complete change. She must reckon with strange and restrictive western clothing, with a new diet (animal milk—another "abomination"), with learning a new language and new customs among a new and foreign people. And she must make all these adjustments in a land where color automatically determines status. The New England village Doro brings Anyanwu to is Wheatley, ostensibly named for an English family Doro supports and a principal cash crop. Butler slips in another quick thrust here for "Wheatley" is an allusion to young Phillis Wheatley, the child stolen from Africa who became known as the "Sable Muse" and was recognized as a significant contributor to 18th-century American poetry. Wheatley, however, is significant for another reason: life in the village cushions the impact of Anyanwu's contact with America's

hardening race and color caste system. Doro's villagers are a racial amalgam—Blacks, Indians, mixed bloods, and whites, a mixture not uncommon in the northeastern states before the increase in the slave trade. Anyanwu finds most of the villagers are friendly and also that village society is tight-knit, functioning roughly in a manner that approximates the familiar rhythms of clan life she had known. Relatives within the compound live with or near other relatives. People who share a common language are allowed to group together. Where no blood or tribal ties previously exist, newly formed families function as extended family and the weak, insecure, or unstable are placed with those who will care for them. The villagers see Doro as a guardian spirit who protects them from Indian raids and like disasters even as he controls their lives. They even make blood sacrifices to him for he takes from among them when he needs a new body. Yet despite the death he inevitably brings, whenever Doro is present in his compound he receives all the homage due a titled tribal elder with many children. And in fact, he has several children within the village.

The most serious clash of wills between Doro and Anyanwu is about the value assigned kinship. Doro's genetics program respects no tradition or socially sanctioned belief. He breeds people, related or not, to improve the pedigree of his stock. When in Wheatley he commands Anyanwu to marry and bear children by his son, and suggests that later she will also bear *his* children, Anyanwu withdraws in total revulsion—a greater abomination she cannot imagine. A century will pass, Anyanwu will have escaped Doro and formed her own special protected community (composed of mutants linked by blood and heightened psychic sensitivity) on a Louisiana plantation where she is the master, before she and Doro can come to civil terms again. They forge a new alliance based on respect and compromise. She recognizes he must kill to live but he learns genuine respect for her feelings and abilities and he also realizes that he must cease killing those of his own who serve him best or any of her close relatives. For Doro to regain Anyanwu's companionship, he must salvage what humanity remains to him.

If kinship is an underlying motif contributing to the dramatic tension in **Wild Seed,** it is clearly the focal point of **Kindred,** the motif underscoring the theme. **Kindred** is outside the Patternist saga, yet it shares with **Wild Seed** three common denominators: Black and white characters who move through an historically viable setting, one which explores the tangled complexities of interracial mixing during slavery and beyond; linkage through phenomenal psychic energy;

an emphasis on blood ties and the responsibilities that result. The bonds of blood in *Kindred* however are not created by exotic mutation nor genetic engineering. They are the result of plain undisguised lust and the raw exertion of power.

Kindred is a neatly packaged historical novel which uses scenes of plantation life and the techniques of the slave narrative to frame the plot. Dana Franklin, the heroine, is a Black woman, a writer who lives in Los Angeles, California, a woman very much of the present. Her family's roots are in Maryland; a fact made all the more pertinent when Dana finds herself traversing time and geography to move between twentieth-century California and nineteenth-century Maryland. The reason she moves is simple—Rufus Weylin "calls" her to him whenever he gets into trouble he cannot resolve alone, be it drowning, or arson, a bad fall, or a beating. Rufus is a child when he and Dana first meet. He is also white and destined to become her great grandfather, several times removed. The agency which moves Dana is never clear. She never understands *how* it happens. The "why" is easier. Whenever Rufus fears for his life, his subconscious mind somehow reaches out to Dana and transfers her to his setting and his time to meet his need. The only way she can return to her era is if she believes a corresponding threat to her own life exists. Time is totally disjointed for Dana during these transferences. There is no correlation between the time she spends in the past, her own history, and the time which passes while she is absent from her present. Dana's only clue to the mystery surrounding these transfers is the blood tie linking her to Rufus; but even the blood relationship is not, for her, a satisfactory explanation for an inexplicable process.

Once Dana knows Rufus' identity and comprehends what his relationship to her will become, she understands her role more precisely. She is to assure the child's survival until he can father the first branch of her family tree. She must serve as his mentor and be his teacher. The task of trying to mold a humane slave holder, in an era where all the accepted social norms mitigate against the possibility, falls to her. And an awesome responsibility it is considering her circumstances: a modern Black woman periodically surfaces in antebellum Maryland over approximately a twenty-year span, with no free papers, no owner to vouch for her, no way to explain her dress, her speech, or her behavior. Her role is to protect a boy/man who is alternately and erratically "generous and vicious." Immediately, Dana recognizes that she is "the worst possible guardian" for Rufus—"a black woman to watch over him in a society that considered Blacks sub-human, and a woman to watch over

him in a society that considered women perennial children" (77). In that age and in that place, Dana is simply a "strange nigger," a fact the child Rufus promptly explains. But because she saves his life and because he realizes they are linked, even though he does not know the extent of their relationship, Rufus, the child, is Dana's unexpected, if unstable, ally.

Quite apart from her role as mentor to Rufus stands Dana's other function. *Kindred,* far more than *Wild Seed,* is an overtly didactic novel, although its artistry is such that one does not realize how much antebellum history gets absorbed. Dana is Butler's tool for sketching a far less romanticized portrait of plantation life from 1815 through the 1830s. She is both a reporter and a respondant for she witnesses and participates in the slave experience. In fact, *Kindred,* is so closely related to the experience disclosed in slave narratives that its plot structure follows the classic patterns with only the requisite changes to flesh out character, story, and action.

Dana's loss of innocence, her discovery that she has slave status is as abrupt and brutal as the same discoveries recorded by Frederick Douglass or Harriet Jacobs in their respective narratives. Tom Weylin is a harsh disciplinarian; he beats his slaves, his horses, and his son with the same whip. On her first visit, he almost shoots the "strange nigger" caught with his son and wife. On her second visit, having seen Rufus' scars, Dana acquires some of her own. Seeking safety away from the big house, she leaves the Weylins' to seek help from the black family destined to become her forbears. Patrollers (and Butler carefully identifies them as young whites charged with policing or "maintaining order" among the slave population) arrive at the cabin first. Ostensibly, they have come to see whether a slave husband is meeting illegally with his free wife. The man is. He has no pass permitting his absence from his owner's plantation. For the crime of visiting his family the slave is beaten, then tied to a tree and whipped savagely while his wife and child watch helplessly. Dana is our hidden mute witness. Yet in order to bring her readers closer to the immediacy of the horror we have just seen, Butler moves Dana rapidly from witnessing slavery to experiencing it, from watching, to feeling, to testifying what life was like for a Black woman, even if she were nominally free. After the slave is dragged away, Dana goes to the assistance of his wife. They talk guardedly for Dana cannot explain who she is or where she comes from; nevertheless, the woman grants her permission to stay. Shortly thereafter, Dana steps outside of the cabin and is captured and attacked by one of the patrollers who had returned alone to rape the slave's wife. He realizes instantly that he has not captured the wife but determines almost as quickly that Dana will satisfy his lust. Degradation, brutality, powerlessness, the commonplace violence directed against Black men and women could be no more sharply delineated. Dana's violent struggle to escape the patroller returns her to her own time.

The third time Dana is called into her own history we are privy to a much broader look at life on the plantation from the master's big house to the slave's quarters. She learns that even "favored" house slaves are given a meager diet of table scraps and corn meal mush, occasionally supplemented by what can be stolen from the plantation's larders. Field hands are supposed to work even harder yet are expected to subsist off even less. Just as almost every slave narrative dramatizes the theme of family separation, Butler also brings this theme to life. Dana is sent to the kitchen to learn from Sarah, the plantation's cook. She learns quickly that Sarah has had three children sold away from her; a fourth she was allowed to keep because the child was born mute, therefore "defective," therefore "not worth much" on the slave market. Both in and out of the kitchen Dana discovers what the typical slave's work day is like, first in the big house and later in the fields. She also discovers how slavery can effect a plantation mistress if the woman has no viable authority. Margaret Weylin is described as temperamental, flighty, beautiful, bored, useless. Her husband controls all of the plantation's business affairs and Margaret is left with nothing to do but lavish unreturned affection on her son because "slaves kept her house clean, did much of her sewing, all of her cooking and washing" (109). Margaret cannot even dress or undress without a slave attendant. During her extended third journey into the past, Dana is called to witness another brutal whipping, this time administered for the offense of "answering back." Shortly thereafter, she is the recipient of the same treatment but her offense is far more serious. She has been caught reading to a slave and almost caught teaching slaves thirsty for knowledge how to read and write. An education was, of course, legally denied slaves. Dana's infraction of this rule was both a courageous and dangerous act. The same hostility which fell on Frederick Douglass' attempts to teach his fellow slaves fell on Dana; Tom Weylin seizes her and whips her viciously. He fears a slave who can read and write will escape by forging a pass; for their part, slaves knew being armed with knowledge was freedom and many took great risks in order to learn.

The large, panoramic slice-of-plantation-life we see in this segment of the novel is deftly handled "fac-

tion," that blend of authentic verifiable historical fact and well-rendered fiction. Butler treats the recurring themes of casual brutality, forceable separation of families, the quest for knowledge, the desire to escape, the tremendous work loads expected of slaves as effectively as any of the narratives or documentary histories discussing the slavery experience. Her use of these details is more than mere costumery, it is part of the "broad delineation of manners and circumstances" inherent in the historical record and essential for developing plot and character.

Kindred incorporates other devices and themes associated with the slave narrative. These narratives repeatedly demonstrate that slavery as a system displayed little regard for marital status among slaves and no respect for the sanctity of the family unit unless a master chose to recognize a family bond. *Kindred* illustrates this. The narratives record ad infinitum the harsh punishment meted out to any slave who dared evince a sense of self-respect, pride, manhood; but if a slave's spirit would not be broken, it could be sorely tried and his body could be broken.[8] *Kindred* illustrates this extreme as well. Although Butler does not belabor the Christian hypocrisy theme, a popular and effective tactic used in many narrative accounts to arouse moral indignation, she does make the novel's climatic denouement turn on the other principal axis of the formulaic narrative, careful attention to socially sanctioned yet unacknowledged miscegenation, illicit sex and lust behind the facade of law and respectability.

Tom Weylin has sired at least three children by slave mothers who are still on his plantation. On Dana's second trip to the past the patroller who attacks her was actually returning to the cabin to molest a free Black woman; when he found himself with Dana instead, the difference between the two Black women never disturbed him. On her third journey back, Dana's husband Kevin is transported with her. Because Kevin is white, he affords her some measure of protection by posing as her master. Ironically, in 1976, while their marriage must withstand some subtle societal disapproval, it is at least legally recognized. In 1819 Maryland, Dana and Kevin dare not admit their marital bond because such a relationship is illegal, unimaginable, and dangerous. Casual sexual liaisons between white men and Black women were permissible but intermarriage was not. White men were expected to be rakes, or at least their licentiousness was tacitly condoned; white women were expected to be chaste (certainly they dare not openly consort with Black men the way their husbands, fathers, sons took liberties with Black women); and Black women, of course, were often treated as mere sexual vessels. A brief glance at an actual narrative describing the entanglements produced by an absence of moral integrity is pertinent and may make Butler's account of events at the Weylin plantation even more credible. *Incidents in the Life of a Slave Girl* bluntly discusses the moral "corruption produced by slavery." Jacobs records how "the slave girl is reared in an atmosphere of licentiousness and fear." She is "bribed" . . . or "whipped or starved into submission" to the will of her master and/or his sons. "The slaveholder's sons, are, of course, vitiated, even while boys, by the unclean influences everywhere around them. Nor do the master's daughters always escape." At this point the Jacobs narrative discloses the forbidden activities of some white women in response to the moral degeneracy surrounding them. Jacobs' testimony is explicit:

> They know that the women slaves are subject to their father's authority in all things; and in some cases they exercise the same authority over the men slaves. I have myself seen the master of such a household. . . . It was known in the neighborhood that his daughter had selected one of the meanest slaves on his plantation to be the father of her first grandchild. She did not make her advances to her equals, nor even to her father's more intelligent servants. In such cases the infant is smothered, or sent where it is never seen by any who knows its history. But if the white parent is the father, instead of the mother, the offspring are unblushingly reared for market. (51-52)

The sexual tension existing at the Weylin home poses both the customary morality/hypocrisy questions and also allows Butler the opportunity to explore another dimension of this tension, sexuality-and-the-white-woman with a little gallows humor. Margaret Weylin discovers that Dana has been sleeping in Kevin's room on a pallet rather than in the attic where other house slaves are expected to sleep. She turns livid with rage. As the Jacobs narrative shows, white men may not be denied their concubines yet they certainly are not supposed to conduct their liasons in the big house; just down in the slave quarters, out of sight. Margaret slaps Dana, screams at her that she is "a filthy black whore!" and protests loudly that hers is a "Christian house." (108) Of course, Dana cannot retaliate but she does think, rather charitably, that for all her flaws, Margaret Weylin must be a moral woman. However, Dana is soon made privy to an irony she had not anticipated. Margaret, although long married, is smitten by a strong attraction to Kevin; she chases him with a barely concealed ardor and is, therefore, extremely jealous of the near connubial relationship Kevin and Dana attempt to maintain. Jealousy based on the unacknowledged sexual

tension between white mistresses and Black slave women linked to white men surfaces frequently in slavery annals.

The most critical sexual relationship in the text however remains the relationship an adult Rufus Weylin forces on Alice Greenwood, a free Black woman on the Weylin plantation. Rufus' feelings for Alice are a mixture of love and lust. He loves her, and he wants her to love him, but he also feels he has a "right" to her and that he is entitled to win her or take her any way he can. Unfortunately, Alice loves a Black man, a slave. Since neither man can openly compete for Alice's affections, this triangle degenerates into an extraordinarily painful relationship, one compounded by rivalry, passion, guilt, love, lust, punishment, pride, power, and implacable hatred. But there are two Black women in young Rufus' life and this adds another level to the sexual tension. Dana and Alice are virtual doubles of each other. Physically, they look alike; intellectually and emotionally, they function as two halves of the same woman, flawed duplicates separated by the dictates of their respective historical time and the resultant sexual-political consciousness each maintains by virtue of their particular social circumstances. In other words, although she is unaccountably displaced in time, Dana retains the attributes of a late twentieth-century woman—knowledgeable, assertive, independent. In contrast, Alice is a nineteenth-century Black woman forced into chattel slavery—by definition her assumed posture is that of ignorance, passiveness, dependence on the will or whim of her owner. Yet even as Butler draws these distinctions they become superficial and the space between Dana and Alice shrinks. For Dana, looking at Alice is like looking at herself, to use Alice Walker's term, "suspended" by historical circumstance.[9] It is as if the folk wisdom of "there but for the grace of God go I" had suddenly been made manifest.

From Dana, Rufus draws a controlled, limited, camaraderie and intellectual stimulation. From Alice he demands sexual attention and actually expects emotional attachment. Although he cannot make her love him, Rufus can and does force Alice to share his bed. And despite the obvious pain that being a witness to (almost a participant in) this crude liason causes her, Dana abets it until Alice gives birth to Hagar, the woman who is the founder of her family tree. (Distasteful as the situation is, Dana must assist Rufus in his conquest of Alice or her personal history, her present, will be irrevocably altered. This is a variant of science fiction's time travel paradox, the problem of the time-space continuum theme.) Eventually, unable to endure the vicious games of Rufus (he pretends to sell her children), her powerlessness, or her concubinage any longer, Alice commits suicide. Almost immediately, a chastened and tortured Rufus then transfers his entire emotional attention to Dana, seeing her as a replicate of Alice, virtually the same woman, this time whole and complete. Because the insidious institution of slavery has given him virtual carte blanche power over Black lives, Rufus has no misgivings, feels no remorse about attempting to seduce or possess Dana in the same manner he won Alice—that is, by cajolery if possible, force or violence if necessary. It does not matter that Dana has saved his life repeatedly, that she has been, in common parlance, a "good" slave for Rufus. Nor does it matter that the "love" he bears for her borders on incestuousness; after all, Dana has been his protector, his confidant, his mentor, and in some respects, his mother and his sister. Since selfish, childish and unstable Rufus can think only of his own immediate needs and wants, and since the system gives him the power to take what he wants—he decides that Dana shall replace Alice and he will not hear her refusal.

Without turning to an actual slave narrative, there probably is no more vivid depiction of life on an Eastern Shore plantation than that found in **Kindred.** The composite rendering is as exact as detailed research could make it. Butler admits to having tempered some of the harshness of the real experience because the slave narratives proved such "grim reading" that she realized she would have to present a "cleaned-up, somewhat gentler version of slavery for there was no entertainment in the real thing."[10] **Kindred,** however, is entertaining and compelling; yet for all the history it enlivens, the average reader absorbs the information without any awareness of an inherently didactic purpose framing an exciting, action filled story. Far from impeding the story line, the didacticism informs it.

Kindred and **Wild Seed** break new ground in science fiction. They are both novels which feature Black characters in major significant roles; they both feature Black women as heroic characters, protagonists who either share power with men or who maintain their right to wield power on an equal basis.[11] Neither of the two women principals yields her basic integrity or submits to male dominance. In each novel we look at a speculative past firmly grounded in an African and African-American social and cultural history. Both **Wild Seed** and **Kindred** mirror Lukács' "broad delineation of manners and circumstances attendant upon events," his insistence upon "dramatic character of action," and his large role voice and dialog within the narrative. Each text is "specifically historical," indeed history is integral to plot, and

each effectively welds function to form giving us precise yet "artistically faithful" images of "concrete historical epochs," whole chapters of African-American history, keeping us spellbound all the while.

Butler's works do something else not generally asked of good historical fiction. They reach an entirely different audience, an established science fiction readership which, taken as a whole, is more accustomed to future histories and alien spaces than it is to authentic African and African-American landscapes. That is, I suppose, one of the benefits of renovation: more people are attracted to the old, the historically significant, recreated and redressed in a new light.

Notes

1. The five novels are *Wild Seed* (New York: Pocket Books—Timescape, 1981), *Mind of My Mind* (New York: Avon, 1978), *Survivor* (New York: Signet, 1979), *Patternmaster* (New York: Avon, 1979), and *Clay's Ark* (New York: St. Martin's P, 1984). Butler's "Speech Sounds" appeared in the Mid-December 1983 issue of *Isaac Asimov's Science Fiction Magazine.* "Bloodchild" is scheduled for a June 1984 appearance in the same journal, and "Near of Kin" was published in *Chrysalis 4,* an anthology edited by Roy Torgeson in 1979. Her first published short story, "Crossover," was published in *Clarion,* an anthology edited by Robin S. Wilson in 1971. Butler calls this one and "Childfinder," a story sold to Harlan Ellison's as yet unpublished *The Last Dangerous Visions,* "student writing." Octavia E. Butler, letter to Sandra Y. Govan, 16 April, 1984.

2. For a full discussion of slave narratives as historical documents see Marion Wilson Starling, *The Slave Narrative: Its Place in American History* (Boston: G. K. Hall, 1981) xviii.

3. The narratives cited are nineteenth century narratives which have been republished and are available in a variety of editions. The texts used here are Frederick Douglass, *Narrative of the Life of Frederick Douglass, An American Slave* (1845; New York: Anchor Books, 1973), William and Ellen Craft's *Running a Thousand Miles for Freedom, or the Escape of William and Ellen Craft from Slavery* (1860; collected in *Great Slave Narratives,* ed. Arna Bontemps [Boston: Beacon P, 1969]), and Harriet Jacobs, *Incidents in the Life of a Slave Girl* (1861; New York: Harcourt Brace, Jovanovich, 1973).

4. Starling, p. 2. The original citation is to "Black Letters," *Graham's Magazine* 42 (January 1853): 215.

5. Several scholars have enlarged upon the principal characteristics of and patterns within the slave narrative. See Richard K. Barksdale, "Black Autobiography and the Comic Vision," *Black American Literature Forum* 15 (Spring 1981): 22-27; John Blassingame, "Black Autobiographies as History and Literature," *The Black Scholar* (Dec. 1973-Jan. 1974): 2-9; and Steven T. Butterfield, "The Use of Language in the Slave Narrative," *Negro American Literature Forum* 6 (Fall, 1972): 72-78. The introduction and comments from various chapters in Butterfield's *Black Autobiography in America* (Amherst: U of Massachusetts P, 1974) also proved useful.

6. Octavia E. Butler, Letter to Sandra Y. Govan, 16 January, 1984.

7. *Ibid.,* Henderson, p. 311

8. Frederick Douglass' *Narrative* provides a graphic depiction of "slave breaking." See chapter ten of the *Narrative,* 63-68.

9. In an interview Alice Walker has argued that Black women in the eighteenth, nineteenth, and early twentieth centuries were "suspended" women. These women "were suspended in a time in history where [their] options were severely limited. And they either kill themselves or they are used up by the men or by the children or by. . . . whatever the pressures against them. And they cannot go anywhere." See Mary Helen Washington, "An Essay on Alice Walker," *Sturdy Black Bridges: Visions of Black Women in Literature.* Eds., Roseann Bell et al. (New York: Anchor Books, 1979) 137-43.

10. Butler to Govan, 16 January, 1984.

11. Butler is fascinated by the question of power. In an interview she said, "I began writing about power because I had so little." Cited in Carolyn S. Davidson's review, "The Science Fiction of Octavia Butler," *Sagala* II, No. 1 (A Howard U Magazine, n.d.). Janice Bogstad devoted an essay to examining this theme called "Octavia E. Butler and Power Relationships," *Janus* 14 (Winter, 1978-79). My own previous essay on Butler, "Connections, Links, and Extended Networks: Patterns in Octavia Butler's Science Fiction,"

Black American Literature Forum 18, (Summer, 1984) also examines this theme.

Works Cited

Butler, Octavia E. *Wild Seed.* New York: Pocket Books-Timescape, 1981.

———. *Kindred.* New York: Doubleday, 1979.

Craft, William & Ellen. *Running a Thousand Miles for Freedom, or The Escape of William & Ellen Craft. Great Slave Narratives.* ed. Arna Bontemps. Boston: Beacon P, 1969.

Douglass, Frederick. *Narrative of the Life of Frederick Douglass, An American Slave.* New York: Anchor, 1973.

Henderson, Richard N. *The King in Every Man: Evolutionary Trends in Onitsha Ibo Society & Culture.* New Haven: Yale U P, 1972.

Jacobs, Harriet. *Incidents in the Life of a Slave Girl.* New York: Harcourt Brace, Jovanovich, 1973.

Lukács, Georg. *The Historical Novel.* New York: Humanities P, 1965.

Starling, Marion. *The Slave Narrative: Its Place in American History.* Boston: G. K. Hall, 1981.

Stepto, Robert. *From Behind the Veil.* Urbana, Illinois: U of Illinois P, 1979.

Williams, Chancellor. *The Destruction of Black Civilization: Great Issues of a Race from 4500 BC to 200 AD.* Chicago: Third World P, 1974.

Janice Antczak

SOURCE: "Octavia E. Butler: New Designs for a Challenging Future," in *African-American Voices in Young Adult Literature: Tradition, Transition, Transformation,* edited by Karen Patricia Smith, The Scarecrow Press, Inc., 1994, pp. 311-36.

For many readers, Octavia E. Butler represents the premiere African-American woman's voice in science fiction. She has achieved cult status as an author whose works speak to a diverse audience who respond to her inclusion of issues of race and feminism in provocative and exciting science fiction. Although Butler is not a "YA" author, she began writing her science fiction as an adolescent. Very significantly, her work has found a readership among young adults, and her books are reviewed and discussed in the journals concerned with young adult literature.

Butler's own adolescent interest in science fiction and her appeal to YA readers may find their origins in the very typical adolescent concern with the outsider, the misfit who does not quite find a niche in the peer group. Butler was raised in the Baptist home of her mother and grandmother; where strict tenets forbade dancing and other activities that customarily interest many young adults. Butler was shy and found it difficult to gain acceptance among those her own age. She turned to books and writing. "I began writing when I was about ten years old for the same reason many people begin reading—to escape loneliness and boredom."[1] She began to write science fiction "simply because I liked to read it," and wrote the "first version of her first published novel, *Patternmaster,* when she was twelve. At thirteen, she began submitting her work to science fiction magazines.—"[2] This adolescent beginning has grown into a body of work that has gained recognition and respect. This recognition includes the Nebula Award in 1985 and two Hugo Awards, one in 1984 and the other in 1985.

Belden and Beckman write that Butler's fiction "should appeal to idealistic teenagers impatient to build a better society."[3] Her nine novels develop patterns and themes that would encourage YA readers to speculate about what such a goal could encompass. Yet, her novels are not simple blueprints for building a better future. Perhaps because she describes herself as "pessimist, if I'm not careful";[4] Butler's writings do not provide easy answers. Rather, she explores issues and ideas that young adults face, not in an imaginative distant future, but rather, in their daily lives.

Butler's works provoke and challenge. The strong language of the novels may deter some from including her works in their collections. Yet, her use of such language, while offensive to some, is not gratuitous; for it reflects the nature of her characters and their settings and situations. Many are outcasts or loners seeking power and their language connotes their status. The "outlaw car family" in *Clay's Ark* speak in a manner befitting their degenerate lifestyle, and even Doro, the powerful protagonist of many of the Patternist novels, uses scatological language as part of his strategy of intimidation.

Butler's use of frank vocabulary is matched by her provocative use of sexuality. She explores and employs all aspects of the sexual. Butler incorporates strong but not necessarily graphic sexual scenes in

the novels. Both heterosexual and homosexual encounters are presented, and some of these are of a violent nature. Rape is a common occurrence, again indicative of the breakdown of society or of the attempt to prove one's power over another. In some of her works, Butler challenges readers with exotic ideas of sexuality. Her alien characters practice a sexuality quite different from an earthly norm. The Oankali in the Xenogenesis trilogy engage in sexual triads, and while accepting alien notions of sexuality may not be too provocative on its own terms, the inclusion of humans in these "menage a trois" may be troubling to some readers. Such strange sexual patterns are not uncommon in adult science fiction because they are but another look at alien beings' biology and culture; they are part of sophisticated explorations of new worlds and their inhabitants. While some may feel such frank language and presentations do not belong in young adult collections, the inclusion of this provocative material is very much a part of the concerns which Butler so strongly addresses in her work.

Butler's themes revolve around issues of personal and societal concern. Her novels treat these concerns in imaginative ways, but Butler frequently addresses them, as well, in essays and interviews which help to clarify her work. When asked to describe herself, Butler responds that she is "black" and a "feminist," and these two words comprise and illuminate much of what she has written. Butler writes of racism and sexism, but does not always focus upon the negative impact of these patterns in society. She also presents the positive aspects of racial and sexual differences. Her major characters are most often strong, black women who survive and even triumph in the difficulties of their time and place. She emphasizes issues of power and the power struggle. Sometimes this exploration of the domination and exploitation of the powerless by the powerful takes on a violent cast in her novels, but it is precisely this theme that provides the most provocative reading. The issue of power encompasses the themes of race, gender, and otherness that challenge readers in her fictional and the real worlds.

Race, gender, power—these are challenging words and issues, and they comprise the patterns that appear repeatedly in Butler's novels. Her nine novels include two series: the "Patternist" series of *Patternmaster* (1967), *Mind of My Mind* (1977), *Survivor* (1978), *Wild Seed* (1980), and *Clay's Ark* (1984); and the "Xenogenesis" trilogy which includes *Dawn* (1987), *Adulthood Rites* (1988), and *Imago* (1989). Another novel, *Kindred* (1979), stands alone.

Throughout these works the themes that concern Butler appear again and again in variations that fascinate readers.

EXPANDING THE LIMITS OF MIND AND MATTER: THE PATTERNISTS

(The publication order of the Patternist novels does not follow the sequence of events that occur within the books. To facilitate an appreciation of the use of Butler's themes and patterns, this discussion will follow the novels in order of events.)

Butler began work on the Patternist books when she was twelve years old. In an interview with Larry McCaffrey, she said that when she was in her teens and was asked about her hopes and dreams, about what she would do if she could do anything she wanted—she answered that she wanted "to live forever and breed people . . . ."[5] Butler stopped believing in an afterlife when she was twelve years old, but became fascinated by the powers of the mind, the psi phenomena. Therefore, during early adolescence, she began to weave these two strands into the pattern that would become her novels; for the Patternist novels do use forms of immortality and psionic powers to explore her themes of race, gender, and power from times past to times future.

Butler creates characters and situations that reflect and embody her major themes. She asks readers to question why power so often resides in the male hierarchy, in which men scramble over each other to be dominant and women are left at the bottom, raped and powerless. In her novels Butler depicts patterns of male dominance over centuries, but challenges the inevitability of this gendered social order by creating strong female challengers in characters such as Anyanwu, Amber, Mary, and Alanna. Butler also ties in the issue of race to complete the triad of concerns. While her strongest female characters are women of color, she comes to show that strength and power reside at the core of one's self and are beyond race. All of this challenges readers with questions such as: Where does ultimate power reside? How far can manipulation of the mind proceed? How ethical is this manipulation? If one has the power to do so, should one be allowed to breed a superrace? Are women ultimately breeders? Are women in power more nurturing? Can humans get beyond color and accept diversity in all its glory? Is there a future for the human race as it now exists? Or must we evolve or be shaped by others into another mode of thinking and being to survive?

Race, gender, and power are at the core of this series of novels and at the core of the character of Doro.

Doro is a 4,000-year-old Nubian whose name is Nubian for "the direction from which the sun comes."[6] He survives through the ages as a predator who kills others to assume their bodies. Assuming male and female forms, he has been all races. Doro breeds people. His mission is to create a super-race of humans with psi powers. It is in *Wild Seed,* the prequel to the series, that his lives begin to unfold. *Wild Seed* is a hybrid science fiction/historical fiction novel, covering the years 1690-1840. It traverses geographical space, as well as time, as the characters appear in Europe, Africa, Colonial and pre-Civil War America.

Butler's settings are fully developed to convey a sense of time and place, and the people who live there. The Africa of the days of the slave trade is depicted as a land of almost idyllic, unique tribal villages whose way of life is periodically shattered by the forays of the slavers. Life there seems suffused with the power of nature, particularly the sun. This contrasts strongly with the images of colonial New York, with its crowds and buildings, and a "civilized" code based on externals, like mode of dress. This is a world in which nature seems less powerful, a world which men seek to control. The pre-Civil War period as described by Butler is truly a world on the verge of chaos, where good and evil seem to have been turned upside-down. The lush landscape of the southland seems to barely hide the uncontrollable power which seeks to destroy that which stands in its way. Butler has selected eras of history which are powerful icons—the idyllic cradle of life in Africa, the birth of a new nation, and the sundering of that nation in a war between brothers. These powerful epochs are appropriate choices for these stories.

Wild Seed begins the story of the struggle for power between immortals, a struggle that begins in Africa, 1690. Doro's breeding project had been proceeding for centuries without contest. As he tours his "seed villages" in Africa, conflicts begin to surface. Slavers have decimated his villages, prime descendants are captured and herded to the coast, and Doro finds himself being drawn by a strong "mental undertow."[7] This strong force is Anyanwu (whose name means "sun"), the woman who will be his equal in the struggle for power and immortality. She is the wild seed, "descended from people whose abnormally long lives, resistance to disease, and budding special abilities made them very important to him. People, who like so many others, had fallen victim to slavers or tribal enemies."[8] Anyanwu is a healer, a shape-shifter, a jumper of rivers, an oracle to her people. She believes "It is better to be a master than to be a slave."[9] She has known power and is not going to relinquish it quickly. To Anyanwu, who has had several husbands over time, even marriage holds threats to her power. Woman's role and place in society plays a dominant role in the life of Anyanwu. She has never met a man with the spirit and power of Doro, and there is mutual attraction, yet simultaneously revulsion.

Doro's seed villages are not immune to danger and destruction. He often loses prime descendants, so he travels gathering those with promise to new places where he can provide protection. Doro has placed loyal, disciplined men in strategic places around the world, ready to serve his needs. One such character is Daly, a white man working for the Royal African Company, a slaver, who tests each slave to determine if any have Doro's inbred powers. Such slaves are saved for Doro, a black man who will use even an institution like slavery to serve his ends.

Doro has enough of his people gathered to fill a "slave" ship. It is captained and crewed by his own people. During the voyage, Doro's powerful sons work the ship and sail it through calm and storm. Each with his own specialty and with their combined powers, the sons save the ship and passengers. Thus they echo African folklore in which Anansi the spider and his sons all use their remarkable powers to help themselves and the people. In these early pages of the series, the emphasis on African myth and lore is strong and brings power and resonance to the books.

Butler again raises the issue of slavery when Doro explains a real slave ship to Anyanwu and contrasts it to his slaver.

> In the benign atmosphere of the ship, all the slaves were recovering from their invariably harsh homeland experiences. Some of them had been kidnapped from their villages. Some had been sold for witchcraft or for other crimes of which they were usually not guilty. Some had been born slaves. Some had been enslaved during war. All had been treated harshly at some time during their captivity.[10]

During the voyage, Doro continues his breeding program, making sure appropriate pairs are matched. So the issues of what is slavery and what is freedom resonate through the novel, as Doro rescues people from the "slavers" and ironically and purposefully enslaves them in his breeding program.

Anyanwu learns more about her shape-shifting abilities as she assumes the bodies of sea creatures like the dolphin. She learns or acquires the special abilities of those she helped or entered, and she is able to

hide from Doro in the assumed animal forms. Doro does not take on the unique attributes of those bodies he assumes. He kills to inhabit those bodies and discards them when they are no longer useful to him.

Doro takes his slave ship to an American town in New York called Wheatley. (Butler often uses names associated with African-American heritage or having biblical "echoes" in this series. Wheatley, Doro's village, is homage to colonial poet Phillis Wheatley. While Isaac is Doro's favored son, Thomas is the doubting outcast. Mary becomes mother to the Pattern, and the Missionary colony is called Canaan, the promised land. Butler's use of such names causes a confrontation with readers. Such time-honored names call up images from the past of piety and purity, but she asks readers to see in a new way what it means to be a loyal son or the mother of a people.) Here all races mingle as Doro continues his breeding. "Wheatley is Doro's American village. He dumps all the people he can't find places for in his pure families on us. Mix and stir. No one can afford to worry about what anyone else looks like. They don't know who Doro might mate them with—or what their own children might look like."[11]

Anyanwu is eager to find her place. She discusses African and Wheatley ways with Doro's son Isaac. Isaac feels social mores are all relative and tells her, "Civilization is the way one's own people live. Savagery is the way foreigners live."[12] Yet Anyanwu is wise to changing mores. She "lived in enough different towns through her various marriages to know the necessity of learning to behave as others did."[13] Anyanwu is a survivor.

The novel passes through time as well as place as it moves to the year 1741. Anyanwu is now a major figure in Wheatley for she has given Doro eight children and Isaac five in the breeding program. Her portrait resembles a black Madonna, but race prejudice is growing in the colonies and some people of Wheatley find the portrait offensive.

Doro continues his breeding work and expands to the Native-American tribes. He feels that "Indians were rich in untapped wild seed that they tended to tolerate, or even revere rather than destroy. Eventually, they would learn to be civilized and to understand as the whites understood that the hearing of voices, the seeing of visions . . . were evil or dangerous, or at the very least imaginary."[14]

In this section of the novel, Butler's characters frequently comment on race. Doro himself seems not to be concerned with race, but other characters reveal their own prejudice or that of their time and place. Doro takes Anyanwu south to mate with Thomas, a white who lives as a wild man. Doro, himself an African, says cruelly to her, " . . . she should not mind the way he lived, since she was from Africa where people swing through the trees and went naked like animals."[15] Thomas, who lives in squalor, curses her blackness and asks if she can turn white. In an echo of slavery he tells her, she is here for breeding and nothing more. Thomas is an anomaly in Doro's program. "Was he really so concerned about her color? Usually Doro's people were not. Most of them had backgrounds too thoroughly mixed for them to sneer at anyone."[16] Those in Doro's breeding program are in virtual slavery to their master and his own designs.

Anyanwu is a survivor who claims, "If I have to be white to survive, I will be white. . . . "[17] As the novel moves to 1840, Anyanwu assumes many other forms to survive—a black dog, a dolphin, a leopard, and an old white man. She now lives on a Louisiana plantation and Doro tracks her there. She, in the form of a white man, is master of the plantation and purchases slaves at auction, especially those who reveal some power. Doro wants to continue his breeding and bring mates for Anyanwu's people.

Death and destruction follow as Butler begins to show how Doro's people may be born with special gifts, but must first survive a transition period before they can be used. As Doro and Anyanwu wage war against each other through their children, the nation's Civil War is about to begin. They agree to a peaceful coexistence. He will no longer try to command her nor interfere with her children. To escape the hostilities between North and South, Anyanwu moves her people to California and takes the name Emma, the grandmother or ancestress. She is the survivor and no one's slave—a powerful black woman with her own destiny and dynasty. Emma Anyanwu represents Butler's heroic female characters, compelling and fascinating to readers.

Emma Anyanwu also appears in the next title of the series, *Mind of My Mind.* Here her role is secondary, that of the wise old woman, the matriarch who guides her extended family in the California city of Forsyth. (The southern California setting, replete with racism, drug addiction, alcoholism, prostitution, and child abuse approximates contemporary times.) Emma presents herself most often as the old grandmother, but her shape-shifting powers still work to her advantage when needed. She and Doro continue their relationship through the centuries—they are still lovers and

co-conspirators in his breeding program. While Emma Anyanwu appears in this novel, it is her grand-daughter Mary who is the central character.

Mary's skin is "a kind of light coffee, . . . gifts from the white man's body that Doro was wearing when he got Rina pregnant."[18] Doro brings Mary to live with Emma, to spare her the abusive situation at home with her mother, an alcoholic prostitute. Doro also recognizes the strength of Mary's psionic powers. She may prove to be the capstone of his breeding program, so he wants Emma to oversee her transition. The novel becomes Mary's story, much of it told in first person, allowing the reader to truly enter Mary's mind.

Other portions of the book are related in third person, as when the stories of other characters unfold or Patternist phenomena are explained. The description of the results of Doro's breeding program makes up a large portion of the novel. Much attention is paid to the rite-of-passage called "transition." This momentous event in the life of Patternists occurs in young adulthood. Those born in the breeding program who show some psionic potential are called "latents." Transition into adulthood with a full flowering of telepathic abilities creates "actives" in the Patternist society. Latents who do not successfully complete this phase often go mad, become violent, die, or must be killed to remove the threat they pose to the Pattern and others. Those characters without any powers or potential are called "mutes." Mutes become the lowest class in the Pattern hierarchy. At one point in the novel Butler describes them as "ordinary people," but their lower class status is made evident when Emma Anyanwu says the word mute "means nigger."[19] Here she is not speaking of race, but rather the perception of roles participated in, within Patternist society.

Racism does become an issue in the novel as characters discuss color and racial diversity. Doro's African roots are chronicled, but he hopes to breed a new "race" through his eugenic program. Mary questions Doro about his origins; and when she learns he is a Nubian from the Nile Valley, she exclaims:

"Black people!"

"Yes," replies Doro.

"God! You're white so much of the time, I never thought you might have been born black."

"It doesn't matter."

"What do you mean, 'It doesn't matter'? It matters to me."

"It doesn't matter because I haven't been any color at all for about four thousand years. Or you could say I've been every color. But either way, I don't have anything more in common with black people—Nubian or otherwise—than I do with whites or Asians."

"You mean you don't want to admit you have anything in common with us. But if you were born black, you *are* black. Still black, no matter what color you take on."

. . . "You can believe that if it makes you feel better."[20]

To Doro, powers of mind supercede all issues of race. His four thousand years on Earth have been filled with a single purpose, the creation of his "master race." All other issues are secondary. In fact, Doro views racial diversity as a positive part of his plan. He has been bringing his most promising offspring from all over the world to North America for hundreds of years for "He had decided then that the North American continent was big enough to give them room to avoid each other and that it would be racially diverse enough to absorb them all."[21] Doro is beyond color. To him strength and power reside in other facets of one's being.

Doro's quest for power culminates in Mary. Like Emma Anyanwu before her, Mary will be a challenge for Doro. She is his greatest creation; and like her grandmother, she proves to be Doro's equal and more. Mary's difficult transition succeeds. Her emergence as an active Patternist gives her power and strength rivaling Doro's, but she is also a nurturing woman in the tradition of her grandmother. It is this nurturing inclination which prompts Mary to gather others to her, especially those young people whose gifts cause them to clash with their parents and who need fostering in other homes. She is not willing to allow gifted young people to be lost in the painful rite-of-passage, even those for whom the process is long and dangerous. Thus Mary begins to enlarge the Pattern.

Mary's own psionic powers are prodigious. She can get beyond others' defenses and shields. She is able to gather other actives and bind them to her without killing them as Doro would have. Mary uses her ability to continue to enlarge the pattern; she is building a true network in a community of active telepaths. She is one who has a sense of community and whose

activities distress Doro, the loner and the breeder. "Together, the 'Patternists' were growing into something that he could observe, hamper, or destroy, but not something he could join. They were his goal, half accomplished. He watched them with carefully concealed emotions of suspicion and envy."[22] Doro's creation is growing beyond him after four thousand years of endeavor.

Doro's resentment of his daughter grows and he seeks to stop her expansionist plans. He wishes no more latents to be brought through transition and wants the Patternists to grow only through births, thereby stressing that he does have an interest in continued breeding efforts. He still feels very much the "master" and intends to kill Mary, if necessary, to continue his plans. Mary realizes that her father now hates her for her individual ability to handle the Pattern. He resents the fact that his children have grown up and don't need him anymore.

Mary and Doro will have to fight for supremacy of the Pattern in the archetypal battle more often seen between father and son. The issue of gender now emerges fully as Doro comes to resent and despise his female offspring for achieving more than he. The conflict between father and daughter draws in and threatens all actives in the net. Mary and Doro both use all their powers, but ultimately, it is Mary's ability to draw additional power from her community of actives that brings her to victory. Mary's use of female nurturance vanquishes her father's macho individualism. With Doro's death, Mary is now the undisputed power of the Pattern. Her position is secure, for Emma Anyanwu dies when she hears of Doro's demise. Doro's dominant world view leads to a lethal trap and downfall. Mary is the new woman of power, another representative of Butler's vision of strong, black women leading the way to a new order.

Another book in the Patternist series, *Clay's Ark*, follows a different path, as it does not deal directly with the Patternists. The novel, set in a near future time from *Mind of My Mind*, chronicles the disaster that befalls Earth and sets the stage for the subsequent novels of the series. The chapters of *Clay's Ark* alternate between the past and the present of the novel and tell of the invasion of an alien plague and its aftermath.

The story begins with the science fiction convention of a space ship returning from a mission in which things have gone awry. The sole survivor of the ship knows things are desperately wrong, but he seeks food, water, and human companionship. The chapters concerning the past chronicle how the extraterrestrial plague established itself on Earth. Eli had been a geologist on the mission to Proxima Centauri. He knows he carries the organism that killed fourteen crew members and that it drives him to seek

> out new hosts for the alien microorganisms that had made themselves such fundamental parts of his body. Their purpose was now his purpose, and their only purpose was to survive and multiply. All his increased strength, speed, coordination, and sensory ability was to keep him alive and mobile, able to find new hosts or beget them.[23]

Anyone he touches might die; but if a person survived the infection it gave him/her the same heightened sense and functions.

Eli seeks food and water at a ranch near the re-entry site and is driven to infect everyone there. Here, alien invasion mixes with racial issues for Eli is a black man. The white ranch family takes him in and one brother remarks to his sister, "If that guy were white, I'd tell you to marry him."[24] Eli becomes part of the family as the issue of plague containment supercedes those of race.

Those who survive begin to change: they can see in the dark, and they prefer to eat live prey. Eli makes the ranch his colony and harem and they remain aloof from the rest of the world. Their children are mutations, born to look like "a gray, hairless monkey."[25] These children are intellectually precocious, and become brown quadrupeds who run with great speed. They resemble the sphinx. This result of the plague could bring about the end of humanity, as it had been known, for these mutants are the future, "the sporangia of the dominant life form of Proxi Two."[26] Those on the ranch are careful about limiting contact with the outside world to minimize the spread of Clay Ark disease.

The alternate chapters set in the present time of the novel focus on the journey of Blake Martin and his two teenage daughters from the sheltered world of the privileged in southern California through the desert to visit grandparents. They drive an "armored, high-suspension Jeep Wagoneer . . . relic of an earlier, oil-extravagant era."[27] Sixteen-year-old Keira has leukemia and is not responding to treatment. They are attacked on the road and taken to the ranch. Life on the ranch resembles that of the nineteenth century, primitive and alien to Blake Martin and his family, for "Like most enclave parents, Blake had done all he could to recreate the safe world of perhaps sixty years past for his children."[28] Through contact with

the ranch family, Martin and his daughters are infected and now the ranchers try to keep them in isolation. Martin and his daughters notice the strange, mutant children and feel they must escape this madness.

They flee the ranch family, but are captured by an "outlaw car family," and so Clay Ark disease spreads. They do escape the car family, but Martin is killed in the process. Thus the novel relates the premise of the origin of the Clay Arks who become enemies of the Patternists later in the series.

In addition to developing the concept of the Clay Arks, Butler uses this novel to comment on social issues. The interracial marriage of Blake Martin and his wife Jorah divides her family who

> did not like her interest in him. They were people who had worked themselves out of one of the worst cesspools in the southland. They had nurtured Jorah's social conscience too long to let it fall victim to a white man who had never suffered a day in his life and who thought social causes were passé.[29]

While daughter Keira felt she had learned a great deal about life "walking down a city street between her mother and father . . ."[30] Butler's extrapolation takes contemporary prejudice and racial tension into the Los Angeles of 2021. She also projects a worsening of societal ills in the future: illegal drugs and weapons, water and fuel shortages, lawless economic ghettos, and worse.

Butler depicts as well, a society's futile effort to fight these ills through religious fanaticism at the turn of the century, even Eli the astronaut had been a child preacher. Car gang members spend time watching videos of this era about the second coming of Christ in which God is a woman, or a dolphin, or a throw-away child, or an alien. Yet, all these ills pale in the face of the crisis of Clay Ark disease described in the epilogue. Cities are burning—San Francisco, Los Angeles, San Diego. Texas oil refineries are in flames. Louisiana residents are shooting strangers, especially if they're black, brown, or Asian. Doctors and nurses are spreading the disease. Some feel it is the end of the world or the beginning of a new order where human beings will be obsolete. *Clay's Ark* is a conventional science fiction story of alien invasion and apocalypse, but Butler uses the novel to voice concern over contemporary issues of racial prejudice, economic class war, depletion of the environment, and degradation of life. All this will have an impact on the Patternists.

Patternmaster is set in an even more distant future. Civilization has been ravaged. Patternists are living in enclaves called Houses. Clayarks threaten their existence in what resembles a guerrilla war, and the struggle for power in the Pattern continues.

The hierarchy of the Pattern has been maintained, perhaps it has become even more stratified. The leaders of the Pattern, Rayal and his wife Jansee, are worshiped as gods, and mutes are truly slaves. In between there are housemasters, apprentices, outsiders, and independents. It is indeed a complex Pattern. "The Pattern was a vast network of mental links that joined every Patternist with the Patternmaster."[31]

The mutes who once led and developed a mechanized society are in eclipse, while the Patternists have ascended to power and a war with the Clayarks. The Clayarks have no telepathic powers and the Patternists cannot enter their minds. Each believes the others are "Not people"[32] and so the warfare goes on and on. When the Clayarks attack Rayal and kill his lead wife Jansee, the conflict reaches a new phase. Rayal is injured and contracts Clay Ark disease. His diminished strength hampers his leadership.

The novel employs the archetype of the competition of two brothers battling to assume their aging father's powers. Young Teray, who has just finished his schooling, is now a threat to his older brother Coransee. Teray wants his own House, not to be an outsider, a permanent servant to those in power. Coransee expects to assume control of the Pattern when Rayal dies. His manipulations make Teray his servant and a muteherd.

Teray does not have the strength to fight Coransee alone. Here Butler creates another strong female character—Amber, an independent healer. She is a strong, brown woman (as her name suggests), who has made her own way through this dangerous world. Amber has much to teach Teray; she guides him on his quest. Amber provides most of the interesting facets of character in the novel. She is a Houseless wanderer, but has valued skill as a healer that makes her less vulnerable in the violent world. She fights the abuse of women in the Houses. She has had to kill to preserve her independence. She rejects marriage and is bisexual. She is a nurturer, a teacher. Amber is a woman who knows her own strengths, her needs and desires, and who is not afraid to work toward her own goals. She is in sharp contrast to Iray, who had hoped to marry Teray right after graduation, but who is just as happy to be with Coransee if he can offer security and worldly comfort. In Amber, Butler provides a feminist character whom many readers cheer. Although Teray eventually prevails against his older brother, he is the hero because a strong woman taught him healing and compassion as a complement to his ability to rule and kill when necessary.

The last of the Patternist novels, *Survivor,* is set in outer space at a Mission Colony called Canaan. The story is told in alternate chapters by Alanna, a colonist from Earth, and Diut, a native of the planet. Connections are made to the past and to Patternist history, although this is a story of mutes. Alanna's parents had been killed by Clayarks when she was eight years old and she was left to forage for herself. She became a wild human, but was drawn back into society when she was caught stealing a cow. The Missionaries Jules and Neila Verrick adopted her to fill the gap of the loss of their own children to Clay Ark disease. The Missionaries were a religious sect who believe the human shape was sacred while the sphinx-like form of the Clayarks was the work of the devil. The Missionaries took to space to escape the Clay Ark plague and to spread their idea of the sacred human form to another world.

Jules and Neila had been mute slaves of the Patternists in Forsyth for twenty-five years before they left to become Missionaries. It was the Patternists of Forsyth who built the starship, using the concept of the "Dana Drive,"[33] which had powered the Clay Ark starship. This combination of particle physics and psionics used human psi powers to fuel and guide the spacecraft. People with strong psychokinetic abilities could not use the Dana Drive for they overcontrolled it. The Missionaries' ship had been powered by a deformed young man, who died in the process. When they journey to Canaan, the Missionaries leave behind the Patternists and Clayarks to try to give human life one last chance.

The Missionaries bring the human form to a new world, but they also bring the seemingly ever present human problems. Racial discrimination again becomes a theme. Many of the Missionaries, who quote scripture and preach strong moral values, still have a difficulty with skin color. When the Verricks adopt Alanna, who is Afro-Asian, the other Missionaries never really accept her. Even the children taunt and fight with her. A contingent led by Beatrice Stamp feels the races should not mix and that Alanna should live "with her own kind."[34] Although the Verricks protect her from the less tolerant members, Alanna never really becomes one of the Missionaries. She is always the outsider, who mouths their words in return for food and shelter.

The colony of Canaan lands in the middle of a war between different tribes of the Kohns, the inhabitants of the planet. The two tribes, Garkohns and Tehkohns, struggle for power in a manner that echoes the war between the Patternists and Clayarks on Earth. In an additional irony, the two tribes engage in a form of racial discrimination, for to them one's color establishes one's role and worth in society. The Kohns are chameleon-like and a rainbow of colors is represented among their people. The Kohns' greatest weapon is their fur, "fine thick alive stuff that changed color and seemed to change texture. It permitted the natives to blend invisibly into their surroundings whenever they wished."[35] The Missionaries see them as "strangely colored, furred caricatures of human beings."[36] The Missionaries' religion allows them to regard the Kohns as lower creatures.

To the Kohns the rainbow of colors comprise their social hierarchy. Bright green are the farmers. Golden green are the artisans (although some are pure yellow). Deep green or blue green are the hunters, while deep blue are the judges and the Hao, the sacred leader. In addition to a basic color, Kohns also express emotion by a temporary change in color. All old Kohns have yellow age spots. Butler does not attempt to resolve the problems color presents for the Kohns, rather she describes it as a fact of Kohn life.

In another echo of Earthly concerns, Butler raises the issue of slavery. The mutes were slaves of the Patternists in Forsyth. They went to a new world secure in their feeling of superiority in carrying the sacred image of the human race to begin a new dynasty. In another ironic touch, the Missionaries side with the Garkohn in the tribal war, thinking they are allies. Yet, the Garkohn use the Missionaries for their own ends, first addicting them to meklah, a yellow fruit of the planet, and then enslaving them and using some in their own breeding program.

Alanna, another of Butler's women of power, grows beyond all this hatred and subterfuge. Since she was never truly accepted by the Missionaries, she has never adopted their intolerance and bigotry. She wants to learn all she can about Kohn culture, both Garkohn and Tehkohn. Alanna becomes a pawn and a prisoner in it all. Her opportunity to learn about Tehkohn culture increases when she is taken prisoner by them.

She alone survives the withdrawal from meklah that the Tehkohn require of all prisoners. This allows her to truly learn and become part of Tehkohn life and culture. After surviving the cleansing from meklah,

Alanna lives with Gehnahteh, a green-gold woman and her husband Choh, who is more yellow in color. They are artisans and with them Alanna begins to learn Tehkohn ways. Although Alanna can have no rank in the Tehkohn hierarchy because she has none of their coloring, she is accepted by them in a way which was impossible with the Missionaries. Alanna learns their language so well, she begins to speak English with a Tehkohn accent. She proves she can hunt, be artistic, and exhibit the wisdom of a judge— all without the expected Kohn coloring. Eventually she marries Diut, the Tehkohn Hao, the man of highest rank in that culture. Diut had at first been repulsed and attracted by Alanna's exotic differences. She bears him a child, a daughter colored a dark shade of green, but with Alanna's round eyes and long hands and feet. Alanna, like Emma Anyanwu before her, has learned to adopt and adapt to the customs of others to survive and yet she is able to remain true to herself and to discover even more of her powers and abilities.

As the Kohn war accelerates, Alanna becomes even more powerful and important to the Missionaries and to the Tehkohn. Alanna and the Tehkohn return to Canaan, where Alanna is damned for her marriage to Diut and her bearing of a half-breed child. Despite her final rejection by the Missionaries, Alanna uses her strength to show them how to withdraw from meklah addiction, join the fight to throw off the oppression of Garkohn slavery, and to find a new life in a valley where no meklah grows. She helps the human colony to survive as thanks to the Verricks. She says, "For a while, I was your daughter. Thanks for that anyway."[37] Unlike the Missionaries and Garkohn who are defeated by their false sense of superiority and intolerance of differences, Alanna and the Tehkohn find true power in their acceptance and celebration of differences.

The entire Patternist series moves through time and space and explores the manifestation and consequences of racial issues. Butler provides no easy answers to questions of race, but her novels in this series suggest that cultures that persist in believing in intolerance come to a dead end, while those that embrace difference flourish. In so addressing these issues, Butler provides the reader with a personal challenge regarding bias and individual response to bias.

In addition, Butler's depiction of the woman of power who is instrumental in spearheading societal change allows for the consideration of a range of feminist ideas. Anyanwu, Mary, Amber, and Alanna are memorable characters, women who establish a new order where females contribute in equal or greater quantities and abilities than males. When Butler declares she is black and a feminist, she does so not only in interviews, but through her fiction as well.

A TIMELESS BOND; A RADICAL ALLIANCE: *KINDRED*

The "stand alone" novel ***Kindred*** treats the issue of racial intolerance and slavery in an historical context. Butler originally intended this novel to be a part of the Patternist series; but she said "it didn't seem to fit, probably because I wanted to be more realistic."[38] She said she wanted to take "a middle-class black— and put him in the ante-bellum South to see how well he stood up" and "I developed an abused female character who was dangerous but who wasn't perceived as being so dangerous that she would have to be killed."[39] Butler's ***Kindred*** is a science fiction/ historical fiction hybrid that uses the conventions of time travel to explore themes of racism and sexism.

Butler's heroic character is Dana, a young black woman, a writer living in southern California, who takes temporary jobs to support herself while she writes. (This aspect of the character is autobiographical.) Dana tells this story and her first person account provides the reader with total immersion into the personal experience of racism and sexism.

Dana and her husband Kevin, a white man, are unpacking books when she is called back in time. Dana is gone only ten to fifteen seconds but during that brief interval she rescues a white boy from drowning in a river. She is almost killed by his parents who don't quite understand what she has done. Thus begins the series of time shifts that draw Dana from 1976 Los Angeles to the Weylin plantation in antebellum Maryland. Through these time jumps, Dana and her husband come to experience directly the impact of slavery on black and white, male and female.

Dana becomes a pawn of time, beckoned to the past when Rufus, her white ancestor, finds his life in danger. Once more Butler uses the theme of the mix of races to demonstrate the irony of racial prejudice. Here also, she uses the science fiction convention of the paradox of encountering one's ancestors in past time and in that meeting affecting one's own existence. Dana realizes she is in the past "Not only to insure the survival of one accident-prone small boy, but to insure my family's survival, my own birth," for "if others were to live, he must live. I didn't dare test the paradox."[40]

Dana is called to the past each time red-haired Rufus's life is in danger, and she remains in the past

until her life in turn is endangered. When Kevin is with her, he, too, is drawn from present to past and back again. Slavery becomes for them not a distanced historical institution but a fact of everyday life. Harsh reality strikes with a vengeance. Rufus calls Dana a nigger and she tries to explain to him that he should refer to her as "a black woman."[41] Dana is accused of not knowing her place. Rufus tells her, "You think you're white. You don't know your place any better than a wild animal."[43] Even Alice, another black woman, tells her, "You ought to be ashamed of yourself, whining and crying after some poor white trash of a man, black as you are. You always try to act so white. White nigger, turning against your own people."[44] Dana is made to work in the fields; she is also whipped. Kevin suffers as he tries to help runaway slaves escape to the North. Both Dana and Kevin learn "Slavery was a long slow process of dulling."[45]

Dana is a woman of talent and confidence, educated and published; and while these attributes work to her advantage in 1976 Los Angeles, they are a liability in the Old South. Here she meets slave women with some power of their own, who may not read or write; but who are able to hold things together in the grip of a double-edged oppression, especially Alice, the free black woman and Dana's ancestor, who loves with power until driven to hang herself by the effects of slavery and Rufus's lust, but not before her daughter Hagar, Dana's great-grandmother is born.

While the slaves suffer from the most obvious hardships and harshness, Butler writes of the effects of slavery on the white slave owners. Rufus has been whipped by his father with the same whip his father "whips niggers and horses with."[46] The Weylins live in fear of their thirty-eight slaves and in ignorance in a home where the whites feel reading is a waste of time. Margaret Weylin, the wife of the slave owner, is nervous and frustrated, jealous of the slave women who might attract the attentions of her husband. The system of slavery benefits no one, except perhaps economically. All spirits are blighted by the racist and sexist patterns.

Dana never really knows what power draws her to Rufus. All she knows is that she "was the worst possible guardian for him—a black to watch over him in a society that considered blacks subhuman, a woman to watch over him in a society that considered women perennial children."[47] Dana knows her sojourns to the past have altered her physically and spiritually. She bears the scars of slavery and has left a part of herself in the 1800s—part of her spirit and part of her arm—literally caught in slavery's grip as Rufus refuses to let go. Kevin, too, carries his scars—on his lined, aged face and in his feeling that life in contemporary Los Angeles was all too soft and easy. Dana and Kevin are caught between two worlds in many ways. The contrasts between past and present are made clear to them both, as they learn how powerless blacks and women were in the ante-bellum South. Yet, they also come to appreciate the similarities of the two times, as they see how people are still held in the bondage of racism and sexism. Butler takes her readers on the trip through time and place to better appreciate the impact of these persistent patterns in all lives—black, white, male, or female; and once again she uses a strong, African-American woman as the character to do so.

SURVIVING DIFFERENCES IN A BIAS-TEMPEST: XENOGENESIS

Butler's themes and patterns of racial and feminist issues continue to weave their way in her latest series, the Xenogenesis trilogy. These novels, *Dawn, Adulthood Rites,* and *Imago,* explore the fate of humanity in a post-holocaust setting. Butler, the self-described pessimist, confronts her readers with the notion that when faced with the ultimate devastation of ecological disaster and the almost certain destruction of the human race, that most humans will still cling to long held prejudice and fear of those who are different. As in her work in *Survivor,* Butler again uses an alien race to provoke humans to confront these issues and to accept dependence on others for continued survival.

In addition to the continued exploration of themes of race and gender, Butler raises even more provocative ideas. The alien Oankali have observed the human race and discovered that a barrier to successful survival lies in two incompatible characteristics. One is intelligence. "That's the newer of the two characteristics, and the one you might have to put to work to save yourselves. You are potentially one of the most intelligent species we've found.... You are hierarchical. That's the older and more entrenched characteristic."[48] Too often these two characteristics are combined in a manner that leads to destruction.

The Oankali are fascinated by what they find in the human race. Their research into human sociobiology finds not only the "mismatched pair of genetic characteristics"[49] of intelligence and hierarchy, but also the compelling "genetic inclination" in many humans "to grow cancers."[50] The Oankali regard cancer as a unique gift, while to humans it has been a scourge. The Oankali are able to stop the disease from harm-

ing humans, while harnessing its properties for work in the regeneration of tissue, as in growing replacement limbs. The Oankali see humans as a remarkable array of incongruities; and as genetic engineers and gene traders, the Oankali find humans a good investment. So much so that it is they who have saved the surviving humans from a dying Earth by placing them in a drugged sleep for centuries while they healed the plant Earth and fortified humans against disease. The Oankali want to bring humans back to Earth, but as traders they exact a price.

In *Dawn,* the process begins as Lilith (another first woman) is awakened from her sleep to the beginning of a new life on a ship orbiting Earth. Lilith is dark skinned, smart and strong, and the Oankali use her to select those humans who will be Awakened for this phase of their experiment. Lilith will be the first "mother"[51] and teacher of the new human race. She is like Emma Anyanwu and Alanna in this role. Genetic engineering Oankali have made her pregnant with the first child of a new Earth, a daughter who is a genetic mix of Lilith, a man named Joseph, and two Oankali. For this is the price the gene traders exact for survival—interbreeding. Humans, including Lilith, will have more to learn, especially what it means to be human. The Oankali mixture will make notions of hierarchy, of superiority of one human to another obsolete. There will be no pure race.

The second novel in the series, *Adulthood Rites,* continues the saga of the regeneration of Earth. This novel is the story of the "constructs,"[52] the children born of the human-Oankali mixture. The Awakened humans still have difficulty in dealing with the aliens. They value human-looking babies, but still resent the fact that they are not fully human. They see the constructs as a threat to the old, pure human race. "Families will change.... A complete construct family will be a female, an ooloi, and children. Males will come and go as they wish and as they find welcome."[53] This new construct race can look different from the human form, especially after adolescent metamorphosis. Margit, a young construct, is angry at the old humans. She declares, "They blame me for not looking like them. They can't help doing it, and I can't help resenting it. I don't know which is worse—the ones who cringe if I touch them or the ones who pretend it's all right while they cringe inside."[54] Butler continues to explore the human tendency toward racism and xenophobia within this new context. The future here serves as a mirror for our contemporary society.

Many of the old human settlers of Earth cling to old ways and ideas. They try to build villages and towns to resemble the past as much as possible. Those who reject the Oankali will die out with their old ways, for almost all humans are infertile without Oankali genetic intervention. The old humans view Lilith and her construct trading village as traitors to the human race. "Human beings fear difference. Oankali crave difference. Humans persecute their different ones, yet they need them to give themselves definition and status."[55]

Akin, the adolescent son of Lilith, dead Joseph, and the Oankali, becomes the hero of the novel. He journeys between construct and human villages and feels he can be an envoy of peace and understanding. He is an idealistic youth, but he finds that his travels have made him unable to find a true bond with either constructs or old humans. He plans for the old humans to try a new settlement on Mars, leaving Earth for the constructs. "Humans would carry their dislike with them to be shut up together on Mars."[56] Perhaps working through the harsh environment there, humans would have to abandon their tendency to self-destruct. Akin is a true hero—the idealist willing to sacrifice a life with those most dear to him in order to carry out his mission to provide a self-destructive race with yet another chance for survival. The work is his rite of passage, as well as, hopefully, that of the human race.

The last novel in the trilogy, *Imago,* is told in first person by Jodahs, the first construct to become ooloi. Jodahs is an unknown factor which could cause pain and death. Without mature control, it could heal and yet, unknowingly, cause cancer. Jodahs, like all ooloi, can manipulate DNA within its body, earning the names "Life Trader" or "Weaver."[57] Since Jodahs is an unknown factor, it must return to the mothership for observation or go into exile on Earth. Jodahs and its family choose Earthly exile.

Jodahs's metamorphosis is not an easy one. It shape shifts from man to frog, to woman. It cures two humans, Tomas and Jesusa, of tumors. Jodahs finds these humans are fertile and as an ooloi it wants to mate with them. Their village of old humans would reject this. This new construct family has a strong will to survive and to help Aaor, another construct ooloi to complete metamorphosis and mate.

More construct ooloi are developing. They are a new species. When the old humans of Pascual, an Hispanic village, realize the ooloi can cure them, they welcome them. More families mate with Oankali, and thus more trader villages develop on Earth. The human-Oankali constructs have inherited the Earth.

Issues of race and gender will become obsolete, as the notion of what it means to be human is transformed.

ON THE VALUE OF THE GENRE TO AFRICAN-AMERICANS

Butler's science fiction has been described as "a literature of survival," with the basic premise "that black people survive the present and participate in shaping the future."[58] Yet, Butler says she is often asked by other blacks, "What good is science fiction to Black people?" Her answer:

> What good is science fiction's thinking about the present, the future, and the past? What good is its tendency to warn or to consider alternative ways of thinking and doing? What good is its examination of the possible effects of science and technology, of social organization and political direction? At its best, science fiction stimulates imagination and creativity. It gets reader and writer off the beaten track, off the narrow, narrow footpath of what "everyone" is saying, doing, thinking—whoever "everyone" happens to be this year.

And what good is all this to Black people.[59]

To all readers, and especially to young adults, Butler's ability to make the less travelled path exciting, to make readers see what it could mean to be truly human, to escape from the "beaten track" of racism and sexism, of trying to be bigger and better in the hierarchy, is a gift to be relished and pondered. Butler weaves strong patterns throughout her novels in which women of color assume power to challenge the established hierarchical thinking concerning race, gender, and the outsider. These are issues of importance which appeal to the adolescent reader, and they make Butler's novels an important contribution to the genre.

Notes

1. "Octavia E. Butler," *Contemporary Authors,* ed. Frances Carol Locker (Detroit, MI: Gale Research, 1978), 73-76:104.

2. Sherley Anne Williams, "Sherley Anne Williams on Octavia E. Butler," *Ms.,* March 1986, 72.

3. Elizabeth A. Belden and Judith M. Beckman, "Extraordinary Viewpoints," *English Journal* 77 (April 1988): 78.

4. Williams, 70.

5. Octavia E. Butler, interview by Larry McCaffrey, in *Across the Wounded Galaxy: Interviews with*

Contemporary American Science Fiction Writers, ed. Larry McCaffrey (Urbana, IL: University of Illinois Press, 1990), 61-62.

6. Ibid., 67.

7. Octavia E. Butler, *Wild Seed* (Garden City, NY: Doubleday, 1980), 3.

8. Ibid., 8.

9. Ibid., 9.

10. Ibid., 60.

11. Ibid., 91.

12. Ibid.

13. Ibid., 98.

14. Ibid., 133.

15. Ibid., 141.

16. Ibid., 147.

17. Ibid.

18. Octavia E. Butler, *Mind of My Mind* (Garden City, NY: Doubleday, 1977), 7.

19. Ibid., 117.

20. Ibid., 60-61.

21. Ibid., 141.

22. Ibid., 113.

23. Octavia E. Butler, *Clay's Ark* (New York: St. Martin's Press, 1984), 30.

24. Ibid., 57.

25. Ibid., 156.

26. Ibid., 181.

27. Ibid., 5.

28. Ibid., 32.

29. Ibid., 160.

30. Ibid., 114.

31. Octavia E. Butler, *Patternmaster* (Garden City, NY: Doubleday, 1976), 17.

32. Ibid., 111.

33. Butler, *Clay's Ark,* 153.

34. Octavia E. Butler, *Survivor* (Garden City, NY: Doubleday, 1978), 31.

35. Ibid., 6.

36. Ibid., 5.

37. Ibid., 185.

38. McCaffrey, 65.

39. Ibid., 65.

40. Octavia E. Butler, *Kindred* (Garden City, NY: Doubleday, 1979), 29.

41. Ibid., 25.

42. Ibid., 163.

43. Ibid., 164.

44. Ibid., 165.

45. Ibid., 183.

46. Ibid., 26.

47. Ibid., 68.

48. Octavia E. Butler, *Dawn* (New York: Time Warner, 1987), 37.

49. Ibid., 36.

50. Ibid., 29.

51. Ibid., 11.

52. Ibid., 247.

53. Octavia E. Butler, *Adulthood Rites* (New York: Warner Books, 1988), 11.

54. Ibid., 15.

55. Ibid., 80.

56. Ibid., 276.

57. Octavia E. Butler, *Imago* (New York: Warner Books, 1989), 6.

58. Williams, 72.

59. Octavia E. Butler, "Birth of a Writer," *Essence,* May 1989, 134.

References

Belden, Elizabeth A. and Judith M. Beckman. "Extraordinary Viewpoints." *English Journal* 77 (April 1988): 78-79.

Blauden, Nellie. "Otherworldly Women: Six All-Star Science Fiction Novelists." *Life,* July 1984, 112-117.

Bogstad, Janice. "Octavia E. Butler and Power Relationships." *Janus* 4 (Winter 1978-79): 28-29.

Butler, Octavia E. *Adulthood Rites.* New York: Warner Books, 1988.

———. "Birth of a Writer." *Essence,* May 1989, 74-79, 132-134.

———. *Clay's Ark.* New York: St. Martin's Press, 1984.

———. *Dawn.* New York: Time Warner, 1987.

———. *Imago.* New York: Warner Books, 1989.

———. Interview by Larry McCaffrey. In *Across the Wounded Galaxy: Interviews with Contemporary American Science Fiction Writers,* ed. Larry McCaffrey. Urbana, IL: University of Illinois Press, 1990, 61-62.

———. *Kindred.* Garden City, NY: Doubleday, 1979.

———. *Mind of My Mind.* Garden City, NY: Doubleday, 1977.

———. *Patternmaster.* Garden City, NY: Doubleday, 1976.

———. *Survivor.* Garden City, NY: Doubleday, 1978.

———. *Wild Seed.* Garden City, NY: Doubleday, 1980.

Davidson, Carolyn S. "The Science Fiction of Octavia Butler." *Salaga* (1981): 35.

Davis, Thadious M. and Trudier Harris, eds. "Octavia E. Butler." In *Dictionary of Literary Biography,* vol. 33, *Afro-American Fiction Writers After 1955.* Detroit: Gale Research, 1984.

Foster, Frances Smith. "Octavia Butler's Black Female Future Fiction." *Extrapolation* 23 (Spring 1982): 37-49.

Govan, Sandra Y. "Connections, Links, and Extended Networks: Patterns in Octavia Butler's Science Fiction." *Black American Literature Forum* 18 (1984): 12-15.

Lefanu, Sarah. *Feminism and Science Fiction.* Bloomington, IN: Indiana University Press, 1988.

Locker, Frances Carol, ed. "Octavia E. Butler." In *Contemporary Authors,* vol. 73-76. Detroit, MI: Gale Research, 1978.

Marowski, Daniel G., ed. "Octavia E. Butler." In *Contemporary Literary Criticism,* vol. 38. Detroit, MI: Gale Research, 1986.

Mixon, Veronica. "Futurist Woman: Octavia Butler." *Essence,* April 1979, 82-87.

Salvaggio, Ruth. "Octavia Butler and the Black Science-Fiction Heroine." *Black American Literature Forum* 18 (1984): 78-81.

Weixlmann, Joe. "An Octavia E. Butler Bibliography." *Black American Literature Forum* 18 (1984): 88-89.

Williams, Sherley Anne. "Sherley Anne Williams on Octavia E. Butler." *Ms.,* March 1986, 70-72.

Burton Raffel

SOURCE: "Genre to the Rear, Race and Gender to the Fore: The Novels of Octavia E. Butler," in *The Literary Review,* Vol. 38, No. 3, Spring, 1995, pp. 454-61.

Just as you cannot always tell a book by its cover, so too you cannot always know a novel by its apparent or even by its declared genre. Is *Crime and Punishment* merely a detective (or mystery) novel? *Huck Finn* simply (as Mark Twain once said of it) "another boy's book," *War and Peace* merely historical, *The Trial* only a *Mittle Europa* Perry Mason drama? Is *Middlemarch* (as its title page proclaims) nothing more than "a study of provincial life"?

A book's transcendence of straightforward genre distinctions can be in part thematic, but is mostly a matter of execution: far more importantly than its intention, what a novel *does* with its chosen materials stands directly at the heart of its achievement, as it also defines its very nature. Whatever his own artistic imbalances, no one knew this better than Henry James: "There are bad novels and good novels, as there are bad pictures and good pictures, but that is the only distinction in which I see any meaning . . . It goes without saying that you will not write a good novel unless you possess the sense of reality; but it will be difficult to give you a recipe for calling that sense into being. Humanity is immense, and reality has a myriad forms . . . and when the mind is imaginative . . . it takes to itself the faintest hints of life, it converts the very pulses of the air into revelations." In this 1884 essay, "The Art of Fiction," James therefore lays down one standard: "The only obligation to which in advance we may hold a novel, without incurring the accusation of being arbitrary, is that it be interesting." Or, as the equally but on the face of it oppositely dedicated D. H. Lawrence put it, in a pair of essays published in 1925, "The novel is the highest example of subtle inter-relatedness that man has discovered. Everything is true in its own time, place, circumstance, and untrue outside of its own place, time, circumstance. If you try to nail anything down, in the novel, either it kills the novel, or the novel gets up and walks away with the nail. . . . The novel is a perfect medium for revealing to us the changing rainbow of our living relationships . . . the one bright book of life."

Operating as I try to do, more or less according to the standards set out by James and Lawrence, I have just finished reading, seriatim, eight of the ten published novels of Octavia E. Butler, initially drawn on by the utterly unexpected power and subtly complex intelligence of her extraordinary trilogy, *Xenogenesis,* but sustained and even compelled by the rich dramatic textures, the profound psychological insights, the strong, challenging ideational matrices of virtually all her books. And in my seventh decade of reading fiction, there are not many novelists, neither those so bubbly light as Wodehouse nor even so broadly and diversely rewarding as Dickens or Balzac, Proust or Thomas Mann, who could have held me so long or so closely. Every one of these eight novels (and I stopped at eight only because I could not easily find her second and third books, some fifteen years out of print) was published under the explicit rubric of "science fiction," but four completely transcend the genre and only one is, though neither weak nor bad, less than absolutely first-rate. Perhaps just as significantly, I do not think any of these eight books could have been written by a man, as they most emphatically were not, nor, with the single exception of her first book, ***Pattern-Master*** (1976), are likely to have been written, as they most emphatically were, by anyone but an African-American. Butler's work, in short, is both fascinating and highly unusual, representing— not only in my mind, but to the growing number of critics and scholars being drawn to it—a richly re-

warding and relatively rare fusion of sensibility, perception, and a driven, insightful intelligence.

That this is serious literature I have no doubt. But I must stress from the start that Butler is not, like some science fiction practitioners, overtly (and is never, like more than a few, over-bearingly) "literary." Her prose is crystalline, at its best, sensuous, sensitive, exact, but not in the least directed at calling attention to itself. The moving final paragraph of the *Xenogenesis* trilogy—the title signifying "the fancied projection of an organism altogether and permanently unlike the parent"—is thus a model of quietly passionate writing:

> I chose a spot near the river. There I prepared the seed to go into the ground. I gave it a thick, nutritious coating, then brought it out of my body through my right sensory hand. I planted it deep in the rich soil of the riverbank. Seconds after I had expelled it, I felt it begin the tiny positioning movements of independent life.

Carefully, expertly crafted, deeply satisfying as it is to the reader of more than seven hundred preceding pages, and tautly, firmly resolving as it does the major plotline question, this is nevertheless determinedly functional, essentially unobtrusive prose—unlike, say, the highly literary writing of Samuel R. Delany (the only other black s.f. writer of major status): "It was foggy that morning, and the sun across the water moiled the mists like a brass ladle. I lurched to the top of the rocks, looked down through the tall grasses into the frothing inlet where she lay, and blinked." Delany makes it work; as Henry James noted, the very good are very good. But more typically, "literary" s.f. prose reads like the early work of a writer who has since learned better, Walter Jon Williams, whose *Ambassador of Progress* opens, with a self-conscious flourish, "In a storm of rain, its brightness a steadier glow among lightning flashes, the shuttle dropped into the high pasture, scattering alarmed cattle who ran in a clatter of bells for the sheltering trees." One can go a good deal farther down the literary ladder; this is for my purposes quite far enough. Plainly, Octavia Butler does not thus tongue a golden-mouthed trumpet, summoning the word-drunk flocks to drink from her overflowing flagons of sweet-scented nectar.

The passionate, abiding importance of the nurturing of new life, which clearly informs the *Xenogenesis* passage I have quoted, equally deeply informs the entire trilogy, as in every book of hers I have read. It seems to me feminist writing at its very best, writing which, like the poetry of Sheryl St. Germain . . . , proudly and utterly comfortably accepts itself as female. That strong, self-assured stance toward the fact of femaleness has been in Butler's work from the very first. The protagonist of **Pattern-Master** is, unlike the central figures in her other work, male. But he is quickly made to realize that the major female figure in the book, the woman "healer" with whom he binds himself, though clearly female and just as clearly both attractive and attracted to him, is "harder than she felt." Soon thereafter, he learns that her sexual interests are not limited to men. And some pages still further, when another female character makes the mistake of assuming that the healer is "his" woman, she is quickly, forcefully corrected. "I'm my own woman, Lady Darah. Now as before." (The two women have had prior contact, professional rather than sexual.) Finally, the protagonist asks the healer, bluntly, "Which do you prefer," men or women? She replies, "I'll tell you . . . But you won't like it. . . . When I meet a woman who attracts me, I prefer women . . . And when I meet a man who attracts me, I prefer men." The protagonist then effectively closes the discussion by annoucing: "If that's the way you are, I don't mind." Nor does he, even though, when he asks her to marry him, she refuses, once again for reasons of independence. "As my lead wife," he argues, "you'd have authority, freedom," but she swiftly responds, "How interested would you be in becoming my lead husband?"

For all its excellences, however, **Pattern-Master** is a smaller, less complex, less far-reaching fiction; in many ways it suggests the sweep and depth of *Xenogenesis* without quite achieving the trilogy's impact. Another striking precursor is **Wild Seed** (1980), which mythologizes Butler's black African heritage in an extraordinary fusion of both pre-slavery African and post-slavery American strands with what seems clearly the most urgent impulse behind all her writing, the drive to define, achieve, and nurture new life. "You steal, you kill," says the witch-like female protagonist, Anyanwu, to the even more wraith-like male protagonist, Doro. "What else do you do?" And he answers, speaking speech-words framed in Butler's beautifully calm prose, "'I build,' he said quietly. 'I search the land for people who are a little different—or very different. I search them out, I bring them together in groups, I begin to build them into a strong new people.'"

But Butler does not deal, as writers with lesser gifts so often do, with *themes*. Her novels teem with fully realized characters, male and female alike, who fascinatingly embody rather than merely represent ideas. Her fertile imagination throws up such intensely functioning, intricately enmeshed human beings that even minor personages take on vivid life—for yet another quality of a major fictive talent is a profound, virtually universal sympathy that permits imagined beings to be exactly what they in fact are, not idea-driven puppets who do only what their creators think the plot requires. The best writers are regularly, even easily, able to inhabit many skins, and to move and speak inside those superficially alien persons as if they were inside themselves. When a wondrously uncontrolled witch-like young woman leaps away from Doro, in terror, and falls heavily on a half-unconscious son of Doro, a man endowed with a propulsive power to move objects outside of his own body, the result is brilliantly, dramatically, tragically in character:

> He gripped Nweke, threw her upward away from his pain-racked body—threw her upward with all the power he had used so many times to propel great ships out of storms. He did not know what he was doing any more than she did. He never saw her hit the ceiling, never saw her body flatten into it, distorted, crushed, never saw her head slam into one of the great beams and break and send down a grisly rain of blood and bits of bone and brain.

Again, this is not fancy writing; it is simply precise and tautly cadenced prose, forceful because it is focused, fictively superbly effective because it is in each and every detail true to the characters' lives. It is the furthest thing from accidental that the high point of such wonderfully accurate truthfulness, in the final pages, deals head-on with, and satisfyingly resolves, the novel's emotional and intellectual core. Anyanwu has fought, all along, to humanize Doro. She has sometimes seemed about to succeed, only again and again to fail. She therefore decides to commit suicide—and just when she is about to die, produces in Doro the reversion to human feeling for which she has so long struggled. But we are not told this in so many words, not at least right away. The novel's final words show us, first Doro's humanization, and then the success of what was not a strategy but Anyanwu's deep, thoroughly comprehensible decision:

> His voice caught and broke. He wept. He choked out great sobs that shook his already shaking body almost beyond bearing. He wept as though for all the past times when no tears would come. when there was no relief. He could not stop. He did not know when she pulled off his boots and pulled the blanket up over him, when she bathed his face in cool water. He did know the comfort of her arms, the warmth of her body next to him. He slept, finally, exhausted, his head on her breast,

and at sunrise when he awoke, that breast was still warm, still rising and falling gently with her breathing.

Butler does not need to resort to artificial icons or frantic adjectives. There is symbolism here, to be sure. But it is fully organic, neither laid on like icing nor, heavily, as with a trowel.

Butler's one comparative failure, *Kindred* (1979), is a much more predictable, far too consciously wrought attempt at a twentieth-century slave narrative. Even in this novel, the stale, overly conscious plot is in good part redeemed by some fine (if not universally three-dimensional) characterization and, hardly surprisingly, by much strongly evocative writing. But *Kindred* is about as close to an unsuccessful book as Butler is capable of producing, just as *Clay's Ark* (1984), though a fine, suspenseful novel, is about as standard a s.f. story as she is likely ever to tell, strongly imbued with her trademark concerns, nurturing and the survival of that most endangered of all species, homo sapiens.

I do not think, Butler being the kind of quietly powerful writer she is, that anything short of an attentive reading of *Xenogenesis* can convey anything like the book's multiple strengths. Not that it is deficient in either technical or substantive accomplishments. Each of the three component novels has a different though connected narrative point of view, the first using as its protagonist a black woman, Lilith Iyapo, the second using a part-human, Akin, and the third, told in the first person, experienced through the persona of Jodahs, also but markedly a part-human. Butler starts with the premise that humans have come very close to killing off one another, as well as destroying the earth humans have inhabited. An extra-terrestrial race, the Oankali, who speak of themselves, cryptically and rather oddly, as "traders," finds and preserves the few survivors. The how and why of that almost miraculous preservation, as also the full flowering of what it means that the Oankalis thus describe themselves, is what the three novels expose for us. The trilogy constitutes a remarkable exposition of eminently plausible emotional and genetic possibilities—imagined, from start to finish, in splendid detail, with a great range of characters both human and alien, and a fascinating unfolding of passionately felt, profoundly experienced events. More than all but a very small handful of "genre" books, *Xenogenesis* deals in basic wisdoms of a totally unparochial nature.

Absolutely nothing is predictable, here. Indeed, it is I think utterly impossible for even the most ingenious

reader ever to catch up to, much less overtake, the author's comprehensive, delicately modulated unfolding of her story. Lilith Iyapo, the first novel's protagonist (she appears in all three of the novels), is by the end of that first book still deeply unsure, on almost all levels, of what she ought to be doing and of what the Oankali truly intend.

> Perhaps they could find an answer to what the Oankali had done . . . And perhaps the Oankali were not perfect. A few fertile people might slip through and find one another. Perhaps. *Learn and run!* If she were lost, others did not have to be. Humanity did not have to be.

She let Nikanj [an Oankali] lead her into the dark forest and to one of the concealed dry exits.

The narrative weight of every one of these sparse sentences is, in context, enormous. Indeed, the small excision I have made in the first sentence is designed to avoid discussing, here, perhaps the most pregnant and yet certainly the hardest to encapsulate in a brief essay of all the trilogy's concerns. We are to learn, in painful detail, that the Oankali are, in effect, no more "perfect" than are humans. Fertile people do slip through, and they do find each other. Lilith is in a sense "lost," but others, as she foresees, are not. At least, not necessarily. And the fascinating ambiguity of "Humanity did not have to be" will only be apparent hundreds of pages into the reading, just as the significance of that "dark forest" (a construct, not located anywhere on earth) and of the "dry exits," or why they are "concealed," cannot be dealt with here. An "answer" is given, by the trilogy's end: it rests, though not visible to someone who has not read the trilogy, in *Xenogenesis*'s final paragraph, quoted near the start of this essay.

Not that Butler, unlike such handy-andy novelists as Robertson Davies, ever plays unfair with the reader, ever conceals or manipulates fictional truth for mere novelistic effect. On the contrary: she is completely forthcoming, absolutely open. Like all her books, *Xenogenesis* provides us with a great deal of straightforward, old-fashioned storytelling, nor is there the slightest attempt at artful trickery. Butler's art is a substantive, not a merely technical one: she plainly cares about her material, cares about her characters, and is too deeply responsible to both to betray them in any way. The intensity of that caring is obvious throughout: here, for example, is a passage from the second of the trilogy's novels, dealing with Akin, a child and partly human, and Tino, an adult and wholly human. The human adult has just remarked on how "everything goes into" Akin's mouth, and how surprised he is that the only partly human child has not poisoned himself, ten times over:

> Akin ignored this and began investigating the bark on the sapling and looking to see what insects or fungi might be eating it and what might be eating them. Tino had been told why Akin put things in his mouth. He did not understand, but he never tried to keep things out of Akin's mouth the way other visitors did. He could accept without understanding. Once he had seen that a strange thing did no harm, he no longer feared it. He said Akin's tongue looked like a big gray slug, but somehow this did not seem to bother him. He allowed himself to be probed and studied when he carried Akin about. Lilith worried that he was concealing disgust or resentment, but he could not have concealed such strong emotions even from Akin. He certainly could not have concealed them from Nikanj.

There is what I can only call a very special tenderness in such writing. (What may seem hard to understand, here, has been in context long since fully explained.) The writer sees herself, in a sense, as a kind of filter through which the fictive experience is transmitted to her readers. But she makes no claims for herself, assumes no privileges not absolutely required by the careful, orderly telling of her story. Just as her prose, sharp, clear, determinedly explicative, asserts no extraordinary claims for itself, so too her narration is made to appear simply "there," eminently apprehendable but in no way forcing itself on the reader. Just as we do not read *Xenogenesis* on account of stylistic pyrotechnics, so too we do not read it for anything but substantive reasons. The people are real, their doings are both believable and continuously interesting, and the stakes, though not fussed over, are obviously very high—I would myself say, with the author, that they could not be higher, involving as they do the present state of humanity and perhaps its future as well.

The following paragraph, which concludes the second section of the trilogy's third book, can perhaps most effectively summarize *Xenogenesis*'s complex effect (showing more clearly than the other passages I have chosen something, too, of the book's scientific alertness). I will not annotate or indeed comment on this quotation, but simply set it forth and hope that, as it should, it leads you to seek out the rest for yourself:

> Tomás [human, male] lifted my unconscious body, Jesusa [human, female] helping him with me now that I was deadweight. I have a clear, treasured memory of the two of them carrying me into the small room. They did not know then that my memory went on recording everything my senses perceived even when I was unconscious. Yet they handled me with great gentleness and care, as they had from the beginning of my change [maturing Oankali experience, a kind of metamorphosis]. They did not know that this was exactly what Oankali mates did at these times. And they did not see Aaor [like the narrator, part-human, part-Oankali] watching them with a hunger that was so intense that its face was distorted and its head and body tentacles elongated toward us.

TITLE COMMENTARY

📖 *PATTERNMASTER* (1976)

Kirkus Reviews

SOURCE: A review of *Patternmaster,* in *Kirkus Reviews,* Vol. XLIV, No. 10, May 15, 1976, p. 612.

This is fine, old-fashioned sf about a distant future in which the earth is ruled by Patternists whose psi powers let them control the "mutes" who have no mental voices and do battle with the Clayarks—strange creatures with four legs and human faces. A brief passage two thirds through the book offers a throwaway explanation of how this state of affairs came to be, but the how and why are less important here than the compelling conflict between Teray and his brother Coransee, both of whom seek to become Patternmaster—the ruler of this strange world. Escape fiction in the best Patterned tradition.

Barbara A. Bannon

SOURCE: A review of *Patternmaster,* in *Publishers Weekly,* Vol. 209, No. 24, June 14, 1976, p. 104.

After centuries of mutations and conflagrations, Earth's survivors have settled down into a neatly stratified system of détente. The Patternists are the elite rulers, linked to one another in a vast mental chain of telepathy and empathy. The Mutes are slaves who do the manual labor. Beyond the Pale of the civilized enclaves of Patternist Houses wander the predatory Clayarks, human-headed, four-legged mutants who can handle rifles with their fore-feet. The reigning Patternmaster is growing old, and his two sons are in hot competition for his job. Teray, the younger, just out of school and still naive, falls into his older brother's superior pattern and seems doomed to extinction until he meets a sexy outsider-Patternist woman who can augment his powers when she "links" with him. The author carefully spells out the ground rules of her unique world, and the ensuing story of love, chase and combat is consistently attention-holding.

John J. Adams

SOURCE: A review of *Patternmaster,* in *Kliatt,* Vol. XIII, No. 3, April, 1979, p. 16.

A great holocaust has divided the humans of America's West coast. The highly telepathic Patternists are men and women able to control, kill and heal with their mental powers. Their slaves and apprentices, however, lack this power. The Patternists are linked to the Patternmaster, an overlord who is able to communicate at will with any individual, as well as call upon the collected strength of all for his own purposes. The enemies are the Clayarks, horrible mutants who rove in murderous bands. The story concerns two Patternist brothers who vie to assume the position of the aging Patternmaster, their father.

Butler's writing is a rich and detailed evocation of the varied mental worlds of the characters. The Clayarks are hinted to have a complex society of their own (some former Patternists who have become mutated) but Butler never develops them beyond their brooding background presence. The action is constant and the tension between the two brothers never lets up.

MIND OF MY MIND (1977)

Barbara A. Bannon

SOURCE: A review of *Mind of My Mind,* in *Publishers Weekly,* Vol. 211, No. 18, May 2, 1977, p. 61.

Doro has survived the past 4000 years through his psychic ability to take over the bodies of others, and has spent much of his time trying to breed a pool of descendants who will possess enough of his talent to form a sort of empire. One of them, Mary, in modern

California, discovers the unique power to form others of the "family" into a mental network which she controls. Encouraged by Doro, who sees this as the nucleus of what he has been working for, she draws half a dozen of them to her—and the mixture is explosive in ways that neither she nor the ageless Doro is able to foresee. Vivid in presenting psychic experience convincingly, the book depends perhaps too much on its special material, with more action taking place telepathically than physically.

Kirkus Reviews

SOURCE: A review of *Mind of My Mind,* in *Kirkus Reviews,* Vol. XLV, No. 8, May 15, 1977, p. 453.

The first chapter in a history that Butler has already taken up at a much later stage in *Patternmaster* (1976). *Mind of My Mind* begins with Doro, a ruthless mutant as old as the pyramids who has spent the last 4,000 years trying to breed a race in his own image. The culminating experiment is his daughter Mary. But, to Doro's astonishment, Mary's first instinct on attaining her full powers is to begin building a mental community—a Pattern—out of the wretched thousands of Doro's half-telepathic failures and partial successes. Despite some ragged moments, Butler is clearly on to a promising vein—something like Zenna Henderson's "People" stories without their saccharine silliness. There's a lot of intrinsic energy in the Pattern idea, and one wants to see where this erratic, gifted storyteller will pick it up next.

Michael S. Cross

SOURCE: A review of *Mind of My Mind,* in *Library Journal,* Vol. 102, No. 14, August, 1977, p. 1682.

This is a diverting novel about a mutant race emerging from humanity. Gifted with psionic powers, the "Patternists" suffer from the disadvantages of psychic sensitivity in the normal world. The novel is concerned with their construction of a telepathic "pattern" that permits them to build their own society. Butler has created some believable characters and placed them in a believable landscape. While neither the ideas nor the plot is new, the novel is readable and entertaining.

SURVIVOR (1978)

Kirkus Reviews

SOURCE: A review of *Survivor,* in *Kirkus Reviews,* Vol. XLVI, No. 2, January 15, 1978, p. 67.

On an alien world, a sect of fundamentalist, anthro-pocentric "Missionaries" are drawn into the affairs of two native communities: the apparently friendly Garkohn and their enemies, the Tehkohn, who preserve a harsh but just hierarchy of which the Garkohn society is a debased mockery. Alanna, foster daughter of the Missionary leader, is kidnapped by the Tehkohn and soon finds a satisfying kinship with their valorous ways. After her marriage to the Tehkohn leader Diut and subsequent recapture by the Missionaries, Alanna must bring about an alliance between the two groups before the treacherous Garkohn can enslave the humans to their own purposes. Butler, a vigorous and nimble storyteller (*Patternmaster, Mind of My Mind*) has yet to prove herself a deeply thoughtful novelist. The Missionary society is a mere cardboard foil to the more vivid portrayal of the Tehkohn, and the one complex figure in the story—Jules, Alanna's loving but xenophobic foster father—is never explored with the thoroughness he seems to deserve. Still, one suspects that this author may give us something really first-rate one of these days.

Joanne Troutner

SOURCE: A review of *Survivor,* in *Library Journal,* Vol. 103, No. 7, April 1, 1978, p. 778.

This is the story of Alanna, a surprisingly adaptive wild human being. She is adopted by members of a religious sect who migrate to an alien world; the Tehkohn and Garkohn, warring nations, also inhabit Alanna's new home. Alanna is kidnapped by the Tehkohn, becomes the bride of their ruler, and returns to her adopted parents to save them from destruction by the Garkohn. The suspense keeps the reader interested and the satire is effective. For avid sf fans.

Elizabeth Barbara Boatner

SOURCE: A review of *Survivor,* in *Kliatt,* Vol. XIII, No. 6, September, 1979, p. 17.

Missionaries fled a dying Earth to find peace on a new world, but found themselves caught between two warring races, one of which seems to befriend them. But Alanna, adopted as a young girl on Earth, discovers that the "friendly" aliens have in fact enslaved the missionaries through addictive foodstuffs, while the "enemy" race offers a chance for freedom and the peace they are seeking. Alanna is torn between the love of her adoptive parents, her alien husband, and the missionaries who had grudgingly accepted her. In the end she must make decisions which she feels are right, but which offer no easy solutions

and which turn her people against her. A well-written story of loyalty on many levels.

KINDRED (1979)

Joanna Russ

SOURCE: A review of *Kindred,* in *Fantasy and Science Fiction,* Vol. 58, No. 2, February, 1980, pp. 96-7.

Octavia Butler's *Kindred* is more polished than her earlier work but still has the author's stubborn, idiosyncratic gift for realism. Butler makes new and eloquent use of a familiar science-fiction idea, protecting one's own past, to express the tangled interdependency of black and white in the United States: the black heroine's great-great-grandfather is a white man who can, half voluntarily, call her back into his time to help him in emergencies; Dana, drawn wholly involuntarily, must save him to preserve her own ancestry, at least until the conception of her great-grandmother—and Rufus is a Southern slave-owner, confused, spoiled, a rapist with a remarkable gift for self-destruction. *Kindred* is a family chronicle set in a small space; the limitations let Butler concentrate on the human relations and the surprising-but-logical interplay of past and present. (What other author would think of taking Excedrin to pre-Civil War Maryland?) Although characterizations in the past are detailed (Rufus as a little boy is especially good) Dana's present-day marriage is sketchy and her aunt and uncle, who disapprove of her white husband, are talked about, not shown. Past events may simply have crowded out the present or Butler may mean to indicate that Dana's present-day difficulties in being black are nothing to her past ones—she gets shut of the appalling Rufus only, finally, by killing him. *Kindred* is exciting and fast-moving and the past occurs without a break in style—a technique that makes it more real—even down to character's speech (Butler describes their accents but wisely doesn't attempt to reproduce them). The end is crossed-fingers hopeful with some chance of sanity "now that the boy is dead" though Dana has assured her own birth at a price: her left arm, lost at "the exact spot Rufus's finger had grasped it." (261)

Kirkus Reviews

SOURCE: A review of *Kindred,* in *Kirkus Reviews,* Vol. XLVII, No. 10, May 15, 1979, pp. 587-88.

Butler is one of those accomplished science-fiction writers (*Mind of My Mind, Survivor*) who tap out their tales so fast and fine and clear that it's impossible to stop reading at any point. And this time the appeal should reach far beyond a sci-fi audience—because the alien planet here is the antebellum South, as seen through the horrified eyes of Dana, a 20th-century black woman who time-travels in expeditious Butler fashion: "The house, the books, everything vanished. Suddenly I was outdoors on the ground beneath trees" . . . in 1819 Maryland. Dana has been "called" by her white ancestor, Rufus—on her first visit, Rufus is a small child, son of a sour slaveowner—and she'll be transported back to Maryland (twice with her white husband Kevin) to rescue Rufus from death again and again. As Rufus ages (the Maryland years amount to hours and days in 1976 time), the relationship between him and Dana takes on some terrifying dimensions: Rufus simply cannot show the humanity Dana tries to call forth; Dana, drawn into the life of slaves with its humiliation and atrocities, treads carefully, trying to effect some changes, but too often she returns beaten and maimed to her own century. And most frightening is the thought that, in the "stronger, sharper realities" of Rufus' time, Dana is "losing my place here in my own time." At one point Kevin and Dana lose one another (Kevin returns haggard, after five years working to help escaped slaves), but finally Dana, fighting off complete possession by Rufus, kills him and that past forever—but not the memories. There is tremendous ironic power in Butler's vision of the old South in science-fiction terms—capriciously dangerous aliens, oppressed races, and a supra-fevered reality; and that irony opens the much-lamented nightmare of slavery to a fresh, vivid attack—in this searing, caustic examination of bizarre and alien practices on the third planet from the sun.

Barbara A. Bannon

SOURCE: A review of *Kindred,* in *Publishers Weekly,* Vol. 215, No. 21, May 21, 1979, p. 56.

It is 1976, and Dana, a young black writer, has just moved into her new California home with husband Kevin, a white novelist. Suddenly, she has the first of many dizzy spells that plunge her back in time to the antebellum Maryland plantation of her slave ancestors. First alone, then with Kevin, she becomes a central figure among Tom Weylin's slaves (working variously as a cook, a teacher and a field hand) and a devoted protector of the erratic Rufus, Weylin's son, whom Dana knows will become her own great-grandfather. Butler has a strong narrative talent, and she brings the daily rounds and cruelties of slavery to vivid life; but the reader grows increasingly uncom-

fortable with the fantasy contrivance that underpins her novel. The recurring time travel is obtrusive, unconvincing and far too easily accepted by the people of 1815. And even given her device, the author never does explore fully the responses of a modern black woman to her family's slave past.

WILD SEED (1980)

Kirkus Reviews

SOURCE: A review of *Wild Seed,* in *Kirkus Reviews,* Vol. XLVIII, No. 12, June 15, 1980, p. 804.

Butler's "Patternmaster" series has been appearing jigsaw-wise rather than in consistent chronological sequence of events; this latest piece fits into the puzzle somewhere before *Mind of My Mind* (1977). Doro, the mysterious and cruel immortal who has been wandering the earth since the days of the Pharaohs trying to breed up a race with abilities worthy of his own, has succeeded only in erratically (and often dangerously) reinforcing various predispositions to telepathy and telekinesis among his selected human strains. Collecting a shipload of African slaves to take to one of his breeding-colonies in 17th-century America, he chances on a female "wild seed"—a second though lesser immortal perhaps generated in the wake of some long-ago experiment of his own. But Doro's new discovery proves to have shape-changing abilities which enable her to rebel against his casual creation and destruction of obedient subjects, and a century and a half later to set up her own kinder equivalent of Doro's communities. Butler, a vigorous narrator, has presented herself with an unfortunate dilemma: should everybody speak characterless 20th-century English or some artificial story-book argot? Better the former, which she chooses—but at the cost of divorcing her characters from any real sense of the supposed historical settings. Good story, not quite the right underpinnings.

Barbara A. Bannon

SOURCE: A review of *Wild Seed,* in *Publishers Weekly,* Vol. 217, No. 24, June 20, 1980, p. 75.

SF does not always take place in the future. This very readable novel by one of the genre's important new talents is set in 17th century Africa, colonial New York State and pre-Civil War Louisiana. Its two unusual and fascinating central characters are both African and immortal. Doro has survived for 3600 years by his ability to take over the bodies of others, putting on new flesh as ordinary men put on new clothes. He's passed the centuries by running a far-flung eugenic program to breed people with special talents (like telepathy). It is this interest which leads him to Anyanwu, a woman who has lived 300 years by using her shape-shifting ability to keep her body young and to take on any human or animal form advantageous to her survival. Anyanwu hates the ruthless way Doro uses his power, but because he threatens her children, she goes with him to America. This novel is an account of the first 150 years of their stormy relationship. It is an exciting and, when Doro finally recognizes his real need for Anyanwu, ultimately, a moving story.

Sister Avalia Lamb

SOURCE: A review of *Wild Seed,* in *Kliatt,* Vol. XVI, No. 1, January, 1982, p. 20.

Desperate conflict between two supranatural beings, Anyanwu, an African witch already 300 years old, and Doro, a something (we never get to know exactly what) who occupies corpses and breeds humans to strengthen traits that serve his nefarious purposes is the basis of this story that ranges from 1690 Africa, 18th century New England, to Louisiana in 1840 and on and on to the Epilogue. It would take a very blasé reader to remain uninvolved in this dreadful power struggle between total evil (Doro) and not so evil (Anyanwu). Unfortunately when one breathlessly reaches the climax expecting a mighty battle to the death, all collapses in compromise, leaving the reader flat and incredulous. Up to that point the story is gripping and credible.

CLAY'S ARK (1984)

Kirkus Reviews

SOURCE: A review of *Clay's Ark,* in *Kirkus Reviews,* Vol. LII, No. 1, January 1, 1984, p. 18.

Despite the basic triteness of its premise and its backdrop: another technically scintillating novel from the author of **Kindred** (1979) and the Patternmaster series. Clay's Ark, the first interstellar spaceship, returns carrying a deadly alien parasite and crashes in the desert; only pilot Eli survives. Transformed by the parasite, he is stronger and faster than before and nearly invulnerable. But the alien unmercifully drives him to infect others. (There's a powerful sexual compulsion too.) So Eli takes over an isolated desert community, hoping to confine the disease there while

shanghai-ing occasional new recruits—such as thoughtful doctor Blake Maslin and his daughters, self-reliant Rane and leukemia-stricken Keira. Soon, then, all three are infected; aware of the alien nature of the parasite, they try to escape. But a vicious bandit gang intervenes . . . and violent complications ensue. The parasite's victims are sympathetic—with superior abilities, tenderness, and the will to fight against their alien-inspired compulsions. On the other hand, these characters *look* terrible; they eat raw meat, carry contagion, produce non-human offspring. And Butler maintains this ambivalence beautifully throughout—in a strong, supple narrative with tense action. Superior science fiction, then, even if many readers will be disappointed by the non-originality of the parasite notion—and by the sketchy, clichéd near-future setting.

Sybil Steinberg

SOURCE: A review of *Clay's Ark,* in *Publishers Weekly,* Vol. 225, No. 1, January 6, 1984, p. 81.

When the first starship returns from the Centauri system, it crashes, deliberately, but there is one survivor, carrying within him an organism that sharpens his senses, increases his strength and subjugates every normal human drive to the demand that the organism be spread. Eli cannot suppress it completely, but with iron will he channels it, contains it, limits it to a few people on an isolated farm, where their mutant quadruped children can be born in secrecy. But the organism demands expansion and from time to time they are forced to kidnap new recruits. Alternating between Eli's story and that of the newest victims—a man and his two adolescent daughters—Butler's plotting is as irresistible as the alien invader itself. This is a genuine SF thriller, as hard to stop reading as *The Andromeda Strain.*

Algis Budrys

SOURCE: A review of *Clay's Ark,* in *Fantasy and Science Fiction,* Vol. 67, No. 2, August, 1984, pp. 34-5.

A book I almost didn't review is Octavia E. Butler's **Clay's Ark.** It is burdened by a discouraging, meaningless dust jacket that looks like an attempt to save money on the designer, the artist, the production cost and the blurb-writing. It is furthermore from a house with a very spotty track record; St. Martin's SF program has no overall feel, no clear direction, and no internal logic. The hand of plonk is all over it, and that does, indeed, affect the warmth of my reception for any St. Martin's book until proven not guilty.

Reading Butler's book thus turns out to be a pleasant surprise. The title does prove to be empty of meaning, but I have the feeling that's not Butler's fault; it hardly sounds like an author's title. *Clay's Ark* (Say it fast, three times. Sounds sweet on the ear, doesn't it?) is the name of the interstellar spaceship that comes back to Earth with a plague aboard; the story has nothing to do with anything ark-like nor with the spaceship per se. We never even see it, or its landing in the southwestern U.S. The story follows the surviving crewman, and then other people he infects over a period of years. *Clay's Plague,* while still far from spot-on, would have been a much better title on any number of counts, and certainly could have been arrived at without burning out too many brain cells.

In any event, the story works. What the crewman infects Earth with is an alien symbiote that transforms the metabolism of humans and causes them to have children of superior physical and mental powers in an alien shape. The nature of the infection is such that its victims cannot effectively prevent themselves from having children and can barely hold down the pace at which they will infect others.

The race of *homo sapiens* is doomed; what has been brought back from the stars is the end of human history. Fighting the grip of the organism, the crewman and his immediate "family" hide out in isolation, attempting to retard the inevitable doom, kidding themselves that they can do this while nevertheless compulsively kidnapping occasional travelers and adding them to the group.

That's what it's about, and Butler creates this tale with verve, originality, and an apparent gift for the circumstantial detail circumstantially told. This latter attribute may instead be a present inability to write in more than one tone of voice, but in any event she never strains for a pitch she's not up to. While rather far from ever reaching a resolution of any kind, this book is an effective piece of work in what might be called the "slice of death" school of SF writing. And there is the possibility a sequel is coming. For all I know, this is itself the middle book in a trilogy, Part One—which ought to have been called *Clay's Ark*—having escaped my gleanings. If so, neither the blurbs nor St. Martin's PR handouts in any way betray this.

If, by the way, Butler's story is built in part on my own "Silent Brother," a story now a quarter-century old, that's O.K. with me; I didn't invent the idea either.

Donna Johns

SOURCE: A review of *Clay's Ark,* in *School Library Journal,* Vol. 31, No. 4, December, 1984, p. 104.

YA—A starship returns to Earth carrying an alien microbe which is deadly to most humans. Those that survive the initial infection are left with an unusual after-effect. Their genetic codes are altered, and their offspring are not completely human. The infected humans have an agonizing compulsion to spread the disease by scratching other humans or, in some cases, by sexual relations with fertile women. Eli Doyle, the only survivor when the ship crashes on Earth, tries to restrain himself from attacking others and spreading the microbe. When the compulsion is too strong, he kidnaps victims and keeps them confined in a remote desert compound so they cannot infect the rest of the Earth. All involved walk a tightrope between a desire to protect their fellow man and the unearthly need to spread the contagion. This bizarre but interesting premise is supported by a compelling plot and some heartbreaking characters.

DAWN (1987)

Roland Green

SOURCE: A review of *Dawn,* in *Booklist,* Vol. 83, No. 22, August, 1987, p. 1722.

This first installment in the Xenogenesis series bodes well for the rest. A band of nuclear holocaust survivors is in the hands of an alien race that offers to save them. The price is high though: the survivors must participate in the evolution of the aliens by bearing children that incorporate some of the aliens' characteristics. Butler is one of the few sf writers who can handle effectively a slow-moving plot that emphasizes characters' emotions. Her command of the language is superior, and her aliens are quite convincing creations.

Matthew S. Moore

SOURCE: A review of *Dawn,* in *Voice of Youth Advocates,* Vol. 10, No. 4, October, 1987, p. 174.

In a story that challenges both the reader's understanding and feelings, Lilith Tyapo finds herself captured by aliens and aboard a craft circling an earth destroyed by nuclear war. The price for her freedom and for the others aboard is cooperation with their captors.

The Oankali, humanoid "gene traders" with tentacles for sense organs, pressure their captives by sense deprivation and "love bombing." Their goal is to establish a new race through sexual intermingling of themselves and the humans. Action covers the mental and physical seduction of the heroine by the Oankali, and the struggle of a group of humans to learn to live together and with the aliens in preparation for colonizing Earth.

Values in the book need comment because they are gender identified rather than attributed to humans in general. Cooperation and willingness to submit to genetic enhancement are distinctly admirable feminine virtues, while resistance to change and adherence to violence are identified as male values.

As a science fiction writer, Butler writes more like Frederick Pohl and Asimov than fantasy spellweavers like Sherri Tepper or Margaret Weiss. *Dawn* has more in common in its subject with Whitley Streiber's "nonfiction" *Communion* than much other SF. Projected to be the first of a "Xenogenesis Series," the book will suit older teens only. Recommended for adult and large teen collections.

Elizabeth A. Belden and Judith M. Beckman

SOURCE: A review of *Dawn,* in *English Journal,* Vol. 77, No. 4, April, 1988, pp. 78-9.

Imagine the Earth made uninhabitable by war, with one group of people selected by benign extraterrestrials and placed in hibernation for safekeeping. You alone are awakened, introduced to the extraterrestrials, and given the responsibility of selecting only a handful of other humans to form the nucleus of a new society which will repopulate Earth.

Twenty-six-year-old Lilith Iyapo finds herself in this situation in Nebula and Hugo Award-winning Octavia Butler's first volume of the Exogenesis Series. If Butler sustains this concept, her sociologically oriented science fiction series should become a classic. *Dawn* certainly should appeal to idealistic teenagers impatient to build a better society.

Butler's style and viewpoint appeal to a wide audience. In common language she presents a complex, concretely realized world and skillfully maintains plot momentum. From word one, she draws readers into Lilith's consciousness and enables us to experience Lilith's confusion, her response to the gray-tentacled Oankali, and her gradual understanding of their plans to revitalize Earth. Watching Lilith select

members of this new society and observing their interactions is a fascinating study of human behavior.

Thought-provoking, exciting reading, especially for those who think they don't like science fiction.

📖 *ADULTHOOD RITES* (1988)

Kirkus Reviews

SOURCE: A review of *Adulthood Rites,* in *Kirkus Reviews,* Vol. LVI, No. 9, May 1, 1988, p. 658.

Second in the Xenogenesis series (*Dawn*), from the talented author of *Clay's Ark* (1984), in which the alien Oankali have descended upon an Earth devastated by nuclear war.

The Oankali, who look frightful but have vast biological talents, have rebuilt both the Earth's biosphere and the surviving humans—giving the humans long, healthy lives while withholding their ability to reproduce without the Oankali's aid. Why? Well, the much-traveled aliens make their living by collecting and interpreting genes—so they *know* that any nascent human civilization will inevitably destroy itself. *Some* humans cooperate with the Oankali (they have a third, neuter, sex, ooloi, that mediates reproduction) and produce "construct" offspring, fusions of human and Oankali. The uncooperative wild humans, unable to bear children, often try to kidnap the construct children despite their nonhuman attributes (sensory tentacles, indeterminate sex, a final repellent-looking metamorphosis, and so forth). The wild humans, then, pose a thorny problem for the kindly Oankali—so when Lilith's young construct son Akin is kidnapped, the Oankali refuse to rescue him (Akin is, however, self-reliant and mature far beyond his human age) in the hope that he will, by coming to understand the wild humans from an Oankali viewpoint, find a solution.

Butler's spare, vivid prose style invites comparison with the likes of Kate Wilhelm and Ursula Le Guin. Add on the intriguing, well-developed ideas here, the solid characters and crisp narrative: Butler in top form.

Genevieve Stuttaford

SOURCE: A review of *Adulthood Rites,* in *Publishers Weekly,* Vol. 233, No. 18, May 6, 1988, p. 98.

Butler's 1984 Hugo and Nebula Award winning novelette ***Bloodchild*** memorably and harrowingly considered human-alien relations reflecting the racial history of this planet. In her followup, Xenogenesis trilogy, of which this is the second volume, the alien Oankali have rescued the dying remnants of humanity after Earth's nuclear war. Now, though, the children of the two reaces, called constructs, are resented and feared by the original survivors. This is the story of one such construct, Akin, who possesses an adult mind and voice before he is two years old. Stolen by a barren human community, he grows up knowing both races. Within a lively and eventful tale, Butler brings Toni Morrison to mind as moving, bitter truths emerge about the obligations and constraints of family and people, as Akin's heightened senses realize what Wallace Stevens called "the blissful liaison between himself and his environment" and, finally, as the author gives us a brief, ecstatic experience of this utopian alternative to human society.

Roland Green

SOURCE: A review of *Adulthood Rites,* in *Booklist,* Vol. 84, No. 20, June 15, 1988, p. 1711-12.

Here is the sequel to ***Dawn,*** in which the author began the tale of the Oankali and their efforts to create part-human synthetic offspring. Akin, son of Lilith (protagonist of ***Dawn***), is kidnapped by the human foes of the Oankali. As the youth learns more of human beings and their motives, he begins to sympathize with their plight. At the same time, he also knows that he is still a hybrid and will need the Oankali's help in order to survive the adulthood rites of his captors. Not as impressive as ***Dawn,*** this remains a well-told tale and a solid building block in a promising sf sage.

IMAGO (1989)

Kirkus Reviews

SOURCE: A review of *Imago,* in *Kirkus Reviews,* Vol. LVII, No. 7, April 1, 1989, p. 508.

Third in the Xenogenesis series (***Adulthood Rites,*** 1988), exploring the impact of the kindly but implacable alien Onkali upon an Earth devastated by nuclear war.

Most of Earth's surviving humans are unable to reproduce without Oankali aid; the aliens, you see, collect and engineer genetic material and will eventually develop a new race, a fusion of human and Oankali. However, from compassion the Oankali have given the humans who reject Oankali aid the planet Mars to colonize and develop as they will. Jodahs, then, is not only a "construct" (mingled human and Oankali) but the first construct ooloi—or third (neuter) sex that mediates reproduction. Jodahs is also well into its final metamorphosis (per the title), when it will grow sensory arms, develop powerful abilities to heal, and feel an overwhelming urge to seek mates. Unfortunately, the Oankali mistrust Jodahs' ability to control its talents. Banished, therefore, from human-Oankali colonies, Jodahs comes across a rare, isolated colony of wild, fertile humans; thus it is able to select mates—siblings Jesusa and Joao—and cure them of inbred genetic defects. But Jodahs' ooloi sibling, Aaor, is less stable and accomplished than Jodahs, and might well die unless mates can be found for it.

Another well thought-out, often absorbing exploration of human-alien sexuality. What's lacking here is narrative tension—a sense that any of this really makes a difference to the larger designs that Butler has previously sketched in.

Sybil Steinberg

SOURCE: A review of *Imago,* in *Publishers Weekly,* Vol. 235, No. 15, April 14, 1989, p. 54.

Although more women authors have enlivened SF writing in the last 20 years, only a few have created work that radically rethinks the male assumptions of the genre: possibly Ursula K. LeGuin, certainly Joanna Russ and, though the least celebrated, Octavia Butler. Her Xenogenesis trilogy, of which this is the final volume, considers a post-holocaust humanity whose only chance for survival is to be absorbed by the alien Oankali. Totally uninterested in domination, this race thrives on a symbiosis that Earthlings find difficult to credit. That distrust hampers the narrator, an ooloi (neuter) named Jodahs, as it tries to find life partners in the same ratio as its five parents: a human couple, an Oankali couple and itself, the essential ooloi who joins all five and melds their genetic legacy. Butler's achievement here is less the abstract reassignment of sexual roles than a warmth and urgency that dramatizes and personalizes these conflicts and transformations.

Roland Green

SOURCE: A review of *Imago,* in *Booklist,* Vol. 85, No. 17, May 1, 1989, p. 1511.

Butler concludes her trilogy of human evolution under the aegis of the alien Oenkali. The Oenkali have three sexes—male, female, and neuter (or olloi)—and the hero of this novel is the first human construct to develop as the latter. Jodahs realizes the need to seek his Oenkali partners while avoiding retaliation from humans who cannot fight the Oenkali but will attack their constructs and sympathizers. A literate, detailed story, very much up to Butler's high standards (although one does wonder if an alien race would be so continuously concerned with human sexuality). Recommended where the previous volumes have found readers.

PARABLE OF THE SOWER (1993)

Sybil Steinberg

SOURCE: A review of *Parable of the Sower*, in *Publishers Weekly*, Vol. 240, No. 49, December 6, 1993, p. 60.

Hugo and Nebula Award-winner Butler's first novel since 1989's *Imago* offers an uncommonly sensitive rendering of a very common SF scenario: by 2025, global warming, pollution, racial and ethnic tensions and other ills have precipitated a worldwide decline. In the Los Angeles area, small beleaguered communities of the still-employed hide behind makeshift walls from hordes of desperate homeless scavengers and violent pyromaniac addicts known as "paints" who, with water and work growing scarcer, have become increasingly aggressive. Lauren Olamina, a young black woman, flees when the paints overrun her community, heading north with thousands of other refugees seeking a better life. Lauren suffers from 'hyperempathy," a genetic condition that causes her to experience the pain of others as viscerally as her own—a heavy liability in this future world of cruelty and hunger. But she dreams of a better world, and with her philosophy/religion, Earthseed, she hopes to found an enclave which will weather the tough times and which may one day help carry humans to the stars. Butler tells her story with unusual warmth, sensitivity, honesty and grace; though science fiction readers will recognize this future Earth, Lauren Olamina and her vision make this novel stand out like a tree amid saplings.

Carl Hays

SOURCE: A review of *Parable of the Sower*, in *Booklist*, Vol. 90, No. 6, November 15, 1993, p. 306.

Although conventional gloom-and-doom scenarios of civilization on the brink of collapse are rapidly becoming passé in contemporary science fiction, original variations occasionally appear to give new life to the form. For instance, Butler's latest novel. Written in diary form, *Parable* chronicles the sometimes grim adventures of Lauren Olamina, an adolescent girl living in a barricaded village in Southern California amid the rampant socioeconomic decay of the early twenty-first century. After her neighborhood is overrun by a cult of drug-demented pyromaniacs, Lauren takes to the road and bands together with other refugees of violent attacks. Withstanding fire and marauding thieves, the group gradually makes its way toward refuge in Northern California, while Lauren wins converts to her homespun "Earthseed" philosophy—a creed espousing community survival for a future among the stars. Sustained by skillful characterizations and an all-too-uncomfortable realism, Butler's narrative holds a mirror up close to our own contemporary blight of moral and economic disintegration and implicitly poses the question, Can we really let it get this bad?

Barbara Hawkins

SOURCE: A review of *Parable of the Sower*, in *School Library Journal*, Vol. 40, No. 7, July, 1994, p. 128.

On Friday, July 30, 2027, Lauren Oya Olamina's California walled neighborhood is burned and plundered by pyro addicts. She and two other teens appear to be the only survivors and join the seemingly endless stream of poverty-stricken people looking for a better life or, at least, for another day. Like her Baptist minister father before her, Lauren carries her faith in her religion, Earthseed, with her. In the insanity of this future world, her faith, practical skills, and determination to survive (whatever the cost) are enhanced by the basic goodness of the folks who expand her group. YAs may see the similarity between Lauren's world and the nightly TV-news coverage of current war-torn nations. They should appreciate this tender coming-of-age story and/or the glimpse into a future they can work to prevent. Romance; science fiction; a strong, black, female protagonist; and a hopeful ending should attract readers to this novel.

Joseph R. DeMarco

SOURCE: A review of *Parable of the Sower*, in *Kliatt*, Vol. XXIX, No. 3, May, 1995, p. 12.

Butler is one of the few African-American women working in the field of SF. Her works are thoughtful, exciting, and well constructed. And here, she does it again. A post-apocalyptic novel that takes place in the 2020s, it is the story of a reluctant prophet, Lauren Olamina, who is also an empath. She is 15 when the novel—written as a series of Lauren's journal entries—opens. We get a vivid sense of the horrible state of the U.S. Local and state governments are ineffectual; the national government, while still funding the space program lavishly, no longer helps the poor and the needy. Crime and violence are rampant. Neighborhoods are walled. Traveling from one neighborhood to another requires group effort and armaments. The gap between rich and poor has widened to mammoth proportions. Electricity, water, gasoline, and other things are at a premium. This is Lauren's world. It is also a world filled with religion and this novel is quite philosophical and religion centered. In it, Butler tackles some serious questions. Lauren is obsessed with her own ideas about religion and has begun setting them down in her book *Earthseed,* which is quoted throughout. After a slow disintegration, Lauren's walled community is destroyed by outsiders. Many of her friends and family are killed and she must make her way in a hellish world. But she has followers and her new religion and she has knowledge. With these she begins her new journey to a more civilized life.

Butler's writing is solid and convincing. Reading these journal entries it is easy to imagine this 21st century nightmare world and the characters peopling it. This is a book that draws readers in quickly and forces them to turn pages to find out what happens next.

📖 *BLOODCHILD: NOVELLAS AND STORIES* (1995)

Kirkus Reviews

SOURCE: A review of *Bloodchild: Novellas and Stories,* in *Kirkus Reviews,* Vol. LXIII, No. 14, July 15, 1995, pp. 989-90.

Essentially a novelist, Butler (*Parable of the Sower,* 1994, etc.) confesses that she finds short fiction arduous and frustrating. So this slim volume collects all her stories and, despite the misleading subtitle, two short essays; each piece is illuminated by a brief but rewarding afterword. The title story—about an isolated planet where, in a relationship of mutual dependence, even love, millipede-like aliens use human bodies to incubate their parasitic young (Butler describes it as her "pregnant man" story)—is justly fa-

mous; although in retrospect it does seem somewhat too compressed. Longer and even better, **"The Evening and the Morning and the Night"** presents a ghastly disease, characterized by self-mutilation, withdrawal, and violence, and its victims' efforts to come to terms with their symptoms. The other stories feature incest (Butler's only non-sf/fantasy tale), alcoholism, and the role language plays in shaping our humanity. Finally, in the first essay, Butler ponders the relevance of sf/fantasy, and writing in general, to black people (she is the only black female sf/fantasy writer of note), while in the second she offers sound advice to aspiring authors: "Persist!"

Splendid pieces, set forth in calm, lucid prose with never a word wasted.

Publishers Weekly

SOURCE: A review of *Bloodchild: Novellas and Stories,* in *Publishers Weekly,* Vol. 242, No. 34, August 21, 1995, pp. 50-1.

Collected in this slim volume is the entire output of short fiction from the pen of MacArthur Award winner Butler (*Parable of the Sower*). "I hate short story writing," Butler admits in her preface; not surprisingly, then, there are only five tales here, ranging in date from 1971 to 1983. Two essays round out the volume: one an inspirational piece about making writing a habit, the other a more personal reminiscence about what it's like to be poor, female, black—and to persist in the writing of SF anyway. **"Bloodchild"** (which won both a Hugo and a Nebula) is a compelling and horrifying novella combining a love story between a human and an alien with a coming-of-age tale; it is, as Butler puts it, a "pregnant man" story. **"The Evening and the Morning and the Night"** concerns genetic disorders, personal responsibility and pheremones; **"Near of Kin"** takes a sympathetic look at a dysfunctional family; and **"Speech Sounds,"** another Hugo winner, depicts a near-future society in which a virus has nearly destroyed people's ability to communicate. Here, too, is **"Crossover,"** Butler's first published story, which deals with the ghostly by-products of hopelessness and drudgery. Following each entry is an enlightening afterword that provides a refreshing look into Butler's writing process and that helps to clarify what excites and motivates this exceptionally talented writer.

Janet St. John

SOURCE: A review of *Bloodchild,* in *Booklist,* Vol. 92, No. 1, September 1, 1995, pp. 47-8.

Referred to as "the grande dame" of science fiction, Butler graces new mansions of thought with her eloquent, distinguished, and poignant prose. This collection of novellas and stories is quirky only in its diversity of subject matter. From what she calls her "pregnant male title story" to a sympathetic tale of incest to a bleak futuristic world of violence and nonverbal communication, Butler's imagination is strong—and so is her awareness of how to work real issues subtly into the text of her fiction. A nice addition is the afterwords that follow each story or novella. Written by Butler, they contain firsthand analysis and discussion of the impetus and influence in her own work. Although this book is little in size, its ideas and aims are splendidly large.

John Lawson

SOURCE: A review of *Blood Child and Other Stories,* in *School Library Journal,* Vol. 42, No. 7, July, 1996, p. 107.

Collected together for the first time are the complete shorter works of the Hugo and Nebula award-winning author. **"Blood Child,"** her "pregnant man story," both a coming-of-age and a love story, revolves around a young man and an alien. In **"The Evening and the Morning and the Night,"** two lovers faced with the stark reality of their deadly genetic inheritance have tough choices to make. The three other selections deal with incest and a dysfunctional family, alcoholism, and a disease that destroys humankind's ability to communicate through speech. The author leaves readers with a glimmer of hope in otherwise bleak situations. Each of the selections has an insightful afterword about Butler's inspiration for writing it and her own thoughts and comments about each one. Two very literate and readable essays about persistence in writing and growing up as a black, female science-fiction writer round out the collection. The youthfulness of some of the protagonists and the contemporary tone of the themes, viewed through a glass darkly, should appeal to YAs. Five intense, thought-provoking tales of people caught up in extraordinary situations.

PARABLE OF THE TALENTS (1998)

Publishers Weekly

SOURCE: A review of *Parable of the Talents,* in *Publishers Weekly,* Vol. 245, No. 42, October 19, 1998, p. 60.

Lauren Olamina, a black teenager, grew up in a 21st-century America that was tearing itself apart. Global warming, massive unemployment, gang warfare and corporate greed combined to break down society in general and her impoverished southern California neighborhood in particular. A victim of hyperempathy syndrome, a disorder that compels its victims to believe they feel others' pain, Lauren found herself homeless and alone in a violent world. Escaping from the urban jungle of Los Angeles, Lauren founded Acorn, a hard-working, prosperous rural community based on the teachings of Earthseed, a religion she herself created and centered on the ideas that God is Change and that humanity's destiny is to go to the stars. Butler's extraordinary *Parable of the Sower* (1996) detailed the aforementioned events. In this equally powerful sequel, Acorn is destroyed by the rising forces of Christian fundamentalism, led by the newly elected U.S. president, the Reverend Andrew Steele Jarret. A handsome man and persuasive orator, seemingly modeled in part on Pat Robertson, Jarret converts millions to his sect, Christian America, while his thugs imprison, rape and murder those they label "heathens," all the while kidnapping their children in order to raise them in Christian households. The narrative is both impassioned and bitter as Butler weaves a tale of a frighteningly believable near-future dystopia. Lauren, at once loving wife and mother, prophet and fanatic, victim and leader, gains stature as one of the most intense and well-developed protagonists in recent SF. Though not for the faint-hearted, this work stands out as a testament to the author's enormous talent, and to the human spirit.

Roberta Johnson

SOURCE: A review of *Parable of the Talents,* in *Booklist,* Vol. 95, No. 5, November 1, 1998, p. 478.

Butler concludes the spiritual and physical journey, begun in *Parable of the Sower* (1993), of Lauren Oya Olamina, an 18-year-old African American who has survived most of her family's demise and a lengthy journey on the dangerous roads of early-twenty-first-century California. She has created her own religion, Earthseed, which empowers people to master change and has as its ultimate goal the colonization of other worlds. Olamina has gathered around her a community of outcasts and wanderers that is beginning to thrive when a fundamentalist Christian wins the presidency. His zealots overrun Olamina's village, enslave the adults with pain-inflicting collars, and adopt the children into Christian American families. Olamina must somehow free herself and her followers and begin another painful journey to find her infant daughter. She is unexpectedly reunited with her brother Marcus, but instead of helping each other, they are on opposite sides of a deep religious chasm.

The novel revolves around the question of which is more important to Olamina: her fledgling religion or her own flesh and blood.

Additional coverage of Butler's life and career is contained in the following sources published by the Gale Group: *Authors and Artists for Young Adults,* **Vol. 18;** *Black Literature Criticism Supplement; Black Writers,* **Vols. 2, 3;** *Contemporary Authors,* **73-76;** *Contemporary Authors New Revision Series,* **Vols. 12, 24, 38, 73;** *Contemporary Literary Criticism,* **38, 121;** *Discovering Authors 3.0; Discovering Authors Modules: Multicultural Authors, Poets; Dictionary of Literary Biography,* **Vol. 33;** *Major 20th-Century Writers,* **and** *Something about the Author,* **Vol. 1.**

Jean Chapman
?-

Australian author, biographer, compiler, reteller, and scriptwriter.

Major works include *The Wish Cat* (1966), *Tell Me a Tale: Stories, Songs, and Things to Do* (1975), *The Sugar-Plum Christmas Book: A Book for Christmas and All the Days of the Year* (1977), *Velvet Paws and Whiskers* (1979), *Capturing the Golden Bird: The Young Hans Christian Andersen* (1988).

INTRODUCTION

Chapman is the author of numerous books reflecting her interest in fairy tales, oral traditions, holiday customs, cats, and her native Australia. Beginning with *Amelia Muddle,* a book of children's stories published in 1963, Chapman has enjoyed a long and varied literary career. Her works have won several awards, including commendations from the Australian Book Publishers Association and the Children's Book Council of Australia.

BIOGRAPHICAL INFORMATION

Chapman was born in Sydney, Australia, the youngest of three daughters born to immigrant parents, and was educated at the National Art School. With an adolescent interest in writing, she gave consideration to a career in literature but did nothing in pursuit of her profession until she was married and became a mother. She began contributing scripts to the Australian Broadcasting Commission Education Programmes and found that she enjoyed writing for children. In an interview published in 1984 in *Something About the Author,* Vol. 34, Chapman offered a glimpse into her creative process: "It's not easy to decide where or when a book begins its life before the first rough draft emerges from my typewriter. Often an idea lurks just around the corner for years, never really maturing, then with some cosseting and nurturing, some loving and hating and bullying, it may grow into a worthwhile story. Writing for me is hard work." Chapman is married to Max B. Chapman, an engineer. They live in New South Wales.

MAJOR WORKS

Chapman's works tend to cover such characteristic subjects as cats, Australian history and storytelling, holiday customs, and fairy tales. Among her most notable cat books are *The Wish Cat, Moon-Eyes* (1978), *Velvet Paws and Whiskers, Cat Will Rhyme with Hat* (1986), and *Grey Cat Magic* (1993). *Moon-Eyes,* for example, follows the adventures of a stray cat who lives in the ruins of the ancient Forum in Rome. *Cat Will Rhyme with Hat* is a collection of cat poems, including works by such authors as T. S. Eliot, J. R. R. Tolkien, and Mark Twain. Another work compiled by Chapman, *Velvet Paws and Whiskers,* contains short stories, songs, and activities grouped around the subject of cats.

Throughout her career Chapman has frequently returned to Australian topics in both her original stories and her compilations, including such works as *Wombat* (1969), *We Live in Australia* (1988), cowritten with Donna Bailey, and *Little Bill Bandicoot: Rhymes and Songs for Australian Children* (1992). In the last-named work Chapman presented a variety of Australian poems set to music, along with dramatic accompaniment so that children could act out the songs.

In the 1970s and 1980s Chapman compiled a series of well-received holiday books, notably *The Sugar-Plum Christmas Book, Pancakes and Painted Eggs,* and *Haunts and Taunts: A Book for Hallowe'en and All the Nights of the Year* (1983). Each of these works combines poems, stories, songs, and crafts depicting holiday customs around the world. According to Patricia Homer in *School Library Journal,* the "overall feel" of the Christmas collection is "one of warmth and gaiety" and the Easter collection provides "a good collection of . . . treats."

Chapman's interest in fairy tales is highlighted in several works as diverse as *Tell Me Another Tale: Stories, Verses, Songs and Things to Do* (1976) and the biography *Capturing the Golden Bird: The Young Hans Christian Andersen.* In *Tell Me Another Tale,* Chapman drew on such traditional tales as Cinderella and Red Riding Hood, combining these stories with related activities. *Capturing the Golden Bird* combines the story of Andersen's early life with ten of his most famous tales, critical commentary, and bibliographic notes. A reviewer in *Junior Bookshelf* considered the work a success and noted that no other writer had "handled the material more succinctly and engagingly than Jean Chapman."

In the mid-1990s Chapman also wrote stories about lonely children finding companionship with animals, as in *Greener Than an Emerald* (1993), in which a boy is isolated on an island with a seagull as his only companion, and *Grey Cat Magic,* in which a lonely boy takes delight in the antics of a cat. Chapman also considered relationships between members of different generations, as in *Favourite Live Thing,* in which an Italian grandmother arrives for a summer visit with two young brothers. Writing in *Magpies,* Annette Dale-Meiklejohn called the book "a delightful tale of cross-generational and cross-cultural relationships."

AWARDS

Chapman has received commendations from the Children's Book Council of Australia for *The Wish Cat* in 1966, for *Tell Me Another Tale* in 1976, and for *The Sugar-Plum Christmas Book* in 1977. *The Wish Cat* and *Velvet Paws and Whiskers* also received design awards from the Australian Book Publishers Association. In addition Chapman was the recipient of an award from the Austrian government in 1970 for a translation of *The Wish Cat* and won special commendation from the Leipzig Children's Book Fair in 1980 for *The Sugar-Plum Christmas Book.* Chapman's *Pancakes and Painted Eggs* was commended as a Christian Book of the Year in 1982, and Chapman herself was given the Lady Cutler Award for services to children's literature in 1990.

TITLE COMMENTARY

THE WISH CAT (1967)

Margery Fisher

SOURCE: A review of *The Wish Cat,* in *Growing Point,* Vol. 6, No. 5, November, 1967, p. 101.

An air of authenticity pervades this story of a young Siamese cat establishing her autocratic rule over a household. The author writes with engaging humour and a complete lack of sentimentality, and lively drawings and nicely posed photographs contribute to a cheerful book.

Bookbird

SOURCE: A review of *The Wish Cat,* in *Bookbird,* Vol. 5, No. 4, 1967, p. 28.

The Wish Cat, a picture story book for seven to 10-year-olds, is a delight for cat-lovers. The naughtiness, imperiousness and gentleness of Lisa, the Siamese who takes over the Lane family, are cleverly evoked by Noela Young's lively drawings and Dean Hay's splendid photographs....

TELL ME A TALE (1975)

Margery Fisher

SOURCE: A review of *Tell Me a Tale,* in *Growing Point,* Vol. 14, No. 5, November, 1975, p. 2751.

Many of the poems, songs and stories in this splendid collection have already been used on Australia's "Kindergarten of the Air", and there is a feeling of immediacy both in the re-tellings of traditional tales and in the singing games and finger-plays suggested for group activity. Interspersed with pieces for re-telling are suggestions for using play-dough, bubble mixture, empty egg-shells and so on. The agreeably idiosyncratic illustrations add zest to the book with their dotty people and equally dotty humanised animals frolicking in clear acid colour and firm line. This is the most lively and imaginative of the many recent books offered for infant classroom, play-school or home.

Books for Your Children

SOURCE: A review of *Tell Me a Tale,* in *Books for Your Children,* Vol. 11, No. 2, Spring, 1976, p. 5.

Here is a... lavish book for the pre-reading stage that will also go on giving pleasure right through until around 10. A wonderful collection of stories, rhymes and songs with related play activities and invaluable recipes for such things as home-made paste and bubble-blowing mixture. The amusing drawings and beautiful design together with the language of the stories, which is not the language of every-day speech, make this a very special choice. It is very important that young children should be hearing language from books as well as developing their own modes of speech.

TELL ME ANOTHER TALE (1977)

Margery Fisher

SOURCE: A review of *Tell Me Another Tale,* in *Growing Point,* Vol. 15, No. 9, April, 1977, p. 3092.

The stories in this second collection for the very young are mainly traditional (Cinderella and Red Riding Hood among nursery favourites, and a number of animal fables). Plenty of finger games, rounds and suggestions for simple activities like cooking frankfurters, making and playing musical instruments and constructing a seed mosaic provide variety. The illustrations, some in colour, are as entertaining as the items that are potentially useful for parents and teachers of under-eights.

The Junior Bookshelf

SOURCE: A review of *Tell Me Another Tale,* in *The Junior Bookshelf,* Vol. 40, No. 4, August, 1977, p. 215.

A bumper book from Australia of stories, poems, jokes, nursery songs, and activities for the young child. Some of the stories are traditional fairy-tales newly told, while some are new. Throughout the book the theme of one item is linked with that of the next two or three following items, so that the child's imagination is strengthened in certain directions. A pleasing book for the family, or the nursery and infant school.

THE SUGAR-PLUM CHRISTMAS BOOK: A BOOK FOR CHRISTMAS AND ALL THE DAYS OF THE YEAR (1977)

Anne Woods

SOURCE: A review of *The Sugar-Plum Christmas Book,* in *Books for Your Children,* Vol. 13, No. 1, Winter, 1977, p. 9.

We have just received a lovely fun collection, **The Sugar-Plum Christmas Book** by Jean Chapman. Illustrated by Deborah Niland. . . . A celebration of Christmas in a collection of stories, songs, pictures, rhymes and things to do for young children—4-10. Could be a real family treasure. Very amusing, highly successful coloured pictures.

Margery Fisher

SOURCE: A review of *The Sugar-Plum Christmas Book,* in *Growing Point,* Vol. 16, No. 6, December, 1977, p. 3231.

Stories, poems, activities reflecting customs from many lands for the twelve days of Christmas are linked by passages from the New Testament, the shepherds and kings and the Nativity providing a fo-

cal point for varied entries. Most of the suggestions for performing carols with percussion or clapping, for making Christmas decorations and delicacies, are familiar enough but Deborah Niland's pictures, quirky but less self-conscious than usual, give the book a new look.

Patricia Homer

SOURCE: A review of *The Sugar-Plum Christmas Book: A Book for Christmas and All the Days of the Year,* in *School Library Journal,* Vol. 29, No. 10, August, 1983, pp. 62-3.

Originally published in Australia, this book is a merry potpourri of Christmas stories, poems, carols and crafts. The Biblical Christmas story is included, as well as many modern and traditional folk Christmas tales, such as "The Nutcracker," "The Little Juggler of Chartres" and "A Visit from St. Nicholas." Most selections lead into a craft, poem, game or carol based on the theme. The illustrations are charming. The directions for the crafts are much too general, giving no specific step-by-step instructions or diagrams to show how things go together, and the number of Briticisms render many descriptions of materials needed incomprehensible to American readers. However, there are things here that are not in other Christmas collections and the overall feel of the book is one of warmth and gaiety.

THE SUGAR-PLUM SONG BOOK (1977)

Margery Fisher

SOURCE: A review of *The Sugar-Plum Song Book,* in *Growing Point,* Vol. 16, No. 7, January, 1978, p. 3248.

The sub-title "Christmas Songs" instead of the more usual "Carols" indicates the wide choice of items, from the time-honoured "Away in a Manger" and that primary school staple "Rocking" to a Negro spiritual and a Chilean crêche-song side by side with "Dame get up and bake your pies" and the "Twelve Days of Christmas". Margaret Moore's one-stave settings for singers include suggestions for simple guitar accompaniment and there is advice on performance with each entry. The quaint, toylike illustrations show a timely control of the artist's sometimes excessive exuberance.

MOON-EYES (1978)

Margery Fisher

SOURCE: A review of *Moon-Eyes,* in *Growing Point,* Vol. 17, No. 4, November, 1978, p. 3427.

The interlaced characters of the story, a stray cat and the city of Rome, are strongly portrayed in vital, descriptive pictures, rich in colour, alternating with marginal and round-text drawings that should help young readers through an extended, discursive text which plays the guide through the streets, into a church and a restaurant, in a nostalgic but persuasive manner.

Anna Biagioni Hart

SOURCE: A review of *Moon-Eyes,* in *School Library Journal,* Vol. 27, No. 1, September, 1980, p. 57.

Moon-Eyes, one of the hungry, stray cats that inhabits the Roman Forum, sets out on a Christmas Eve journey to find shelter and warmth. He ends in comfort among the straw of a Franciscan church's nativity scene, with ample food and security as the parish mouser. Attractive pen-and-ink sketches, some with a color wash, illustrate every page of this story. The author is knowledgeable about Italian life and customs, but her awkward prose doesn't give life to the setting or narrative. A sentence or two is simply unintelligible: "'scram! he said, stamping his feet. 'scram! Il gatto, hop it!'" Her use of 12 Italian words does little but annoy since the nouns interrupt the action without enlightening readers. The book's endpaper glossary is attractive but incomplete. Italian words are partially explained without connotations and additional comment that might have sparked this promising but disappointing book.

Bulletin of the Center for Children's Books

SOURCE: A review of *Moon-Eyes,* in *The Bulletin of the Center for Children's Books,* Vol. 34, No. 2, October, 1980, p. 28.

First published in Australia, an oversize book is lavishly illustrated with pictures in black and white and color; a Christmas story set in Rome, this describes the adventures of a scrawny, half-feral cat, Moon-Eyes. Trapped on a ledge, the little cat is tense when a child pets him, but his fear fades away and he begins to purr with joy as he is stroked. He follows the child when she leaves, is treated harshly when he gets into a restaurant and then into a Christmas manger scene. Finally he comes into a church and there sleeps in the warm straw of the Christmas crib. A worshipper is horrified, but the kindly priest says that it isn't an insult to the Holy Family, it is just another animal in Christ's manger. And so Moon-Eyes becomes the church cat, loved and content. The pictures are nicely composed and softly colored; the story is uneven in pace and verges on sentimentality, but it's adequately told.

Children's Book Review Service

SOURCE: A review of *Moon-Eyes,* in *Children's Book Review Service Inc.,* Vol. 8, No. 14, August, 1980, p. 135.

Moon-Eyes, a Roman Forum cat, knows no other life than the cold impersonal one of a stray cat until he unexpectedly experiences the warmth of a little girl's touch. The book not only presents an engaging story, but also very clear, accurate physical descriptions of the cat's actions and reactions to people and situations. The very descriptive language combined with the length of the story may make it inappropriate for the intended audience; however, the book will be enjoyed by those children who are able to appreciate the language, and be satisfied with a minimum of illustration. A glossary is included to help with the many Italian words that are used throughout the story.

VELVET PAWS AND WHISKERS (1980)

Margery Fisher

SOURCE: A review of *Velvet Paws and Whiskers,* in *Growing Point,* Vol. 19, No. 1, May, 1980, p. 3695.

Velvet Paws and Whiskers would make a good standby for bedtime reading, since this anthology of cat-pieces ranges from songs and nursery rhymes for the youngest to anecdotes and longer poems which older children could read for themselves, while they could also take up the suggestions for cooking, model-making and other activities. The book is copiously illustrated in the chunky, semi-grotesque style by now familiar; the Niland cat is as recognisable as the Burningham dog, with a similar half-human repertoire of facial expressions. Both in black-and-white and in strident paint the pictures add an extra flavour of humour and fantasy to the light-hearted items. Author and illustrator reveal themselves on the back end-paper as cats of jocose and friendly aspect, another point to attract children to browse through the book for themselves.

The Junior Bookshelf

SOURCE: A review of *Velvet Paws and Whiskers,* in *The Junior Bookshelf,* Vol. 44, No. 4, August, 1980, pp. 186-87.

This is basically a book of ideas, united (sometimes only loosely) by the theme of cats. There are also nursery rhymes, traditional songs with the melody line, folk tales, fairy tales and a few more modern ones. They are all retold in a somewhat uniform junior-school classroom style (for which place this is an obvious source-book: a pity if thereby children are deprived of the illustrations). There are too many "pussies" for most tastes, and an unfortunate confusion over the use of "may" and "might", while the value of the instructions for things to do is somewhat variable, as are the explanations of "cat"-phrases, and some of the questions directed at the reader would have benefited from an answer at the end of the book. Despite all this, however, much useful material has been brought together here, and its presentation almost wholly redeemed by Deborah Niland's outstanding illustrations in black and white and soft colours. Her vigorous knowing cats riot round the pages, humorously transforming the most mundane snippet of information, while a small dog appears frequently as a kind of cheer-leader at the bottom of the pages: altogether delicious.

Margaret L. Chatham

SOURCE: A review of *Velvet Paws and Whiskers,* in *School Library Journal,* Vol. 29, No. 7, March, 1983, p. 172.

This is an anthology of 24 short stories about cats, with verses, songs and activities which have a tenuous connection to the stories. The contents are either readily available elsewhere ("The Owl and the Pussycat") or eminently forgettable (discussion of cat's cradle with only a single drawing to even hint at how it's played). Chapman flattens all the stories with a style that knows only two means of emphasis—repetition and exclamation points. When she gives instructions, both the Australian vocabulary and the lack of complete sentences make them hard to follow. The cheerful, colorful cartoon illustrations and attractive format cannot rescue this dismal book.

📖 *PANCAKES & PAINTED EGGS: A BOOK FOR EASTER AND ALL THE DAYS OF THE YEAR* (1981)

Margery Fisher

SOURCE: A review of *Pancakes and Painted Eggs,* in *Growing Point,* Vol. 20, No. 3, September, 1981, p. 3951.

A collection based on Easter festivals and traditions, with a few stories ('The Selfish Giant' being one),

seasonal poems, recipes for pretzels, hot cross buns and pancakes, instructions for decorating eggs, and explanations of the ceremonies associated with, for example, Maundy Thursday and Palm Sunday. Illustrations in cheerful colour alternate with quaint black and white figures, and on many of the pages a rabbit comments caustically on the entries. An exhilarating collection for children round seven or eight.

Denise M. Wilms

SOURCE: A review of *Pancakes and Painted Eggs: A Book for Easter and All the Days of the Year* and *The Sugar-Plum Christmas Book: A Book for Christmas and All the Days of the Year,* in *Booklist,* Vol. 79, No. 12, February 15, 1983.

Chapman offers two seasonal anthologies that will aid librarians struggling to meet heavy Christmas and Easter demands. Each book offers a blend of stories, poems, lore, songs, and simple craft and game activities. *Pancakes and Painted Eggs* begins appropriately with the story of Christ's death and resurrection, but its contents speak not only to the Christian feast but to spring and renewal as well. Activities include blowing eggs, knitting a lamb, making candles, or baking a rabbit cake. Stories are mainly pieces of folklore, though Oscar Wilde's "The Selfish Giant" appears too. Songs are presented with only a melody line. *The Sugar-Plum Christmas Book* follows a similar pattern, with the Nativity story appearing early on, but with secular legend and lore also getting a nod. Santa is not a prominent figure; sample contents include instructions for making snowflakes and a pink sugar mouse, a retelling of *The Nutcracker,* and assorted verses and songs, which are not necessarily familiar ones. The books are sturdy and generally attractive. Light cartoon drawings, some in color, provide clean illustration. Handy in the right place.

Patricia Homer

SOURCE: A review of *Pancakes and Painted Eggs: A Book for Easter and All the Days of the Year,* in *School Library Journal,* Vol. 29, No. 8, April, 1983, p. 111.

This Easter anthology includes explanations of customs through song, poetry, prose and activities. The book is illustrated with full-color cartoon-like figures and animals. Directions for crafts and recipes are all well explained and diagrams are given for construction. Some choices seem a bit odd. It is as if the stories were chosen only because they fit in with one of the book's subthemes: i.e., new clothes—"The Emperor's New Clothes." Poets include William Blake, Christina Rossetti and Coleridge; there are also anonymous and traditional poems. On the whole this is a good collection of Easter treats.

SUPERMARKET THURSDAY (1986)

Naomi Lewis

SOURCE: A review of *Supermarket Thursday,* in *Times Educational Supplement,* No. 3649, June 6, 1986, p. 54.

In *Supermarket Thursday* . . . the reliable Jean Chapman provides five stories for under-fives: doll nearly lost in wrong shopping basket; trying out newly learnt counting skills on the stairs; night noises (wuff, wuff, waa waa—that's baby crying, milkman, paperboy); plenty of dialogue, sound and detail. Nice stuff for nice parents or teachers to read to the restless young. They can all be read a second time and a third and that's the test. With pleasant ordinary pictures by Astra Lacis.

THE TALL BOOK OF TALL TALES (1986)

Stephen Corrin

SOURCE: A review of *The Tall Book of Tall Tales,* in *Times Educational Supplement,* No. 3657, August 1, 1986, p. 21.

Jean Chapman's volume of tall tales, in a format to match its title, is a spanking gallimaufry of walloping fibs: the further removed from the possible the jollier they get. Mrs Chapman belongs to the breed of born storytellers, it's no wonder the National Book League nabs her the moment she lands here from down under. Apart from Australia, various countries are represented—Italy, Russia, Ireland, France and Germany. Tales about the dead, fear of the dead or the dupes of pretend ghosts are narrated with a robust raciness and a certain stylish panache. Baron Münchausen looms large, even putting his name to one of the stories.

CAT WILL RHYME WITH HAT: A BOOK OF POEMS (1987)

Carolyn Phelan

SOURCE: A review of *Cat Will Rhyme with Hat: A Book of Poems,* in *Booklist,* Vol. 83, No. 11, February 1, 1987, p. 894.

A fine collection of cat poems, some written especially for children, though most are not. The 49 poets represented here include such noteworthy writers as John Ciardi, Elizabeth Coatsworth, Walter De la Mare, T. S. Eliot, Eleanor Farjeon, X. J. Kennedy, Rudyard Kipling, Eve Merriam, Christopher Morley, Ogden Nash, J. R. R. Tolkien, Mark Twain, William Wordsworth, and W. B. Yeats. Divided into seven thematic sections, this offering is illustrated with a full-page drawing at the beginning of each division. Parnall's graceful, shaded work is somehow more personal and more humorous than the spare, clean lines of his familiar pen-and-ink illustrations and effectively introduces each section without intruding upon the reader's vision. Varied in mood and style, the verses are linked by a common theme with definite child appeal.

Judy Greenfield

SOURCE: A review of *Cat Will Rhyme with Hat: A Book of Poems,* in *School Library Journal,* Vol. 33, No. 7, April, 1987, p. 92.

Readers need not love cats to enjoy these 61 poems about them. Don't be misled by the title, taken from a four-line verse by Spike Milligan. This is *not* an easy reader. It includes challenges such as T. S. Eliot's "Macavity: The Mystery Cat," W. B. Yeats' "The Cat and the Moon" and Ted Hughes' "Pets." Lighter pieces include Ogden Nash's "The Kitten" and Doug McLeod's "Kitty." More obscure is "Pangur Ban" by an unknown 8th-Century monastic student and translated from Gaelic. The variety makes this a lively and interesting single theme collection. Each one of its eight sections focuses on a type of cat (kitten, witch's cat, Tom). Parnall's amusing full-page pencil illustrations introduce each section. Sources are listed in front, with title, author, and first line indexes in back.

Carolyn Phelan

SOURCE: A review of *Cat Will Rhyme with Hat,* in *Book Links,* Vol. 87, No. 6, November 15, 1990, p. 644.

This cat anthology . . . , introduces each section with a spare pencil drawing that perfectly captures a feline mood or activity; the individual poems conjure their own images.

□ *CAPTURING THE GOLDEN BIRD: THE YOUNG HANS CHRISTIAN ANDERSEN* (1988)

The Junior Bookshelf

SOURCE: A review of *Capturing the Golden Bird: The Young Hans Christian Andersen,* in *The Junior Bookshelf,* Vol. 52, No. 2, April, 1988, p. 98.

The life-story of Andersen has been told before for young readers, but none, I think, has handled the material more succinctly and engagingly than Jean Chapman. This Australian writer has researched her subject on the ground in Denmark, and she captures the atmosphere of a small nineteenth-century town and uncovers the inhibitions imposed by provincialism and poverty on a child who is strong on genius and lacking in direction. Ms Chapman concentrates on the early years, which are so much more interesting and important than the years of fame, and she keeps her story deliberately short in order to make room for ten of the tales, chosen from different stages of the writer's development. To each of these she appends a short evaluative and bibliographical note, written in a tone which will appeal equally to children and adult readers. Altogether a job done imaginatively and well. Sandra Laroche's illustrations—chapter-heads for the biography, full-page for the tales—are in spirited silhouette, rather like the scissorcuts which Andersen himself loved to do. They are most deftly done, and have something of the blend of sentiment and self-mockery which is the Andersen hallmark.

□ *COCKATOO SOUP* (1988)

Belle Alderman

SOURCE: A review of *Cockatoo Soup,* in *Booklist,* Vol. 85, No. 4, October 15, 1988, p. 420.

This anthology, filled with verse, stories, customs, songs, games, riddles, crafts, and more, has been collected from various cultures and previous generations, beginning with Aboriginal lore and ending in mid-twentieth century. Copious, attractive illustrations.

□ *MY MUM'S AFRAID OF LIONS* (1990)

The Junior Bookshelf

SOURCE: A review of *My Mum's Afraid of Lions,* in *The Junior Bookshelf,* Vol. 54, No. 5, October, 1990, p. 228.

Here are six chapters in the life of Katie, a little girl in the real world with a taste for fantasy. She indulges this in the first story when, bored with a minor illness, Katie conjures figures from television—cricketers and a lion—to leave the set and come into her room. The writer is at her least happy in this story. The others are of more homely events, such as a very small adventure in the supermarket, a bring-and-buy sale at school (Katie buys back her own contribution)—realistic magic with the Tooth Fairy, a seaside holiday, and a vacuum-cleaner monster.

Short-stories for young children are always in short supply, and there should be a warm welcome for these charming and apparently artless little tales, each about the right length for bedtime reading. Ms Chapman is very sound on child behaviour. Her portraits are full of affection without a trace of sentimentality. Young readers will have no difficulty in recognising themselves while laughing at Katie's small dilemmas. Astra Lacis' illustrations, about half of them in colour, are a good accompaniment.

□ *LITTLE BILLY BANDICOOT: RHYMES AND SONGS FOR AUSTRALIAN CHILDREN* (1992)

Hugh McCann

SOURCE: A review of *Little Billy Bandicoot: Rhymes and Songs for Australian Children,* in *Magpies,* Vol. 7, No. 4, September, 1992, p. 24.

Verse for children should be a source of delight in language and in reading. Shared properly, adults and children can enjoy the beginning of joyful language study. Verse is one of the important ways in which early readers can be assisted into delight in saying and savouring words, sharing and reading. Verse allows child and carer to focus on the sounds and rhythms of language.

This collection provides examples of verse which have musical versions, verse which can be accompanied by action—finger play and movement—verse which has been written in Australia. It also provides examples of verse from around the English-speaking world including the word play which belongs to nonsense verse. Accompanying many of the choices there are suggestions of what activities parents or carers might try out to add to the pleasures of verse.

The illustrations are strewn throughout the text, placed closely to each of the verses. They will assist many young readers and encourage them to look more closely at some of the verses.

Both Jean Chapman and Sandra Laroche have contributed quite widely to literature for the young. Jean Chapman, who has contributed to television and radio for children, has been honoured for her contributions to literature for children in Australia.

This is an attractive book which provides a linguistically helpful collection for use with children.

GREENER THAN AN EMERALD (1994)

Alan Horsfield

SOURCE: A review of *Greener than an Emerald,* in *Magpies,* Vol. 9, No. 3, July, 1994, p. 28.

This book is set on a remote tropical island where Kem, a young boy, lives alone. He does not fully appreciate the natural beauties of his world. He enjoys solitude but is never lonely and rejects approaches made by a pesky young sea gull to befriend him. The island is almost destroyed by a violent storm and Kem and the gull are separated. Only then does Kem come to terms with his surroundings and animals which share his battered world. Kem witnesses the small changes in nature that herald the island's regeneration. Through his efforts he also takes part in the change by rebuilding his fragile world. He has a serious self-sufficiency that is a little unreal. There are no flashy, spontaneous smiles. There is none of that vivacity that one associates with such children. I felt a little uncomfortable with the idea of a lone child, with no family or extended family, somehow abandoned to a comfortable but futile existence.

OFF TO SCHOOL (1996)

Liz Waterland

SOURCE: A review of *Off to School,* in *Books for Keeps,* No. 96, January, 1996, p. 6.

It's a little disconcerting to find that the name of the publisher is three times the size of the title and author on the cover but, with that reservation, this is an excellent book for the teacher or parent of a reception-aged child. Seven stories about everyday happenings in Lisa's school year will be interesting and informative for any four- or five-year-old, and those a little older will enjoy the feeling of recognition if they read it for themselves. Many children will wonder if the school Santa is the real one or not!

FAVOURITE LIVE THING (1994)

Annette Dale-Meiklejohn

SOURCE: A review of *Favourite Live Thing,* in *Magpies,* Vol. 11, No. 4, September, 1996, pp. 31-2.

In this brief novel Chapman presents a delightful tale of cross-generational and cross-cultural relationships as two young boys make room in their lives for their Nonna. Nonna is visiting from Italy and the story opens with the preparations for her arrival which, as the family lives in a small unit, means the boys must share a room. The manner in which each boy reacts is realistically and sympathetically presented and provides the base for their character development throughout the story.

As the story progresses the boys learn to come to terms with *Kissing Nonna,* as the younger brother privately calls her, and to love her for who she is. Nonna demonstrates considerable humour, love and resourcefulness, especially as the day of the school *faint* approaches and Mark needs cakes for his class stall and, even more tricky, Paul needs a favourite live thing for his class contribution. All seems to be settled when disaster occurs and Paul's entry is missing. The solution is found by Paul himself and provides a lovely conclusion to this well-told tale.

Favourite Live Thing is part of the *Storybridge* series which is aimed at the middle primary school aged reader. This novel certainly fits that area, with its well-defined and believable characters of both genders and all ages and its storyline which introduces a sub-plot without complicating the reading task for this age-group. Its cover should appeal to the target audience and its contents should ensure peer-recommendations; it would also work well as a class read-aloud in middle primary classes.

Additional coverage of Chapman's life and career is contained in the following sources published by the Gale Group: *Contemporary Authors,* **Vols. 97-100 and** *Something about the Author,* **Vols. 34, 104.**

David Diaz
1958-

American illustrator.

Major works include *Neighborhood Odes* (1992), *Smoky Night* (1994), *Wilma Unlimited* (1996), *The Inner City Mother Goose* (1996), *The Disappearing Alphabet* (1998).

INTRODUCTION

Diaz is the illustrator of *Smoky Night*, the surprise winner of the 1995 Caldecott Medal. Combining an expressive color palette with such collage elements as breakfast cereal and wire hangers, Diaz's illustrations gave a sense of immediacy to Eve Bunting's simple story of a child observing the Los Angeles riots in 1992. Although some commentators found the subject ill-suited to young readers, the illustrator maintained that "the book could have a positive effect and help erode barriers of prejudice and intolerance. And above all, it was a book that could be part of the post-riot healing process."

BIOGRAPHICAL INFORMATION

Diaz was born in Fort Lauderdale, Florida. He met his wife, Cecelia, in eleventh grade and attended Fort Lauderdale Art Institute. Diaz and his wife moved to California in 1979, where he worked a variety of odd jobs, including Fotomat operator, while he tried to gain assignments as a freelance illustrator. The Diazes have three children.

Before illustrating books for major publishers, Diaz created numerous unpublished books documenting his life and travels. Incorporating found objects into his signature thick-outlined paintings, these works anticipate the style of his professional career. Furthermore, it was this work that landed Diaz commissions illustrating Gary Soto's *Neighborhood Odes*, as well as Bunting's *Smoky Night*, both for Harcourt.

MAJOR WORKS

In *Neighborhood Odes*, Gary Soto's poems explore aspects of living in a Hispanic part of the city. Diaz's

black-and-white paper cut-outs complement twenty-one poems about fireworks, tortillas, the library, and other subjects. His work on *Smoky Night*, by contrast, is full of eccentric color choices. People's faces range from blue to green to purple. The reviewer from *Publishers Weekly* said, "Even the artwork here cautions the reader against assumptions about race." Loaded with collage elements that add detail and mystery, the illustrations for *Smoky Night* bring out elements suggested by the words of the story in unexpected ways. For example, when Bunting writes about a man "staggering under a pile of clothes taken from the dry cleaners," Diaz shows the man, but another part of the page comprises a photographic view of the crinkling plastic bag covering the clothes and the twisted wire forming the hook of a hanger. These illustrations supplement the text rather than commenting on it, and their earnest and heartfelt tone does not mean they are dull. Hazel Rochman, writing in *Booklist*, called the artwork "powerful—pulsating and crowded; part street mural, part urban collage."

Not all of the criticism of *Smoky Night* was favorable. Selma G. Lanes, in *The Horn Book Magazine*, complained that Diaz's pictures "are so tasteful and low-key, given the charged subject matter, that we are hardly aware of what is happening." Writing in *Teaching and Learning Literature*, Michael Patrick Hearn sneered, "I never imagined a riot could appear quite so benign as this."

Wilma Unlimited: How Wilma Rudolph Became the World's Fastest Woman tells the life story of the famous athlete, focusing on the childhood obstacles that threatened her dreams. Rudolph suffered from scarlet fever and polio, and doctors predicted she would never walk without metal braces. Diaz zeroes in on these braces, and they become the silent, menacing villain of the story, finished for good when Rudolph takes three Olympic gold medals in 1960. Diaz also designed the type for this book. A reviewer from *Horn Book* wrote that the illustrations capture the athlete's "physical and emotional determination, as well as the beauty of her body in motion."

Eve Merriam wrote *The Inner City Mother Goose* in 1969, and the harsh, frank book had a profound impact on children's literature. Among the most-quoted lines from this modern classic are: "Now I lay me down to sleep / I pray the double lock will keep." For the 1996 edition, the publisher Simon & Schuster included an introduction by the prominent African American author Nikki Giovanni and new illustrations by Diaz. Carolyn Phelan of *Booklist* celebrated how the "images, almost mythic in their sense of representing more than individual people, seem to move with the rhythm of the verse."

In *The Disappearing Alphabet*, the poet Richard Wilbur imagines what would happen if, one by one, the letters of the alphabet were taken away. Without an N, for example, "Birds would have WIGS instead of WINGS." The illustrations, termed "friendly" and "eclectic" by *New York Times* reviewer David Sacks, show a different side of Diaz's artistic temperament, which is often associated with the multicultural melting pot of the American city.

AWARDS

Smoky Night won the 1995 Caldecott Medal, awarded by the American Library Association.

AUTHOR COMMENTARY

David Diaz

SOURCE: "Caldecott Medal Acceptance," in *The Horn Book Magazine,* Vol. LXXI, No. 4, July-August, 1995, pp. 430-33.

Superstition runs deep in certain publishing companies. For instance, the word Caldecott is taboo. If that word is mentioned with reference to a particular book, it will jinx it. I am so thankful to the people at Harcourt for not uttering "that word" over **Smoky Night**! Because early one morning this past February, something quite extraordinary happened in my life. I was honored as the recipient of the 1995 Caldecott Medal. Every day I am overwhelmed with joy and gratitude for this prestigious award. My son Jericho, who is twelve, said, "I have always heard of other families being famous, but I never thought it would happen to us!" But my five-year-old son, Ariel, wonders, "How come I didn't get a Caldecott? I draw better than Dad."

I recall 1966, sitting in my first-grade class and receiving a mimeographed work sheet. The class had

just come in from squinting into the clear blue Florida sky, trying to pick out a wisp of vapor trail from one of the space launches at Cape Canaveral. On the mimeographed paper there were twelve squares, and within each square a drawing. Underneath each drawing was a word that could be completed with a vowel. Near the center of the page were the letters N_SE and above them the profile of a nose. I filled in the blank with the vowel O and afterward drew lines to the nose that made a profile of a face. That was when I first realized I wanted to be a "draw-er." I had no idea what an illustrator, designer, or art director was. What I knew was that I had found my gift: drawing pictures.

There were a few things in high school that propelled me toward a career in illustration. One was meeting Cecelia, my wife. After a year of sarcastic banter, we became close friends. The focus of my time in art class became seeing how much I could distract her from her weavings and batiks. But she taught me about color and how to see color. About the colors you can miss if you're not paying attention. Like the color of black licorice when you bite into it—a kind of greenish, brownish, yellow black. At the time my work was dominated by grays and muted tones. Cecelia opened my eyes to vivid color, and I began to use it.

The second key thing was having a great art instructor, Sandra Tobe. She had a gift for motivating students, and she encouraged us to enter numerous competitions. She showed us that there were jobs out there doing artwork. Money for pictures! Through her I was introduced to Duane Hanson, the hyperrealist sculptor. I apprenticed with him for years, through high school and art school. While working for Duane, I was exposed to a lot of the superrealist movement through his personal collection. I was drawn to the movement, and my work—very tight realistic pieces—reflected it. I labored intensely, sixty to eighty hours, over a drawing six inches square. I drew tiny circles with a razor-sharp pencil to create a rich, gradual tonal quality, almost like a photograph. Until, while working on an assignment at three a.m., I thought, "Why not just take a photograph? Think of all the time it would save." Determined to find another approach to drawing, I began to experiment with a variety of techniques. A turning point finally came when I saw the German Expressionist show at the Guggenheim in 1980. I saw beautiful work that conveyed the emotion of the artists with immediate, direct line. Bold, simple, loose brush strokes.

Another influence on my development as an artist was the work of William Steig. I found a copy of his book *Male/Female* (Farrar) in a used bookstore. I was immediately drawn in by the depth of characterization he conveyed in so few lines. I sought out other Steig books. As I became more acquainted with his drawings, I saw an evolution in his work that I recognized, as he moved from tightly rendered pieces toward a looser line.

In 1979, when I arrived in San Diego, I began to show my portfolio and to receive editorial assignments. Although the pay was low, these assignments allowed me a lot of room for experimentation. I had the freedom to work in a variety of mediums: oil, acrylics, pen and ink, watercolor, woodcuts, scratchboard—as many as I could find. Typically, at the end of an assignment, there would be some materials left over. I would take those and make a small piece as a thank-you for the art director who had given me the job. I'd send it along with the completed work. The response to these pieces was very positive, and I realized I'd hit upon a very effective way of promoting my work. These personal gift pieces allowed me to find my own direction in drawing and to become comfortable with the way I drew naturally. And, of course, the ideas I worked out in these personal pieces found their way into the work I did for assignments. These gift pieces eventually evolved into limited edition books that Cecelia and I collaborated in producing at the end of the year.

There is nothing like receiving a piece made by hand. Part of the ethic of the arts-and-crafts movement was the idea that as you were surrounded by pieces made by hand, your life would be enriched. Furniture, ceramics, textiles, and books all bore the mark of the craftsman's hand. These "touch of the hand" pieces were a format for my personal work and sometimes resulted in assignments specifically requesting a new style.

The distinction between work for assignments and personal work narrowed. In 1989 I began to experiment with a series of bold, loose, brush-stroke faces. My goal was to create an image without hesitation, lifting the brush from the surface as few times as possible. I believed that once I hesitated with the brush stroke, I'd pause to question what I was doing rather than complete the piece in one stream of thought. I wanted to put down on paper exactly what I had imagined. I experimented with this style for about three years. In 1992, while visiting my brother in Brazil, I worked on a series of faces as we traveled down the Amazon River. That series was incorporated into our year-end book *Sweet Peas.* We combined the faces with text and with objects found and

made. For example, we bound in one spread a latex glove, in another a postcard from the 1930s. One page was a piece of waxed paper. During that year, Diane D'Andrade at Harcourt Brace contacted me to illustrate *Neighborhood Odes* by Gary Soto. I stopped by Harcourt's office to give her a copy of *Sweet Peas.* When she saw it, she said, "I have a manuscript I haven't known who to assign to! Seeing what you've done here, I'd like you to take a look at it." Of course, the manuscript was *Smoky Night.* I saw its possibilities right away. Eve Bunting had taken a timely subject and had handled it in a truly sensitive and thoughtful way. I felt the book could have a positive effect and help erode barriers of prejudice and intolerance. And above all, it was a book that could be part of the post-riot healing process.

I wanted to do *Smoky Night.* And I wanted the art to have the same dignity as the manuscript. Although I had done hundreds of faces and images in this style, I was challenged by the job of carrying out character continuity through the book. I wanted *Smoky Night* to achieve a balance between the text, the design, the painted illustrations, and the collaged backgrounds. I wanted each element to add to the book and to create a cohesive unit.

One decision I made was to use the same color palette for all the characters in the story. I did this to avoid any indication of ethnic background, and to let their personalities speak for themselves.

I would like to thank the members of the Caldecott Committee for selecting and awarding *Smoky Night* the Caldecott Medal.

I want to thank Eve Bunting for her wonderful manuscript.

At Harcourt Brace I'd like to thank Rubin Pfeffer, who, when he had reviewed the folded and gathered sheets for *Smoky Night,* called me to say, "*Smoky Night* is a book that raises the level of what a children's picture book can be"; Louise Howton, for the freedom to design and create *Smoky Night;* Diane D'Andrade, my editor, who had the vision and insight into my work to give me *Smoky Night* to illustrate; William Steig for pointing the way; and, most of all, my sweet wife, Cecelia, who always believed and knew what could be.

Jackie Peck and Judy Hendershot with David Diaz

SOURCE: An interview in *The Reading Teacher,* Vol. 49, No. 5, February, 1996, pp. 386-88.

Soon after *Smoky Night* was named the 1995 Caldecott Winner, questions about its suitability for young readers were raised. David Diaz, whose illustrations won the award, gave his view of this controversy in an interview with *Reading Teacher* associate editors Jackie Peck and Judy Hendershot.

[David Diaz:] There's been some controversy about whether a book dealing with this subject . . . should be considered a children's book. . . . I think that . . . kids today . . . need to have as much information as possible to deal with issues. *Smoky Night* handles this issue in a way that's really thoughtful and considerate, and the purpose of the book is to cause discussion, to cause evaluation of attitudes towards people who are different than you. And it really accomplishes that.

[*Reading Teacher:*] *How does an illustrator handle a sensitive issue, such as the violence of an urban riot, thoughtfully and considerately for young readers? For David, it involved moving beyond a particular setting of time and place to capture the broader sense of the story.*

I didn't go to Los Angeles. I didn't go to the site. Typically the way that I illustrate is, you know, I'll sit down with a roll of tissue paper and just begin sketching. I try not to use references in an attempt to simplify a lot of images. . . . There's no time in the book when Los Angeles is mentioned at all. And I think that will help this book transcend the next time.

David began work on **Smoky Night** *by breaking the text into 14 segments that captured 14 individual scenes because "that's typically how long a children's picture book is." Then he began to sketch the scenes.*

I did brush stroke drawings of [the scenes] and submitted them to Harcourt Brace. They were approved. Then the next part was designing the book and I approached [it] with the idea of creating these collage backgrounds for the book . . . if we could come up with a photography budget for it.

Harcourt Brace budgeted the funds "and the collages just kind of grew." David allowed "space on each spread for the typography" and then designed the collages and shot them to size.

The collage backgrounds reflect David's work in media other than illustration.

I do ceramics as well as illustration. . . . There's ceramic work in there. Almost everything here is from

a recycled product. There's newspaper shredding, handmade paper, post-waste board.

These materials were purposefully chosen by David to maintain the integrity of the story.

What I wanted to do, essentially, with the design . . . was to create this book that had these same elements appearing over several pages . . . say, the shredded newspaper thing that appears in a couple of different spreads. It created this book that wasn't just text and illustration. It became this one, big cohesive unit. . . . I just wanted it to be continuous throughout, that feeling of . . . chaos in the background. And then in some of them where . . . they deal with the friend of his mother and where they've got the cat, the mood and the background changes to match the illustration.

Surprisingly, this incredibly effective use of mixed media was the first time David used collage in his work. "It was all experimentation, I must say that."

David told us that **Smoky Night** *was completed about 18 months before the formal presentation of the Caldecott Award in June, 1995. Readers of picture books often wonder about how long an illustrator works to complete a book. We asked David about the length of time he spent working through the entire* **Smoky Night** *process.*

It was in the office for about 9 months, and during that time I worked on other projects as well. . . . It goes back and forth with the editor, you know, experimenting with the book and the design.

We were also curious about how David originally connected with the **Smoky Night** *project. He explained that Harcourt Brace was "one of the first clients I had out of art school when I came to San Diego." David estimated that he had designed 75 book covers for Harcourt Brace. Then in 1992 he illustrated a book of poetry,* **Neighborhood Odes** *by Gary Soto. The editor of this project, Diane D'Andrade, later saw another of his books,* **Sweet Peas,** *a limited edition collection of drawings (now unavailable) David did when in Brazil visiting his brother on the Amazon.*

They were brush stroke, figural, loose lines . . . and along with [them] I used typography and other elements injected into the bindings of each spread in the book. So [Diane] saw that book and said, "You know, I've had this manuscript here for a couple of months and haven't known who to assign it to. And I really like what you've got going on here. I'd kind of like you to . . . read it over and tell me what you think about doing it. . . . I'd like you to do it." So that was **Smoky Night.**

We told David we thought the illustrations showed influences of or similarities to French expressionistic or Fauvistic work, such as that of George Roualt. David graciously responded.

Oh no! You know what's funny is that . . . the comparison is well taken. But when I created these pieces I had no interpretation of any particular style in mind. It just seemed . . . the appropriate way to represent these characters. I tried to use the same color palette throughout on all the different characters so that there's no indication of any ethnic background or nationality. There are only two times in the book where a last name is given—and that's Mrs. Kim and Mr. Rodriguez—and other than that, the characters are open to interpretation . . . each person can be like pink and green and yellow and blue all at the same time.

The loose brush strokes seen in **Smoky Night** *illustrations are a style David has been developing through his personal work of the past 3 years. His goal is to* "continue to have a loose brush style and to stay fluid throughout the entire piece. It's evolved into this style and I think that in the book that I'm doing now it takes another step, going in a new direction."

David is a risk-taker whose experiments with design and form have yielded successful outcomes. In his work, new directions are expected. The integration of the collage backgrounds to the illustrations and text worked well together in **Smoky Night,** "so I think that can be done in different ways for different books."

David isn't sure that **Smoky Night** *will influence his future work, but he plans to be doing books for a long time.*

There'll be other books with Harcourt, HarperCollins. I'm doing a book with Dial. I have a book with Simon & Schuster as well.

In other ways, however, the influence of **Smoky Night** *is certain, and David articulated it for us.*

It's an important book. There are so many people that I've met that have . . . used the book with young children and taught about the riots.

Recognizing its potential appeal beyond readers in the U.S., we asked David if **Smoky Night** *has been offered on the international market. He said some*

copies were sent to England and Canada, and he too anticipates a wider audience will develop.

I think this book ultimately . . . is a great book to use to cause young children to . . . question why they might feel a certain way, to begin thinking critically. . . . It would be neat if it would just create conversation with kids about what differences are and what their sameness is. That'd be great.

Smoky Night *has prompted conversation and provoked questions, but David hopes there are 'teachers who aren't hindered by some of the controversy . . . [who] pick the book up themselves and read it and see how great a book it is." We think many teachers already have.*

TITLE COMMENTARY

📖 *NEIGHBORHOOD ODES* (1992)

Publishers Weekly

SOURCE: A review of *Neighborhood Odes,* in *Publishers Weekly,* Vol. 239, No. 15, March 23, 1992, p. 74.

The Hispanic neighborhood in Soto's 21 poems is brought sharply into focus by the care with which he records images of everyday life: the music of an ice cream vendor's truck, the top of a refrigerator where old bread lies in plastic, dust released into the air when a boy strums a guitar. . . . Diaz's woodcuts complement the poems perfectly: the silhouettes are fanciful and dynamic but do not draw attention from the words on the page.

Ellen Fader

SOURCE: A review of *Neighborhood Odes,* in *The Horn Book Magazine,* Vol. LXVIII, No. 3, May-June, 1992, p. 352.

David Diaz's contemporary black-and-white illustrations, which often resemble cut paper, effortlessly capture the varied moods—happiness, fear, longing, shame, and greed—of this remarkable collection.

📖 *SMOKY NIGHT* (1994)

Publishers Weekly

SOURCE: A review of *Smoky Night,* in *Publishers Weekly,* Vol. 241, No. 5, January 31, 1994, p. 89.

Bunting addresses urban violence in this thought-provoking and visually exciting picture book inspired by the Los Angeles riots. Although they're neighbors, Daniel's cat and Mrs. Kim's cat don't get along. Nor do Daniel and his mother shop at Mrs. Kim's market. "It's better if we buy from our own people," Daniel's mother says. But when Daniel's apartment building goes up in flames, all of the neighbors (including the cats) learn the value of bridging differences.... Diaz's dazzling mixed-media collages superimpose bold acrylic illustrations on photographs of carefully arranged backgrounds that feature a wide array of symbolic materials—from scraps of paper and shards of broken glass to spilled rice and plastic dry-cleaner bags. Interestingly, Diaz doesn't strongly differentiate the presumably Asian American Mrs. Kim from the African American characters—even the artwork here cautions the reader against assumptions about race.

Hazel Rochman

SOURCE: A review of *Smoky Night,* in *Booklist,* Vol. 90, No. 13, March 1, 1994, pp. 1267-68.

Bunting says she wrote this story after the Los Angeles riots made her wonder about what riots mean to the children who live through them. A boy and his cat look down from the window at people rioting in the streets below. His mother explains that rioting can happen when people get angry: "They want to smash and destroy. They don't care anymore what's right and wrong." The boy says that they look angry, but they look happy. too. He sees them looting Mrs. Kim's grocery store across the street; his mother's building burns, and everyone has to rush out to the shelter. The boy's cat is gone, and so is Mrs. Kim's cat, but a kind fire fighter finds both animals; they were hiding together.... Diaz's art is powerful—pulsating and crowded; part street mural, part urban collage. In each double-page spread, the background is a photograph of found objects and debris in a variety of textures and jagged shapes. On the right-hand page is an acrylic painting like a view through a heavy window, with thick lines and bright neon colors showing a multicultural cast. In fine contrast, the story is told quietly from the child's point of view, safe with his mother despite the fear, reaching out to the neighborhood community within the chaos.

Louise L. Sherman

SOURCE: A review of *Smoky Night,* in *School Library Journal,* Vol. 40, No. 5, May, 1994, p. 89.

Daniel and his mother watch through their window as an urban riot is in progress. She tries to explain what is happening as he sees the laughing people break into the neighborhood stores and rob them.... Diaz illustrates the story with bold, dark, stylized acrylic paintings framed by collage backgrounds of various textured objects usually reflecting the text. When the rioters loot a dry cleaners, for example, the background is wire hangers and plastic film. The pictures are more arresting than appealing, but they invite discussion and will stimulate thoughtful responses to this quietly powerful story.

Ellen Fader

SOURCE: A review of *Smoky Night,* in *The Horn Book Magazine,* Vol. LXX, No. 3, May-June, 1994, p. 308.

Daniel's mother explains that the rioting in the street outside their apartment "'can happen when people get angry.'" The aberrant behavior of the people who are smashing windows, cars, and street lights and the looters who look angry and happy at the same time fascinate Daniel. When the smell of smoke wakens the two of them during the night, they flee to a shelter with other residents of their building. Daniel is frantic because he cannot locate his cat, Jasmine. Mrs. Kim's mean orange cat, who always fights with Jasmine, is missing, too. Daniel and his mother don't have too much to do with Mrs. Kim and do not shop at Kim's Market because "Mama says it's better if we buy from our own people." Eventually, a fire fighter appears at the shelter with one cat under each arm, claiming to have discovered the cats "holding paws" under the stairs of the burning building. When the cats drink from the same dish, Daniel observes that the animals might not have previously liked each other because they didn't know each other. Silence follows Daniel's innocent comment, until his mother introduces herself to Mrs. Kim: "'My name is Gena. Perhaps when things settle down you and your cat will come over and share a dish of milk with us.'" Clearly, the African-American woman's attempt to reach out to the Korean-American woman is a result of surviving the riots together and understanding the commonality of their lives. Although the CIP page mentions that these events took place during the recent Los Angeles riots, young readers may need some additional explanation, since the setting is not mentioned anywhere in the book. Diaz's bold artwork is a perfect match for the intensity of the story. Thick black lines border vibrant acrylic paintings that are reminiscent of Picasso's early work, especially in the composition of the characters' faces. Diaz's work also evokes images of the French impressionist Georges Rouault and of the early books of John Steptoe, both of whom used black to outline individual elements in their paintings. Diaz places these dynamic paintings on collages of real objects that, for the most part, reinforce the narrative action. For example, a painting of Daniel observing someone looting a dry cleaners is superimposed on a collage composed of wire hangers and clothes wrapped in clear plastic. Because each double-page spread is so carefully designed, because the pictorial elements work together harmoniously, the overall effect is that of urban energy, rather than cacophony. Both author and illustrator insist on a headlong confrontation with the issue of rapport between different races, and the result is a memorable, thought-provoking book.

Donnarae MacCann and Olga Richard

SOURCE: A review of *Smoky Night,* in *Wilson Library Bulletin,* Vol. 69, No. 3, November, 1994, p. 118.

People who believe that sociological concerns are outside the librarian's proper domain should consider how speedily current events turn up in kindergartners' books. Eve Bunting's **Smoky Night,** for example, deals with what Bunting calls the "Los Angeles riots." She interprets these events with a fictional text but ignores entirely the impulse behind the rebellion of 1992—namely, the beating of Rodney King. She ignores the court's exoneration of the participating Los Angeles police officers, and thereby suggests to African Americans that they must bring up their children in a world of officially sanctioned brutality. Every blow that landed on Rodney King's head was trivialized by the jurors—treated as irrelevant; when an author makes no reference to this central issue, how can she interpret the rebellion fairly? According to Bunting's text, the issue is "hooligans" and how to deal with them. Also the issue is Korean/African American misunderstandings and how they might be resolved (e.g., people should get together the way two cats drink from the same bowl in this narrative, one "Korean" cat and one "African American" cat).

But getting together, in this case, depends upon first countervailing the miscarriage of justice that has just occurred in the King/police trial. Instead of addressing the injustice, Bunting puts these words into the mouth of an African American mother as she explains the "rioting" to her son: "It can happen when people get angry. They want to smash and destory. They don't care anymore what's right and what's wrong." She uses her mouthpiece, Mr. Ramirez, to voice this simplistic conclusion: "Those people are

hooligans . . . Hooligans!" The one friendly African American firefighter who helps evacuate a building does not offer a real balance to the book's repeated images of black-instigated looting and threats to life.

Perhaps picture books are not the right medium for analyzing urban history, but if writers decide to take on the challenge, the public can require responsible coverage and can object to the wastefulness of strong visuals when the narrative material is unworthy. Creative illustrations add only a note of contradiction to this work. David Diaz has made effective backgrounds of crumpled fabrics and papers and then placed over the reproduction of these textured grounds some stylized, boldly outlined paintings. Unfortunately, such talented work tends to validate an ill-conceived project.

Renée Olson

SOURCE: "Newbery, Caldecott Medals Go to New Creators," in *School Library Journal,* Vol. 41, No. 3, March, 1995, pp. 108-09.

Sharon Creech and David Diaz were named the recipients of the 1995 Newbery and Caldecott Medals February 6 during a press conference at the 1995 Midwinter Meeting in Philadelphia. . . .

Diaz, illustrator of **Smoky Night** (Harcourt Brace), written by Eve Bunting, won the 1995 Caldecott Medal for the most distinguished American picture book published in 1994.

"**Smoky Night** is dramatic and groundbreaking," said Grace W. Ruth, chair of the Caldecott Award Selection Committee. "Diaz uses thickly-textured, expressionistic acrylic paintings to portray a night of urban rioting from a child's perspective."

Selma G. Lanes

SOURCE: "Violence from a Distance," in *The New York Times,* May 21, 1995, p. 25.

Children and adults, we live in volatile and perilous times. From the bombing of the Oklahoma City Federal Building to the nerve-gas attack in the Tokyo subway, the world has come to accept deliberately orchestrated as well as mindlessly random acts of violence as familiar, everyday components of our lives. With almost daily exposure to horrors we can do nothing about—they have, after all, already taken place by the time we see and hear about them on ubiquitous television newscasts—we are rendered impotent. By slow degrees, we become impervious to normal human reactions of revulsion and outrage. Overexposure induces numbness. As the film director Marcel Ophuls has chillingly observed, "No violence, real or fictional, is taken seriously any longer. It's all just imagery—video clips."

It is in this context that *Smoky Night,* a troubling and curiously affectless picture book, becomes comprehensible. Eve Bunting, who has written more than 100 children's books, both fiction and nonfiction, for various age levels, here bravely attempts to give us a child's-eye view of the rioting in Los Angeles three years ago. The text chronicles one evening's sorry spectacle of crime and violence from a relatively safe, dispassionate distance. ("Mama and I stand well back from our window, looking down," the boy hero begins. "We don't have our lights on though it's almost dark. People are rioting in the street below.")

Though Ms. Bunting writes about wanton vandalism, looting and arson, her prose remains disconcertingly detached and nonjudgmental. Perhaps as apologia for this disquieting neutrality, there is another early quote from the young narrator: "Mama explains about rioting. 'It can happen when people get angry. They want to smash and destroy. They don't care anymore what's right and what's wrong.'" And, somehow, neither do the book's readers. As innocent onlookers, all we want is to keep out of the path of the maelstrom. We partake of the powerlessness of victims and, for a thoughtful child, this may be little short of nightmarish.

Thus, the text presents a decided challenge to an illustrator, particularly one new to picture books. David Diaz takes up the gauntlet boldly, however, on two fronts. First, there are tasteful, low-key pictures, one to each double-page spread. Contained within heavy black borders, the figures in each frame are also outlined in black. The effect is reminiscent of stained-glass windows, a resemblance enhanced by the artist's almost translucent palette of mellow blues, purples and greens. For the most part close-ups, his images have a stopped-in-time, near-abstract quality. We focus on faces and are distracted from the ugly events being depicted. In one picture, a boy brandishes a baseball bat menacingly above his head. On the following page we see a smashed store window and three figures, facing us, reaching in to steal some shoes. There is also an off-putting quality of pantomime about the work, at one remove from the awful reality of the subject matter.

More troubling still is Mr. Diaz's second graphic contribution. Each picture is inset within an elaborate, double-page photographed collage. Into these constructions Mr. Diaz has crammed a rococo array of objects: broken glass, corrugated cardboard, plastic bubble wrap presumably ripped from stolen appliances, shoe soles, wrinkled wax paper, burlap and other fabrics, wooden match sticks, nails and a luscious variety of marbleized and handmade papers that smack more of the artist's studio than the streets of Los Angeles. (Even the book's text is printed on photographed paper fragments of different textures and shapes.) A page dealing with the sacking of a neighborhood grocery has a collage composed entirely of cold cereals liberated from their packaging: Raisin Bran, Kix, various berry-shaped bits. Another page describing a looter "staggering under a pile of clothes he's taken from the dry cleaners" has a backdrop of plastic dry-cleaning bags and wire hangers. There is something bordering on the repellent about this prettified evocation of destruction and chaos. It is also a monumental job of assemblage and photography.

This bravura one-man graphic circus clearly dazzled the 1995 Caldecott Committee of the American Library Association, which in February named Mr. Diaz the recipient of its 58th annual Caldecott Medal as "the illustrator of the most distinguished picture book for children published in the United States during the previous year."

Diana West

SOURCE: "P.C. Mommy Knows Best," in *The American Spectator,* Vol. 28, No. 7, July, 1995, pp. 64-5.

Nothing like a night of looting and torching to bring together cat-loving Korean grocers and their boycotting black neighbors. So concludes *Smoky Night,* written by Eve Bunting and illustrated by David Diaz. A children's picture book for the brave new world set amid the Los Angeles riots, *Smoky Night* is not so much a storybook as a message book. While its message might (charitably) be described as childish, the book itself is inappropriate for actual children. That didn't stop the American Library Association from recently honoring *Smoky Night* with its coveted Caldecott Award, joining the book's reputation to that of such past winners as *Madeline's Rescue* and *Where the Wild Things Are.*

The book opens as young Daniel and his Mama watch a mob pillage and burn the neighborhood outside their apartment window. With features outlined in black, the blue-lavender faces of the boy and his mother are emotionless, vacantly focused as though absorbed by motion on a television screen. Mama's words are as impassive as her face: "[Rioting] can happen when people get angry," she explains to her son. "They want to smash and destroy. They don't care anymore what's right and what's wrong."

Mama and Daniel's surprising composure is shared by almost every character depicted in **Smoky Night,** lawless and lawful alike. On one page, a foursome lugs a looted television, their faces—lips together, eyes calm—betraying none of the primitive glee or even the often-attributed rage behind their thievery and destruction, even as one wields a bat, poised to smash something beyond the picture. Turn the page and, against a none-too-subtle collage of badly-worn soles, see a sober-faced trio display newly looted shoes. Even the Korean grocer, one of the few characters painted with a mouth-opened burst of emotion, shouts with frozen rage as she stands before her ransacked store (collage: spilled cereal and broken fortune cookies) across the street from Daniel and Mama. (They never shop at her store; "Mama says it's better if we buy from our own people.")

The second half of the book hangs on Daniel's concern for his missing cat Jasmine (note the Oriental wink of a moniker), with whom he is reunited at the shelter he and his mother come to share with their neighbors. Among them is Mrs. Kim, the Korean grocer, whose cat, it turns out, has befriended Daniel's.

"Look at that!" Mama is all amazed. "I thought they didn't like each other."

"They probably didn't know each other before," I explained. "Now they do."

Everyone looks at me, and it's suddenly very quiet.

"Did I say something wrong?" I whisper to Mama.

"No, Daniel." Mama's tugging at her fingers the way she does when she's nervous. "My name is Gena," she tells Mrs. Kim. "Perhaps when things settle down you and your cat will come over and share a dish of milk with us."

And with a stroke—poof—antagonism and hatred in the ghetto vanish. Nothing against happy endings, nothing against fairy tales, but **Smoky Night** has wrapped itself in a hard-edged mantle of reality, thus staking a claim to instruct its readers in the ways of the world. That mantle, it turns out, has been tailored

to fit a bowdlerized model of human nature in order to teach the rudiments of a political agenda.

THE INNER CITY MOTHER GOOSE (1996)

Carolyn Phelan

SOURCE: A review of the *Inner City Mother Goose,* in *Booklist,* Vol. 92, No. 16, April 15, 1996, p. 1432.

Anyone who thinks that "inner city" and "Mother Goose" are incompatible hasn't read a good collection of the rhymes to a child at bedtime and wondered, "Maybe I should skip this one . . ." These traditional rhymes have been violent from the beginning, and their origins often lay in social commentary. The *Inner City Mother Goose* makes no pretense of appealing to children. Someday, perhaps, the rhymes' biting, ironic commentary will be so far removed from reality that they become nonsense, but that day seems no closer than it was 27 years ago when the first edition of *The Inner City Mother Goose* was published as an adult book. The 1970 *Booklist* review called its verse "lacerating little rhymes, worlds removed in mood and content from the traditional Mother Goose poems." Most of the verses were illustrated with striking, gritty black-and-white photographs.

Now published as a young adult book, the new edition includes a number of poems written after the first. It also omits several from the original book. Acrylic paintings by Caldecott-winner David Diaz illustrate 10 of the verses. Although the more sophisticated art in the first edition may actually have greater appeal to young adults, Diaz's small, intense paintings create portraits rich in composition, color, and gesture. The images, almost mythic in their sense of representing more than individual people, seem to move with the rhythm of the verse.

WILMA UNLIMITED: HOW WILMA RUDOLPH BECAME THE WORLD'S FASTEST WOMAN (1996)

Publishers Weekly

SOURCE: A review of *Wilma Unlimited: How Wilma Rudolph Became the World's Fastest Woman,* in *Publishers Weekly,* Vol. 243, No. 18, April 29, 1996, p. 73.

"No one expected such a tiny girl to have a first birthday," begins this inspiring biographical sketch of a

Illustration by David Diaz from Smoky Night, *by Eve Bunting*

legendary track star. Born in 1940 in Tennessee, the chronically sickly though "lively" Rudolph contracted polio just before her fifth birthday. Though not expected to walk again, the fiercely determined girl persevered with her leg exercises; by the time she was 12, she no longer needed her steel brace. Eight years later, Rudolph represented the U.S. in the 1960 Olympics in Rome, where, despite a twisted ankle, she became the first American woman to win three gold medals during a single Olympic competition. Krull's (*Lives of the Musicians*) characteristic, conversational style serves her especially well here. Through her words the nearly superhuman Rudolph seems both personable and recognizable. Rendered in acrylic, watercolor and gouache, Caldecott Medalist Diaz's (***Smoky Night***) imposing, richly hued illustrations have a distinctive, cubist feel. The artist's bold design superimposes this art against sepia-toned photographs of relevant background images: playground sand, wooden fence slats, the gravel of a running track. This juxtaposition yields busy, effectively tex-

tured pages, flawed only by the text's curiously embellished font—the letters look as though they have been speckled with either ink blots or dust. A triumphant story, triumphantly relayed.

Michael Cart

SOURCE: A review of *Wilma Unlimited: How Wilma Rudolph Became the World's Fastest Woman,* in *Booklist,* Vol. 92, No. 17, May 1, 1996, p. 1503.

Wilma Rudolph was a wonder. Though partially paralyzed by polio as a child, she managed—through indomitable spirit and unlimited determination—to transform herself from a disabled 5-year-old to a world-class runner at age 20, the first woman ever to win three gold medals in a single Olympics. . . . Enhancing the text are Caldecott medalist Diaz's richly colored, stylized illustrations that—though painted— have the look and permanence of wood carvings. These single- and double - page pictures are set on sepia-tone backgrounds that, like his Caldecott Medal-winning art for *Smoky Night* (1994), Diaz assembled and photographed. He has also created a striking new font called Ariel for the display and text type. Both Krull's words and Diaz's illustrations are celebrations of an inspiring life that deserves to be remembered.

Ann Welton

SOURCE: A review of *Wilma Unlimited: How Wilma Rudolph Became the World's Fastest Woman,* in *School Library Journal,* Vol. 42, No. 6, June, 1996, pp. 116-17.

[This book recounts the] story of Wilma Rudolph, the prematurely born black child who, despite suffering from polio, became the first woman to win three Olympic gold medals. The narrative could very easily slip into sentimentality. It is to Krull's credit that though her telling is affecting, it is also crisp and matter of fact, very much in the spirit of Rudolph's deep day-to-day determination. However, the real impact of this book lies in the potent melding of powerful prose with Diaz's stunning artwork. His watercolor and acrylic illustrations with definite black outlining create a stained-glass effect, and the paintings themselves are backed on sepia photographs that relate to the text. For example, narrative about Wilma's bus trips to Nashville is matched with an illustration showing the girl and her mother at the back of the bus. This in turn is superimposed over a photograph of a bus tire. Children will listen raptly to this inspirational tale, which is especially appropriate for this Olympic year.

Ellen Fader

SOURCE: A review of *Wilma Unlimited: How Wilma Rudolph Became the World's Fastest Woman,* in *The Horn Book Magazine,* Vol. LXXII, No. 5, September-October, 1996, pp. 616-17.

An inspiring picture book tells the story of the indomitable Wilma Rudolph, who, although she weighed only a little more than four pounds when she was born and contracted polio when she was five, went on to become the first American woman to win three gold medals at a single Olympics. The book's design is similar to that of the Caldecott medalist's *Smoky Night,* in that brightly colored acrylic, watercolor, and gouache paintings are placed against equally dynamic sepia-toned photographic backgrounds, creating juxtapositions that thoughtfully extend both the text (which is in an unfortunately distracting typeface) and the pictures in the foreground. Diaz creates illustrations of Rudolph that artfully capture her physical and emotional determination as well as the beauty of her body in motion.

📖 *GOING HOME* (1996)

Barbara Kiefer

SOURCE: A review of *Going Home,* in *School Library Journal,* Vol. 42, No. 9, September, 1996, p. 171.

Mama and Papa are ecstatic to be going home to Mexico for the Christmas holidays, but Carlos and his sisters, who have been raised in a labor camp on a farm in the U.S., have difficulty understanding their parents' longing for this unfamiliar place. After the old station wagon crosses the border, however, excitement builds, and when they finally reach La Perla, a noisy and joyous family reunion takes place. After all the guests have left, Mama and Papa steal outside and dance barefoot in the street. Their amazed children then begin to understand the sacrifices their parents have made for them. Bunting conveys her message softly, leaving the major role to Diaz. His distinctive style is well suited to the setting and the mood of the book. End papers feature closeup photographs of brilliant "artesanias Mexicanas," decorative objects, figures, and other popular arts found in the market places. This "arté popular" then forms the background on which the paintings and type are placed. Diaz uses color, shape, and line to evoke the anticipation of the trip and the joy of arrival. Even the layout effectively mirrors the emotional energy and tension of the story. A lovely journey home for Mama and Papa and their children, and for readers, a journey to understanding.

Publishers Weekly

SOURCE: A review of *Going Home,* in *Publishers Weekly,* Vol. 243, No. 39, September 23, 1996, p. 76.

Diaz's fiesta-bright artwork ignites this joyous tale of a Mexican American family's sentimental journey. For the parents, the Christmastime trip to their Mexican home means a longed-for reunion with family and friends; for their son Carlos and his sisters, the trip is a big unknown: although they were born in Mexico, they don't remember it—their parents moved the family to California "for the opportunities," and work long, hot days harvesting crops while their children go to school. "Home is here," Carlos's mother tells him as they pack. "But it is there, too." By journey's end, Carlos has a better understanding not only of "home," but also of his parents, and of the depth of their sacrifice. . . . The fiery colors and bold lines of Diaz's woodcut-like illustrations lend a strength and nobility to these scenes. Employing the same mixed-media technique used so effectively in the Caldecott-winning *Smoky Night,* his previous outing with Bunting, he sets his artwork within photographic backdrops that show gaily painted pottery, folk art figurines, Mexican Christmas decorations, festive flowers and other shiny holiday trinkets. A veritable feast for the eyes, this South-of-the-border treat stirs the soul as well.

Susan Dove Lempke

SOURCE: A review of *Going Home,* in *Booklist,* Vol. 93, No. 3, October 1, 1996, p. 357.

In a family that has moved to California from Mexico to work, the parents may call one place home, the children, another. When Carlos and his family go to his parents' village for Christmas, Carlos realizes the sacrifices his parents have made in leaving behind a beloved home to do brutally hard work so that their children may have better lives. . . . Diaz uses photographs as borders (this time mainly of folk art objects) for his paintings, just as he did so effectively in his 1995 Caldecott winner, *Smoky Night,* also written by Bunting. However, the theme here is not the chaos of a riot, and the overall effect is cluttered and frustrating, as his fine paintings are overshadowed.

Kathleen Krull

SOURCE: A review of *Going Home,* in *The New York Times,* May 11, 1997, p. 24.

[A serious theme,] adroitly rendered by way of . . . [a] magical conclusion, comes from the team that collaborated on *Smoky Night,* for which David Diaz won the 1995 Caldecott Medal for illustration. Eve Bunting's text for *Going Home* is a short story about how love of one's adopted country does not necessarily replace love of the old one. A California family of legal farm workers journeys home for Christmas—and "home" for young Carlos's parents is still Mexico. This is such a hard concept to grasp (for adults or children) that stories dramatizing it are precious. As "Going Home" makes clear, Mexicans differ from previous generations of immigrants in the proximity of their homeland—so close that immigration no longer exacts the emotional damage of permanently cutting ties. Many are able to cross to "el otro lado," the other side, for holidays and vacations, and some even choose to move back to Mexico. The history of this particular family unfolds over four days of driving to reach their small village, as Carlos struggles with questions about the meaning of home. Then he observes a family reunion so emotional, so joyous, that it culminates in a dreamy scene where Papa and Mama dance in the street in their pajamas—and magically float into the sky with bliss. The narrative never loses sight for a second of what this all means to a small child, and the ultimate underlying message is one promoting tolerance and understanding, a common Eve Bunting theme.

David Diaz's intricate extension of this poignant Christmas story begins with a typeface of his own design, called Jericho, and features stylized oil paintings of symbolic moments. His framing technique makes use of one bold border of razor-sharp black designs reinforced with dramatic hues, and a second border of glittering photographic backgrounds, taking advantage of the Christmas setting to display the tones and textures of traditional Mexican folk art from this time of year.

JUST ONE FLICK OF A FINGER (1996)

Hazel Rochman

SOURCE: A review of *Just One Flick of a Finger,* in *Booklist,* Vol. 92, Nos. 19-20, June 1, 1996, p. 1718.

"I wanted to be bad, so bad no one would mess with me." The setting is a bleak city neighborhood, but every bullied kid will understand Jack's wish. In simple free verse, he tells how he tries to stay out of trouble, but Reebo is out to get him. Jack steals his dad's revolver ("as he [sleeps] off his latest beer") and wonders if his dad would care if anything happened to him. Jack's friend, Sherms, does care, and he's appalled when Jack appears with the gun. Jack is white; both his friend and his enemy are black. Sure enough, the bully confronts Jack, Sherms tries to intervene, the gun goes off, Sherms is wounded—but then everything works out all right in the end. Diaz's dramatic, framed mixed-media paintings of schoolyard friendship and confrontation are like larger than-life street murals, almost comic book in style with huge eyes and exaggerated gestures. As in his Caldecott winner, *Smoky Night* (1994), the background evokes a kind of feverish excitement with neon-lit graffiti, peeling walls, flashing color.

Publishers Weekly

SOURCE: A review of *Just a Flick of a Finger,* in *Publishers Weekly,* Vol. 243, No. 34, August 19, 1996, p. 67.

Speaking with a staccato, rap-like cadence, the teenage narrator of this stark picture book for middle-graders sets the scene: "The rule / at my school / is you're a fool / if you can't get / your hand on a gun." So when his nemesis, Reebo, gets in his face, the narrator steals a revolver from his father's drawer as the man sleeps off his beer. . . . Adopting a design reminiscent of Diaz's **Wilma Unlimited,** this book superimposes his stylized paintings of harsh, tension-filled scenes against backgrounds of digitally manipulated photos. These present a variety of images, some recognizable and some abstract, reproduced in neon colors that command as much attention as the author's message.

Julie Cummins

SOURCE: A review of *Just One Flick of a Finger,* in *School Library Journal,* Vol. 42, No. 9, September, 1996, p. 204.

The issue of adolescents taking guns to school is intensely played out in narrative and depiction. The verselike text is hip street talk and the bold, craggy images are recognizable as Diaz's style. . . . Designed to convey a gut reaction akin to that of the characters, the layout affixes black-framed scenes of action on the recto pages and highlighted, goldenrod blocks of text on the verso against vivid, amorphously splotched backgrounds. Added to the look is a type style created by Diaz that makes some letters more pronounced and puts dots inside the o's (looking up the barrel of a gun?). The peculiar stylization is distracting to the flow of reading. Though the subject is serious, the heavy tone edges close to dramatization but lacks emotion. The title admonishes, the message shrouds the story, and the brazen loudness of the artwork borders on overkill.

DECEMBER (1997)

Jane Marino

SOURCE: A review of *December,* in *School Library Journal,* Vol. 43, No. 10, October, 1997, p. 40.

[*December* is a] story singular in its originality; its artwork; and its contemporary, multilayered theme that is ultimately filled with joy and peace despite its stark setting. On Christmas Eve, a homeless boy and his mother share their small cardboard-box home with an elderly stranger. The next morning, she is gone. And outside, the child thinks—but cannot believe—he sees an angel like the one on his December calendar page. The story ends a year later, when his situation has changed. His mother has a job and they have moved to a small apartment. It is then he observes that his calendar angel wears a rose just like the one the stranger had put on his Christmas tree. The message of charity as a risk worth taking in a dangerous world is a sobering, thoughtful holiday message. So deft in her writing, Bunting creates a mood or expresses an emotion with a simple sentence or phrase. Diaz's now-familiar angular, almost stained-glass figures dominate illustrations that are set against backgrounds so striking in their creativity and complexity that they would overwhelm a lesser story. The artist uses a mix of media and repetitive patterns to create unusual designs that give each backdrop a multidimensional look. One of a very few holiday books that has both art and writing so strong that they effectively mesh to create a truly unique title.

Publishers Weekly

SOURCE: A review of *December,* in *Publishers Weekly,* Vol. 244, No. 41, October 6, 1997, p. 57.

The creators of the Caldecott-winning **Smoky Night** offer a fresh approach to a holiday story of hope. A homeless mother and son's luck turns after they welcome a mysterious downtrodden guest into their home on Christmas Eve. This familiar theme, rooted in a number of ethnic folktale traditions, is updated to the 20th century and set in the streets of an unnamed city. Bunting's prose, in the boy's first-person narrative, is particularly moving, and the strong lines of Diaz's muralistic acrylic, watercolor and gouache artwork—inset over wallpaper-like backdrops of photographed collages—underscore the urban flavor.

BE NOT FAR FROM ME: THE OLDEST LOVE STORY, LEGENDS FROM THE BIBLE (1998)

Publishers Weekly

SOURCE: A review of *Be Not Far from Me: The Oldest Love Story,* in *Publishers Weekly,* Vol. 245, No. 12, March 23, 1998, p. 95.

Kimmel (*Hershel and the Hanukkah Goblins*) presents a collection of Bible legends—culled from the

Bible and the Midrash (a body of literature that amplifies and explains biblical texts)—within a fresh framework: the age-old story of love between God and his people. Kimmel skillfully crafts his work as character studies of 20 important Biblical figures. . . . Mixed-media paintings by Caldecott Medalist David Diaz (*Smoky Night*) feature black cut-paper silhouettes of each hero highlighted in the text. Bold-colored borders and contrasting soft, watercolor backgrounds add a sense of power and intensity.

Ilene Cooper

SOURCE: A review of *Be Not Far from Me: The Oldest Love Story, Legends from the Bible*, in *Booklist*, Vol. 94, No. 15, April, 1998, p. 1318.

[*Be Not Far From Me*] centers on various heroes and heroines from the Bible, beginning with Abraham and ending with Daniel and including many biblical figures often ignored in children's Bible stories, for example, the prophets Isaiah, Amos, and Hosea. The retellings of the stories themselves are quite wonderful. . . . Power also appears in the artwork of Caldecott medalist David Diaz, which is arrestingly different from his previous work. The collage-style art, featuring cut silhouettes of black and light papers set against softer backgrounds, is dynamic. The whole book, in fact, is elegantly and thoughtfully designed.

Patricia Lothrop-Green

SOURCE: A review of *Be Not Far from Me: The Oldest Love Story, Legends from the Bible*, in *School Library Journal*, Vol. 44, No. 6, June, 1998, pp. 162-63.

These stories about 19 men and 1 woman are subtitled "Legends from the Bible," but the fabric of the book is canonical, adding details and incidents from ancient midrashic tradition. . . . Diaz provides 20 full-page bold, massy silhouettes, placed against delicate watercolor backgrounds and set off by vibrant black- and color-edged borders. Color inserts enliven the cut-out shapes, giving some a stained-glass effect. A few figures, minus necks, seem to have lost control of their floating heads, but the style is particularly good at suggesting tendrils of hair, wooly tunics, and curling flames. Colorful end maps contrast the Middle East at three ancient periods with today.

📖 *THE LITTLE SCARECROW BOY* (1998)

Publishers Weekly

SOURCE: A review of *The Little Scarecrow Boy*, in *Publishers Weekly*, Vol. 245, No. 29, July 20, 1998, p. 218.

Hewing to an earthy palette of cornfield yellows, oranges, and greens, with shades of blue for contrast, Caldecott Medalist Diaz (*Smoky Night*) makes a dramatic departure, in a winsome interpretation of Brown's previously unpublished tale. In typical Brown fashion, a strong and loving family bond is at the core of the story, which tells of a happy scarecrow trio. "Old man scarecrow is teaching his son the family business, and although the scarecrow boy is eager to ply his trade, his father tells him repeatedly "No, little boy. / You can't go. / You're not fierce enough / to scare a crow. / Wait till you grow." But one day the lad can't resist giving his new skills a try, and nearly comes to grief. Not until his sixth attempt, making his fiercest face of all, does he finally drive the crows away from the fields, This warmly evoked coming-of-age tale, marked by repetitive phrasing and even pacing, makes for a superior read-aloud, enhanced by the timeless, leisurely quality in Diaz's watercolor, gouache, and pencil illustrations. The patched look of the scarecrow characters echoes the patchwork of the fields and multicolored corn. With his round head and chubby body, sprouting straw from every sleeve and pocket, the scarecrow boy will enchant young readers; the "faces" he makes are a droll caricature of the kind of grimaces children concoct, as his button eyes strain at their threads, his fingers pull cloth lips back to reveal straw "teeth," and so on. This scarecrow boy may be made of straw, but he's all heart—and so is this picture book.

Carolyn Phelan

SOURCE: A review of *The Little Scarecrow Boy*, in *Booklist*, Vol. 95, No. 1, September 1, 1998, p. 124.

A little scarecrow wants to go out into the cornfield with his father to make faces and scare crows, but each time he asks, old man scarecrow replies, "No, little boy. / You can't go. / You're not fierce enough / to scare a crow. / Wait till you grow." After he's grown a bit, the boy runs off to the field early one morning to scare the crows. Although the text is not Brown's best, its rhythm, internal rhyme, and sense of a small child's longing provide a strong enough base for the soaring, intensely colorful illustrations. Although very different from Diaz's usual style, the pictures energize the text. Large in scale and seemingly backlit by the summer sun, the scarecrows are intriguing characters with their mobile faces, buoyant bodies, and genial take on life. An old crow proves itself a bit of a menace, but nothing the little scarecrow can't handle, with his inborn courage and his talent for making faces. Expect preschool audiences to make a few faces of their own in delighted mimicry of the young hero.

Kathy Piehl

SOURCE: A review of *The Little Scarecrow Boy,* in *School Library Journal,* Vol. 44, No. 11, November, 1998, p. 76.

Diaz provides wonderful illustrations for a story Brown wrote in the 1940s. Little scarecrow boy longs to accompany his father, old man scarecrow, to the cornfields to frighten the crows. Instead, he has to remain home to grow and to practice the terrible facial expressions his father teaches him. Convinced that he has mastered the six fierce faces, he slips out early one morning and confronts a big black crow in the field. These encounters test the youngster's mettle, but he succeeds in frightening the bird, filling his father with pride. Brown's masterful use of repetition and rhythm creates a fine read-aloud story. The warm watercolor illustrations incorporate straw and patchwork to evoke a Midwest summer day in this sunny coming-of-age story.

THE DISAPPEARING ALPHABET (1998)

Publishers Weekly

SOURCE: A review of *The Disappearing Alphabet,* in *Publishers Weekly,* Vol. 245, No. 33, August 17, 1998, p. 70.

If the alphabet started to disappear, as the premise of this inventively witty book sets up, then the world as we know it would, too. Wilbur (*Opposites*), a Pulitzer Prize-winning poet, starts at the beginning and imagines what life would be like without each of the 26 letters: "If [B] were absent, say, from BAT and BALL,! There'd be no big or little leagues AT ALL." In addition to pondering words without particular letters, Wilbur playfully points out the symbols' other important functions (e.g., in music, "If there were no such thing as C! Whole symphonies would be off key"; or in reference to the roman numeral M in mathematics, "If M should vanish, we would lose, my dears,! MINCE PIE, MARSHMALLOWS, and a thousand years"). Diaz (*Smoky Night*), in a clever quip, employs cut-outs as his medium; the rainbow-hued silhouettes set against a white background serve to either amplify or clarify the text. For the destruction of the letter Q, for example (as a result of which "Millions of U 's would then be unemployed"), Diaz pictures a wrecking ball aimed at a giant Q while the

ground is littered with discarded Us. And, in W, for a more obscure reference to the watermelon shape in Cassiopeia, Diaz enlightens readers with a picture of the constellation. With plenty of brain-tickling words to grow on and a plethora of visual puns, watch this one vanish from the family bookshelf.

Jennifer M. Brabander

SOURCE: A review of *The Disappearing Alphabet,* in *The Horn Book Magazine,* Vol. LXXIV, No. 5, September-October, 1998, p. 618.

The celebrated poet and author of *Opposites* (rev. 8/73) and *More Opposites* plays once again with words, here surmising in twenty-six poems what might befall us should we lose the alphabet. "What if there were no letter A? / Cows would eat HY instead of HAY. / What's HY? It's an unheard-of diet, / And cows are happy not to try it." Of course, we'd lose more than words, as the introductory poem states: "And since it is by words that we construe / The world, the world would start to vanish, too!" Similarly, readers will laugh at the nonsensical wordplay while catching a glimpse of the formative—and transformative—power of language. The tone of mild astonishment suits the subject matter, as Wilbur's poems are filled with small, satisfying surprises. A small slip in one poem, which ponders what we'd call the elephant without the letter E, includes the (impossible) possibility, "Hey, you!" David Diaz's slick computer-generated art is bold and appropriately playful. Each letter hides in the background, sliding toward or off the edge of the page. Black silhouettes, contrasted sharply with glowing colors, are shadowy figures ready to slip away into the night along with the alphabet. Other illustrations contain opposites of the silhouettes—cutout-like figures in jewel tones against white backgrounds. One can't help wondering how Wilbur's own simple drawings might have more accurately—and with less spectacle—captured the poems' droll humor and allowed readers more room for their own imaginings.

Michael Cart

SOURCE: A review of *The Disappearing Alphabet,* in *Booklist,* Vol. 95, No. 6, November 15, 1998, p. 585.

The premise of Pulitzer Prize poet Wilbur's rhyming alphabet is simple: suppose the letters began disappearing, one by one. "Some words would soon look ragged and queer / (Like quirrel, himpanzee, and choochoo trai) / While others would entirely fade away . . . " First published in *The Atlantic Monthly,* these 26 sprightly exercises in wordplay are witty and inventive but generally too sophisticated for the usual alphabet book set. Older kids and adults will enjoy them, however. The same is true of the computer-generated illustrations by Caldecott medalist Diaz: they're visually arresting exercises in design, and their coloration is gorgeous. Unfortunately, they're more decorative than narrative, tending to be too literal renderings of a text that would, in its whimsicality, seem to invite more freewheeling artistic invention than this.

Additional coverage of Diaz's life and career is contained in the following source published by the Gale Group: *Something about the Author,* **Vol. 96.**

Rudyard Kipling
1865-1936

(Full name Joseph Rudyard Kipling) English short story writer, poet, novelist, essayist, and autobiographer.

Major works include *"Wee Willie Winkie" and Other Child Stories* (1888), *The Jungle Book*s (1894), *Captains Courageous* (1897), *Kim* (1901), *Just So Stories for Little Children* (1902).

The following entry presents criticism of Kipling's novel *Kim*. For information on Kipling's complete career, see *CLR,* Volume 39.

INTRODUCTION

The most popular writer of his age, Kipling endures as one of the best known and most influential children's writers in English literature, and *Kim* is considered his finest work. The story of a young British orphan raised as an Indian, *Kim* portrays the boy's journey to self-realization and understanding of his dual heritage. *Kim* is particularly praised for combining Kipling's knowledge and love of India with political intrigue, picaresque adventures, and an insightful depiction of the boy's psychological development. In an assessment of the novel published in 1957, critic Nirad C. Chaudhuri claimed *Kim* as "the finest novel in the English language with an Indian theme," and Robert F. Moss praised it as Kipling's "final splendid testament to the India of his youth." For many, however, Kipling's politics and personal outlook are inseparable from his literary legacy, and the scrutiny his views invite have helped to make him, in the words of Shamsul Islam, "perhaps the most controversial figure in English literature." In particular, Kipling's endorsement of the British colonial system—evident especially in *Kim*—has been regarded as narrow-minded and racist. Rather than denying these claims, Kipling's defenders point out that he wrote in a wide variety of genres and styles, and that among his body of work there is much to be savored.

BIOGRAPHICAL INFORMATION

Kipling's father, John Lockwood Kipling, was an architect, teacher, and minister who took his wife, Al-

ice, with him when he went to serve the British Empire in India. Rudyard Kipling was born in India but returned to England to be educated from the age of six. Shortly before turning seventeen, he returned to India and began writing for newspapers. His first poems and short stories appeared during this time.

In 1892, Kipling married Caroline Starr Balestier, an American woman, and the couple had three children. The eldest, Josephine, died of influenza while the family was living in Vermont. In America, Kipling wrote both *Jungle Books* and began *Kim,* but then he returned to England in 1906. Kipling's son John was killed on the battlefield in World War I; the war often recurred as a subject of his later fiction and poetry.

As Kipling's work became widely known, he made every effort to resist the trappings of fame. He repeatedly refused knighthood and discouraged the formation of a "Kipling Society." After several years of poor health, he died of internal hemorrhage in 1936. Kipling's ashes were installed in London's Westminster Abbey, beside the memorial to Charles Dickens.

PLOT AND MAJOR CHARACTERS

Considered Kipling's finest achievement and described by Angus Wilson as "one of the oddest masterpieces ever written," *Kim* tells the story of Kimball O'Hara, an Irish orphan who is raised in poverty in India by a half-caste woman following the death of his parents. Kim gains knowledge of the ways of the bazaar and often serves as an errand-boy to a horse dealer who is also employed as a British spy. By chance Kim meets a holy man who is searching for a sacred river into which Buddha himself is said to have shot an arrow. Kim offers to assist the Lama in his quest, and the two set off together, with Kim secretly engaged in delivering a message for his employer the spy. Kim, too, is in quest of a "red bull on a green field," an image he ultimately learns is the emblem of his father's regiment. Kim is taken in by white society when they learn of his real heritage, and he is sent away to school. He maintains his relationship with the Lama and returns to his work in espionage, helping to foil a Russian plot. Because of Kim's dual identity as both the son of a British officer and an Indian street urchin, the novel includes a wide range of characters from all levels of society. Structurally, the quest of the holy man for the sacred river is seen to parallel Kim's quest for a personal identity. The character Kim, and the book as a whole, both refrain from criticizing the imperial system that oppresses the Indian people. Concluding his analysis in 1972, Chaudhuri summarized that Kipling "stands supreme among Western writers for his treatment of the biggest reality in India, which is made up of the life of people and religion in the twin setting of the mountains and the plain. These four are the main and real characters in *Kim*."

CRITICAL RECEPTION

Kipling's literary reputation has seen many ups and downs. Only five years after Kipling's death, literary critic Edmund Wilson observed that he had "in a sense been dropped out of modern literature." The qualities that made him popular—his plain and direct style, his zest for stories of adventure, and his view of the world that placed England at the very center—all went out of fashion. However, Kipling is constantly being rediscovered by new generations of readers, thanks especially to Hollywood, which has returned often to his works, basing numerous live action and animated films on them. In the decades since Kipling's death, *Kim* has continued to enthrall young readers and to gain critical esteem. Writing in 1963, critic J. I. M. Stewart commented that in the novel "Kipling's own brilliant powers of memory and evocation are . . . enlisted, as too rarely, in what is entirely a labour of love. The result is a book that knits a lavishly achieved picaresque narrative to a central figure who almost brings off the ultimate feat of escaping from the pages in which he is created." Praising another aspect of *Kim* in 1982, Moss wrote, "There is no doubt that *Kim* is the most intimate revelation of Kipling's inner self, as much a spiritual autobiography as Wordsworth's 'Prelude'; the book is an attempt to seize all the jagged, confusing, remarkable fragments of his psychic life and incorporate them into a great fictional kaleidoscope. But the brilliance of the novel may have more to do with its depth than its breadth, with the excavations Kipling was able to make into his own soul."

AWARDS

Kipling was offered, but refused to serve as Poet Laureate in 1895; he also refused an Order of Merit Award. He received honorary degrees from many universities. In 1907, Kipling became the first English recipient of the Nobel Prize for Literature.

TITLE COMMENTARY

KIM (1901)

Helen Master

SOURCE: "What Spring Brings," in *The Horn Book Magazine,* Vol. XIII, No. 3, May-June, 1937, pp. 135-38.

Most of the poems listed for children as "Spring poems" are of what one remembers seeing, hearing, thinking, rather than of what one did. There is a wide place for thought and reflection of course, but it seems to me that Spring brings an interest in activity which it is quite possible to satisfy by stories as well as by poems. . . .

Of course *Kim* has all times and weathers in it, and I'm told that there is no Spring in India, which seems a little sad, and yet *Kim* is a story which fits particularly well into what Spring brings. It is a great story of a quest and a finding: for the lama, his River of the Arrow; for Kim, the Red Bull on the Green Field and all that that involves. Kim first decides to become the lama's *chela* and to go on the pilgrimage with him because, as he tells Mabub Ali, "I am tired of Lahore city. I wish new air and water." There it is!

But *Kim* also brings another attribute of Spring to me, that peculiar lengthening out of daylight which marks the withdrawal of winter. Quite suddenly and unexpectedly it comes. Where yesterday you accomplished some part of the day's routine in the dark, today you find yourself doing it in the light. That light is strange and yet familiar. You see it once every year; it is the first evening of Spring. It is what we feel when we sing the "Easter Day" hymn whose Latin words Venantius Fortunatus wrote some thirteen hundred years ago,

> "Months in due succession, Days of lengthening light.
> . . . "

It is what children mean when they say they have to "go to bed by day." Stevenson knew. And Kipling knew when he wrote the description of the end of day coming to Kim and the lama as they travel south along the Grand Trunk Road. Near the beginning of Chapter IV it is, and if you grow weary for Spring in the midst of winter, take down the book and read. It may be that each evening of an Indian day the year through is like this one; I do not know. But I do know that it is the only beginning of North American Spring for me. The light is right, the sounds are right, the smells though unfamiliar are right, the coolness of the air is right. Kim says, "Look, the sun is sloping," and the lama says, "Who will receive us this evening?"

Nirad C. Chaudhuri

SOURCE: "The Finest Story about India—in English," in *The Age of Kipling,* edited by John Gross, Simon and Schuster, 1972, pp. 27-36.

[In *Kim,* Kipling] wrote not only the finest novel in the English language with an Indian theme, but also one of the greatest of English novels in spite of the theme. This rider is necessary, because the association of anything in English literature with India suggests a qualified excellence, an achievement which is to be judged by its special standards, or even a work which in form and content has in it more than a shade of the second-rate. But *Kim* is great by any standards that ever obtained in any age of English literature.

This will come as a surprise from a Bengali, Kipling's *bête noire,* who heartily returned the compliment, and I shall add shock to surprise by confessing that I had not read *Kim* till about three years ago. The only work by Kipling which I had read before was *The Jungle Book.* I read it first when I was only ten years old, and I have never ceased reading it. It is now as much a part of me as are the Arabian Nights, Grimm's Fairy Tales, and Aesop's Fables, or for that matter the Ramayana and the Mahabharata. But I never had the courage or inclination to pass on to Kipling's other books, for I had heard of his 'imperialism' and contempt for Bengalis. I thought I should be hurt by an aggressive display of Anglo-Saxon pride, and while British rule lasted I should have been, because the contempt was both real and outspoken. Anyone curious to sample its expression might as well read a story called **'The Head of the District'** . . . .

There was no originality in Kipling's rudeness to us, but only a repetition, in the forthright Kiplingian manner, of what was being said in every mess and club. His political fads were explicit, and he was never sheepish about them. But his politics were the characteristic politics of the *epigoni,* when the epic age of British world politics was already past, and the British people had ceased to bring about great mutations in the history of the world. . . .

Kipling's politics, which even now are something of a hurdle in the way of giving him a secure place in English literature, and which certainly brought him under a cloud during the last years of his life, are no essential ingredient of his writings. Kipling the writer is always able to rise above Kipling the political man. His imagination soared above his political opinions as Tolstoy's presentation of human character transcended his pet military and historical theories in *War and Peace.* Of course, quite a large number of his themes are drawn from what might legitimately be called political life, but these have been personalized and transformed into equally legitimate artistic themes. It is the easiest thing to wash out the free acid of Kiplingian politics from his finished goods.

Coming to particulars, *Kim* would never have been a great book if it had to depend for its validity and appeal on the spy story, and we really are not called upon to judge it as an exposition in fiction of the Anglo-Russian rivalry in Asia. Kipling's attitude to war and diplomacy had a streak of naïveté and even claptrap in it, which made Lord Cromer, in whom high politics ran in the blood, once call him, if I remember rightly, a cheeky beggar.

The spy story in *Kim* is nothing more than the diplomatic conceit of an age of peace, in which people enjoyed all kinds of scares, including war scares, and even invented them, in order to have an excuse for letting off some jingoistic steam, to ring a change on the boredom of living in piping times of peace. India in the last decades of the nineteenth century was full of all sorts of fanciful misgivings about Russian intrigues and the machinations of the Rajas and Maharajas, which the clever darkly hinted at and the simple credulously believed in. There is an echo of this even in one of Tagore's stories in Bengali.

But in *Kim* this political mode, which Kipling seems to have taken more seriously than it deserved to be, is only a peg to hang a wholly different story, the real story of the book. . . .

[*Kim*] is the product of Kipling's vision of a much bigger India, a vision whose profundity we Indians would be hard put to it to match even in an Indian language, not to speak of English. He had arrived at a true and moving sense of that India which is almost timeless, and had come to love it.

This India pervades all his books in greater or lesser degree and constitutes the foundation on which he weaves his contrapuntal patterns. In certain books this foundation is virtually the real theme, and so it is in *Kim*. But the book is specially important in this that through it Kipling projects not only his vision of the basic India he knew so well, but also his feeling for the core and the most significant part of this basic India. . . .

Kipling was equally at home in our plains, hills, and mountains, and like all great novelists he remains firmly ecological. There are in *Kim* not only entrancing descriptions of the Himalayas but a picture of the green phase on the great plain that is uncanny in its combination of romance and actuality. We Indians shall never cease to be grateful to Kipling for having shown the many faces of our country in all their beauty, power, and truth.

As regards the human material the best choice in India is always the simplest choice, namely, the people and their religion. . . .

Kipling's artistic and spiritual instincts led him to these elemental and inexhaustible themes, although he may not have been wholly original in his choice, for in this as in many other things he was controlled by the general bias of British rule in India towards the commonalty. But whether completely original or not he stands supreme among Western writers for his treatment of the biggest reality in India, which is made up of the life of people and religion in the twin setting of the mountains and the plain. These four are the main and real characters in *Kim*.

Faith G. Norris

SOURCE: "Rudyard Kipling," in *British Winners of the Nobel Literary Prize*, edited by Walter E. Kidd, University of Oklahoma Press, 1973, pp. 14-43.

Even in 1907 there were those in England and the United States who cast upon Rudyard Kipling a cold and critical eye and who obviously felt no enthusiasm about the announcement that the Swedish Academy had selected him as that year's recipient of the Nobel Prize in Literature. There were outspoken detractors like the Scots literary critic Robert Buchanan, and there were silent denigrators like the editor of the *London Times,* who confined himself to the bare news announcement that Kipling was the choice for the award. . . .

In the view of the spokesman for the Nobel committee, Rudyard Kipling was not only a talented poet, story writer, and novelist but also a man who "had acquired a complete knowledge of the ideas and mentality of the Hindus," with the result that his account of their "customs and institutions" had done more to contribute to a knowledge of the India of England than had "the construction of the Suez Canal."

In addition, the giver of the speech which went with the award praised Kipling as an "idealist" of the concept of empire. Though before 1907 certain British and American liberals had attacked Kipling as a spokesman for "vicious jingoism," the speechmaker expressed the view that Kipling deserved praise for having done more than any other writer of "pure literature" to make tighter "the bonds" uniting England to its colonies.

When one considers that the decision to give Kipling the Nobel Prize was in large part due to the pressure exerted upon the committee by a small band of Englishmen, one is at first skeptical of the above quotation and of even more extreme, flowery tributes to Kipling. At the same time, one has to recall that he had been both a critical and a popular success in France, Germany, and Scandinavia since the late 1890's. At the time he won the award, for example, Sweden's distinguished woman novelist, Selma Lagerlöf, who was herself to receive the medal in 1909, announced that her most recent work, *The Marvelous Voyage of Nils Hölgersson,* owed a great debt to Kipling.

By English and American critical standards did the man who received the award in 1907 deserve to be so honored? The answer is yes, especially if one takes into account both the aesthetic and the political ideals of 1907. Much of his work still has value in our own time, but the rest deserves a far less harsh judgment than it usually receives, if one examines it from the standards of his world, not ours. . . .

[During] the quarter century between his seventeenth birthday and his winning of the Nobel Prize, the man who had once been called a "precocious pup" had written far more, and in a wider variety of genres, than many another author does in a period twice as long. Readers may at once object that quantity is no substitute for quality—that Flaubert's literary heritage was minuscule when compared to that of Dumas. One can also argue that much of the early Kipling is imitative: his rhythms and alliteration are often those of Swinburne; his horror stories echo the manner of Edgar Allan Poe.

At the same time, though one may condemn as lacking in quality much that Kipling wrote before 1907 or dismiss it as "imitative" in style, any fair-minded reader should realize that, to every form he attempted, he brought originality of subject matter. Indeed, because of that last aesthetic fact alone he deserved the Nobel Prize. For much of Kipling's fresh subject matter exhibited, in terms of 1907, the "idealistic" character which Alfred Nobel had hoped the winners of the literary prize would possess.

In the field of the novel [Kipling] was less successful [than as a short story writer]. Of his four long works only one met with both popular and critical acclaim in its own time (before 1907); That book, *Kim,* is the only one still widely read. Even *Kim* (1901), has suffered the fate of often being lodged in children's libraries and considered a book for boys because its protagonist is a lad in his early adolescence. Yet it no more deserves such a lot than does that other great work about a boy of approximately the same age, *Huckleberry Finn.* Like Twain's novel, the color and excitement of the story, together with the simplicity of style, render *Kim* a book which an adolescent can enjoy. But just as Huck Finn's wanderings down the Mississippi are more appreciated by adults than by the young, so should be Kim's journeyings from city to city in India and the passes of the lower Himalayas.

For *Kim,* like *Huckleberry Finn,* is far more than an adventure tale. It is the story of a precocious lad's search for his identity and also a study of how the conventional mores of a number of societies appear to a youthful observer who violates the "accepted" morality of adults and yet at the same time is far more ethical than they are. Like Huck, Kim lies, cheats, steals, smokes by the time he is twelve, and has for school and its discipline nothing but contempt. At the same time, Kim, like Huck, is a loyal and even tender protector of an elderly man of a different race, a dignified but simple soul to whom the conniving of the earth would do harm were it not for the protagonist's intervention. Although both Huck and Kim find much in their respective older companions that baffles them, neither boy mocks the customs or superstitions of the mature innocent whose search for freedom they seek to aid. True, Kim feels a certain condescension toward the lama he befriends because the boy is white and the old man is Tibetan. In just the same way, of course, Huck exhibits toward Nigger Jim a certain condescension. But in both cases the boys' superiority seems based not so much on racist feeling as on the fact that the two young rogues have learned more of the evil ways of the whites, because they themselves are white, than have their nonwhite companions. Even if there are a few instances in which the two lads lord it over their companions simply by dint of belonging to the white race, one has to take into account the era which each work was describing. For the United States in which Huck is supposed to grow up, he is remarkable in his acceptance of a runaway slave; for the 1880's in which Kim is supposed to dwell, he is just as remarkable in his preference for the ways of nonwhites to those of the race to which by birth he belongs.

It has often been argued that Kim plays a double-dealing game with the lama in that the supposed "disciple" uses his old Buddhist "master's" search for a mystic river of "soul freedom" as a means to work at the same time for the British Intelligence Service. Valid though this objection is, Kim's actions in regard to the lama are consistent with the boy's devious character, as consistent as Huck's in regard to Nigger Jim. Like Huck, Kim is a picaro with a strong urge for excitement. Is it not natural, then, that such a fictional character combine altruism with self-seeking? In both cases is it not obvious, considering the protagonist's race, that ultimately he must abandon the way of life which has formed the novel's heart, that a day *must* come when free and easy association with one of another color will no longer be possible? Given this fact, plus the precocious shrewdness with which Kipling endows Kim, it seems only natural that the boy should early render service and loyalty to British Intelligence, since a day has to come when he must abandon his "Indian" way of life so that he may win full acceptance by his "own kind."

The simplicity of style in **Kim** resembles Twain's masterpiece. Intrusions of the author's own opinions are few, and the descriptions of towns or countryside are no longer than necessary to convey atmosphere and information essential to events in the plot. Typical of Kipling's word pictures is the following account of the spot in the Himalayan foothills where they meet the two Russian spies, one of whom brutally attacks the weakened lama and so hastens the old man's near approach to death in the novel's last pages:

> At last they entered a world within a world—a valley of leagues where the high hills were fashioned of the mere rubble and refuse from off the knees of the mountains. Here one day's march carried them no farther, it seemed, than a dreamer's clogged pace bears him in a nightmare.

Thanks to these two sentences we find believable the exhaustion which overtakes Kim, as well as the lama, following the encounter with the Russians, an exhaustion which drives them out of the mountains and once more into the plains, a move essential to the novel's close. Such a piece of writing compares well with Twain's paintings of scenes along the Mississippi. Like Twain's writing it presents no barriers to a reader who has grown up on Hemingway and Steinbeck but who finds wearisome the involuted word paintings of Dickens. Nor is this passage atypical. At no time does Kipling become so lost in painting his myriad pictures of the India of the mountains and the plains that he forgets his first task—to tell us of Kim's adventures with the lama.

Kim also stands comparison with another widely read example of the picaresque novel, *Don Quixote*. Granted that Kim is a mere lad and Sancho Panza an adult, the fact remains that the old man whom each rogue both serves and uses for his own ends is a seeker after an ideal of perfection in a way that Nigger Jim is not. In contrast to the unearthly moral purity of the old man in each story are the misdemeanors of the younger companion. Furthermore, in a world as corrupt as it is, there is something pathetic about the nobility of both Don Quixote and Kim's lama. It is this very pathos of the two old visionaries that brings out the best in their earth-bound companions. Throughout **Kim** the young rogue is content to achieve his ends by trickery and lying—until the lama is struck by the Russian spy. Then at once the lad's reaction is a spontaneous leap to the old man's defense, a physical attack upon an assailant both bigger and better armed than he. Furthermore, despite the many notes of ludicrous comedy in both *Don Quixote* and **Kim,** the conclusion of both these works lacks the happy quality of *Huckleberry Finn*. To say this is not to imply that any novel with a happy ending must perforce be less admirable than one with a conclusion that leaves one troubled and puzzled.

Although Kipling does not actually show us the lama at the moment of death or Kim turning his back forever on the carefree days of playing Hindu or Moslem beggar boy, the conclusion does suggest that the old Tibetan is nearing his last days on earth; and Kim has been so successful in his final espionage mission for Colonel Strickland that, once the "master" is dead, the lad will dissociate himself from the Buddhist way and will soon become a full-time agent of the British Intelligence Service. The old man, though, knows nothing of Kim's other life and thinks only that the discovery of what the lama believes *is* the mystic river will enable both master and disciple to be baptized in its waters and thus freed forever of the evils of lust, anger, and ignorance. With Kim baptized, as well as himself, the dying old man is content. But knowing the boy as we do, we cannot believe that either the "master's" teachings or the washing in the river will make the young rogue pure. Hence the final sentence of the book is as poignant in its way as is the end of *Don Quixote:* "He [the lama] crossed his hands on his lap and smiled, as a man may who has won salvation for himself and his beloved."

There is one more interesting facet of **Kim** which seems worthy of tribute, though it has not received it. This is the fact that the novel is also the story of a youth involved in an identity crisis, groping for values. Although Kipling gives us none of the long introspective passages that we find in *Portrait of the Artist as a Young Man* or *Tonio Kröger,* he nonetheless implies several times that, as he grows older, Kim is deeply troubled about who and what he is. From the opening page he and we know that both his dead parents were white, despite the fact that he lives with a slatternly Hindu, dresses in Indian clothes, has dark skin, and can speak in various Indian dialects better than he can in English. As the years pass, Kipling depicts his young protagonist asking himself, "Who *is* Kim?" On one occasion the author even intrudes into the story with the comment, [Kim] considered his own identity, a thing he had never done before, till his head swam." Although loyalty and affection draw him to follow the wanderings of the pure old lama as he seeks the river, Kim knows full well that he is no true *chela* ("disciple"). Even the lama's financial sacrifices only serve to confuse Kim further: by paying for Kim's education in a Catholic boarding school, the lama introduces him to a world of British clothes and values, one where Kim looks down with the same contempt on his half-caste fellow pupils while certain of his other classmates sneer at him for knowledge of Indian ways and a preference for Indian over British clothing.

Yet even as Kim rebels at the school against British dress and standards, he knows that he *is* a sahib, that his future lies with the rulers, not the ruled, and that the lama's hard-sought "salvation" from the "wheel of life" can never be his. The cheerful street urchin, the illiterate orphan of the first page has changed by the end: shadows of the prison house of adult Western life are falling upon him even as the shade of death is stealing over the lama. Never again will the boy earn his living in the same free manner that he enjoys while begging for his Tibetan "master."

Also like *Don Quixote, Kim* is not faultless. The order of many of its episodes grows out of no logical necessity; an event that occurs in Chapter VIII could take place just as easily in Chapter III. Certain of its characters are nonessential, and so are certain of its scenes; their sole function seems to be to fulfill a wish on Kipling's part to paint as many Indian cities and rural areas as possible. Such qualities, however, are standard ingredients in any picaresque novel, and to condemn them as faults may perhaps be as foolish as to complain that an orange does not have the texture and flavor of a pear.

It may be that the presence of such faults is the reason for the relatively low critical esteem in which the picaresque novel as a genre tends to be held. Yet it remains a literary form which has produced three works that are likely to be read as long as men delight in books: *Huckleberry Finn, Don Quixote,* and *Tom Jones.* To this great trio I would add Kipling's *Kim.* Granted that many a contemporary reader may not approve of the British intelligence system as depicted in the work, the same kind of objection can be made to aspects of the others of the great trio. The same eternal qualities of *Huckleberry Finn* and *Don Quixote* which give pleasure in the twentieth century exist in *Kim.*

Angus Wilson

SOURCE: *The Strange Ride of Rudyard Kipling: His Life and His Works,* The Viking Press, 1977, pp. 130-32.

It is rare to find readers, Kipling fans or others, who are not captivated by *Kim;* it is equally rare to find many who can offer any detailed account of their enjoyment of the book. "Oh! *Kim,* of course, is a magical book," is the usual general account that follows a detailed discussion of his other works. And so it is . . .

I know of no other English novel that so celebrates the human urban scene (for English novelists are all touched by the Romantic country worship) except for that utterly dissimilar book, *Mrs Dalloway;* and when one reads of Kim's thoughts, "this adventure, though he did not know the English word, was a stupendous lark", one is reminded of the opening passage of Virginia Woolf's novel (Clarissa's thoughts as she steps out into the streets of London): "What a lark! What a plunge!" It is a note of delight in life, of openness to people and things that is maintained throughout the novel and is the essence of its magic.

Kipling's passionate interest in people and their vocabularies and their crafts is, of course, the essence of the magic of all his work. But in all the other books it tends to be marred by aspects of his social ethic—by caution, reserve, distrust, mastered emotion, stiff upper lips, direct puritanism or the occasional puritan's leer, retributive consequences, cruelty masquerading as justifiable restraint or bullying as the assertion of superiority. None of these is present in *Kim.*

Kipling's social ethic, it is true, is there in Kim's apprenticeship to "The Game", the British Secret Service in India. This is the way that, as a sahib's son, he will serve the British cause. This has stuck in the gullet of many liberal critics. . . .

True, Kim will be serving British rule, but this must be read within the context of Kipling's belief that the two higher values in this book—the richness and variety of Indian life and the divine and spiritual idiocy of the Lama—can only be preserved from destruction by anarchic chaos or from despotic tyranny by that rule. . . . Kim, by his involvement in The Game, can help to preserve that holy man whose spirituality he can glimpse and love but never hope to achieve. And let us note, it is a game, however terrible a one, in which Kim, by his strange street-arab status of friend of all the world and night climber across rooftops, is peculiarly associated—a game in which he must be able to carry maps in his head and remember a hundred objects seen and be able to pass disguised as twenty or so other people. These powers make him perfect material for a spy; the same powers made Kipling a great writer of fiction.

But, if the moralising side of Kipling is only lightly present in *Kim,* implicit in The Game, the corruption of Kim's world is always implicit rather than stated. The world Kim moves in is no ideal one. Only the Lama in his innocence mistakes the generous prostitute for a nun. It is a world of lies—Kim knows the Lama for a rarity because he tells the truth to strangers. Physical danger is constant and real. Human life is not held in high regard—Mahbub Ali is prepared to sacrifice Kim's life to get his message to Creighton, yet he loves Kim strongly and jealously. Few of the fifty or so vividly realised characters are without his or her faults, but most are made generous and loving by contact with Kim and the Lama. Yet Kim is never above the ordinary dishonesties and tricks of daily life. As the Lama says, "I have known many men in my long life, and disciples not a few. But to none among men, if so be thou art woman-born, has my heart gone out as it has to thee—thoughtful, wise and courteous; but something of a small imp."

And it is not Kim's virtues alone that win him the friendship of all the world. He is remarkably physically beautiful and, in a way that is successfully kept by Kipling from being fully sexual, flirtatious with all and sundry. It is part of his worldly guile. The prostitute in the train is won over by him as is the other prostitute who dresses him up when he escapes from St Xavier's School; the Sahiba's motherliness has an earthy tinge; the woman of Shamlegh yearns for him. In Lurgan's shop, as I have said, the jealousy of the Hindu boy has obvious sexual overtones; as I think does the jealousy of the horsedealer, Mahbub Ali, for Kim's overriding devotion to the Lama. Yet all this sensuality is without an explicit sexual tinge. I do not believe that this is Victorian self-censorship upon the part of Kipling. It is certainly not an avoidance of the subject in a book ostensibly intended for the young, for the scene where a prostitute tries to steal from Mahbub Ali is quite explicit. It is, I think, one more aspect of the purposeful attempt by Kipling in this novel to create a world that is real and ideal at one and the same time. Nor is the absence of overt sex offensively evasive as a modern critic might think. It is just a natural part of the innocent-corrupt world in which Kim lives.

As to evil it is strikingly absent, as may be measured by the unimportance of the "villains", the Russian and French spies. They are bad men, we know, for they offer violence to a very good man, the Lama. But their retribution is not the savoured brutal one of so many of Kipling's stories. They merely pass out of the novel, mocked by all the Himalayan villagers as they make off with their tails between their legs. Their humiliation is like that of Trinculo and Stephano on Prospero's magic island in *The Tempest* and we bless the babu Hurree Singh, who mocks

them, as we bless Ariel. In default of true evil, we must judge the English chaplain, Bennett, as the villain, for he lacks all concern for freedom and variety, virtues so surprisingly celebrated by Kipling in this book. It could be said that this absence of real evil prevents *Kim* from vying with the great novels of the past as a "mature" book; but, in compensation, it must surely be said that this creation of an innocent world of guile makes it an unequalled novel.

Nirad Chaudhuri has said that *Kim* is the very best picture of India by an English author, and I am sure he is right. But rich and convincing though the varied Indian characters are, and splendid though the evocations of the Indian scenes are from the Jain Temple outside Benares to the Himalayan foothills, it is yet Kipling's own India as Kim is Kipling's own street-arab and the Lama Kipling's own Buddhist. Many Indian critics, notably K. Jamiluddin in *The Tropic Sun,* have pointed out that Buddhism is a very strange choice of religion to represent India, from which it has been absent for centuries. No doubt, Kipling was a bit influenced in his choice by his desire to draw on his father's special knowledge; but I think he was even more concerned to pose his own version of self-abnegation against his own version of commitment to the world as represented by Kim. The Lama and Kim make a most delectable Prospero and Ariel. And it is no sparring partnership for either, since the Lama's greatest erring from The Way is in his attachment to his Chela, and Kim comes close to exhausting his adolescent physical strength in bringing his master down from the mountains. The story of Kim and the Lama is, in the last resort, beneath all its superbly realised human and topical detail an allegory of that seldom portrayed ideal, the world in the service of spiritual goodness, and, even less usual, spiritual goodness recognising its debt to the world's protection. It is the culmination and essence of all the transcendence that Kipling gained from his Indian experience. In it alone of all his works he does ask, "Who is Kim?", although he cannot answer the question. In a sense, his answer is the book itself, for it is the best thing he ever wrote.

Rosemary Sutcliff

SOURCE: *Kim,* in *Children's Literature in Education,* Vol. 13, No. 4, Winter, 1982, pp. 164-70.

I can claim no remembrance of the first time I read *Kim,* or rather, of the first time *Kim* was read to me, for I was one of those fortunate children possessed of a parent—in my case my mother, which was just as well, since my father, being a sailor, was liable to be away from home for two years at a time—who loves reading aloud and does it beautifully. I can only say that by the time I was eight or thereabouts, the book was a long-familiar and much-loved part of my life, as were the *Just So Stories, The Jungle Books, Puck of Pook's Hill,* and *Rewards and Fairies.* I loved them all equally, though in slightly different ways, and I think I still do. Yet it is *Kim* that has a permanent place along with *The Secret Garden, The Wind in the Willows,* Professor Gilbert Murray's translation of the *Hippolytus,* and half-a-dozen more, on my bedside windowsill.

Quite why, I do not know. I am in much the same predicament with regard to *Kim* as my first editor with regard to *The Wind in the Willows,* who told me long ago when we were both new to our careers, that he could not judge how good the book was because he loved it so much.

Since that first meeting with *Kim,* whenever it may have been, I have read and reread it many times; not, maybe, regularly once a year, yet I doubt if I have ever gone much longer than three years between readings, and I do not think that I have often gone two. My feeling for the book has of course changed with the passage of time, but it has never grown less. Always the delight has been there, waiting for me. Last week, rereading the book for the first time for a purpose (a purpose, that is, apart from the pleasure of reading it), I was nervous. Would the purpose drive out the delight? Break the spell? I pulled out the battered volume—my Grandmother's, when it was new—greeting as usual the elephant with the lotus flower held in the tip of his trunk, whose embossed head decorates the cover, turned somewhat hesitantly to page 1, and began to read.

> He sat, in defiance of Municipal Orders, astride the gun Zam-Zammah on her brick platform opposite the old Ajaib-Ghar, the Wonder House as the natives called the Lahore Museum. Who hold Zam-Zammah, that 'fire-breathing dragon', hold the Punjab; for the great green-bronze piece is always the first of the conqueror's loot.

And instantly the delight was there, and the old spell weaving itself again.

On the surface, *Kim* is a spy story, and such plot as it has, which is not much, for Kipling himself described it as being nakedly "picaresque and plotless", as are a surprising number of the great stories of the world, concerns a boy's education to be a Secret Agent in the service of the Raj; and that is probably the level at which a child first reads it, with undertones of

magic lying sensed but unrecognized beneath. But the plot is little more than a thread on which to string jewels as curious and entrancing as any in the shop of Lurgan Sahib, "The Healer of Sick Pearls." This is why the large-scale and vastly expensive film made from the book some twenty or more years ago, as watched for the third time by me on TV recently, is merely the husk, though a colourful and entertaining husk, with all the peculiar essence of Kipling's story drained out of it.

The film is a spy story, its climax the hero's encounter with Russian spies among the High Hills of the Frontier. But the book is so much more, and the encounter is merely an incident on the way, though admittedly one which forms a turning point in the quest of Kim and his Lama. For the story is, among so many other things, a Quest story—of the Lama for his sacred river, and release from the Wheel of Things, of Kim for his true self.

This is a quest that takes them drifting among the drifting vagabond life of India too far down to be coloured by any question of State or politics. Kipling's account of this life is so evocative that reading it, one catches the scent of dust and withered marigolds and the smoke of dung fires where the village elders gather under the peepul tree in the dusk:

> The lama, very straight and erect, the deep folds of his yellow clothing slashed with black in the light of the parao fires, precisely as a knotted tree trunk is slashed with the shadows of the long sun, addressed a tinsel and lacquered ruth (ox-cart) which burned like a many-coloured jewel in the same uncertain light. The patterns of the gold-worked curtain ran up and down, melting and re-forming as the folds shook and quivered in the night wind; and when the talk grew more earnest, the jewelled forefinger snapped out little sparks of light between the embroideries. Behind the cart was a wall of uncertain darkness speckled with little flames and alive with half-caught forms and faces and shadows.

This description of a night scene on the Grand Trunk Road expresses perfectly two of the aspects of *Kim* that linger most strongly in the mind. First, its preoccupation with light. Kipling could never visualize any incident without its setting of light and weather, time of day, and season of the year, but in *Kim* more than any other of his books, one is constantly aware of this play of changing light, windy sunlight brushing across the tawny grass of a hillside, the chill grey of dawn on waking camp on a railway siding, the smoky flare of torches, white peaks lifting themselves yearning to the moonlight while all the rest is "as the darkness of interstellar space".

Secondly, there is its sense of crowding riches—riches so vast that they overflow untidily in all directions and much could not be used at all, though one senses them behind what actually appears, a shifting background "speckled with little flames and alive with half-caught forms and faces and shadows".

Kipling himself, in his autobiography, describes the process of smoking over the book with his father:

> Under our united tobacco it grew like the Djin released from the brass bottle, and the more we explored its possibilities, the more opulence of detail did we discover. I do not know what proportion of an iceberg is below the water-line, but "Kim" as it finally appeared was about one tenth of what the first lavish specification called for.

And that is exactly the impression that the reader gets.

I suppose it must have been about the time that I started to write, and my awareness of the working of the craft in others was therefore beginning to waken, that I first realized the kinship that undoubtedly exists between *Kim* and *The Jungle Books*. Kimball O'Hara, whose father was a Colour-Sergeant in an Irish regiment and his mother a nursemaid in the Colonel's family, and who, after the death of his parents, was brought up—insofar as he was brought up by anyone except himself—by a half-caste woman who smoked opium "and pretended to keep a second-hand furniture shop by the square where the cheap cabs wait", is in the same position as Mowgli, a boy belonging by birth and heritage to one world, thrown into and accepted by another, and faced in the end with the same choice to be made. Mowgli has to choose between the Jungle and the Village, Kim between the world of action for which he has been trained, and the timeless Eastern world he knows in his bones and in his heart's core. And though we are not actually told so, we know that like Mowgli he will go back to the Village, leaving the Jungle behind him, and that he too will break something within himself in doing so. But because of the very nature of the world for which he has been trained, he will remain always just a little a citizen of two worlds, with all the strains and stresses and heartbreaks that such a position entails. For to be even just a little a citizen of two worlds must of necessity mean to be not completely a citizen of either.

Like Mowgli, too, Kim has his sponsors in his adoptive world, and in his case, in the world of the Secret Service, the Great Game, also. First and foremost there is the lama himself, the most completely good character that Kipling ever created; the only perfectly good character, I think, that I have ever met between the covers of a book, who contrives also to be unreservedly attractive—generally speaking, human beings, actual or fictional, need a fault or two before it is possible to love them. Then there is the masterful old dowager of Saharumpore, the owner of the jewelled finger aforementioned, who emerges vividly and irrepressibly and outrageously among the rest, though she remains (more or less) behind her embroidered curtains and is never actually described at all. Mahbub Ali, the lean and ferocious horse dealer with the dyed red beard, is the only one of Kim's sponsors to stand for him in both worlds, and is believed to be based on a friend of Kipling's early days, a Pathan of "indescribable filth but magnificent mien and features", who brought him the news of Central Asia beyond the Khyber Pass. Lurgan Sahib, "The Healer of Sick Pearls" and another player of the Great Game, was also based on a real character, the keeper of a curiosity shop in Simla, Alexander Jacob by name, a man of Turkish ancestry, and possessed of uncanny powers. And for the fifth and last, there is the soft-bellied Bengali babu (clerk) with the heart of a lion—for surely no courage can match that of the man who is always afraid. Ironically, he is the clever, half-Westernized Hindu whose kind later spread to form a "middle class" which India had never had before, and from which much of the backing for Self Rule was to come.

But this, having little feeling for politics, Kipling could not foresee. Nor could he foresee that by that time the word "Empire" would begin to take on shameful undertones. Empire building and holding, all the things that much of his work seems to stand for, would be widely considered a disreputable occupation. Further, he could not foresee that because he stood for these things, the charge of jingoism would be flung at him by people who had not noticed that the accent of his work is on Service, rather than mere mastery. His **"A Ballad of East and West"** would be quoted in support of the charge: "Oh East is East and West is West and never the twain shall meet", by people who had taken the lines out of context, without reading far enough to see that the verse ends:

> But there is neither East nor West,
> Border nor breed nor birth,
> When two strong men stand face to face
> Though they come from the ends of the earth.

I can sympathize, as Kipling could, with the Native's hunger to have his land and his culture to himself again (I have made that clear enough in some of my own books). But born and bred as I have been in the tradition of the so-called Fighting Services, I feel very close to Kipling in most of his values. I do not think that an Empire is necessarily a good thing, but I do not feel that it is necessarily something to be ashamed of either. I can appreciate also, from the same Service background, his opinion of people behind desks or in pulpits at home, who have no clear idea of what things are actually *like* at the scene of action, but who know exactly how everything should be done nevertheless. I can appreciate his feeling for the difference between the outsider, sometimes to be considered as "fair game" by the initiated, and the individualist and rebel, to be encouraged within reason (Kim belongs very much to the second of these two categories).

So, in the later part of his life, in the years after his death, and by some people even today, Kipling was and is looked on as the jingoistic upholder of an oppressive Raj. And yet the Bengali writer Nirad C. Chaudhuri could claim that *Kim* was not only "the finest story about India in English", but also that the book was the outcome of Kipling's vision of a larger India than meets the most penetrating outward eye, "A vision whose profundity we Indians would be hard put to it to match, even in an Indian language, not to speak of English. . . . We Indians should never cease to be grateful to Kipling for having shown the many faces of our country in all their beauty, power and truth."

Kipling loved India, and not with a love that stemmed from the outside looking in, but very much from within, from the long hot fever-smelling nights when as Assistant Editor of the *Civil and Military Gazette* published at Lahore, and still in his late 'teens, he would explore the ancient Muslim city crouched under its ghost-ridden fortress from which Ranjit Singh, the Lion of the Punjab, had ruled his short-lived Sikh kingdom. On such nights, no one could sleep much, and most of the life of Lahore went on in the streets and on the rooftops. These nighttime prowlings were to bear fruit and flower later:

> He (Kim) knew the wonderful walled city of Lahore from the Delhi Gate to the Outer Fort Ditch; was hand-in-glove with men who lead lives stranger than anything Haroun al Raschid dreamed of; and he lived in a life wild as that of the Arabian Nights, but missionaries and secretaries of charitable societies could not see the beauty of it. His nickname through the wards was 'Little Friend of all the World'; and very often, being lithe and inconspicuous, he executed commissions by night on the crowded rooftops for sleek and shiny young men of fashion. It was intrigue, of course—he knew that much, as he had known

all evil since he could speak—but what he loved was the game for its own sake, the stealthy prowl through the dark gullies and lanes, the crawl up a water pipe, the sights and sounds of the women's world on the flat roofs, and the headlong flight from house-top to house-top under cover of the hot dark.

And his contact with "White Man's India" was not Vice-regal Lodge or the Simla parties, for which he had a splendid contempt, but the company at the Lahore Club, where tired representatives of Army, Education, Canals, Forestry, Engineering, Irrigation, Railways, Medicine and Law met and talked in great detail each their own particular brand of "shop".

The only "shop" which he does not seem to have drunk in with joyful avidity was that of the Church. He had above all, no use for the Missionary, however valiant and well-meaning, who did not understand native culture or traditions or allow for the possibility of other truths than his own. He had a deep religion of his own, but it was not particularly a Christian religion. And he stated his own belief in his splendid **"Hymn to Mithras"**

> Many roads Thou hast fashioned
> All of them lead to the Light.

And in *Kim,* when he wishes to make a saint, he makes him a Buddhist, not a Christian.

The lama possesses charity in its broadest sense of love with understanding and acceptance; the two Army Chaplains, one Anglican, one Roman Catholic, good, well-meaning men both of them, are entirely lacking in that quality. But even the lama only gains his vision of his Sacred River after, for love of Kim his Chela, he has denied his own philosophy of unattachment to earthly things and the severing of all human bonds.

Kim is a strange, beautiful book, written on many levels, and beneath the Secret Service adventure story, and below the spread of constantly changing scenes, curious incident and laughter, and the delights of smell and sound and colour, the raggle-taggle riches and the half-glimpsed glories, at the deepest level of all, it is a story that has to do with the Soul of Man; a story whose real theme is love.

Robert F. Moss

SOURCE: *Rudyard Kipling and the Fiction of Adolescence,* St. Martin's Press, 1982, pp. 142-47.

Two years after the publication of *Stalky & Co.,* . . . Kipling's myth of boyhood arrived at its culmination.

Reunited with his parents and finding at last a permanent home in the English countryside, Kipling was able to create a final, splendid testament to the India of his youth. In *Kim,* the adolescent strain, cultivated from Mulvaney and his friends through *Stalky & Co.,* reached its most dramatically successful form. More than any of Kipling's other boys—certainly more than his adolescent men—Kim comes across as he was intended. Kim's instinct for where adventure is to be found, his gift for self-preservation in the midst of adversity, his game-playing, his love of professionalism—all these are superbly rendered. He receives his education in the streets of India, in an Anglo-Indian school, in the secret training grounds of the Great Game. Fundamentally, it is the same education that Kipling's other heroes receive, but here there is less emphasis on brutalization of the learner and more on the joy of learning. In addition, Kim is the only one of Kipling's heroes who is educated both indirectly, through sink-or-swim immersion in reality (like Dick and Cheyne, Sr) and directly, through formalized pedagogy (like Mowgli, Stalky and the soldiers). But the real profundity of *Kim* lies in Kipling's handling of the search for identity. Always uncertain as to his real destiny, Kim's odysseys are all, in some sense, a quest to find his true self, an attempt to assess the conflicting demands of two radically different ways of life. In the first two-thirds of the book, the clash Kim feels is between his Western heritage and his Eastern upbringing. In the latter portion of the novel, however, the conflict alters considerably; it is no longer a choice between East and West, but between the Game, which is both Eastern and Western in nature, and the Search, which is exclusively Eastern. At virtually all points in *Kim* the conflicts are viewed through the hero's troubled soul; never are they merely painted backdrops.

There is no doubt that *Kim* is the most intimate revelation of Kipling's inner self, as much a spiritual autobiography as Wordsworth's "Prelude"; the book is an attempt to seize all the jagged, confusing, remarkable fragments of his psychic life and incorporate them into a great fictional kaleidoscope. But the brilliance of the novel may have more to do with its depth than its breadth, with the excavations Kipling was able to make into his own soul. There he examined the warring forces of his personality with the longest, most penetrating scrutiny he ever gave them. Through Kim, he probed his dual attachments to the life of action and the life of art; to progress and permanence; to Eastern mysticism and Western pragmatism; to sensuality and asceticism; to the hard-nosed

Yorkshire naturalism of his father and the leaping Celtic poetry of his mother.

Yielding himself up fully to his art at last, Kipling succeeded in combining the cultural complexity of [*Captains Courageous*] with the psychological depth of the Mowgli stories. His achievement was further enhanced by the sympathetic, loving picture of the Indians in *Kim,* proof against the blanket accusations of racism that his works have always had to face. Though Kipling went on to create other magnificent works in various modes (**"Dayspring Mishandled"** and **"The Gardener"**, for example), *Kim* marks the end of the most fruitful and best remembered phase of his career, a journey toward artistic fulfilment that began with the inauspicious *Soldiers Three* and ended with this remarkable novel.

Mark Paffard

SOURCE: "Illustrating the Native Feature," in *Kipling's Indian Fiction,* St. Martin's Press, 1989, pp. 80-102.

> The foolish person in search of a little disinterested information about things may find the so-called Indian Mutiny an unexplained historical phenomenon and eagerly hope for some enlightenment on the subject from a writer who is 'illustrating the native feature'. He will get little or none from Mr Kipling. . . . He will find the scantiest mention of or even allusion to the social movements of the natives.

So argued the radical poet Francis Adams in 1891. In effect he combines two points here—that Kipling wilfully ignores Indian politics, as represented by the Indian journalism of Bombay and Calcutta, and by the newly-formed Indian Congress; and also that he sees Indians only in the mass, as 'raw, brown, naked humanity', as Kipling puts it in **'The Conversion of Aurelian McGoggin.'**

The correctness of the first point is not at issue. Kipling had no time for the Indian's point of view, and his early journalism dismisses the political consciousness emerging in the big cities as an aberration. The second point involves critical judgement, although only a radical like Adams could have raised it in the nineties. Another distinguished early critic, Richard Le Gallienne, writes without irony of 'the romance of the English government in India.' Since then the critical perspective has undoubtedly been changed by Kipling's most popular and sustained account of India in *Kim* (1901). Still, it is questionable whether Adams himself would have accepted that Kipling's treatment of 'natives' had fundamentally altered in this characteristic passage from Chapter 4 of *Kim:*

> They met a troop of long-haired, strong-scented Sansis with baskets of lizards and other unclean food on their backs, the lean dogs sniffing at their heels. These people kept their own side of the road, moving at a quick, furtive jog-trot, and all other castes gave them ample room; for the Sansi is deep pollution. Behind them, walking wide and stiffly across the strong shadows, the memory of his leg-irons still on him, strode one newly released from jail; his full stomach and shiny skin to prove that the Government fed its prisoners better than most honest men could feed themselves. Kim knew that walk well, and made broad jest of it as they passed. Then an Akali, a wild-eyed, wild-haired Sikh devotee in the blue-checked clothes of his faith, with polished steel quoits glistening on the cone of his tall blue turban, stalked past, returning from a visit to one of the independent Sikh states, where he had been singing the glories of the Khalsa to college-trained princelings in top-boots and white cord breeches. Kim was careful not to irritate that man; for the Akali's temper is short and his arm is quick.

Descriptive moments like these have impressed several twentieth-century critics with the richness and diversity that Kipling in *Kim* finds in India. Yet despite the generosity of detail, and the obvious love of colour and movement that Kipling shares with us, he is still dealing here with India en masse, the Indian *crowd.* There is no doubting his affection for the *characteristic* moments of Indian life—in this respect his recording of Indian smells, and especially of Indian cooking, is even more impressive; but it falls short of entailing the respect of equals and the acceptance of the Indian as a real individual. Time and again Kipling draws Indian characters so deftly that they remain in the memory, but do so explicitly as *types,* so that the reader actually recalls them by means of a label: 'the Jat farmer' or 'the Amritsar courtesan'. As Arnold Kettle has pointed out, the two foreground figures who explore India in *Kim*—a British boy and a Tibetan lama—are *both* foreigners.

One of the delightful things about Kim himself is that his education appears to consist of a series of holidays. We are seduced by his whole-hearted approach to India, but it must not be forgotten that India is so enjoyable precisely because it is all at his disposal. Although Kim learns a great deal, he does not have to unlearn this attitude in order to take on adult responsibilities when he goes to work for the government. He is perfectly suited by his 'native' background to the education that Kipling designs for him; for if India is still a foreign land in *Kim,* there

is a new emphasis on the need for its rulers to know and respect it—in much the same way, one might say, as an educated gentleman in the nineteenth century had to know Italy or France. We find, for example, some vehement criticism of one British attitude typical of lower-class white men. Of the drummer-boy who is temporarily put in charge of Kim we are told that 'He did not care for any of the bazaars that were within bounds. He styled all natives "niggers"; yet servants and sweepers called him abominable names to his face, and, misled by their deferential attitude, he never understood.' To some Anglo-Indians, at least, this must have been a vaguely alarming comment. The 'real' sahibs, however, are in an altogether different case. All are, indeed, experts on Indian languages and customs. Such a sahib is Creighton, the spymaster who recruits Kim to the service: 'No man could be a fool who knew the language so intimately, who moved so gently and silently, and whose eyes were so different from the dull fat eyes of other sahibs.' Among such men ignorance is a cardinal sin. Creighton explicitly warns Kim that recruits who 'contemn the black man' and 'feign not to understand him' have their pay cut for ignorance.

The extent to which Kipling is willing to modify traditional British prejudice and isolationism is reflected in the school to which Kim is sent, which is Catholic and mainly attended by the children of well-to-do Eurasian parents. These boys have the advantage of knowing India far more intimately than the upper echelons of the 'pure' English who stay within their cantonments. Nevertheless, 'When tales were told of hot nights, Kim did not sweep the board with reminiscences; for St Xavier's looks down on boys who "go native" altogether. One must never forget that one is a Sahib, and that some day, when examinations are passed, one will command natives.' In his account of the school Kipling thus gives his seal of approval to the Eurasian establishment. We should be reminded here of the 'second fighting-line of Eurasians' that he envisages in **'His Private Honour'.** Clearly such approval has to be treated with caution, for the racism of Kipling's day, as indeed of our own, is not always so clear-cut as to be instantly identifiable, but comprises a system that makes numerous distinctions. Kipling may accept the Eurasians who attend public school and are destined for careers in medicine, law, or administration as sahibs, but not the signaller Michele D'Cruz in **'His Chance in Life',** who has only one drop of white blood in him. Nor will he necessarily allow that miscegenation is ever really desirable. Race, class, and caste tend to overlap to create distinctions, but 'racial purity' remains fairly fundamental. It may seem odd that in the first draft of *Kim* one of Kim's adversaries is described by Kipling as a 'nigger', but the criticism levelled at the drummer-boy in the published version is that he does not *distinguish* between 'niggers'—Holderness's 'Dravidians' and 'coolies'—and other Indian races. Again, in the published version, the Afghan Mahbub Ali nearly stabs Kim because he calls him 'Kala Admi'—a black man—but refrains upon remembering that Kim, although he looks like a native, is a pure white sahib. What is true is not that Kipling has become non-racist in outlook, but that his attention is on the 'better' representatives of various racial groups: those whom he imagines may work in harmony with the British government, rather than those who pose a nuisance or a threat. But if Kipling's racism has altered only by degrees, there is a wholesale change in his imaginative assimilation of India. Throughout his career, since, for example, 'The Story of Muhammed Din', Kipling had often written about particular Indians with affection and respect. In Lahore he had belonged to a freemason's lodge that included representatives of almost every race in India. In all this work, however, racial characteristics are quite unalterable, and the British are inevitably 'superior' in the long run. In *Kim* the British retain their superiority, but for the first time they have something to learn from the 'simple, tolerant folk' of India. In the preface to *Life's Handicap* Kipling finely remarks that 'when man has come to the turnstiles of Night all the creeds in the world seem to him wonderfully alike and colourless'. There is an abundance of colour and of different customs in *Kim,* and its impact is such that Kipling is doing more than observing and celebrating the difference. There is at least scope for a more complex characterisation of members of other races; a sense that they may also change and develop with experience. The relationship of Kim with the lama is at the heart of this shift in attitude, but it shows itself in small things as well as large ones. When the detective Strickland first dons native disguise in **'Miss Youghal's Sais'** (1888) he is unable to stomach native tobacco, but Kim smokes it for preference.

It is nevertheless the white men who hold all the threads of the 'Great Game' of espionage which in Kim's phrase, 'runs like a shuttle through all Hind'. The expression 'Great Game' originated in the context of the First Afghan war of 1839, and then became current as a description of British Eastern diplomacy in general, so that its use in *Kim* relocates it and indirectly asserts the political primacy of India and its north-west frontier. The actual system of espionage described in *Kim* is based on fact, down to

the terminology of 'players' and 'games', and the use of a wooden rosary to count the paces in clandestine survey work. Though they are trustworthy 'players', Kipling's agents are controlled from a centre which processes their information.

Among his native friends Kim is the 'Friend of all the World' and 'Friend of the Stars', and the India he finds is there, like these enjoyably Oriental appellations, to be enjoyed and savoured. It is appropriate to such enjoyment that the book should have an episodic feel. In his autobiography Kipling described it as 'nakedly picaresque' and cited Cervantes. The allusion is fitting in the other sense that the India traversed by Kim and the lama is a peasant society; much of the colour and good humour with which it is described is made possible by the endearing simplicity of its inhabitants, who become progressively more simple as the story moves into the mountainous regions near Nepal and Tibet. Kipling's account of his inability to 'make a plot' is somewhat disingenuous, for the book is tightly organised around a clear double structure. Kim and the lama undertake two journeys together, each of which ends in a discovery. In the middle there is a hiatus covering the time that Kim spends at school. The first part of the novel leads to the discovery that Kim is a sahib; the second is concerned with discovering what it means to be a sahib. In typically Victorian fashion the discovery of a new identity involves a need to be educated into new social norms, and this is what the hiatus between journeys stresses. The fascinating jewel-dealer Lurgan who trains Kim in espionage skills is in the end a superior kind of schoolmaster: "'By Jove! O'Hara, I think there is a great deal in you; but you must not become proud and you must not talk.'" It is only when the new lessons have been sufficiently rubbed in that Kim can set out with the lama again, but bearing this time not only his cheerful ability to blend in with Indian life but also his formal qualifications in espionage work and, most importantly, his sahib's mentality. Kim is now on equal terms with his fellow-agent, Mahbub Ali, whose pawn and messenger he has been. The pleasant paradox of *Kim* is that his burgeoning sahibdom brings him closer to his people, the Indians themselves.

'And who are thy people, Friend of all the World?'

'This great and beautiful land', said Kim, waving his paw round the little clay-walled room where the oil-lamp in its niche burned heavily through the tobacco-smoke. 'And, further, I would see my Lama again. And further, I need money.'

This statement to Mahbub is important, signalling that Kim is destined to become not merely one of the better type of sahibs, but a sahib of a virtually new type; one with a real and deep affection for India. The affectionate irony with which 'this great and beautiful land' is contrasted with the smoky interior is a reinforcing measure; India as we have seen it through Kim's eyes *is* beautiful. Sahib though he is, Kim also needs the lama, and it is through serving as his disciple that he finds fulfilment and is integrated with his people. For although the lama is not of India, he represents the spirit of India. In one of the most assured passages in the book the lama's wanderings while Kim is at school are sketched in, and he is described 'coming and going across India as softly as a bat'. Bat-like movement, flitting, responding to echoes, could well serve as an image for the people of India in **Kim**. It contrasts with the symbol of benevolent British domination, the railways, whose presence is constantly felt in the book. 'The government has brought on us many taxes', observes a farmer from the Punjab, 'but it gives us one good thing—the *te-rain* that joins friends and unites the anxious. A wonderful matter is the *te-rain*.' Kipling's style subtly reflects the contrast between the indirections and the relaxed quality of the Indian way of life and the ordered world of the British. 'They entered the fort-like railway station, black in the end of night; the electrics sizzling over the goods-yard where they handle the heavy northern grain-traffic.' The same elegant balancing of clauses and use of assonance is employed to create the 'Indian' quality of the Jain temple at Benares:

> The Oswal, at peace with mankind, carried the message into the darkness behind him, and the easy, uncounted Eastern minutes slid by; for the lama was asleep in his cell, and no priest would wake him. When the click of his rosary again broke the hush of the inner court where the calm images of the Arhats stand, a novice whispered, 'Thy *chela* is here', and the old man strode forth, forgetting the end of that prayer.

It is very important that Kipling seeks, through his prose, to portray in **Kim** an India that has its own inward movement and rhythm. Kipling described his method of literary composition in **Something of Myself**, in which he progressively deleted from his first draft until he was left with what was essential. It is a method that has been deprecated as well as praised, on the grounds that what the resulting style gains in vigour and compression is lost in possible ambiguity, and that the net result is too inflexible an instrument. In **Kim,** too, Kipling's passion for figures with

sharply etched outlines, and for the *mot juste,* impose limitations on the India he portrays, as in this description:

> Then they met Sikander Khan coming down with a few unsaleable screws—remnants of his string—and Mahbub, who has more of horse-coping in his little finger-nail than Sikander Khan in all his tents, must needs buy two of the worst, and that meant eight hours of laborious diplomacy and untold tobacco.

This, too, is elegant; but here it is impossible not to be aware of the narrator's voice and its controlling power—as, for example, in the faintly ironic 'laborious diplomacy and untold tobacco'. The ways of Muslim horse-dealers are, one feels here, fixed to all eternity. The Indian scene that emerges is at times too predictable, and too plastically subservient to Kipling the craftsman and Kipling the imperialist. Mahbub Ali is, indeed, the wily and ferocious type of Pathan that we meet throughout Kipling's work. If we see only his virtues in **Kim** this does not mean that he ever steps beyond the cocoon of racial characteristics, into which his paternal feelings for Kim neatly fit. Both he and Kim's other secret service mentor Hurree Chunder Mookerjee are 'supermen' to some extent. Thus Mahbub is shown restraining his *native* instinct for bloodletting in order better to conceal his identity, just as Hurree is shown overcoming his *native* timidity when his work as an agent demands it. 'Watch him', Kipling exhorts us, 'all babudom laid aside'. It is only the super-spy who can doff, but not alter, his racial type; but Hurree is also as much an old Roman as a Bengali: 'Rolled in the Babu, robed as to the shoulders like a Roman emperor, jowled like Titus'—an impression which Lockwood Kipling's original illustration strongly confirms.

It is only through the lama that we sense an India freed from preordained characteristics and able to develop independently. He represents a simplicity that, convenient though it may be to Kipling, seems to go deeper than typecasting. It is at the point in the book where the lama, laden with his spiritual difficulties, returns to the simple life of the mountains that we come across a scene that Edmund Wilson rightly described as unmatched in Kipling.

> Then they thawed out in the sun, and sat with their legs hanging over infinite abysses, chattering, laughing, and smoking. They judged India and its government solely from their experience of wandering Sahibs who had employed them or their friends as shikarris. Kim heard tales of shots missed upon ibex, serow, or markhor, by Sahibs

twenty years in their graves—every detail lighted from behind like twigs on tree-tops seen against lightning.

Whatever its weakness, Kipling's sharp, unambiguous style—unconsciously imaged for us here in the simile of the twigs—renders convincingly this basic sense of uncomplicated human community. Descriptive passages like this, and the portrayal of the lama in the Jain temple illuminate Nirad C. Chaudhuri's remark that Kipling 'stands supreme among Western writers for his treatment of the biggest reality in India, which is made up of the life of people and religion in the twin setting of the mountains and the plains.' Against this setting the sign that the lama discovers in his torn chart can be presented as valid on its own terms: 'Kim stared at the brutally disfigured chart. From left to right diagonally the rent ran—from the Eleventh House where Desire gives birth to the Child (as it is drawn by Tibetans)—across the human and animal worlds, to the Fifth House—the empty House of the Senses. The logic was unanswerable.' We are not expected to take this literally, but it would obviously be a grave mistake to dismiss it as 'native superstition'; a mistake which is in fact made by the Russian spies who are the tokenistic villains of *Kim.* The same is true of the lama's final 'discovery' of his sacred river after his final meditation. While we do not literally believe in the river, as Kim himself clearly does not, we recognise a spiritual state which has, above all, contributed to Kim's education.

> About the end of the first century B.C. there was something of a split in the ranks (of Buddhism) resulting from an attempt to restore it to a popular basis. This led to the evolution of the Boddhisattvas, beings who on the threshold of Nirvana set aside their entry into the final state of bliss and remained in the sinful world out of compassion for others to whose salvation they became devoted. . . . Whatever the merits of this development it inevitably led to the growth of myths attendant on the peculiar virtues of each one of them. The way was open to a compromise with Hindu teachings.

There is clearly a possible analogy between the action of the Bodhisattvas and the sacrifice of Christ, and it is noticeable that in *Kim* the Bodhisat is always mentioned as a single individual, as he is in Kipling's poem 'The Buddha at Kamakura' (1892). In those verses the Christian pantheon seems to influence Kipling further, as the single Bodhisat is amalgamated with the father-figure of the Buddha. It is certainly the action of the Boddhisattvas that the lama imitates in his own mind at the end of *Kim.* His

account is counterpointed by the commonsense view of the other characters, who see an old man tumbling into a brook and having to be fished out; yet the comicality of the lama never really diminishes respect for his special qualities. At the last, Kim 'peered at the cross-legged figure, outlined in jet-black against the lemon-coloured drift of the light. So does the stone Bodhisat sit who looks down upon the patent self-registering turnstiles of the Lahore Museum.' With this the entire novel wheels back to its opening scene, and it does so with some intent, for the museum is presided over by the kindly curator (whose resemblance to John Lockwood—Kipling the father—was recognisable even at the time of publication) who serves the lama as the model of the kind of sahib he would like Kim to become. As Edmund Wilson has pointed out, Kim is clearly destined to be rather more of a soldier than a scholar. The argument, however, that Kim's career as a spy is a 'betrayal' of the Indian people is misconceived. The Indians of *Kim* are not looking for independence, and nothing about the Indian world that Kipling depicts contradicts the notion that spying is an honourable service to them. It matters that Kim's own question, 'What is Kim?' changes to 'Who is Kim?'—that the affectionate mood of the novel is geared to a vision of India in which sahibs and natives no longer occupy entrenched positions. But such a vision presupposes that the Indians are willing subordinates to the British. The remark of one of the Russians that 'It is *we* who can deal with the Orientals' is exposed as fatuous, but the underlying implication is that if British were substituted for Russian, then the remark might embody truth.

Every aspect of *Kim* reveals its purpose as a blueprint for India as a country under permanent and beneficient British rule. The gentle ways of the lama complement rather than challenge this conception. Yet although the figure that Kim sees outlined in jet black is akin to the final price in the colourful jigsaw puzzle India that Kipling has constructed, he emerges with a rare degree of individuality. The two journeys through which Kim finds his place in the world are also learning experiences for the already wise lama. There is a mystery behind his very simplicity, and the story of Kim's growth to adulthood is finally of less interest than the shadows he casts. As Kim's mentor, the lama is joined by the 'sahiba', the rich widow and grandmother who presides over the final unity. She stands, in the scheme of *Kim,* for India on its benevolent physical, rather than spiritual side. Like Kim and the lama, she too is seeing India on a jaunt, for it is a curious fact that the thronging, colourful world of *Kim* does not in the end contain any real account of Indian people engaged in their ordinary working lives. With the Sahiba we encounter a manner of describing India that is familiar from Kipling's earlier work: 'The patterns on the gold-worked curtains ran up and down, melting and reforming as the folds shook and quivered to the night wind; and when the talk grew more earnest the jewelled forefinger snapped out little sparks of light between the embroideries.' This takes us back to Mulvaney's description of the princesses in **'The Incarnation of Krishna Mulvaney'**, or to the jewel-hoard in **'The King's Ankus',** which Angus Wilson has aptly described as written in a 'restrained Yellow-Book manner'. The Orient stirs seductively for a moment in the description of the Sahiba's conveyance, but in the very few such moments when the sensuous hints at the sensual, Kim's magic charm is such that they bring him pure relief: 'Kneaded to irresponsible pulp, half hypnotised by the perpetual flick and read-justment of the uneasy *chudders* that veiled their eyes, Kim slid ten thousand miles into slumber'.

In the end the tolerant, celebratory mood of *Kim* is surely both a gain and a loss. The tension beneath the surface of his early work, caused by a real struggle to mould at least some of the actualities of civilian and army life into an acceptable yet desirable picture of India has gone. The 'evil presence' of those early stories is still officially supposed to exist in *Kim,* but it is reduced to meaninglessness by the pronouncement that the boy Kim 'had known all evil since he could speak'. In reality Kim is always too much the almost disembodied Puck figure, the 'Friend of the Stars', for the process of his growth to be made interesting. His fulfilment is to realise that he is simply part of the everyday world: 'Roads were meant to be walked upon, houses to be lived in, cattle to be driven, fields to be tilled, and men and women to be talked to.' Kipling seems to have ignored the fact that one cannot make a *bildungsroman* out of such a plain tale. But although *Kim* is a blueprint that produces an arbitrary resolution of the conflict between India and the British, it produces an 'India' which is more than the result of sheer manipulation. The unexpectedness of the lama's interventions in particular give it, within the obvious limits that Kipling imposes, an independent life. It is through the lama, too, that Kim himself acquires a vitality rare among the heroes of what the book essentially is: Victorian boys' fiction—'I have known many men in my so long life, and disciples not a few. But to none among men, if so be thou are woman-born, has my heart gone out as it has to thee—thoughtful, wise, and courteous, but something of a small imp.'

Jessica Edwards

SOURCE: "Rudyard Kipling: *Kim.*" *Inkblot Magazine,* Spring, 1999. Retrieved May 17, 2000 from http://www.dreamsbay.com/inkblots20b2/kim.html.

Of Kipling, George Orwell once said, "I worshipped [him] at thirteen, loathed him at seventeen, enjoyed him at twenty, despised him at twenty-five, and now again rather admire him. The one thing that was never possible, if one had read him at all, was to forget him." I only hope that I have the opportunity to share so many years with Kipling as Orwell spent. Many of us have grown up familiar with Kipling's classic works **The Jungle Books** and **Just So Stories,** but upon growing older have seen Kipling's writing pass out of our lives like that of so many other childhood authors. And while I despair at that loss, that is the topic for another essay. Kipling, though, should be reclaimed by adults and *Kim* is a tremendous place to start.

Imagine yourself in India at the turn-of-the-century, a country full of soldiers and skirmishes, where the British think they rule, but the native people know better. Enter Kim, the orphan of an Irish soldier, raised as a street child: smart, free and mischievous. Include a Tibetan lama searching for the river of life. Add intrigue and secret conspiracies, horse dealers and murder and you begin to piece together the recipe of Kipling's greatest work.

Writing for his contemporaries, Kipling magnificently tells a story that has both political and literary merit. Though Kipling believed in the British Empire and in British supremacy, he saw the dangers inherent in ruling India. From his childhood in Bombay and his love for India, he understood that permanent occupation by soldiers was the only way that the British would maintain control in India. Using *Kim,* Kipling tried to warn the world of the burgeoning power of the Indian people, of their patience and cleverness in waiting to reclaim their country. There are difficult passages in *Kim* for a modern reader. Through our eyes, Kipling seems horribly racist and sexist; implying that British men are vastly superior to all other humans. While we would rather absolve all of our heroes of the things we think they did wrong, I refuse to release Kipling. He was racist and sexist, but these are important to the reading of his novels, especially *Kim.* It shines with pure intentions and a true desire to find a solution that both allowed India its freedom and maintained the superiority of the British.

Perhaps most interesting about *Kim,* in light of Kipling's political views, is the reverence with which he treats Indian cultures and religions. The spirit of India is carried through his words, across these oceans and centuries to each reader. Kipling's personal sense of awe at the peace that can be achieved through devotion and teaching is what sets this novel apart from his others. He guides us through *Kim* like a teacher of a new religion slowly initiating a new student, gradually revealing further mysteries—each time making the revelation more personal and more inspiring. *Kim* is a page-turner that rivals any modern junk novel, but it adds the depth that one is more likely to find in intellectual reading. *Kim* begs a second reading, almost before the first reading is done. Kipling intended it this way, for as his characters find, nothing is as it first seems. The heart of all things should be examined.

Additional coverage of Kipling's life and career is contained in the following sources published by the Gale Group: *Authors and Artists for Young Adults,* **Vol. 32;** *Concise Dictionary of British Literary Biography, 1890-1914;* *Contemporary Authors,* **Vols. 105, 120;** *Contemporary Authors New Revision Series,* **Vol. 33;** *Discovering Authors; Discovering Authors 3.0; Discovering Authors: British; Discovering Authors: Canadian; Discovering Authors Modules: Most-studied Authors, Poets; Dictionary of Literary Biography,* **Vols. 19, 34, 141, 156;** *Major Authors and Illustrators for Children and Young Adults; Major 20th-Century Writers; Poetry Criticism,* **Vol. 3;** *Short Story Criticicm,* **Vol. 5;** *Something about the Author,* **Vol. 100;** *Twentieth-Century Literary Criticism,* **Vols. 8, 17;** *World Literature Criticism,* **and** *Yesterday's Authors of Books for Children,* **Vol. 2**

Elizabeth Laird
1943-

New Zealand novelist and short story writer.

Major works include *The Miracle Child: A Story from Ethiopia* (1985), *The Road to Bethlehem: An Ethiopian Nativity* (1987), *Red Sky in the Morning* (1988; also published as *Loving Ben,* 1989), *Kiss the Dust* (1991), The Little Red Tractor Series (all 1991).

INTRODUCTION

Laird writes works for children and young adults that reflect her Christian faith, her interest in folklore, and her love of gardening, among other pursuits. She has based several of her stories on what she has learned and experienced during extensive travels in Africa and the Middle East. Laird's most personal book, *Loving Ben,* emerged from the emotional hardship she underwent during her younger brother's illness and death. She is also the author of books for young readers, including the "Cubby Bears," the "Little Red Tractor," and the "Toucan 'Tecs" series.

BIOGRAPHICAL INFORMATION

Laird's family emigrated from Scotland to New Zealand; she later drew on this material in writing her novels for adults. Laird herself was born in Wellington, New Zealand. From a young age, she kept a diary, recording her emotions and writing down her earliest imaginative works. A formative event in her early years was the birth of her younger brother, Ben, later the namesake of *Loving Ben.* The baby had brain damage and only survived a few years.

Laird did not immediately produce the book that captured this painful experience. First, she followed her wanderlust; at eighteen years old, she went to Malaysia and worked as a teaching assistant in a girls' school. Next, she studied the French language in Paris. After that, she moved to Addis Ababa. Ethiopia was a peaceful, and, in comparison with the ensuing decades, prosperous nation at the time, and Laird's experiences included working at another school, horseback riding, and researching folk traditions dating back hundreds of years. The author's travels have also taken her to India, Iraq, and Lebanon, and she

has become adept in several languages. Laird is married to another writer, David Buchanan McDowall; the couple live in Surrey, England, and have two sons.

MAJOR WORKS

The Miracle Child and *The Road to Bethlehem* are rooted in Laird's Ethiopian sojourn. Based on the legends surrounding a thirteenth-century saint, the first book is noteworthy as much for the text as for the accompanying illustrations—reproductions of eighteenth-century paintings executed by Ethiopian monks. In *The Road to Bethlehem,* Jesus' mother Mary is a powerful character in her own right, performing miracles while fleeing King Herod into Egypt.

Laird's young adult novel *Kiss the Dust,* inspired by her experiences in Iraq, is a far more realistic story of terror and flight. The heroine is Tara Khan, a twelve-year-old Kurdish girl whose family relocates from Iraq to Iran in order to escape political oppression. Descriptions of the violence and brutality surrounding the girl are considered appropriate only for mature readers. Tara tries to grow accustomed to the strictures of Muslim life, but soon she is moved again, this time to England, where she experiences further culture shock. In the *New York Times,* Elizabeth Cohen wrote, "*Kiss the Dust* is filled with wonderfully researched ethnographic details about both Kurdish and refugee culture, and opens a door to a foreign world."

Loving Ben revisits Laird's memories of her brother. Like the protagonist of the above-mentioned book, Anna is twelve years old. In the story Anna gains insight into her own family through her acquaintance with another family facing a similar situation. Her confusion and grief at the condition of her brother's disabilities and his eventual death are presented forcefully, according to the critics. "Anna's voice," said one reviewer, "rings true throughout as she moves from awkwardness and judgmental statements to mature empathy."

Although she is capable of tackling difficult subjects, Laird can also relate to young children. "The Little Red Tractor" series presents the adventures of a farmer named Stan and a tractor named Duncan. In *The Day the Ducks Went Skating,* Stan and Duncan save a family of ducks from a fox. In *The Day Veronica Was Nosy,* a calf gets in Duncan's way, but Stan acts quickly. *Rosy's Garden,* published in 1990, is another work for young children. Laird uses the story of a girl and her grandmother to convey information and anecdotes about flower gardening.

AWARDS

Red Sky in the Morning won a Burnley Express Book Award, and *Kiss the Dust* won the Sheffield Children's Book Award and the Royal Dutch Geographical Society's Glazen Globe prize.

GENERAL COMMENTARY

Margery Fisher

SOURCE: A review of *The Doctor's Bag* and others, in *Growing Point,* Vol. 21, No. 3, September, 1982, p. 3951.

Children learning to read will find Elizabeth Laird's books (*The Doctor's Bag* and others) simple enough, but parents should note that the words are in no way graded and depend on the recognition of whole words, some of them polysyllables. The series is launched for 'preschool and early readers' but I find the books more suitable for children over the first stages, to use for practice. Certainly the books are persuasive enough with their vivacious, relaxed, highly topical pictures of domestic happenings in which nursery moods of fear, envy and irritation are sharply reflected.

TITLE COMMENTARY

THE MIRACLE CHILD: A STORY FROM ETHIOPIA (1985)

Richard Pankhurst

SOURCE: "Famine into Feast," in *Times Literary Supplement,* November 29, 1985, p. 1356.

The British expedition of 1867-8 against Emperor Tewodros II of Ethiopia led to the extensive looting of his mountain fortress at Magdala. The booty, which required fifteen elephants and nearly 200 mules to transport, included over 500 Ethiopian manuscripts, many finely illustrated. Most ended up at the British Museum (and thus later the British Library) while others found their way to the Bodleian in Oxford, the Royal Library at Windsor Castle and other libraries in Britian. Many other manuscripts passed into the hands of private collectors, the most notable of whom was Lady Meux of Theobald's Park, Waltham Cross, a collector of North African antiquities, who financed the publication of several Ethiopian texts, with English translations by the Egyptologist Wallis Budge.

One of Valerie Meux's manuscripts was a beautifully illustrated account of the eighteenth-century life of the medieval Ethiopian saint Takla Haymanot. Budge's translation, with a facsimile of the original, appeared in 1906 entitled *The Life of Takla Haymanot* and consisted of two immense volumes. Lady Meux bequeathed her manuscripts to Emperor Menilek of Ethiopia, but her will was contested, so that they were never repatriated. The life of Takla Haymanot was sold to an unidentified purchaser, and its present whereabouts is a mystery.

Elizabeth Laird has been inspired by Budge's edition to produce a children's book, with encouragement from the Ethiopian Orthodox priest in London, Abba Aregawi. *The Miracle Child* is attractively illustrated with over thirty coloured reproductions from Budge's volumes. These pictures, which seem as fresh as when they were painted, are good examples of Ethiopian art produced by churchmen, who, though still unfamiliar with perspective, were breaking away from their Byzantine traditions and exclusively religious models. There are quaintly realistic scenes of banquets, ploughing and the watering of cattle, as well as of leopards, monkeys, birds and crocodiles—besides two of Takla Haymanot standing on one leg and sprouting wings.

The story, which is simply written for twentieth-century children not familiar with Ethiopia, tells of various miracles. One, which is today sadly topical—and the subject of two illustrations—describes a medieval Ethiopian famine when "the grain jars were empty", the oil "was all used up", and "poor and rich alike had nothing left to eat". Takla Haymanot, then a child, was "very sad". The day of the Archangel Michael had come, and his mother had no food for the feast. The child crawled to the baskets, and as he touched each one it overflowed. His mother was soon singing for joy, for she had all she needed for the feast. Miracles of this kind are woefully absent in today's world, but *The Miracle Child* will play its part in overcoming the present Ethiopian famine, for royalties and profits are donated to Oxfam's Ethiopian Famine Relief Fund.

Jean Mercier

SOURCE: A review of *The Miracle Child: A Story from Ethiopia,* in *Publishers Weekly,* Vol. 228, No. 24, December 13, 1985, pp. 53-4.

Abba Aregawi Wolde Gabriel is a priest of the Ethiopian Orthodox Church in England who contributed to Laird's enthralling account of St. Tekla Hymanot, a revered hero of his people since the 13th century. Illustrating the book are glorious paintings, faithfully reproduced from an illuminated manuscript on which an unknown monk recorded the saint's miracles. The regal colors, the expressions that animate the people in the pictures, proclaim the artist of the 1700s as a man with great gifts dedicated to religious works and, particularly, to St. Tekla Hymanot. There are moving scenes of the holy person frustrating evil, being saved from danger by the Archangel Michael, healing the sick, reviving the dead and bringing food to his starving people when Ethiopia suffered from

famine as it does today. The author and publisher will donate profits from the book to Ethiopian famine relief groups.

Tom S. Hurlburt

SOURCE: A review of *The Miracle Child: A Story from Ethiopia,* in *School Library Journal,* Vol. 32, No. 5, January, 1986, p. 69.

While depicting the life of St. Tekla Haymanot, *The Miracle Child* also gives insight into a rich and ancient society that most children know about only from the recent reports of the famine that has engulfed Ethiopia. The first miracle performed by St. Tekla Haymanot, a 13th-century monk, was as an infant, when he replenished the food supply in his village by merely touching empty baskets during a severe famine. The story (which is still popular in Ethiopia) tells of his lifelong committment to prayer and good deeds as he healed the sick, raised the dead and converted the evil. The text is accompanied by reproductions of primitive paintings by an 18th-century artist whose identity is not known. Along with each illustration is an explanatory caption giving the meanings of the various symbols and formats that are used in the paintings. These notes add to a further understanding of Ethiopian culture and Christianity. Also of interest are the African features of all characters depicted in the illustrations, including Jesus and the Archangel Michael. Author's and publisher's profits from the sale of this book are to be donated to Ethiopian famine relief groups.

Ilene Cooper

SOURCE: A review of *Miracle Child: A Story from Ethiopia,* in *Booklist,* Vol. 82, No. 10, January 15, 1986, p. 758.

Although few children will be familiar with Tekla Haymanot, one of Ethiopia's premier saints, they should be intrigued with the life of this miracle worker who healed the sick and fed the hungry. Told in a folkloric style, the narrators recount how Tekla Haymanot's parents longed for a child and, after an unusual experience with Saint Michael the Archangel, a son was born to them. The boy went on to perform many miracles and later, as a man, was revered for his devotion to God. Legend has it that while praying in a small cell he stood for so long that one of his legs withered and fell off, so he stood on the other for seven more years, praying unceasingly. The book is illustrated with Byzantine-style paintings taken from an eighteenth-century illuminated manuscript painted by an anonymous Ethiopian monk. Children, who may be unacquainted with this art style, will find it unusual, but perhaps arresting. The pictures are captioned in detail, adding dimension to the story.

📖 *THE ROAD TO BETHLEHEM: AN ETHIOPIAN NATIVITY* (1987)

Susan Helper

SOURCE: A review of *The Road to Bethlehem: An Ethiopian Story,* in *School Library Journal,* Vol. 34, No. 2, October, 1987, p. 34.

Laird has gathered many Ethiopian tales surrounding the Nativity into a single narrative, beginning with Mary's birth and childhood and ending with the Holy Family's early wanderings to escape Herod's wrath. Bold typeface matches the equally striking artwork, orange-framed paintings in bright colors from 18th-century illuminated manuscripts. Helpful captions identify Ethiopian artistic conventions such as the use of cloth strips to identify important people and depicting wicked people by showing them in profile. Like the John Bierhorst/Barbara Cooney collaboration on a Mexican Nativity (*Spirit Child* [Morrow, 1984]), this beautiful and unusual book presents yet another version of a well-known story. Nonetheless, librarians may have difficulty moving this story from one of the earlier Christian countries off the shelf because of the esoteric illustrations and the somewhat lengthy text. Profits from the royalties of this book will be donated to Oxfam for famine relief in Ethiopia.

Kirkus Reviews

SOURCE: A review of *Road to Bethlehem: An Ethiopian Nativity,* in *Kirkus Reviews,* Vol. LV, No. 9, October 1, 1987, pp. 1464-65.

A sensitive retelling by Laird (***The Miracle Child,*** 1985) of an Ethiopian nativity originally written by a fourth-century bishop of Cyprus.

Illustrated with Ethiopian paintings from 18th-century illuminated manuscripts, Laird's adaptation reveals cultural nuances of one of the oldest Christian civilizations. While close to the traditional story, it also contains pieces of folk tales and legends about the life of Mary and the birth of Jesus found outside the New Testament, creating a combination of folk and Bible stories that is highly effective and eminently readable. Evocative paintings, rich in red and gold,

on pages with large white borders, accompany the coherent, rhythmic text. Each striking painting is captioned by explanatory notes regarding its style and content.

As a holiday story, a Bible story, or a comparative folk story, this well-designed volume is a valuable purchase for any collection—and far above the usual holiday fare.

Publishers Weekly

SOURCE: A review of *The Road to Bethlehem,* in *Publishers Weekly,* Vol. 232, October 9, 1987, p. 84.

With unique style and skill, Laird has compiled an Ethiopian nativity based on a composite of ancient texts which recounts the familiar epic of Joseph and the Virgin Mary, Christ's birth and the flight into Egypt. Informative explanations of symbolic content and historical detail accompany vellum paintings, photographed from the British Library's collection of period manuscripts. These interpretations help the reader understand an exotic culture and its ways. There is much to digest: a foreword by Terry Waite; a summation of Christianity's origins in northern Africa; and the modern translation itself. This book will best suit readers whose curiosity will be aroused by such an intriguing subject, or those mature enough to appreciate the intricacies of the effort.

Ilene Cooper

SOURCE: A review of *Road to Bethlehem: An Ethiopian Nativity,* in *Booklist,* Vol. 84, No. 4, October 15, 1987, p. 398.

As she did in her first book, ***The Miracle Child*** . . . , Laird uses the art and literature of Ethiopia to present a unique view of some of Christianity's most cherished stories. In an interesting author's note Laird describes how various tales about the life of Jesus circulated from Christianity's earliest days. The stories in this volume come from different parts of the ancient world and were recorded in Ethiopia; she has woven these into a vivid, folkloric piece that traces the life of Jesus through his ancestors to his birth and the Holy Family's sojourn in Egypt. The Byzantine-style art is reproduced from eighteenth-century illuminated manuscripts; captions explain much of the art's symbolism. A unique offering—especially touching is the introduction by Anglican envoy Terry Waite, at this writing missing in Lebanon.

Diane Manuel

SOURCE: "Bible Heritage for Young Readers," in *The Christian Science Monitor,* Vol. 80, No. 6, December 3, 1987, p. 27.

The Road to Bethlehem: An Ethiopian Nativity, told by Elizabeth Laird . . . , draws on several folk legends from one of the world's oldest Christian countries. Based on Gospel narratives, this tale of Mary, Joseph, and Jesus is embellished with distinctly regional accounts of Mary's lineage and of two thieves who try to steal her child.

Vibrant red-, green-, and gold-tone paintings from 18th-century illuminated manuscripts give primitive vigor to the story and are used to explain unfamiliar religious customs. Laird's poetic text holds its own on the richly illustrated pages with a tempo made for reading aloud. A note indicates that a percentage of the book's earnings will be donated to Ethiopian famine relief groups.

Betsy Hearne

SOURCE: A review of *The Road to Bethlehem: An Ethiopian Nativity,* in *The Bulletin of the Center for Children's Books,* Vol. 41, No. 5, January, 1988, p. 94.

Adapted from Ethiopian nativity stories and illustrated with paintings from 18th-century illuminated manuscripts, this will serve as an art history resource as well as a Christmas book. The text weaves familiar New Testament motifs with popular legends and miracles into a cohesive narrative. When Mary escapes to Egypt with the baby Jesus, she cures many illnesses: "The dumb spoke, the lame ran, the deaf heard and the blind could see." The radiant paintings project much of the book's impact and are more vividly reproduced than those in Laird's book about St. Tekla Haymanot in ***The Miracle Child: A Story from Ethiopia.*** Each picture, captioned with helpful commentary, is intense in color and beautifully balanced with rhythmic shapes and traditional patterns.

📖 *RED SKY IN THE MORNING* (1988; ALSO PUBLISHED AS *LOVING BEN,* 1989)

Dawn Woods

SOURCE: A review of *Red Sky in the Morning,* in *Books for Your Children,* Vol. 23, No. 2, Summer, 1988, p. 19.

Anna is excited when her mother is expecting another baby, as it will give her the opportunity to show she is grown up and can take care of her father and younger sister.

Unfortunately, when Ben is born he is handicapped, and changes the lives of his whole family.

Ben becomes ill and Anna's grief is acute. She acquires a job looking after Jackie—another handicapped child, and teaches not only Jackie, but Jackie's brother, that handicapped people are human too.

The range of emotions expressed by Anna, from her love of her brother, impatience with her sister, concern over her mother's loneliness, to her first teenage crush over a boy, are most touchingly described and the moments of humour make this a book to appeal to everyone over the age of 10.

Mary Cadogan

SOURCE: A review of *Red Sky in the Morning,* in *Times Educational Supplement,* No. 3753, March 6, 1988, p. 49.

In ***Red Sky in the Morning*** the secure pattern of Anna's home life is disrupted by the birth of a brother, Ben, who suffers from hydrocephalus. His severe mental and physical handicaps make heavy demands upon his family: Anna's mother becomes tense and withdrawn; her father begins to spend a lot of time outside the home, and her younger sister Katy is jealous of the unending and special attention that Ben requires. Surprisingly it is Anna, the "dummy" of her class, who is best able to cope with her retarded brother.

From the beginning, Anna has a deep, spontaneous affection for Ben, and a capacity to feel empathy with him. Through the relationship she develops from a rather shallow character into a robustly interesting one. Ben's innocence and sense of joy also eventually have a positive effect on the other members of Anna's family, although the book offers no contrived false hopes or happy ending. It is, quite simply, a wonderfully moving story about the power of love, which unfolds through Anna's wryly unsentimental first-person narrative. Almost certainly, family responsibilities in the context of serious retardation have never been treated more perceptively in a children's story.

The Junior Bookshelf

SOURCE: M. H., A review of *Red Sky in the Morning,* in *The Junior Bookshelf,* Vol. 52, No. 4, August, 1988, p. 197.

This is a very sensitive first novel. The 12-year-old narrator Anna, who chats guilelessly away to the reader, has a humorous understanding (though perhaps beyond her years) of events and people. A much-longed-for baby brother comes before her mother can reach hospital and is brain-damaged. Anna loves the handicapped child, but finds it difficult to adjust to his effect on the family's life. She guards him ashamedly from her schoolfriends and boyfriends, and is short-tempered with 10-year-old Katy, her sister, who still plays for their parents' attention (though she comes to see that Katy, whom their mother favours and spoils, is reacting as she did herself at that age). She also watches her mother almost lose their father through her preoccupation with Ben, the slovenliness of her appearance and of the house. In fact, Anna is instrumental, after Ben's death, movingly described, in bringing the family together again. Several adults in the story help her in this new understanding of human nature: the wise poetry-loving English mistress Mrs. Henderson, the shopkeeper, and the sensible low-profile vicar who knows how to run a youth club are sufficiently real, and the story homely and natural enough for the wisdom of the moral lessons conveyed to be palatable. In fact, Anna's Saturday job and her subsequent minding of another handicapped child provide her with something of a general guide to life and death, to human behaviour, even to aberrations such as kleptomania. She uses her new experience in her turn to help others, like the handsome, unwilling elder brother of handicapped Jackie. It is what you might call a wholesome book without being 'pi'; it is also very readable.

Keith Barker

SOURCE: A review of *Red Sky in the Morning*, in *The School Librarian*, Vol. 36, No. 3, August, 1998, p. 108.

Elizabeth Laird's **Red Sky In The Morning** explores not only the taboo topic of death but also the taboo topic of handicap. Anna, the heroine of the novel, is twelve when her brother Ben is born with severe mental and physical retardation. The fact that Anna loves and cherishes him despite all the odds makes his death half-way through the book all the more moving. The writer does not attempt to hide the less glamorous aspects of looking after a disabled child, nor does she dismiss the attitudes of others and the effect such an event has on a marriage and family life. However, she is burdened by the voice she gives Anna who appears far too naïve and immature for her years and whose main contribution to child psychology appears to be a fundamental belief in 'bottom spanking'.

Barbara Chatton

SOURCE: A review of *Loving Ben,* in *School Library Journal,* Vol. 35, No. 13, September, 1989, p. 252.

When Anna Peacock is 12, her brother Benedict is born. Ben is hydrocephalic, loving, and playful, but incapable of doing what most infants can do, and is easily susceptible to illness. Anna instantly loves her brother but soon realizes that her family life and friendships will be changed by his birth. In a wry first-person narrative, Anna talks about her life with Ben as well as her own self-image, her schoolwork, friendships, and her first job during the two years of Ben's life and the year after he dies. Anna's voice rings true throughout as she moves from awkwardness and judgmental statements to a more mature empathy with others and acceptance of herself. Discussion of handicaps, death and bereavement, and religious belief are carefully integrated into the story and emerge as natural concerns of Anna and her family rather than as issues to be addressed lightly. An additional strength of this book is the well-rounded portrayal of adult characters. Anna's mother, alternately distracted and affectionate; Mrs. Chapman, the generous and insightful shopkeeper who helps Anna to understand herself and her brother better; and a sympathetic minister all help Anna to grow up. Readers might want to compare this with McNair's *Commander Coatrack Returns* (Houghton, 1989), also about a relationship between an older sister and a handicapped child.

Zena Sutherland

SOURCE: A review of *Loving Ben,* in *The Bulletin of the Center for Children's Books,* Vol. 43, No. 2, October, 1989, p. 36.

"Hydrocephalus," the doctor had said just after Ben was born, but Anna (twelve at the time) loved him dearly, spent as much time as she could with him, and was happy that some of her friends understood how sweet a child her baby brother was. Anna is the narrator, so that her feelings about Ben and, two years later, about his death, have an immediacy and poignancy that are moving. It is in part because of her love for Ben that she later becomes devoted to a child she's helping to care for, and toward whom she is protective. The book deals with a sensitive subject and a touching relationship but it never becomes saccharine, and it unfolds with pace and purpose.

Kirkus Reviews

SOURCE: A review of *Loving Ben,* in *Kirkus Reviews,* Vol. LVII, No. 19, October 1, 1989, p. 1476.

An unusually perceptive first novel, reminiscent—in its treatment of the loss of a baby and its sensitively drawn portrait of a whole family and its interaction—of Ellis' *A Family Project* (1988).

Ben is hydrocephalic, destined to be a very slow learner, yet charming, happy, and well-loved—especially by his doting mother and by Anna, his older sister, who is 12 when the story begins dramatically with his birth at home. A prickly, strong individual, Anna is a loner who tends to put down her little sister despite their underlying affection for each other. Initially, the family conceals Ben to avoid the inevitable callous remarks; yet when Anna's classmates (long alienated by the chip on her shoulder) find out about him, they respond with friendship. After Ben's death, at three, Anna's grief is again complicated by others' assumptions: that his loss is a blessing, that her mother is the one who mourns. Anna's own sorrow is lessened when she volunteers to care for a four-year-old Mongoloid child, Jackie; in the process of showing Jackie's family that Jackie, like Ben, can take joy in learning, Anna happens on some truths about herself.

This beautifully balanced, well-told story was a runner up for the Carnegie. Unfortunately, in its American edition, the British setting has been suppressed with tampering, inconsistent, unnecessary revisions, leaving a sort of generic family set nowhere real. Happily, however, most of its appeal is intact.

Publishers Weekly

SOURCE: A review of *Loving Ben,* in *Publishers Weekly,* Vol. 236, No. 17, October 27, 1989, p. 70.

When Anna's baby brother is born at home, nothing seems right. Then her father explains that the baby is probably handicapped. Anna asks if he'll be able to do all the usual things: play, go to school, talk, laugh. "He'll be able to laugh," the doctor says. "Oh, yes, I'm sure he'll laugh." Thus begins Laird's first novel for young readers, a painful, moving account of Anna's relationships with her family and her world after Ben's birth. Ben is a hydrocephalic, and while Anna adores him; she also avoids mentioning what he's really like to her friends, afraid of their casual cruelty. How Anna and her family cope with life with—and then life without—Ben will be certain to move readers, in this praiseworthy addition to literature on the handicapped.

Pat Thomson

SOURCE: A review of *Red Sky in the Morning,* in *Books for Keeps,* No. 75, July, 1992, p. 26.

This was a runner-up for the Children's Book Award. The story of Anna's baby brother, Ben, who was only to live for two years, was painful for the children to read and many said they cried, but it won their hearts and their respect.

'Severe mental and physical retardation' the hospital letter said, and Anna is torn between her love for Ben at home and her reluctance to tell her friends about him at school. One by one, she tackles the hurdles, finding courage and growing herself. When it comes, Laird does not avoid the issues which surround the death. They are frankly dealt with. Perhaps the Award readers responded to the openness, not so often found in children's books. Finally, we see Anna with a new holiday job, using all she learned from her brother on another child who needs her, and herself 'a hundred times older . . . a thousand times wiser'.

SID AND SADIE (1988)

Margery Fisher

SOURCE: A review of *Sid and Sadie,* in *Growing Point,* Vol. 27, No. 6, March, 1989, p. 5132.

The simplest of journeys (a girl collects her small brother at a neighbour's house and leads him home) is enlarged in pictures which show the children stamping in puddles, finding a penny on the ground, scared by a prowling cat as darkness brings shadows and ending up under the light where Mum is waiting for them. The lucid, expressive text is supported by relaxed, naturalistic water-colour scenes which convey a sense of family affection and show the firm alliance between different ages. A real family book.

G. B. Harrison

SOURCE: A review of *Sid and Sadie,* in *The School Librarian,* Vol. 37, No. 2, May, 1989.

Out of a very ordinary situation—older sister fetching home a younger brother from the childminder—Elizabeth Laird has produced a prose poem which is very appealing. Many children will be able to relate to the walk home in winter, late in the afternoon. There is the comfort of a family relationship, some teasing fun, a bit of tension and a sense of unease before both are back safely in their own house. The author captures the atmosphere with a fine economy of carefully chosen words, laced with some sensitive repetitions. Children who can already read will curl up and enjoy the book by themselves; younger ones will enjoy having it read to them while inside an encircling arm.

The accompanying illustrations by Alan Marks offer a visual delight in water-colour on every page-spread. Colour, line and expertly chosen angles of view all complement the words. A delightful book at a very reasonable price.

ROSY'S GARDEN: A CHILD'S KEEPSAKE OF FLOWERS (1990)

Carolyn Phelan

SOURCE: A review of *Rosy's Garden: A Child's Keepsake of Flowers,* in *Booklist,* Vol. 86, No. 4, March 15, 1990, p. 46.

This unusual treasury of flower lore includes information, activities, and legends set within the fictional framework of a little girl coming to spend the summer with her old-fashioned, garden-loving grandmother. Happy to share her knowledge and lore of flowers, Granny tells Rosy the meanings of flower names, remembrances from her childhood, customs and legends from many lands, snippets of English verse, and directions for making rose water, potpourri, face lotion, and various foods prepared with herbs. While lovely, rather sentimental watercolor paintings set in an English cottage garden predominate, Ichikawa shifts styles intriguingly in some of the artwork. A Dutch interior, where candlelight and firelight illuminate the characters, illustrates a story of seventeenth-century tulip madness, while a Persian folktale is interpreted in a mannered style with brilliant colors reminiscent of Persian miniatures. While many will find the overall tone a trifle sweet, others will like the book very much indeed.

Carolyn Jenks

SOURCE: A review of *Rosy's Garden: A Child's Keepsake of Flowers,* in *School Library Journal,* Vol. 36, No. 7, July, 1990, p. 61.

The garden of the title actually belongs to "Granny," with whom Rosy spends a happy summer as "Chief Assistant," learning about flowers and their folklore and uses. One of the things Rosy learns is how to make potpourri, and that word best describes this book. Grandmother's reminiscences, flower poems, some history and legends of individual flowers, the meanings of their names, and a few recipes are scattered randomly throughout, seemingly as a vehicle

for Ichikawa's beautiful, botanically correct watercolors. The total effect is an unfocused but pretty book of limited use.

The Junior Bookshelf

SOURCE: A review of *Rosy's Garden,* in *The Junior Bookshelf,* Vol. 54, No. 4, August, 1990, p. 170.

Rosy's Garden is largely an excuse for the artist's delicate paintings of flowers and flower-like children. They are very pretty but a vein of sentimentality runs through them, which some children may reject. The book, with words by Elizabeth Laird, is really an anthology of garden-pieces, little anecdotes, poems, scraps of information and flower-lore. The link is provided by Granny who teaches Rosy the mysteries of gardening and herbs. It all depends how you react to this style of drawing. The pictures are reproduced with due regard to their fine colouring.

Miriam Martinez and Marcia F. Nash

SOURCE: A review of *Rosy's Garden: A Child's Keepsake of Flowers,* in *Language Arts,* Vol. 67, No. 8, December, 1990, p. 854.

Rosy goes to spend the summer with her grandmother, which means a summer spent in Granny's beautiful garden. She learns many things about the plants in the garden during their time together. Tulips were once the most precious flowers in the world; Greeks thought the buds of delphiniums looked like dolphins and so named them *delphinos*—the Greek word for dolphins. This book is a study in integration. The information which Rosy and the reader gather is imparted through stories, songs, poems, and games integrated into this lovely, gentle story of a summer shared by a grandmother and granddaughter. Satomi Ichikawa's detailed pastel watercolors will make readers reluctant to leave this beautiful country garden.

THE LITTLE RED TRACTOR SERIES (1991)

Publishers Weekly

SOURCE: A review of *The Day Patch Stood Guard* and *The Day Sidney Ran Off,* in *Publishers Weekly,* Vol. 238, No. 2, January 11, 1991, p. 100.

The daily comings and goings on Gosling Farm may not amount to much in the scheme of things but, like veterinarian James Herriot's Yorkshire escapades, therein lies their charm. This pair of gentle stories, the initial offerings in the Little Red Tractor series, are modest in scope, played out on the small canvas of English farm life. Duncan the red tractor and his owner, Stan, get into the kinds of scrapes one might expect in such a bucolic setting—an escaped piglet, a smash-up against a tree, a young sheepdog testing his mettle. Reeder's whimsical watercolors are laced with humor and skillfully reflect the pastoral scenes—most especially in the case of an otter on a riverbank at twilight. As a promising start for what looks to be an appealing series, these books should have no problem finding an enthusiastic audience.

The Junior Bookshelf

SOURCE: A review of *The Day Sidney Was Lost,* in *The Junior Bookshelf,* Vol. 55, No. 2, April, 1991, p. 61.

Gosling Farm is the setting for the Little Red Tractor books. It forms part of a stretch of countryside where traditional farmland is interrupted by places such as Tawny Owl Wood, Stumpy's Mill and Heronwood Lake. Only the silos and farm machinery show that this is a modern farm. The tractor helps Stan the farmer to care for his crops and animals. On this occasion, Sidney the piglet has wandered away from his sty. Together, Stan and the tractor trace his steps and bring him home. Their efforts are shown in watercolours of warm summer shades. Although the tractor does not really come to life as a character, the story should appeal to some of the many children attracted to farms and farm machinery.

Carolyn Phelan

SOURCE: A review of *The Day Patch Stood Guard* and *The Day Sidney Ran Off,* in *Booklist,* Vol. 87, No. 19, June 1, 1991, p. 1879.

Originally published in England, these picture books from the Little Red Tractor series tell of events on Gosling Farm. In the first tale, Duncan the tractor rolls down a hill, crashing into a tree. When the farmer tells his sheepdog to "guard poor Duncan," the dog does so, spending the night in the garage where the tractor awaits repair. In the second book, the farmer rides around the farm on Duncan, hoping to find his runaway pig, Sidney. Although the tractor is never personified with human thoughts or actions, it does, nevertheless, become a character in the gentle stories. Suiting the mild, good-natured tales in tone, the pleasing pen-and-watercolor artwork portrays country life with simplicity and affection.

Nancy Seiner

SOURCE: A review of *The Day Patch Stood Guard* and *The Day Sidney Ran Off,* in *School Library Journal,* Vol. 37, No. 9, September, 1991, p. 236.

Two quiet stories of minor mishaps. Stan, a no-nonsense English farmer, lives a peaceful life on Gosling Farm with Patch, his sheep dog, and Duncan, a red tractor. In a simple world where the sky is always blue and problems are easily solved, Stan looks after his farm and respects the needs of his wild animal neighbors. In *The Day Patch Stood Guard,* Duncan rolls down a hill and crashes into a tree. Patch watches over the tractor until all repairs are completed. In *The Day Sidney Ran Off,* Stan hops on Duncan to follow a runaway pig, ultimately ending up in a puddle. While the stories unfold with little attention-grabbing drama, their child appeal is assured by the winning personalities of the animals and the major role played by the tractor. Lively cartoon-style watercolors add much; the drawings, in various sizes, capture the action and nuances of the stories. A pictorial highlight is the map of the countryside on the endpapers. Language is simple, but colorful. Beginning readers will be able to master the short sentences, although they will need some help with some unusual words. Older preschoolers who like long stories will enjoy these slices of farm life. Nonessential, but pleasant additions.

Nancy Seiner

SOURCE: A review of *The Day the Ducks Went Skating* and *The Day Veronica Was Nosy,* in *School Library Journal,* Vol. 37, No. 12, December, 1991, p. 96.

Two concise, interesting stories that show a small part of a farmer's day. As children follow the plot, they will also gain insight into Stan's work and see his devotion to animals. In the first story, Stan and his tractor, Duncan, break up the ice in the pond so that the ducks can be safe from a hungry fox who is closing in on them. Expressive prose and carefully detailed illustrations convey the story's humor, as well as the drama of the ducks' danger. Watercolors in predominantly blue, white, and gray reflect the winter's chill. In the second story, Stan must swerve Duncan into a tree to avoid hitting a curious calf. Then, as Veronica investigates the tree, she disturbs a nest of hornets. After stinging her, the hornets turn on Stan, who finds safety in Duncan's glass-enclosed cab. Mellow browns, golds, and oranges bring an autumn glow to the carefully created pictures of rural life. Illustrations reflect the action, amplified in both closeups and larger scenes; on one page, four rondeles show the hornets as they crawl over Duncan's hood and exhaust pipe, look into his windows, and try to sting his tires. Beautifully written text combining short and long sentences offers a realistic view of nature.

THE PINK GHOST OF LAMONT (1991)

Chris Stephenson

SOURCE: A review of *The Pink Ghost of Lamont,* in *The School Librarian,* Vol. 40, No. 2, May, 1991, p. 61.

This is ostensibly a story about a group of neighbouring children devising and producing a Victorian melodrama, but there is much more to it than that. The narrator, ten-year-old Robert, is jealous of the maternal attention lavished on his little brother Martin, who can fake tummy-aches at will. Their mother has been in a state of depression since the death of the boys' father. The house they have moved into is dirty and neglected, and she is reluctant to ask anyone in. Putting on the play enables the family to come to terms with its problems. The brothers are drawn closer together by it; Robert acts out his fantasies of deprivation in it; and their mother is galvanised into clearing up the place and asking her new neighbours round to watch the performance of it.

Two sisters also take part in the play. Like those of the boys, their personalities are well fleshed out and aptly expressed through dialogue. The heavy themes of the book are handled with a light touch, and the process of play-making is the source of much humour. A thoroughly enjoyable and worthwhile read.

KISS THE DUST (1991)

Susan Perren

SOURCE: A review of *Kiss the Dust,* in *Quill and Quire,* Vol. 57, No. 6, June, 1991, p. 28.

"Sulaimaniya, Iraq, Spring, 1984" is the title of the first chapter of Elizabeth Laird's newest book, **Kiss the Dust.** Thirteen-year-old Tara, the central character of this novel, is the eldest daughter in a family of prosperous Iraqi Kurds; she leads an indulged, if cloistered life and has every expectation of continuing this comfortable existence into adulthood. All of this changes when her businessman father, who is secretly working for Kurdish independence, is tipped off that he is about to be arrested by the Iraqi secret police. The family is forced to flee, leaving all their possessions behind—first to an ancestral village in the Lagros mountains and later, when bombing makes that village unsafe, across those mountains into hostile Iran and a refugee camp, and eventually to political asylum and greatly reduced circumstances in Britain. Tara is forced into early adulthood to survive and to ensure her family's survival.

This is not a great book, but it is certainly a timely one. Based on the experience of the writer, who spent a year living in Iraq, the story feels somewhat contrived—as though the author has dressed up facts and made fiction of them. One of the consequences of this is weak characterization. However, the book's virtues are its timeliness, its ability to convey a sense of place and daily life in that troubled area of the Middle East, and its mirroring of Tara's struggle for autonomy with that of Kurdistan. In both of these cases the struggle carries a heavy price.

Sharon A. McKinley

SOURCE: A review of *Kiss the Dust,* in *Children's Book Review Service Inc.,* Vol. 20, No. 12, Spring, 1992, p. 142.

Tara and her family are Iraqi Kurds. Tara's father has been working with the Pesha Murga resistance group and her brother goes to fight with them. The rest of the family narrowly escapes the police as it heads for their ancestral village in the mountains. There Tara must trade her life of luxury for an old way of life with no modern conveniences. After a bombing raid devastates the village, the family makes the dangerous journey to Iran that ends in a bleak refugee camp. Eventually the family makes its way to England where Tara must adapt all over again. When one wonders if things are getting a bit melodramatic, one remembers that the gripping tale is taken from true accounts, and that the horror and suffering is probably all too real.

Kirkus Reviews

SOURCE: A review of *Kiss the Dust,* in *Kirkus Reviews,* Vol. LX, No. 8, April 15, 1992, p. 539.

Here, Laird, author of a poignant first novel about the effects of a hydrocephalic baby on his family (**Loving Ben,** 1989), portrays the journey of a Kurdish refugee family—a story based on the real experiences in the mid-80's of Iraqi Kurds now living in England.

For Tara, 13, and her family, their ordeal is cruel and often life-threatening, yet they are among the lucky ones. Wealthy "Baba" (secretly a power in the Kurdish military) still has money even after repeated searches, while "Daya" manages to smuggle her jewels. Escaping the police as they leave their luxurious home in a city in northern Iraq, they take a taxi to their primitive vacation house in the mountains. For Tara, the return to village ways is almost as much of a shock as the bombs that eventually drive the family over the border into Iran, to a refugee camp infested with bedbugs and assaulted by deafening prayers rasped from a loudspeaker. Eventually, Baba makes contact with relatives in Teheran and passage to London is negotiated.

Ever-present dangers maintain suspense—from a brutal street-killing Tara witnesses to her older brother's miraculous escape; meanwhile, Laird builds a sympathetic picture of the embattled Kurds and a compelling portrait of Tara and the sobering changes wrought in her and her family by the events, including her first startled response to a free society ("attractive and exciting . . . but frightening . . . as if things might suddenly get out of control"). An important contribution to the growing number of refugee stories.

Publishers Weekly

SOURCE: A review of *Kiss the Dust,* in *Publishers Weekly,* Vol. 239, No. 20, April 27, 1992, p. 269.

Laird weaves compelling facts about the conflicts between the Arabs and the Kurds into her gripping tale about one family's escape to freedom. After witnessing a teen's brutal murder and meeting a wounded revolutionary, 12-year-old Tara begins to realize the extent of persecution in her native Iraq. When her Kurdish father is sought by the secret police, Tara and her family abandon their home and head north to the mountains. Their refuge is short-lived, however; bombs begin to drop and they flee across the Iranian border to a primitive refugee camp. Stripped of their dignity and still not out of danger, the family plots to leave the continent, despite slim chances of asylum. The author personalizes the Kurdish experience by sensitively portraying Tara's feelings of loss, degradation and uprootedness. Although some readers may find the girl's initial naïveté as hard to swallow as her abrupt awakening to violence, most will overlook these minor weaknesses as the story's tension rapidly mounts. Even those familiar with political problems in Iraq and Iran may be shocked by the graphic depiction of tyranny—and may sense that despite their

hardships, Tara's family fares better than many people who risk their lives for independence.

Robert Strang

SOURCE: A review of *Kiss the Dust,* in *The Bulletin of the Center for Children's Books,* Vol. 45, No. 10, June, 1992, pp. 267-68.

In this exciting, behind-the-headlines story, Tara and her family are Kurds living in the Iraqi city of Sulaimaniya. It's 1984, and Iraq is engaged in war with Iran while at the same time battling Kurdish insurgency. As Tara's father's involvement with the *pesh murga* (Kurdish fighters) becomes apparent to the government, the family is forced to leave their comfortable life in the city and go to the Kurdish-controlled mountains, the first step in a long journey to safety. Excepting an occasionally romanticized note, the novel easily incorporates cultural and political details within the fiction, and dots of everyday realism, often provided by Tara's baby sister Hero, balance the drama. Fast-paced and easy to read, the story has a number of book-talkable episodes, such as the scene where Tara's family crosses a treacherous mountain range to reach the (relative) safety of Iran. The author's brief afterword describes the terrible recent history of the Kurds; the novel itself charges the facts with human interest.

Hazel Rochman

SOURCE: A review of *Kiss the Dust,* in *Booklist,* Vol. 88, No. 20, June 15, 1992, p. 1825.

Stories about "foreign" places risk two extremes: either they can overwhelm the reader with reverential details of idiom, background, and custom, or they can homogenize the culture and turn all characters into American mall babies. Laird's docunovel about a Kurdish teenager caught up in the Iran-Iraq War in 1984 isn't much rooted in the particulars of Kurdish culture. The focus is on the universality of the character and the experience. We are quickly swept up into a fast-paced refugee story about someone—just like us—forced to flee home, school, and safety. Tara Hawrami lives with her middle-class family near Baghdad. Political struggles swirl in the background. She's interested in friends, videos, grades, shopping. But the fierce oppression comes into her home and excitement mounts as the Hawramis escape over the garden wall from the secret police, live through bombing raids in the mountains, flee over the border to Iran, endure a series of harsh refugee camps, and finally find asylum in Britain. Laird does show some subtle aspects of class and cultural conflict: for example, in most ways, Tara is further from the simple mountain Kurds than she is from her Arab city neighbors. When she gets to Iran, she resents having to wear the black chador veil; then, in Britain, she's shocked by the bold, revealing fashions. Kids will grab this for the adventure story, and even if they don't learn much about what it's like to be Kurdish, they will feel for the individual beyond the media sound bites of mass suffering.

Susan Knorr

SOURCE: A review of *Kiss the Dust,* in *School Library Journal,* Vol. 38, No. 7, July, 1992, p. 90.

A fictional account of a Kurdish family during the Iran-Iraq War in the mid-1980s, when many Iraqi Kurds who had been struggling to establish a homeland were forced to take refuge in Iran and other countries. Laird focuses on 13-year-old Tara, an urban girl who finds herself fleeing with her family from Iraqi secret police, then living in a wartorn village and surviving in an Iranian relocation camp before finally escaping to England. While Laird dispels many of the stereotypes young people may have of the Middle East by showing Tara as a thoroughly modern girl who loves to ride in her family's Mercedes or watch her VCR, there are times when observations about Kurdish heritage and struggle emphasize differences in clothes rather than examining ideology or religion. Often, cliched phrases are jarring distractions from the location and mood of the story. Still, the author clearly shows the changes wrought in a young girl who comes to an awareness of the struggles of her people and leaves behind the comfortable, spoiled existence she'd known. Because Tara remains connected to her family at all times, and rides in a car and shops during excursions from the relocation camp, Laird's account of Tara's plight may sound, at times, less desperate and frightening then other refugee novels that focus on separation and severe deprivation, such as Tamar Bergman's *Along the Tracks* (Houghton, 1991). But in some ways those contemporary elements may have even more impact for readers who will be forced to realize that atrocities are not relegated to the past and that freedom is not easily won.

Pat Atkinson

SOURCE: A review of *Kiss the Dust,* in *Book Report,* Vol. 11, No. 2, September, 1992, p. 49.

Tara, almost 13, lives with her family in the city of Sulaimaniya, Iraq. She enjoys a comfortable life in a large house with her parents, older brother and younger sister. Her life is much like that of many American teenagers, focusing on friends, school and television. Her family are Kurds and she knows the political situation is not good, but her family has not had any problems. All of this changes when word comes that the Iraqi secret police are after her father. The family must leave their affluent home and flee to the mountains of Kurdistan. On the journey, the mother becomes very ill, and Tara must care for her. The family has little food and lives in filthy shelters as they try to reach relatives in Iran. Eventually they get help from relatives and are able to get passports to London where they plan to start a new life. This excellent story reveals much about the culture of the Kurdish people, as well as some of the customs of Iran and Iraq. It will give readers a better understanding of the trauma in the Middle East. Tara's growth from a spoiled child to a responsible young adult is a good model for adolescent readers.

Luvada Kuhn

SOURCE: A review of *Kiss the Dust,* in *Voice of Youth Advocates,* Vol. 15, No. 4, October, 1992, pp. 225-26.

This story is set in Iraq in 1984 and 1985 and relates the events in the lives of a family of Kurds struggling against the oppressive government in Iraq. Kurdish people have distinct traditions and customs, but they have never had a country of their own.

Tara, almost 13, is protected by her family from the realities of the war until the day she sees a young Kurd shot down in the street by soldiers. Very soon thereafter she learns that the secret police are after her father and that her whole family must leave their home and hide out in the mountains of Kurdistan in northern Iraq.

For all her life, Tara has lived in a beautiful home, attended school, and generally lived the life of a well-to-do teenager in modern Iraq. Suddenly she finds herself in a one-room house in a primitive village, carrying water and helping with the countless chores of village life in the midst of constant danger. Her innate courage and pride in her family carry this young girl quickly into maturity.

Fast paced and exciting, this novel deals with people who have only recently become a part of the average American's scope of knowledge. The horrors of war are not glossed over, but the emphasis is on family and growing up in the face of danger. This family of refugees triumphs, but the reader is left with a clear understanding of the hundreds who have not been so fortunate. The author has researched the Kurdish customs well and based the story on wartime events and a real Kurdish family.

Dean E. Lyons

SOURCE: A review of *Kiss the Dust,* in *Kliatt,* Vol. XXVIII, No. 4, July, 1994, p. 9.

In 1984, 12-year-old Tara Hawrami is enjoying her pampered and protected urban life in Iraq when she is suddenly confronted with the reality of the persecution of the Kurds by the government. Soon the Iraqi secret police come for her father, who is warned in time to escape. Her older brother heads for the hills to join the *pesh murgas.* Before long, she, her 3-year-old sister, and their mother have to make a harrowing dash for the mountains of Kurdistan. For a while they are safe there, but then bombing raids destroy whole villages around them and parts of their village. Her father is once more in imminent danger of capture. They make a dangerous, exhausting, nighttime horseback trek through the mountains to seek asylum in Iran. With her mother seriously ill, Tara must take on responsibilities she never imagined in order to keep the family going in the refugee camp.

I am in no position to know for sure, but it appears that the facts and ethnographic details in the story have been carefully researched. An Afterword offers two pages of factual information regarding the situation faced by the Kurds. Written from Tara's viewpoint, the book is suitable for middle schoolers and should enlarge the scope of their understanding.

Julia Eccleshare

SOURCE: "Breaking down the Barriers," in *Books for Keeps,* No. 104, May, 1997, p. 4-5.

The horrors of ethnic cleansing or minority persecution at a national level are [very hard] to tackle in fiction. Dangers of sentimentality and romanticism abound. Elizabeth Laird skilfully treads a fine line in *Kiss the Dust* which explores the plight of the Kurds. Tara and her Kurdish family live prosperously in Iraq but their apparently normal life is underpinned by danger especially as Tara's father is active in the movement for Kurdish independence. The family is forced to flee, first to the mountains and then, when that becomes too dangerous, to Iran where they are refugees. As the war between Iran and Iraq escalates they are no longer safe and must travel on to En-

gland on a one-way ticket knowing no one and with nowhere else to go. Though at times Laird comes close to presenting an action adventure, she pushes her story on so that it becomes a book about tolerance and compassion rather than merely a drama.

One of the strengths of *Kiss the Dust* lies in the insight that it gives young British readers into the former lives of those who become refugees here. Refugees are usually at the margins of the society they move to but this is not necessarily a reflection of the lives or status they once enjoyed.

HIDING OUT (1993)

Joanne Schott

SOURCE: A review of *Hiding Out,* in *Quill and Quire,* Vol. 59, No. 7, July, 1993, p. 59.

On the last day of a tense two-family holiday in France, Peter finds his first real pleasure, a cave in which he lets his imagination loose. He creates a home there, somewhere he can live on his own. When both families' cars depart and he is mistakenly left behind, Peter's survival skills shrink; the cave as a necessity is less inviting. His discoveries surprise him. He can make a snare but cannot tighten it on the rabbit he traps, shouting at it instead to be more careful. Stealing food, however, is far easier than he ever thought.

Stephane, odd man out in another family on holiday, discovers Peter, watches him, and fantasizes companionship with a kindred spirit. Peter becomes aware of Stephane, too, and knows it is he who left toffees and precious matches for him in the cave. The story follows Peter's parents also, before and after they realize he is missing. Momentum increases and the paths of all the story's participants, including some villagers, converge. When Peter is found, he leaves behind his Swiss army knife for Stephane, who recognizes it as a gift from a friend he has never met. Suspense and our inherent interest in Peter's successes and failures at surviving on his own make good storytelling material. But the changes in Peter's perception of himself are just as interesting as the concrete events, and certainly played a large part in making this the winner of Britain's Children's Book Award.

David Self

SOURCE: A review of *Hiding Out,* in *Times Educational Supplement,* July 16, 1993, p. 22.

From all the hype, you might think the makers of the *Home Alone* films had discovered a new plot—but the theme of children coping (or not coping) on their own is at least as old as *Coral Island.* . . .

In Elizabeth Laird's **Hiding Out,** Peter is about twelve and belongs to the sort of family that holidays in a rented house in the Dordogne. Indeed, his story begins on their return trip across France. Another family has been holidaying with them and bickering has developed between the adults with Peter's mother suspecting her husband is too interested in the other mother (whose husband has left her).

After a picnic lunch, the families tetchily drive off in their two cars each thinking Peter is in the other one. Separated *en route,* it is only at Dover that they realise they have left him behind in an area whose name they do not know. The spine of the story concerns his highly practical attempts to survive in a cave and to live off the land.

This well-told story is convincing, even when explaining away Peter's reluctance to seek out the locals, and is perhaps at its best when describing his aborted attempt to snare a rabbit. "The first rabbit he had ever known suddenly popped into his head. It had been a picture on a mug which someone had given him for his first birthday. The rabbit had been wearing a little blue coat . . ."

J. A. Tweedie

SOURCE: A review of *Hiding Out,* in *Books for Your Children,* Vol. 28, No. 3, Autumn-Winter, 1993, p. 22.

This gripping story takes its theme from every child's nightmare—that of being lost on a family outing.

Peter Castle finds himself accidently abandoned in rural France after his family have stopped for a picnic on the way to catch the ferry back to England. Afraid to seek help, he takes refuge in a cave and begins a lonely struggle for survival.

His activities are described with fascinating detail—catching a fish without tackle, creating equipment from rubbish—nothing is left to the imagination. I lived through every difficulty with Peter—willing him to succeed. I was also forced to share his private fears—a crevice in the cave becomes a snake pit, a tree in the moonlight is a monster. Would his family have left him behind if they really cared?

Elizabeth Laird's atmospheric storytelling keeps up the suspense until the very last page—a book you won't be able to put down.

David Bennett

SOURCE: A review of *Hiding Out,* in *Books for Keeps,* No. 86, May, 1994, p. 15.

I can see why this won the Smarties Young Judges Award. It meets a lot of wish fulfilment—parents left to their confusing lives, holing up in a cave, in this case in France, and going feral.

When I read the cover blurb, I couldn't imagine how anyone would succeed in making me believe that parents could leave their child behind by mistake—credit to Ms Laird; she did it admirably.

As well as the action and tension, there's a thoughtful under-current of how isolated from each other parents and their offspring can be without necessarily recognising it.

SECRET FRIENDS (1997)

Adrian Jackson

SOURCE: A review of *Secret Friends,* in *Books for Keeps,* No. 103, March, 1997, p. 23.

This is a marvellous and moving short novel from the author of the award winning **Kiss the Dust** and the wonderful **Red Sky in the Morning**

On their first day at secondary school, Lucy starts a nervous conversation with new classmate, Rafaella and, without meaning to be hurtful, calls her 'Earwig' because of her big ears. Rafaella then finds herself teased and cut out of social contact at school—not, interestingly, because she is 'foreign' as Lucy thinks of it, but because of her ears. Lucy guiltily joins in this ostracism, but outside school she becomes Rafaella's secret friend, meeting her kind parents (so much warmer than her own) and sharing in her excitements. The ending is a shock, delicately and skilfully handled so that the reader is swept up in the drama in the most moving way. This short novel about, among other things, friendship, bullying and betrayal, is beautifully handled, a treat to be enjoyed by readers of all ages and a treat to read aloud—a box of tissues at the ready. It is illustrated with powerful and evocative pencil drawings.

Hazel Rochman

SOURCE: A review of *Secret Friends,* in *Booklist,* Vol. 95, Nos. 9-10, January 1, 1999, p. 878.

Lucy likes Rafaella and feels welcome in her warm "foreign" family, but Rafaella is an outsider at school, and Lucy cannot risk being seen with a social outcast; in fact, Lucy feels guilty for giving Rafaella the insulting nickname "Earwig" because of her large protruding ears. From that first school yard encounter, the teasing scenarios will draw middle-graders right into the story. Unfortunately, the climax becomes unwieldy melodrama when Rafaella dies of a heart defect while undergoing corrective surgery for her ears, and Lucy blames herself bitterly. The power of the story is the honesty of Lucy's first-person narrative, her uneasiness as a bystander to the bullying, torn between shame and pity, despising the in-crowd, not brave enough to be with her friend in public. What adds unexpected depth to the outsider theme is Lucy's envy of Rafaella's happy family, a place of refuge for Lucy from her own cold home.

Linda Bindner

SOURCE: A review of *Secret Friends,* in *School Library Journal,* Vol. 45, No. 3, March, 1999, pp. 210-11.

Without meaning to, Lucy tags Rafaella with the nickname Earwig on her very first day at Dale Road Middle School, and the name sticks. Though Lucy knows she has hurt this stranger, she is too passive to stop the taunting right away, and the girl's ears do stick out. Despite the teasing, Rafaella's initial aloofness, and Lucy's desire to be in with the popular crowd, Lucy is fascinated with the new girl and intrigued by her family, who come from an unidentified foreign country. The girls become secret friends during the hours away from school. Then, just before Christmas, Rafaella tells Lucy that she'll have a surprise for her after the holiday. It is only after Rafaella unexpectedly dies during cosmetic surgery that Lucy realizes how much she likes Rafaella and how badly she has treated her. Lucy's shame and grief come across in spite of the book's lack of engaging conversation, and though the plot is a bit predictable, the message of being proud of and standing up for your friends is no less powerful. The book's brevity and lack of detail might effect how well it captures the attention of the intended audience, but the characters and theme are memorable. Laird's story makes a good companion piece to Mary Downing Hahn's longer and more fleshed-out story on the same theme, *Daphne's Book* (Clarion, 1983).

JAY (1997)

Books Magazine

SOURCE: A review of *Jay,* in *Books Magazine,* Vol. 11, No. 3, July 8, 1997, p. 5.

Teenage years can be the best years of your life . . . or they can be riven by highly-charged emotion and hormone-induced stress. Twelve year-old Lucy, ill and forced to stay at home, watches her older brother Jay rush headlong towards crisis and disaster, eventually realising she must play a part in the drama that is her home life. Strong contemporary fiction from this award-winning author.

THE LISTENER (1997)

Steve Rosson

SOURCE: A review of *The Listener,* in *Books for Keeps,* No. 106, September, 1997, p. 25.

Graffix is a new series of almost comic book stories, highly illustrated with line drawings, which will prove useful with reluctant readers—especially boys. . . .

Football features . . . in **The Listener.** Gavin desperately wants to watch Johnny Mason make his debut for United but he has to go and stay with Grandma in her isolated cottage. Gran has a fall on the moors and the nearest house where Gavin can get help is occupied by Johnny and his busty, blonde bimbo of a girlfriend. It is Johnny's deaf sister Shelley, the listener of the title, who helps Gavin and brings about a satisfactory resolution to the tale.

FORBIDDEN GROUND (1997)

Sarah Mears

SOURCE: A review of *Forbidden Ground,* in *The School Librarian,* Vol. 45, No. 4, November, 1997, p. 213.

A love that challenges convention: this is the theme of Elizabeth Laird's latest novel. Hannah lives in North Africa. She has moved with her family from her native village to the cosmopolitan town and now she struggles to find an acceptable compromise between the moral values she has long held and the more relaxed attitudes of her friends in town—struggles which come to a head when she meets Simi.

This is a very restrained story; emotions and passions are tightly controlled. Few Western teenagers in Hannah's position would suffer the turmoil she experiences over what seems to us so chaste a relationship; and this is reflected in the sparse language and subtle shifts of emphasis within the story. Hannah develops emotionally and intellectually as the tale progresses and she begins to reach an understanding of her life and her position within society. A readable story which provides a view of life in a modern Islamic community.

📖 *A FUNNY SORT OF DOG* (1998)

Ethel E. Ashworth

SOURCE: A review of *A Funny Sort of Dog,* in *The School Librarian,* Vol. 46, No. 1, Spring, 1998, pp. 34-5.

Uncle Pete, home from sea, brings Simon a dog that he bought cheap from a man at the dock. The dog has a rough, rasping tongue, sharp claws and a long tail with a dark tip, so Simon christens him 'Tip'. But it is not long before it becomes apparent that Tip is no ordinary dog but, in fact, a lion cub! After a few most unusual happenings, Simon and his mother are forced to the decision that Tip must go to the Safari Park to be kept safe and happy. A later school visit there, and an understanding farewell to Tip, leave Simon feeling quite lion-like himself and altogether braver against bullies.

📖 *ON THE RUN* (1998)

Chris Stephenson

SOURCE: A review of *On the Run,* in *The School Librarian,* Vol. 46, No. 1, Spring, 1998, p. 34.

Hania, in *On the Run,* is left with her grumpy grandfather when her parents go away to avoid conscription to the Nationalists in a civil war. As the story opens her self-esteem is at rock bottom—her only moments of happiness are when she has to feed the chickens, because they appreciate her and don't snap and grumble at her all the time. Only when she has

coped with hiding a wounded freedom fighter and nursing him back to health in the barn does her grandfather (who unbeknown to Hania supports the banned freedom movement and has secretly been searching for the injured soldier himself) begin to accord her the respect that she deserves. The strong and enterprising character of Hania is contrasted with that of her frivolous, chatty schoolfriend, Rita, whose comings and goings serve to increase the tension of the plot by compounding the danger of discovery. Evocative line illustrations work with the text in portraying the range of emotions felt by the various characters. The whole thing is somewhat far-fetched, but ultimately a heart-warming moral tale.

📖 *ME AND MY ELECTRIC* (1998)

Lois Keith

SOURCE: A review of *Me and My Electric,* in *Books for Keeps,* No. 112, September, 1998, p. 22.

Me and My Electric is an inspired idea for a book. It came out of a Save the Children Fund conference called 'Invisible Children' which was attended by writers, publishers, directors and programme makers who acknowledged the invisibility of disabled children in their work. This book aims to rectify some of that. Seven disabled young people were linked with seven well established children's authors, Elizabeth Laird, Jacqueline Wilson and Rachel Anderson among them, to help them to tell the stories of their lives. The adult reader might be able to glimpse the writer's hand—all the stories are readable and well structured, but the content of these funny, energetic, powerful stories is the children's own. In her introduction Laird quotes a disabled person (I like to think it was me), saying to her 'We don't want people to say how awful life is for us, or how wonderful we are, but how we are different and how we are the same.' That is what these stories are all about. An essential read.

Additional coverage of Laird's life and career is contained in the following sources published by the Gale Group: *Contemporary Authors,* **Vol. 128;** *Contemporary Authors New Revision Series,* **Vol. 65; and** *Something about the Author,* **Vol. 77.**

Jess Mowry
1960-

American novelist, short story writer, and dramatist.

Major works include *Rats in the Trees* (1990), *Way Past Cool* (1992), *Ghost Train* (1996), *Bones Become Flowers* (1999).

INTRODUCTION

The author of gritty street fables, Mowry presents the lives of kids in the city and the daily threats to their survival and their dreams. Mowry bases his literary works on his own experiences and those of the children he has encountered as a social worker in Oakland, California, achieving realistic language and scenarios that some readers find disturbing. Ishmael Reed has called Mowry "the Homer of inner-city youth"; he has also been compared to Charles Dickens for his intense focus on the tribulations of children in the real world.

BIOGRAPHICAL INFORMATION

Mowry was born in Starkville, Mississippi, and raised in Oakland. His father, a crane operator, was black, and his mother was white, though he never knew her. Attracted to literature at a young age, Mowry took a special interest in Herman Melville's *Moby-Dick,* but he dropped out before high school and began to serve as a drug dealer's bodyguard. For the next several years, he led a violent life that would be echoed in his fictional work, especially in *Rats in the Trees,* his literary debut, a collection of short stories.

Mowry left the drug world and tried working as a mechanic, a truck driver, and a tugboat engineer. His principal source of income, however, came from the aluminum cans he would collect and carry to the recycling center. This was how he supported himself, his partner Markita Brown, and their four children. At the time Mowry began writing, the family was living in an abandoned bus that doubled as a drop-in center for troubled teenagers in poverty- and violence-stricken west Oakland.

A ten-dollar typewriter enabled Mowry to get his stories down on paper. The literary magazine *Zyzzyva,* a

longtime outpost for rebellious West Coast literature, was the first to publish his work. Literary recognition came as a surprise. "I'm getting published by these magazines with guys like college professors," he told the *Los Angeles Times.* "There'd be the list in the back, 'so and so is a professor teaching creative writing,' and there's Jess Mowry. 'Graduated eighth grade.' I'm wondering what people think." Even after *Rats in the Trees* came out, Mowry and his family were still living below the poverty level. In 1990, however, a $30,000 advance from the publisher Farrar, Straus, & Giroux eased somewhat their financial hardship.

Nevertheless, the author has maintained his close ties to the community and has generally refused to accept the trappings of celebrity if he thinks it will in any way compromise his integrity. For example, he has refused to lead reporters on tours of the ghetto and to give readings to audiences he suspects of misinterpreting his work or condescending to his characters. He has turned down substantial offers from companies like Disney, when he thinks he or his community might be exploited. Mowry has maintained this guarded stance as subsequent works have gained wider audiences and been optioned for film productions.

MAJOR WORKS

The nine stories that make up *Rats in the Trees* all focus on the life of a teenage boy named Robby. Robby becomes involved with the Animals, an interracial gang. Despite its limited distribution, the book caught the attention of critics and, eventually, major publishing houses. A reviewer for the *Wilson Library Journal* wrote, "Rarely has street life been so encapsulated in its own language."

Way Past Cool opens with a drive-by shooting and proceeds to detail the events of two days in a clash between rival gangs, the Friends and the Crew. Mowry focuses on the lives of Deek and Ty, a teen drug dealer and his bodyguard. Ty's brother Danny plans on entering the same high-risk, high-stakes world, but Ty intervenes. *Six out Seven* was written before *Way Past Cool* but published afterwards. It tells the story of what happens to Mississippi teenager Corbitt Wainwright when he moves to Oakland. Mowry explores the economic circumstances that compel Wainwright to join a gang called the Collectors. Reviews of both books praised the language and dialogue, while criticizing their uneven structure.

Mowry has described his success as a chronicler of urban youth, most notably in *Way Past Cool,* as "both a blessing and a curse. A 'blessing' in that I was able to tell the truth and show the world a view of how the U.S. treats [black street kids] . . . but a 'curse' in that I seem to be expected (by the 'mainstream' publishers) to write this kind of 'ghetto fiction' for evermore." Wary of presenting urban youths in exclusively violent, albeit realistic, situations, Mowry wrote *Ghost Train,* a supernatural mystery story. Haitian Vodoun figures prominently into the plot. This subject returns in his 1999 novel, *Bones Become Flowers,* which the author has called "the BEST writing I have done to date." Mowry's continued concern over economic exploitation is further explored in this young adult novel set in Haiti.

AWARDS

Rats in the Trees won Mowry a PEN-Oakland Josephine Miles Award.

AUTHOR COMMENTARY

Jess Mowry

SOURCE: "Stupid Rejection Letters to a Black Author," in *Voice of Youth Advocates,* Vol. 20, No. 5, December, 1997, pp. 308-10.

I'm sure that every author at one time or another has had the urge to write a short article (or publish a large book, as the case may be) to show the world their collection of stupid rejection letters. There are probably as many motives for wanting to do this as there are authors. Some of those motives might include outrage, despair, incredulity, perhaps even disgust. Ironically, often those writers with the most rejections—the hopeful young (or not-so-young) beginners—usually have the kindest collection: theirs are usually just the standard little forms, saying some variation of "thank you for your submission, but the material does not fit our current needs." This may be a good thing—ambiguity is seldom as discouraging as benightedness.

I think it's safe to say that all authors, great and small, have had their material rejected more than once—even Stephen King (but at least he can afford to laugh about it). However, most authors who have managed to gain some degree of renown—authors with at least a few books to their credit, and their names not totally unknown in the world of major publishing—are the ones most likely to receive the infamous short, polite (and often obtuse) note from an editor explaining why it was felt that this work could not be published. While these letters are often signed by a senior editor, one would sometimes prefer to think that they were actually written by an intern or perhaps somebody in the mail room. And while every author must feel at some time or another that their work is "misunderstood," many must also wonder if the work was actually read or just skimmed over during a power-lunch. Perhaps, too, many authors have sometimes speculated if their work was being censored or suppressed because it went against the grain of mainstream beliefs or attempted to shatter certain established stereotypes.

While I'm sure that most authors have been tempted to make some of their "best" rejection letters public, there also is the cold, hard fact that the publishing world is a very small place, and it is almost certain literary suicide to bite the hand that feeds you—or to even make growly sounds. In the case of "minority" authors such as myself, one always feels as if one is walking a very tenuous tightrope across a very deep pit if one even dares to suggest that their work has not been treated with the utmost kindness and dignity. Anyone who has ever read Ralph Ellison's *Invisible Man* (Vintage, 1993) ought to remember the scene in Dr. Bledsoe's office when the protagonist threatens to "tell" of his treatment, and the good Doctor just laughs and asks "who" he is going to tell (and by logical extension, who is going to care if he does). Obviously there are many more issues involved here than a badly written letter. However, in writing this piece for *VOYA*, I only wish to "tell" of my own rejection letter experiences as an author of stories for black young adults and to let the facts speak for themselves to anyone who cares to listen.

I began writing in 1988 for my own kids and for the street children of West Oakland who hung around a sort of youth center run by a dedicated and caring woman. Many of these kids wanted to read, and would read independently and outside of school, but had little they could relate to as far as actual reading material. Yes, there are several noted black children's and young adult authors. But the complaints I kept getting from the kids usually boiled down to either the stories were too tame (for lack of a better word) and/or the writer had no clue as to what (current) life in the innercity was like for a kid, or (worst of all) that the only reason you knew the characters in this or that book were "black" was that the author had mentioned it once.

Maybe white suburban kids feel the same way sometimes, but I'm sure you'd agree that they have a much wider range of books to choose from and identify with. Shocking as it may seem to some people, there are many black kids who haven't the slightest interest in basketball, and many more who would like to read a black ghost story, sci-fi, adventure, or fantasy; once upon a time I had a dream to write at least one of each kind. Anyhow, I started writing "real" stories about "real" black kids in West Oakland for real black West Oakland kids. Since life is not a Disney movie, I won't try to say that the response was phenomenal—readers of *VOYA* are, after all, librarians and educators who work with young people and know for a fact that a grunt of assent, the shrug of a shoulder, a murmured "it was okay," and sometimes even a smile from a young reader speaks volumes. All the praise I needed was to see the kids reading. Period. I got lots of criticism from them, and also lots of constructive advice. I learned what few established black writers seem to know (or at least will dare to write)— black kids like character descriptions that include physical attributes and the many shades of color that make them beautiful (seems logical). Black kids like reading about other black kids who do things besides play basketball, or join gangs, or do drugs. And most of all, I learned that black kids like reading about other black kids who are kind, gentle, intelligent, and who manage to triumph over a sometimes harsh environment despite these handicaps.

Some of you might be familiar with my most generally popular novel, *Way Past Cool* (Farrar, 1993). It is currently in its seventh trade paperback printing here in the U.S., and is also in eight other languages besides English. In many ways, this was a raw and brutal book for which I make no apology because it was written for a certain audience (innercity black kids) at a time when crack was first flooding their neighborhoods. That it was released in hardcover less than a month before the Rodney King Rebellion (or "riot," depending upon your point of view) was certainly timely, and I'd be the first to admit that it didn't exactly hurt the book's sales. But, *Way Past Cool* was only one story about a certain group of kids in a certain situation in a certain time and place. If I may be allowed to make the rather grandiose comparison, one would not read John Steinbeck's *The Grapes Of Wrath* and think that this book was representative of all white people in the United States. Steinbeck went on to write many other stories about many other people, some of them poor people (*Cannery Row*) some of them "ordinary" (his little known *The Wayward Bus* is my personal all-time favorite). Point is, *The Grapes of Wrath* was one story, and Steinbeck was "allowed" to move on from there.

Lest you think I'm rambling, let me return to the beginning of this piece and pull things together—how does all this relate to stupid rejection letters? Well, as I've just said, *Way Past Cool* was one story; it depicted a certain amount of violence, and some might even say perpetuated certain stereotypes about black innercity kids. Yet I felt it was a story that needed to be told, and one of the risks a black author takes when writing for his or her intended audience is that the work will fall into the "wrong" hands and be used against them. It is, after all, absurd to imagine that a black book will only have black readers—nor, I daresay, would *Cool* have been published "mainstream" had the publisher thought it would only be of interest to black people. It was never my intention to keep "re-writing" *Way Past Cool* for the rest of my life (guns, gangs, drugs, and violence—the everready equation for books about black innercity kids) any more than it was Steinbeck's intent to keep on re-writing *The Grapes Of Wrath*. *Way Past Cool* was followed by *Six Out Seven* (Farrar, 1993), another book about guns, gangs, drugs, and violence, although from a different perspective, being that half of the book was set in rural Mississippi; and I tried to get more into the root causes of "guns, gangs, drugs, and violence" (which surprisingly to some, are not causes but effects—nor did black innercity kids invent them). Though currently in its third trade paperback printing, *Six* did not do as well "mainstream" as *Cool*. My most recent book about innercity kids is *Babylon Boyz* (Simon & Schuster, 1997/*VOYA* April 1997). The reviews so far have been good to excellent, and my publisher was "delighted" with the book. Please don't misunderstand: I'm proud of *Boyz*—it, too, tells a story that I felt needed to be told. However, it also contains three murders, a beating, and a retrospective rape, as well as (guess what?) guns, gangs, drugs, and (obviously) violence. Now remember, this is a book the publishers were "delighted" to publish.

My next submission to this particular publisher was (and probably always will be now) a story called *Skeleton Key*. Since I hope it will be published some day by somebody, I won't give away the plot or the ending. Suffice to say that it deals with drug addiction, child abuse, and homelessness. But while the main character, a thirteen-year-old black boy, is beaten by a man in the beginning, he manages to get through the story, sign his mother into rehab, find a friend, meet a girl, and put his life back on track with hope for a future without packing a gun, joining a gang, or killing anybody. (Nor does he play basketball.) Here's a quote from the rejection letter:

> *We feel . . . that the readers we would reach with this book would be white kids for whom this book would feed their stereotypes of black innercity kids. We think they wouldn't see themselves in this book, and those kids who would wouldn't have access to the book.*

Okay, a book with three murders, a beating, a rape, guns, gangs, drugs, and violence (*Babylon Boyz*) doesn't do all of the above, while a book (*Skeleton Key*) with little graphic violence and a young black male working out his problems more or less peacefully—although not necessarily within the letter of the law or traditional American values—does? Perhaps the most frightening thing about this letter is the reference to who will have "access" to the book. If that doesn't enrage a lot of dedicated librarians, I might as well give up.

Care to hear a few other rejection comments from other houses?

> *We didn't feel it lived up to Mowry's talent as demonstrated in **Way Past Cool** and **Six Out Seven.***

Personally, I feel that the actual writing is much better in *Key*, and of course *Cool* and *Six* were my most "violent" books—I suppose that's one form of "talent."

> *I felt that the story was motivated primarily by a desire to frighten or scare.*

I won't even try to touch that one.

> *Mowry's prior novels were well-received because they had a* Lord of the Flies-*type sensibility: adults are absent, and the children turn to violence because of their urge [URGE!?!] to survive—while Robby and Timon [characters in* **Skeleton Key**] *are tender, they are not terribly compelling characters. . . . such a departure from Mowry's territory that I doubt his audience would be interested in reading it.*

I would assume that this editor is a white person, yet she feels confident that my "audience"—innercity black kids—would not want to read about "tender" characters. Upon what experience is her judgment based? Come to think of it, who is she to define my "territory?"

There are more, but since I have a feeling that these are now four major Young Adult publishers who will never publish anything of mine after this betrayal, I think I'd best quit while I still have some semblance of a career left. In the almost two years between the time *Boyz* was bought as a manuscript and its reaching the shelves in May '97 as a book, I've written two other novels besides *Skeleton Key*—one set in Alaska, and the most recent set in Haiti—both of which deal with the treatment and exploitation of children in the world. The Haitian novel is the absolute best writing I've done to date; and yet the rejection letters for these books have about the same theme: not a one mentions "bad writing, poor plotting, structure, pacing," etc., the standard ambiguous reasons to reject a manuscript. They simply say in so many words that "Mowry's audience would not be interested." Still, I can't resist showing you what now takes its place in my collection as the stupidest rejection letter of all time; this concerning one of the "non-ghetto" novels:

> *I'm afraid I can't get excited about* **The Wolf's Sun** *[spelling correct] because I have a natural aversion to happy father-son relationships; not having had one myself, I can't read about it or effectively promote it.*

This guy is choosing books for our kids, folks! And check out his criteria! Could it be that "happy father-son relationships" feed stereotypes? And, by the way, what's so "natural" about such an aversion?

If this tale should sound a bit familiar, consider that it's also the predicament in which many black recording artists and filmmakers find themselves—if we try to promote the positive, our music is not recorded and our films are not produced. So, in the case of perpetuating stereotypes, and perhaps promoting racism based on ignorance among our children—children of all colors—who really has the final say?

My agent told me recently, "You have a lot of fans in the publishing biz, but you're not giving them what they want." Apparently what they want is guns, gangs, drugs, and violence. Anyhow, there you have it: my stupid rejection letter story. It might be funny if not for the disturbing implications in regard to what types of books black kids are being permitted to "access," what young adult publishers are choosing to publish for them, and what a black writer is being "allowed" to write for his audience. After all, it used to be against the law to teach black kids to read: maybe it's now against the law to teach them to think.

GENERAL COMMENTARY

Cathi Dunn MacRae

SOURCE: A review of *Rats in the Trees*, in *Wilson Library Bulletin*, Vol. 65, No. 7, March, 1991, p. 113.

He was "a normal, happy street kid" growing up in Oakland, California. His white mother left when he was three months old. His black father, a scrap yard crane operator who loved to read, took him from Mississippi to Oakland to raise him alone, "blowing all the stereotypes." In fourth grade, he antagonized his teacher by reading ahead in assigned books. After eighth grade, he quit school to become a drug dealer's bodyguard. By seventeen, he left the drug world behind, having become sick of seeing friends die on the streets. He tried jobs as a mechanic, a truck driver, a tugboat engineer; but, collecting aluminum cans made better money. With his four children and their mother, Markita, he lived in an abandoned Greyhound bus in a junkyard, which doubled as a drop-in center for youth.

. . . Until the purchase of a used typewriter for ten dollars changed everything. He began to write about

his experience. Perhaps it was his avid reading that did it, he concedes. Books let him know there was another world out there.

This is not the story line for a new young adult novel on inner-city gang life. Not exactly. It is thirty-two-year-old writer Jess Mowry's own life, which he mines extensively in his three books *Rats in the Trees* (John Daniel & Co., 1990), *Children of the Night*, and *Way Past Cool.*

Without a colleague's help scouting small press booths at a past American Booksellers Association convention, I would never have discovered Mowry's first book, *Rats in the Trees,* or learned how a reviewer can be haunted by the reviewed. A series of incisive linked stories about the short life of runaway Robby, who becomes involved with the Animals, an interracial Oakland gang of boys barely in their teens, *Rats* still shook me long after I wrote its review . . . The work has since received the PEN-Oakland Josephine Miles Award and has been listed in "Books for the Teen Age" by the New York Public Library.

I received Mowry's newest novel from his first major publisher, Farrar, Straus & Giroux, as I was searching for a young adult author to speak at an American Library Association program addressing issues in multicultural YA publishing called "Connections—YA Publishers, YA Librarians, YA Readers: Linking Multicultural Needs."

In reply to my invitation, I received a plump, heavily taped package from Mowry's Oakland address. Inside were his two most recent books, a folder stuffed with clippings, and a two-page single-spaced letter—a most graceful decline of my invitation. It explained why he was too poor a speaker to accept, while eloquently addressing each of the panel's issues.

Like his books, Mowry's letter moved me to tears. In it I saw a private, sensitive man, compelled to mirror in writing his alien world for outsiders to see, but unwilling to visit our reality, where four hundred librarians would simply spell discomfort. Were some of those librarians—afraid to promote his gritty, violent, four-letter-word-spattered books to the youth for whom they were intended—part of the problem?

In his letter, Mowry agreed that such librarians may be

> one of the main reasons why there are very few books for "my" kids to read and relate to. I say *one* reason, because it is pretty obvious that to be

young, male, and black in this society is to be an endangered species. . . . Point of fact is that these kids are not *supposed* to be able to read. . . .

. . . the issue goes . . . much deeper . . . into the reality that there is an active and growing war on black males in this society. The Rodney King rebellion . . . was actually us shaking the bars of our cages. . . . One of the most deadly attitudes being drummed into our kids is this idea of "bad" and "cool," and that it's not "cool" to read. . . .

As I see it, we need *black* publishing and *black* distributing especially for our inner-city youth . . . books and reading material of every sort and subject written *by, for,* and *about* black kids, and this we don't have.

Most of the writers of the nearly thirty articles Mowry sent me are also deeply affected by his testaments. *Way Past Cool* stirred a *Los Angeles Times* reviewer "to a real anger. It's proof that literature is far from dead. Unless you are emotionally dead yourself, you simply cannot read about fourteen-year-old kids who are discussing Capt. Kirk one minute and talking about taking dirt naps, their term for being killed by a dealer, or buying a new Uzi the very next."

If Mowry himself had not sent me his second book, *Children of the Night,* an original paperback from a small African-American publishing company, I would never have seen it. Enter Mowry's alternative universe, a West Oakland neighborhood where thirteen-year-old Ryo is luckier than many because he has a mother, Tracy, who loves him and surrounds him with other caring adults to compensate for his lack of a father. Tracy must work endless hours in Brownie's Cafe, with little time off to spend with Ryo in their drab, windowless apartment. During Ryo's meals at the café, kind-hearted Vietnam veteran Brownie and his regular customers offer Ryo advice and support, marveling at his intelligence and common sense, which set him apart from his neglected peers.

Of course, Ryo cannot remain unaffected by his surroundings. Hanging out with his best friend, his "homey" Chipmunk, an enormously fat boy who still manages to be an ace on a skateboard, Ryo begins to see no way out. Dressed in shabby clothes, he endures the sneers of rich white "squid-kids" at the mall while window-shopping a skateboard that he cannot afford. Far beyond recreation, a board is a safe way to navigate the dangerous streets. "There's all kinds of ways to be hungry," Ryo thinks. "An' money seem to be the only thing what fill you up."

There is only one way to get the money to escape from his city cage with his mother—by working for drug dealer Big Bird.

Sensing Ryo's talents, sixteen-year-old Big Bird grooms him for inside work, giving special treatment that includes a ride in Big Bird's Piper Cub, beyond airplane buff Ryo's wildest dreams.

Despite his bedazzlement, however, Ryo soon becomes disenchanted with Big Bird's "rock house," which speeds boys as young as eight into crack addiction. How else, though, can Ryo earn a hundred bucks a day toward his dream? It takes Chipmunk's death in a drug run to propel Ryo to destroy Big Bird and so save himself.

Mowry believes that the pivotal age of thirteen is when ghetto children first see "what is," the dreadful reality around them. Through the voice of café owner Brownie, Mowry rails against the traps confining these boys, tired of "having nothing, being nothing, and seeing nothing ahead." While mourning for Chipmunk and the other lost ones, the reader roots hard for Ryo, hoping he will be one of the survivors. Our hope is kept alive by Suntop, a nineteen-year-old pimp who hangs out at Brownie's. A fan of ElfQuest graphic novels, Suntop believes in magic, swearing that he makes magic happen, sometimes through his ladies the "Elf-Princesses," who bring happy moments to this dark world.

When Ryo turns to Suntop for comfort after a crack-crazed friend is shot, the seventeen-year-old "Elf-Princess" Firefox is part of Suntop's cure for Ryo's blues. Ryo's sexual awakening with Firefox is a ritual coming-of-age, timed for the night before he discovers Chipmunk's body, giving Ryo the power to make a stand.

Though Mowry strongly depicts drug lords as evil predators on the weak and innocent, Suntop's prostitutes and magic rituals (really a form of positive thinking) are just as clearly a force for good. Such values are part of what makes this inner-city underworld so foreign to the rest of us; we must be careful to judge that world by its own rules, not ours. As Brownie says, the problem is "people not believin' what's goin' on in places like this . . . as long as they can keep it in places like this."

In *Way Past Cool,* Mowry simply moves down the block from *Children of the Night* to similar Oakland turf controlled by other versions of Ryo and Chipmunk, a gang of five innocuously called the Friends. Gordon, the oldest at thirteen, is the leader, but elusive, mystical Lyon is the power behind Gordon's throne. Like Chipmunk, Gordon is a fat skateboard expert; obesity represents status in a place where people often go hungry. The other Friends are the quarrelsome twins Ric and Rac and younger Curtis, who wears dreadlocks as his parents dream of moving to Jamaica.

The book opens with a bang as the Friends are "drive-byed," shot at from a careening van on their way to school. Hiding behind dumpsters, only little Curtis gets hurt by flying debris. Upset that his gang's one cheap pistol jammed and his homework papers got dirty, Gordon fears a scolding from his teacher more than the shooting.

When the Friends learn that their rival gang, the Crew, has also been drive-byed, they realize that both gangs were set up by Deek. At sixteen, Deek, their local drug dealer, lords it over them with his bodyguard, Ty; his Uzi; and his Trans Am.

In alternating chapters, the point of view shifts between the friends and Ty, Deek's reluctant bodyguard, who plans to work for difficult Deek just another month to earn money for his mother and siblings. Yet, Ty wonders if he can hold out that long. Enraged, Ty attacks his twelve-year-old brother, Danny, to keep him from applying to Deek for a job. Deek's casual murder of the two boys he hired for the drive-bys—injecting them with battery acid, which they think is cocaine—further alienates Ty.

As the two gangs join forces to plan revenge on Deek, Danny tries to save Ty from their wrath. Suspense mounts to an unbearable pitch, reaching a climax in an abandoned car wash, where a cop and several gang members are killed.

Stuck between impossible choices, Ty is the central force in this novel, marked by Mowry's identification with him from his own bodyguard days. As with Ryo in *Children of the Night,* Ty's spirit is bolstered the night before the battle by his sexual encounter with Markita (named after Mowry's own partner of sixteen years' standing). Her warmth and decency make Ty realize that love is worth the fight.

The structure of the two novels, from conflict buildup to injection of sexual power to climactic battle, is astonishingly similar. Both books end full of hope for the future, weakening their strong trajectories that forecast little hope. With its concentration on Ryo, *Children* seems more integrated. Since Suntop keeps chanting that if you follow your heart "there is never no hope" (echoing Mowry's letter), its positive ending is not unexpected. *Way Past Cool* is a darker book whose ending works less well, though it reveals Mowry's heart. Like Suntop in *Children,* Lyon is the shamanistic character in *Cool,* invoking magic and heart following. But unlike Suntop, Lyon is killed. It is only Ty who sees "way past cool," the ironic ghetto compliment, by realizing that strutting young gangs fight something "so huge and powerful and so far beyond their understanding that they might as well have been trying to stop a tank with a BB gun." To Ty, that power resides in a pyramid with rich whites on top and blacks on the bottom.

The similarity of characters, plot, setting, and themes in the two novels does not diminish either one. Both are vibrant, mesmerizing evocations of an underworld that the classes above ignore. Insider Mowry captures that world with descriptions of ugly places and desperate people so lyrical that they force us to really see what we would rather not. Mowry writes organically, it seems, his words fusing into one whole. His own life is so solidly enmeshed in his work that perhaps we need a new word for it. Such social commentary is actually "docufiction."

Mowry's critics compare him to writers from Shakespeare to James Baldwin, from Twain to Warren Miller. Mowry himself is utterly unpretentious, such a product of his milieu that he cannot participate in our world's ways. Money and possessions mean little; his publishers begged him to get a cellular phone. He makes few personal appearances, accepting a less lucrative British book contract to avoid an author tour. Interviews are sparse, conducted by phone or in a Denny's restaurant; he won't "give tours of the ghetto." After receiving a $30,000 advance on *Way Past Cool* from FSG and a $75,000 Disney film option, he moved his family to an apartment, but he still uses the Greyhound bus as an office. He upgraded his ancient Royal typewriter to an old IBM. He puts most of his money back into his community by helping neighborhood kids, one of whom caught him collecting cans again, staying "in practice" for a change in fortune.

His books themselves tell what youth in all universes need to know. Mowry is self-deprecating about even that. "The thing is that there can't be much of a secret to writing if I can do it. Maybe it's just that I've come up with a new angle—looking at these kids as human beings instead of . . . hardened animals."

Mowry refers to his young gang characters as "The Little Rascals with Uzis." His own old gang name was Buckwheat. When a journalist asked him why he gives his money away, Mowry joked, "Buckwheat does Mother Teresa. Maybe it's that old Buddhist saying that once you don't want it, you can have it all. I write for the kids. The best thing was when a guy called me from L.A. and said he was working with these teenagers at the second-grade level who were reading my stories all the way through."

Ishmael Reed

SOURCE: "The Activist Library: A Symposium," in *The Nation,* New York, Vol. 255, No. 8, September 21, 1992, pp. 293-94.

Jess Mowry began writing as a result of ties with what might be called an extended family of kids with whom Mowry came in contact during a storefront storytelling workshop in Oakland. Discovering that there was a dearth of books with which young blacks could identify, he began making up street stories for the consumption of his workshop members. Eventually he wrote them down. His three books—*Rats in the Trees* (John Daniel), *Children of the Night* (Holloway House) and his most recent novel, *Way Past Cool* (Farrar, Straus & Giroux)—were the result.

Mowry presents the educational establishment with a direct challenge. With his own meager funds he has persuaded those kids deemed incorrigible—children who've been forgotten by the system—to read books and become interested in intellectual activity, a feat that not only some inner-city schools but suburban and private schools have failed to accomplish.

The brilliant word play of rap music and the prose of Jess Mowry, the Homer of inner-city youth, indicate a full-blown word renaissance among black youth and the white and brown youth whom they inspire. The question for educators is why it's happening in the streets and not in the schools, and why Mowry, a grammar-school dropout, is so successful in motivating inner-city youth to take as much interest in language as they do in basketball, with a budget that would amount to less than the lunch tips of a commission convened to investigate why Johnny can't read.

TITLE COMMENTARY

📖 *RATS IN THE TREES* (1990)

Kirkus Reviews

SOURCE: A review of *Rats in the Trees: Stories,* in *Kirkus Reviews,* Vol. LVIII, No. 3, February 1, 1990, pp. 131-32.

[*Rats in the Trees* contains] nine interrelated stories about a runaway boy who survives for a time in inner-city Oakland—in a less-than-polished first collection, but one that evocatively creates a milieu where almost everyone is either in trouble or on the edge.

Robby is a 13-year-old black who leaves Fresno by bus (**"Welcome to Oakland".**) because he's going to be sent to a foster home. But he discovers quickly (**"One Way"**) that "The ocean was just as worn-out and thrashed as everything else . . . "; and meets fat Donny ("I figure everybody gots somebody they wanna kill"), who explains the local gang scene: drugs, violence, exploitation. **"Passing Rite"** brings an outsider, Chuck, into the neighborhood (as a staffer at the local center) so that we can get some sociological perspective: "they were a new and primitive race evolving fast from garbage." They attend "War Zone Elementary or Death Camp Jr. High." Then Robby is finally accepted by The Animals, who are involved mostly with skateboards and beer, though drugs and violence are also prevalent. In **"Prev,"** the gang beats up a guy from "Silicone land" who tries to pick up one of them, and in **"Fire,"** Robby gets a gun and shows up well in a firefight. The predictable finish fast approaches: in **"Wolf-Boy,"** Eric, with the gift of prophecy, looks into the future: "we old kids already . . . But we nuthin', man. We goin' nowhere"; and in **"Werewolf Night,"** Robby is killed, and life goes on when Eric takes his skateboard.

An honest look into an ugly, depressing scene: Mowry's style is rough, but the nicknames, slang, and jive ring true. Finally, then, it's a book more interesting for sociological than for literary reasons.

Publishers Weekly

SOURCE: A review of *Rats in the Trees: Stories,* in *Publishers Weekly,* Vol. 237, No. 9, March 2, 1990, p. 78.

Mowry's first book at once saddens, overwhelms and charms as it explores a realm unto itself—urban gangs. A youth counselor in Oakland, Calif., fluent in street language, the author delivers nine polished and interrelated short stories about Robby, a 13-year-old runaway who lands in Oakland with five dollars and a skateboard. He is befriended by the Animals, a gang of dangerous but nevertheless vulnerable youths. Mowry repeatedly demonstrates how uneasy frailties surface despite hard veneers: characters wash down Ding-Dongs with beer, swear in pig Latin or unsuccessfully try to mooch matches from a convenience-store clerk even as they tote .45 pistols. The Animals accept violence, knowing they cannot avoid fighting a local tough in a gun battle considerably less glamorous than "anything on TV." Often these teens simply hang out and talk frankly, pondering the trivia of daily life as well as death and survival, wondering why "the world lies, man. 'specially to kids."

Cathi MacRae

SOURCE: A review of *Rats in the Trees,* in *Wilson Library Bulletin,* Vol. 65, No. 7, March, 1991, p. 113.

Like the youths in the drop-in center where he works, Mowry rides a skateboard. The used typewriter on which he created these related stories and his few extra years of age may be his only differences from them. Rarely has street life been so encapsulated in its own language.

Through the grit of dingy alleys comes Robby, fleeing a Fresno foster home to land in Oakland. After winning a place in the interracial gang the Animals, Robby finds Oakland as hopeless as Fresno. Even the gray polluted ocean is hype. According to a worker at the center, boys like Robby represent "a new primitive race evolving fast from garbage." Mowry's stories decode that race's language, if we can stand to listen. The lives of these Animals, all in their early teens, are ugly and cruel. They beat a child who apes them, begging to join them, and then kill a rival gang leader in their first gunfight, shockingly unlike what they expected from TV. As they deck and roll their boards to the next alley, Robby muses, "Sometimes I just get the feelin' stuff ain't what it's really supposed to be like. . . . I wonder if squid-kids [prosperous whites] are happy, man?" His awareness makes Robby one of the few who might find his way out, until his shattering, inevitable end.

This small press trade paperback will shock readers with a terrifying reality more unvarnished than many of us can handle. Amid its violence and four-letter words is the beauty of the undaunted human spirit, the yearning for decency and hope. The Animals' loyalty to each other is all the love they experience, unless librarians have the courage to make their story available to those who dare to really see.

WAY PAST COOL (1992)

Kirkus Reviews

SOURCE: A review of *Way Past Cool,* in *Kirkus Reviews,* Vol. LX, No. 3, February 1, 1992, p. 137.

Black teen gangs in West Oakland are the subject of Mowry's first novel—a long cry of pain and rage over conditions in the ghetto.

A fast-moving start (a bunch of kids on their way to school are sprayed with bullets from a passing van) is followed by a very slow-moving story about two early-teen gangs; 16-year-old drug-dealer Deek and his bodyguard Ty; and a teen mother, Markita, working at Burger King to support herself and her baby. Deek, who is evil incarnate, has hired the Big Boys in the van to give both gangs a good scare; the gangs, observing their "rules," have a meet and decide that Deek must be killed. This duly happens, in a climactic firefight that lasts forever. A parallel storyline centers on Ty, a lost soul who regains his humanity when he stops his kid brother Danny from becoming another street-corner dealer and tries to stop Deek from murdering the Big Boys ("they knew too much"). Markita finds him sobbing in an alley and takes him home; they make love, and a schmaltzy ending suggests that they have a future together. Mowry uses this lumbering vehicle to make some familiar points: that his feral, gun-toting homeboys are still kids who do their homework and ache for love; that ghetto life is "a long line of cages"; that "black death means nothing to nobody"; and that the drug culture has devastated black pride and solidarity.

Mowry (the story collection **Rats in the Trees,** 1990) does know the territory, but, given his overheated prose, his cry from the heart too often sounds like an out-of-control scream; for a restrained treatment of this material, there's always *Boyz 'n the Hood* (John Singleton's impressive 1991 movie debut).

Donna Seaman

SOURCE: Donna Seaman, a review of *Way Past Cool,* in *Booklist,* Vol. 88, No. 14, March 15, 1992, p. 1337.

Jess Mowry sees the trash-strewn, junked car-lined streets of Oakland as a fog-shrouded land of the damned, a hell for children whose sins are being black and poor. Here boys just reaching puberty have already chosen the way of the gun, banding together in gangs for protection and camaraderie. They'll kill, but they're still open to love. Mowry's heartbreaking gang bangers call themselves the Friends and include fat Gordon, whose malapropisms are both funny and depressing, magical Lyon, who believes in the power of the heart, and a goofy pair of twins named Ric and Rac. A well-armed drug dealer, who's reached the impressive age of 16, decides to stir up trouble for the Friends. His reluctant enforcer and bodyguard, Ty, goes along with the program until his younger brother gets involved. As Ty witnesses and experiences willful violence and cold-blooded cunning, he struggles with his rage at the hunger and desperation that transform children into junkies and killers. There's no glamour here, no celebration of the gang look or the gang life; Mowry is all compassion and fury. His streetwise dialogue has astonishing emotional depth while his masterful evocations of setting and atmosphere create an aura of unreality that makes the reality of this urban underworld all the more appalling. Powerful, gritty, and transcendently hopeful.

Daniel Max

SOURCE: "'Cool' Author Gives Hollywood a Cold Stare," in *Variety,* Vol. 347, No. 3, May 4, 1992, p. 310.

Jess Mowry, the Oakland, Calif.-based author of the remarkable new novel *Way Past Cool,* is making a career out of biting the hands that feed him. But far from alienating his supporters, Mowry has touched a chord in the publishing industry, the media and, most importantly, book buyers.

The outspoken Mowry, who never finished grade school and takes care of Oakland ghetto kids when he's not writing, at first nixed all publicity for his novel. But he has finally agreed to interviews, and now *Way Past Cool,* the story of an Oakland gang just published by Farrar, Straus & Giroux, is jumping out of stores wherever his potshots have run.

Scratch most ghetto scribes and you find a writing school grad, but Mowry is the real thing. Echoing the blacks who rioted in Los Angeles after the Rodney King verdict, Mowry accuses the white establishment of deliberately keeping blacks from power: "We had something going in the '60s but they found a better way to control it."

Mowry believes race plays a part in his publisher's delay in exercising the option on his next book. "Being a black book, we got to go through this. A white author with my track record, they'd snap up my option like that."

When Hollywood came courting the 32-year-old author, Mowry committed Hollywood's version of a mortal sin: He refused to take a meeting.

"Basically I was livin' on the street or in the truck," says Mowry. "How fucking stupid to get on a plane and fly down to L.A. to talk with those people. I didn't have a clean pair of jeans. Not that I'd do it now either."

"Those people" were Don Simpson and Jerry Bruckheimer, who have a development office at Disney. Mowry's then agent, Sandra Dijkstra, along with Ron Bernstein of the Gersh Agency, had set up a deal that called for Mowry to write the screenplay for *Way Past Cool.*

The indie producers found Mowry so hard to work with that they walked away, leaving the project to Hollywood Pictures, which has hired a white screenwriter—per Bernstein. Mowry wound up with a $75,000 option.

Bernstein says Mowry wanted an impossible degree of control over the material. "[Simpson and Bruckheimer] weren't going to be at the mercy of a writer who . . . wanted to remake the business. I cannot tell you the number of memos, faxes and phone calls that went back and forth trying to satisfy him. Jess had a view of Hollywood that just didn't dovetail with reality."

Mowry objected to the contract most of all. "I wasn't wantin' to do the screenplay on their terms. Read one of their contracts. Thirty pages of fine print: Now and forever on earth as it is in heaven, and if space aliens come down and want to rent videos it's in there."

Mowry kissed off the sizable screenplay fee, and his objections to the Disney contract made Hollywood howl when they ran with an *L.A. Times* interview.

Bernstein notes the L.A. riots may make a green light for the movie less likely.

Others echo Bernstein's bafflement at the visitor from Other America. "It's almost like dealing with an author from another country," says Helen Atwan, publicity director at Farrar, Straus.

The author was taught a love of books by his father, and he's used his money to benefit the kids he looks after and to help local families in need. He says he didn't know interviews were obligatory to book publishing and that the whole commercial apparatus of publishing caught him by surprise—and disgusts him.

"What Mowry is saying is what we're all thinking," adds a book editor at a mass market house on condition of anonymity. "The industry has sold out. It's about nothing today; it's about money."

Mowry's own publisher endorses some of his criticisms.

"I like Jess and I respect what he stands for and what he does and the way he wants to handle things," says publicist Atwan, a 16-year veteran of the business.

"I think in principle he's correct." says Roger Straus Sr., president of the company that bears his name. "The industry has never been more unfriendly to literary publishing."

Mowry has now been interviewed by the *New York Times*—an honor more likely to fall to Farrar, Straus's dozen Nobel Prize winners than a neophyte novelist—and *Entertainment Weekly,* the *San Francisco Examiner, Details,* the *Los Angeles Times* and, finally, *People.*

"I was on the verge of telling the *New York Times* to use [black writer] Kevin Powell's interview," says Mowry, "or to forget the whole thing. There's few enough of us. Of course FSG went apeshit over that one."

Mowry's interviews—such as they are—sell books, especially on the West Coast where most of the publicity has run. Stores there report re-orders up to five times elsewhere.

"It's a definite phenomenon on the West Coast," reports Sally Dedecker, VP of marketing for Ingrams Book Co., a major wholesaler. "There's a huge distinction between east and west."

And since authors who won't play by the rules are news, there will doubtless be a second wave of publicity with the paperback release. Farrar, Straus, which has a $150,000 paperback minimum bid, or "floor," will profit from the $30,000 book come what may. It has printed 15,000 hardcover copies.

Mowry nixed Ed Bradley's request for an interview on CBS' "Street Stories" because he won't allow his neighborhood to be shown; he fears someone may kidnap one of the kids he cares for. "If he's from where he says he is, he ought to know," says Mowry of the black newsman.

Meanwhile, Mowry has just fired Dijkstra, one of the hottest agents of the '90s thanks to clients Amy Tan and Susan Faludi. Mowry discussed signing with black agent Marie Brown, but instead chose Molly Friedrich—known to some in the industry as "Six-Figure Moll." She is also on a roll thanks to the success of authors Jane Smiley and Terry McMillan, who introduced author and agent.

Dijkstra had sold *Way Past Cool* in six countries, including a remarkable $50,000 sale to Italy's Einaudi. England's Chatto & Windus (a Random Group publisher) bought in for £30,000 but said it would cut the offer in half when Mowry refused to tour. Before Dikjstra could renegotiate, Mowry faxed a note to the publisher giving his assent.

"If money was the bottom line, I'd never have a complaint with [the Dijkstra Agency]. But you can't talk writin' with them," Mowry says.

His next project is currently on submission. Dijkstra says FSG isn't waiting for *Way Past Cool*'s performance, as Mowry believes, but rather for more pages to read before deciding. Editors frequently exercise particular caution on the followup work to an autobiographical novel. Mowry's next book is set half in Mississippi and half in Oakland. Dijkstra says she has an offer for the new book from the paperback floor holder in case FSG doesn't opt in.

Mowry's choices have already cost Dijkstra in the vicinity of $50,000 in lost commissions. Still she says: "He's an angry man [but] a brilliant writer. We were proud to be part of this."

People Weekly

SOURCE: A review of *Way Past Cool,* in *People Weekly,* Vol. 37, No. 24, June 22, 1992, p. 66.

He cruises the mean streets of Oakland in a battered '59 GMC truck crammed with garbage cans, paintbrushes and family snapshots stuck in the visors. At Marcus Books, an African-American bookstore, Jess Mowry hops out and, in seeming disbelief, pauses at the window where his novel, *Way Past Cool,* is the featured display. The store manager greets him and asks him to give a reading. "I ain't never read for nobody," says Mowry. "I wrote the book for black kids, and I 'spect white people won't buy it."

Not so. *Way Past Cool,* a gritty tale of life among two rival Oakland gangs—"Little Rascals with Uzis," Mowry calls them—is a success. The *Los Angeles Times* called it a "wrenching" novel that "crackles with authenticity." Jonathan Galassi, editor-in-chief of Farrar, Strauss & Giroux, Mowry's publisher, likens Mowry to Dickens. Disney bought the film option for $75,000, and paperback rights may go for $150,000.

Mowry, 32, disdains the role of rising literary light. He's testy and elusive. No reporter has seen his home or family, his mailing address is a post office box in Santa Cruz, and he's reachable only on a cellular phone. According to Mowry, the facts of his life are these: He was born in Mississippi to a white mother and black father (he won't name them) who soon split. Father and son moved to Oakland, where Mowry dropped out of school at 13. For a time he protected a drug dealer, toting a pistol. But he also read voraciously. "My father showed me books were cool," Mowry says.

Working as a mechanic and scrap collector, Mowry began writing in 1988. His first book, **Rats in the Trees,** won a PEN award in 1990. But the success of **Way Past Cool** has left him torn. Though he can better support his family, which he claims includes companion Markita Brown and their four children, ages 8 to 16, fame and fortune have made him feel a misfit in his old neighborhood. Mowry wants to keep writing—he's at work on a book about his Southern roots—but beyond that, anything is possible. "For all I know," he says, "we may move to Kenya."

SIX OUT SEVEN (1993)

Kirkus Reviews

SOURCE: A review of *Six out Seven,* in *Kirkus Reviews,* Vol. LXI, No. 15, August 1, 1993, p. 960.

Lumbering in on the heels of his highly acclaimed debut, **Way Past Cool** (1992), Mowry unloads a ponderous tale about African-American youth in peril—as lavish in its attention to lingo as it is weakly plotted.

In the tiny Mississippi community of Bridge-End, a cluster of cabins on a decaying road to nowhere, Corbitt and his buddies Lamar and Toby are learning about sex and race, while on the mean streets of Oakland, California, boy-mountain Lactameon ("Tam") skillfully maneuvers his bulk through the maze of tight squeezes and close calls that his neighborhood offers its children. With Corbitt's father just jailed for fighting Bates, an old racist pedophile across the river, Corbitt feels the burden of lingering racism more acutely than his sidekicks and eventually tangles with the white man—an encounter that proves fatal when Bates's shotgun fires. Tam has his share of troubles, too, when the gang claiming him as its mascot hits a crack house that deals mostly to kids but that's run by a boy whom he considers a friend;

caught in the middle, he does a delicate balancing act, and in the process is adopted by one-eyed urchin Ethan, who makes a living servicing travelers in the bus depot. When Corbitt runs away from home, he comes to Oakland, where he connects with Tam through Ethan, but in spite of their friendship, he is pulled into the heart of 'hood darkness and is forced to lead a deadly assault on a new crack house.

With far more attitude than velocity, the harsh realities of rural and urban black America hit home relentlessly, but leave few lasting impressions: a painfully long and, for Mowry readers, a now-familiar saga of lost childhood innocence.

Sybil Steinberg

SOURCE: A review of *Six out Seven,* in *Publishers Weekly,* Vol. 240, No. 32, August 9, 1993, p. 450.

Mowry's powerful third novel returns to the Oakland street scene of **Way Past Cool** to tell another coming-of-age story set among the black gangs of urban America. This time, however, his tale concerns a boy from the rural South seeking an escape from his oppressive small-town life. Bright, handsome Corbitt Wainwright sees little opportunity in Bridge-End, Miss. When his father is sent to jail for attacking a white man and he himself becomes involved in a deadly dispute over a catfish, Corbitt flees the town in hopes of finding a better life in California. Instead, he becomes caught up in the world of guns, gangs and crack. Save for Lactameon, a gifted, sensitive gang mascot whose obesity sets him apart from the regular homeboys, California might have been another dead end for Corbitt. When they eventually come together, Lactameon finds Corbitt carpentry work setting up a crack house and the two conspire to rescue a starving one-eyed urchin named Ethan from early death on the streets. Mowry has an unerring ear for gritty street talk, a graphic sense of place and an unflinching view of American urban life. Influenced by rap music, gangster movies, street slang and the ghosts and magic of a distant African past, he synthesizes a dazzling new sort of literary adventure fiction.

Donna Seaman

SOURCE: A review of *Six out Seven,* in *Booklist,* Vol. 90, No. 2, September 15, 1993, p. 128.

We were knocked out by Mowry's last novel, **Way Past Cool** . . . , a transcendent tale of gang life on the blasted streets of Oakland, and certainly have respect for what he's attempted here, but this novel is a far more diluted and didactic affair. Mowry has set up a parallel between the struggles of urban gang-bangers and the conflicts of a young black man living in a tiny Mississippi community. In each realm, poverty and prejudice choke expectations and dreams. The link between these circumscribed worlds is Corbitt, the best and the brightest of Bridge-End. Tall, very dark, and intense, Corbitt has been forced to recognize the depth and insidiousness of white fear and hatred as his father is sent to jail without having committed a crime and a violent confrontation forces Corbitt to flee to California. Corbitt's Oakland double is Lactameon, a hugely fat and appealing homeboy every bit as decent, honest, independent, and strong as Corbitt. Once these two young heroes join forces, the pace of this far too preachy novel picks up a bit, and catharsis is achieved. This is an interesting near miss. Mowry has burdened his fine characters with too many messages and tried, unsuccessfully, to blend mysticism with polemics. But we do give *Six Out Seven* at least a four out of seven and hope that Mowry will try again.

Shelley A. Glantz

SOURCE: A review of *Six Out Seven: A Novel,* in *Kliatt,* Vol. XXIX, No. 1, January, 1995, p. 10.

Mowry has created some of the most unforgettable characters in literature in this novel. The book centers on 13-year-old Corbitt, a bright black boy from rural Mississippi. As his story begins, his father has been sent to jail for assaulting a white man who had molested a young boy. Corbitt tries his best to keep himself together during those summer days, with help from his two best friends and the girl for whom he has feelings. The chapters chronicling his struggles alternate with chapters relating the life of Lactameon, known as Tam, also black, also bright, and also 13, who lives in the Oakland ghetto. As their parallel stories are told, the reader is made aware that they will eventually cross paths. They do, when Corbitt runs away from Mississippi and meets Tam and Ethan, his eight-year-old sidekick, as he steps off the bus in Oakland. Because of his very dark skin, Corbitt is considered an African by his city counterparts. His intelligence and creativity serve to convince them even further of this attribute. The few weeks he lives on the city streets awaken Corbitt to the plight of the young black male in America today. He sees new acquaintances shot to death, or die from drugs and neglect. The lives of the gang members Corbitt comes in contact with are changed so much by him that many of them leave the gang and begin working in a

local children's shelter, but not before they avenge the death of a friend.

Mowry's writing reflects today's news stories, but his characters will remain with readers forever. Unfortunately, many of them die much too young. All of these children drink and smoke, most carry guns or knives, but many of them are turned off by drugs, especially the crack cocaine which kills some of the characters. Corbitt and Tam are the most mature characters and take on many of the characteristics and nurturing roles we expect of adults. When Corbitt returns to Mississippi, he is accompanied by Ethan, who has been abandoned by his parents. This novel is one that will move all readers and affect them for the rest of their lives.

GHOST TRAIN (1996)

Publishers Weekly

SOURCE: A review of *Ghost Train,* in *Publishers Weekly,* Vol. 243, No. 38, September 16, 1996, p. 84.

The author of the explosive *Way Past Cool* now takes aim at a younger audience, offering another gritty, keenly perceptive portrait of inner-city life but framing it as a ghostly tale. Haitian immigrant Remi knows that life will be different in Oakland, Calif., where refrigerators, hot running water and TV are taken for granted. But when he and his parents move into an apartment in a ramshackle Victorian house, the last thing the 13-year-old expects is to be haunted by a recurring vision of murder. Every night, while his mother and father sleep, Remi (who has "always had a certain affinity for the supernatural") hears a "fantôme" train "panting puffs like the breath of some huge jungle beast." From his window, he witnesses the ghosts of two railroad men, one white and one African American, acting out a deadly scenario. He and his streetwise neighbor, Niya, draw together to uncover an injustice half a century old. Containing more substance than most thrillers for this age group, this horror story is underscored by strong social commentary on poverty, waste and materialism.

Deborah Stevenson

SOURCE: A review of *Ghost Train,* in *The Bulletin of the Center for Children's Books,* Vol. 50, No. 4, December, 1996, p. 145.

Remi has just moved from Haiti to Oakland for the eighth grade, and he finds America a strange world.

Strangest of all is the train that noisily ploughs past his apartment in the middle of the night—on tracks that haven't been used for decades. He finds a friend in Niya, a neighbor girl, and the two begin to investigate the phenomenon, uncovering a hidden wartime murder. The story is neatly turned and nicely finished, and Mowry manages to address some serious issues of racism (like Remi and Niya, the ghost was black, and his murder was racially motivated) while keeping the style simple. The writing tends to be naïve, with characters receiving extensive description instead of characterization, Remi's speech contrivedly amusing with its blend of precise formal English and Oakland slang, and the social commentary rather heavy-handed. It's still an entertaining urban mystery, however, and young readers will appreciate Remi and Niya's setting things right.

Susan L. Rogers

SOURCE: A review of *Ghost Train*, in *School Library Journal*, Vol. 42, No. 12, December, 1996, p. 139.

Old-fashioned suspense co-exists with a modern-day setting in this short, easy-to-read, and very successful mystery. On Remi DuMont's first night in his new home, a train thunders past his window and he watches a murder being committed. Remi, 13, is a recent immigrant from Haiti to Oakland, CA. He shares his father's interest in *voodun* and the supernatural. He soon realizes that the late-night train is a ghost train and the murder reenacted on it nightly actually happened more than 50 years ago. As the boy and his new friend Niya investigate, they put together the pieces of an unsolved crime and an unexplained disappearance. They then step into the past to try to right a long-standing wrong. Niya introduces Remi to the slang and customs of the "hood" while he shares some of his knowledge of Haitian French and family history with her. Their conversations are realistically sprinkled with four-letter words never used by Joe Hardy or Nancy Drew (in English or French) and show an innocent, healthy appreciation of one another's sexuality, but also have moments of righteous indignation at the plight of poor minorities. Social concerns are swept aside as the mystery gains momentum and Remi, Niya, and readers are caught up in a hair-raising, life-and-death struggle with a murderer and with time itself. The ending is surprising and satisfying, but has a tinge of sorrow.

Ann C. Sparanese

SOURCE: A review of *Ghost Train*, in *Voice of Youth Advocates*, Vol. 19, No. 6, February, 1997, p. 330.

In a departure from the brutal realism that characterizes his adult novels, Mowry's first YA novel is a supernatural time-travel thriller involving two thirteen-year-olds who witness, enter and then solve a murder that occurred half a century before.

Remi, a new immigrant from Haiti to Oakland, California, is awakened on his first night in his new country by a train roaring past directly outside his bedroom window. The train veers away from crashing into his building at the last moment and turns into what seems to be a foggy shipyard. Remi soon discovers that no train has run by his window in many years, and the shipyard closed long ago. The following night, the scene is repeated at exactly the same time, but this time Remi sees the murder.

With his already established connection to the supernatural (his father is an expert in Haitian Voodoun), Remi has no problem in accepting the possible existence of a *fantôme*, and involves his new American friend, Niya, in the intrigue. They begin to put the pieces together and through their intervention, a fifty-year-old mystery involving their landlady's husband and son is unraveled.

Niya and Remi are likeable enough, but underdeveloped as characters. The dialog sometimes has a stilted quality that interferes with the smoothness of the story. But the novel's strength is in its plot. From the opening scene, the suspense pulls the reader along to the climactic last chapter, where danger gives way to a satisfying resolution.

An unusual weave of mystery, ghost story, Haitian culture, action and chaste romance for younger teens.

BABYLON BOYZ (1997)

Publishers Weekly

SOURCE: A review of *Babylon Boyz*, in *Publishers Weekly*, Vol. 244, No. 5, February 3, 1997, p. 107.

The author of *Way Past Cool* offers another piercing view of inner-city life in this hard-hitting, suspenseful novel set in Oakland, Calif. Dante, born to a mother on crack, has a bad heart but his father can't afford the operation he needs; Pook wants to become a doctor; and Wyatt, whose mother owns a restaurant, weighs about 300 pounds. They've been friends since childhood, and all three want nothing more than to escape their crime-ridden neighborhood, where everyone around them seems like "little black ants…waitin' to get stepped on an' too stupid to see it." The boys cannot find a route to their dreams—until they discover two packets of cocaine worth thousands of dollars. The moral dilemma that arises from their find is only one of the issues explored in this fast-paced, increasingly tense drama. Others include Pook's homosexuality, the homelessness of a younger boy the trio befriends and the ineffectiveness of a local rehab center run by a psycho-babbling counselor. Using dialogue that feels so genuine it nearly jumps off the page, Mowry personalizes the ghetto experience while clearly defining the conflicts, strengths and vulnerabilities of his characters, major and minor. His powerful images of violence and survival illuminate shadowy corners of contemporary urban America.

Bill Ott

SOURCE: A review of *Babylon Boyz,* in *Booklist,* Vol. 93, No. 12, February 15, 1997, p. 1020.

Mowry, author of the fine adult novel **Way Past Cool** (1992), injects new life into one of YA fiction's standard formulas: the alternative family under attack from a hostile world. Here that world is Babylon, an inner-city neighborhood in Oakland, and the family consists of three boys as alienated from their peers as they are from mainstream society: Pook, whose nimble athleticism and well-cut body make his open avowal of homosexuality all the more inexplicable to most of his homophobic classmates; Dante, whose damaged heart is a death certificate waiting to happen unless prohibitively expensive surgery can be performed; and Wyatt, who is so fat he can hide a handgun under the folds of his belly. All three harbor dreams of escaping Babylon, and those dreams seem within reach when the boys recover a cocaine-filled suitcase discarded by a dealer on the run. As the story unfolds, we watch the boys, struggling over whether to sell the drugs, move from exhilaration at simply having a choice to acceptance of the difficulty of making it. What drives this novel isn't the melodramatic and sadly familiar elements of its plot but the striking individuality of its cast. Each of the boys rises above the stereotypical aspects of his character to become, not emblems of hard life in the ghetto, but vivid reminders that we are all more than the sum of our situations. Behind every incident, including some relatively explicit sex scenes, is the conviction that details matter. Mowry ends his novel with neither triumph nor tragedy, but with an affirming vision. . . .

Kirkus Reviews

SOURCE: A review of *Babylon Boyz,* in *Kirkus Reviews,* Vol. LXV, No. 8, April 15, 1997, p. 645.

Mowry allows young readers to hang with the Babylon Boyz, an inner-city posse: Dante, a 14-year-old "crack baby" with a heart condition; Pook, a fearless, gay street fighter; and Wyatt, witty and able to slip a gun past the school's metal detectors by packing "heat" in his rolls of fat.

The world these teens inhabit is portrayed in gritty, vivid, and cruelly realistic terms, right down to the drugs, homelessness, and casual gun play. Babylon, situated on San Francisco Bay, has a textbook case of urban rot, and while the novel follows the boys' lives after they chance upon a block of cocaine, it is the milieu and people that take center stage; Mowry's depiction of the boys at home and at school is unerring as they struggle in the predacious environment. He doesn't sugar-coat reality; there is graphic sex (both Pook and Dante are "deflowered") and violence (a local drug dealer's brains are blown out as Dante watches). While the decision about whether or not to sell the drug is removed from the boys' hands—the white criminals get it back—they do argue among themselves about the money it could provide. The lack of sympathetic white characters—Mowry depicts them as timid, unfeeling, or in the case of the police, sadistic and prejudiced—reduces the impact of the novel's climax, where the boys deliver a homeless teenager's baby, and makes questionable the overall theme of mutual acceptance, understanding, and love.

Deborah Stevenson

SOURCE: A review of *Babylon Boyz,* in *The Bulletin of the Center for Children's Books,* Vol. 50, No. 10, June, 1997, p. 368.

Oakland is a rough place for young African-American men, and these three kids have it even worse for being outsiders even among their classmates: Wyatt is substantially overweight, Pook is gay, and Dante, born to a crack-addicted mother, has heart problems that make exertion dangerous. Their tight friendship helps them survive, but that may change when they find a substantial package of pure cocaine and must decide whether to sell it, thereby poisoning people, or to destroy it and forego the badly needed money. Grim, atmospheric, and passionate, this is a compelling portrait of life against astronomical odds. Mowry is occasionally a bit programmatic with his plot, but he can also be marvelously inventive: Dante begins attending drug rehab under false pretenses (he just wants the associated in-class candy privileges), has his first (not entirely satisfactory) experience with sex, and ends up unintentionally finding a boyfriend for Pook. It's a hard-edged, well-written description (Mowry is particularly adept at dialogue) of a violent world with tough choices (Dante fears he's "a house nigger himself who might be selling everyone down the big river"). Kids who relished Myers' *Scorpions* will want to have a look at life on the other coast.

Beth Wright

SOURCE: A review of *Babylon Boyz,* in *School Library Journal,* Vol. 43, No. 9, September, 1997, p. 222.

When 14-year-old Dante and his friends find a suitcase full of cocaine, they face an excruciating decision: whether to flush the stuff, or to sell it. Selling the cocaine would bring the money they all desperately need, particularly Dante, who was born with a bad heart because his mother was a crack addict, but they know it would also add to the drug problems already affecting their Oakland, CA, neighborhood. Racist white cops and exploitative adults who get rich by playing off of these needy, often homeless kids all add to this affecting story that revolves around the ills of contemporary society. With its realistic, gritty dialogue; violent deaths; and semi-explicit sex scenes, this is definitely a book for mature teens; those readers will find authentic, unforgettable characters and descriptions that make the boys and their community come alive. Set among the rough streets of a modern Babylon, this is ultimately a story about family, friendship, love, and of kids living in poverty and victimized by drugs but still trying to make the right choices in their lives.

Florence M. Munat

SOURCE: A review of *Babylon Boyz,* in *Voice of Youth Advocates,* Vol. 20, No. 2, June, 1997, p. 112.

Dante, Pook, and Wyatt are teenage friends who live in a section of Oakland called Babylon—a landscape of run-down housing, wharves, gang violence, and drug dealing. Dante's crack-addicted mother died when he was born, her habit bequeathing him a dam-

aged heart. Pook, a homosexual Adonis, wants to go to medical school but has no money. Wyatt is a 300-pound amateur photographer and pet owner who loves to eat at his mother's shipyard cafe. Rounding out "the posse" are Kelly, a Korean American who deals in guns and liquor; Jinx, a slow-witted crack addict in rehab who begins a relationship with Pook; and Radji, a homeless Aborigine.

One night Dante and Pook see a drug dealer named Air Touch throw a suitcase from his car while being pursued by police. The homeys retrieve the case, assuming it contains money. Instead, they discover the case contains pure cocaine—enough to send Pook to medical school and allow Dante to have the heart operation he needs. But the boys know that if they sell the drugs they'll be contributing to the further deterioration of their neighborhood and its people. They have a choice: to sell or to flush?

This realistic urban novel is about choices. Life in Babylon seems to offer none to these teenagers, until the cocaine comes along. But by the book's end, the boys realize they have more options than they had originally perceived. To that degree the resolution offers hope, even to these children who have witnessed and done things no child should ever have to see or do.

Mowry, who has written several adult novels, including ALA Best Book for Young Adults *Way Past Cool* (Farrar, 1993), stumbles through the initial characterizations, but then the plot takes over and delivers riveting action until we feel we're walking the mean streets of Oakland with Dante. The characters speak a dialect that contains some profanity and ethnic slurs. There are scenes that depict sex, drinking, murder, a police beating, and the delivery of a baby. There also are scenes of tenderness and camaraderie among the boys. While it's sometimes difficult to read about this subject matter, toning it down would have sadly compromised the story's realism. Instead, Mowry has delivered a realistic, tenacious tale of urban hopes and dreams.

Additional coverage of Mowry's life and career is contained in the following sources published by the Gale Group: *Authors and Artists for Young Adults,* Vol. 29; *Contemporary Authors,* Vol. 133; and *Something about the Author,* Vol. 109.

Jill Paton Walsh
1937-

(Full name Gillian Paton Walsh) English novelist, editor, and author of picture books.

Major works include *Fireweed* (1969), *Goldengrove* (1972), *Unleaving* (1976), *A Parcel of Patterns* (1983), and *Gaffer Samson's Luck* (1984).

INTRODUCTION

Jill Paton Walsh is best known as an author of award-winning historical fiction for older primary graders and young adults. In works set in various periods of English history, including the Middle Ages, the Victorian era, and, most frequently, the period surrounding World War II, Paton Walsh examines such themes as the nature of heroism, the meaning of community, and the effects of war. In addition, she has also written contemporary realistic fiction, science fiction, and picture books for children, and short stories, novels, and mysteries for adults. Paton Walsh has won the praise of numerous critics and reviewers, including Sheila Egoff, who commented in her *Thursday's Child,* that of the many "skilled and sensitive writers [for young people], Walsh is the most formally literary. Her writing is studded with allusions to poetry, art, and philosophy that give it an intellectual framework unmatched in children's literature."

BIOGRAPHICAL INFORMATION

The daughter of Patricia Dubern and John Llewellyn Bliss, a pioneering television engineer, Paton Walsh was born in Finchley, a north London suburb, in 1937. A breech birth left her with limited movement in her right arm, a condition that she has called "of great importance, not in any physical way, but psychologically. In the first place, all my life the people around me have supposed I would not be able to do things—like carrying trays, or standing on my hands—which I found, as soon as I tried them to be perfectly possible for me. And this has left me with a life-long disposition to have a shot at things." Paton Walsh grew up in a family in which improper grammar was corrected and in which "everyone was without prejudices against or limited ambitions for girls."

For a period during World War II, she was evacuated with her mother and three siblings to her grandparents' home in St. Ives, Cornwall, and the rocky coastal environment has become one of the predominant settings in her works. She was educated at St. Michael's Convent, a Catholic grammar school in North Finchley, and at St. Anne's College, Oxford, where she studied English with a concentration on medieval literature and philology. At Oxford Paton Walsh attended lectures by C. S. Lewis and J. R. R. Tolkien and later noted that "the example they set by being both great and serious scholars, and writers of fantasy and books for children was not lost on me." Paton Walsh was awarded a master's degree with honors in 1959. She also met her future husband, Antony Paton Walsh, at Oxford and married him in 1961. After completing her studies, Paton Walsh took a position teaching English at Enfield Girls' Grammar School in Middlesex. She remained there until 1962, when she gave birth to the first of her three children. It was while Paton Walsh was at home with her infant son that she turned to writing as a source of intellectual stimulation and as a respite from round-the-clock baby feedings. According to Paton Walsh in *Something about the Author Autobiography Series (SAAS),* "As plants need water and light, as the baby needed milk, I needed something intellectual, cheap and quiet. I hauled out of the cupboard an old portable typewriter that my brother had given me. . . . I began to write a book. It was a children's book. It never occurred to me to write any other kind." Although that first book was rejected, Macmillan children's book editor Kevin Crossley Holland advanced Paton Walsh £50 for the rights to publish her next work. *Hengest's Tale,* an epic based on fragments of *Beowulf,* was published in 1966. Since that time Paton Walsh has written a succession of award-winning children's novels. From 1978 to 1986 she was a visiting faculty member of the Center for the Study of Children's Literature at Simmons College in Boston. Together with John Rowe Townsend she founded Green Bay Publishers in 1986. She continues to write at her homes in Cambridge and near St. Ives. According to Paton Walsh, "A writer is what I shall be as long as there is a daydream in my head, and I have strength to sit up and type."

MAJOR WORKS

In several of her works Paton Walsh has used turbulent historical settings which act as catalysts for the emotional growth of her characters. Through extensive research she presents authentic details and evokes a true sense of time and place. Paton Walsh based her first novel, *Hengest's Tale,* on a character from Old English myth. This suspenseful story concerns the maturation of Hengest, a fifth-century Jute torn between honor in battle and loyalty to a childhood friend. Her second novel, *The Dolphin Crossing* (1967) is set along the English coast as two teenage boys, one wealthy and one a Cockney evacuee, join together in the evacuation of British troops from the Battle of Dunkirk. In *Fireweed* Paton Walsh again portrayed the struggle of two teenagers during World War II. Bill and Julie, who meet in an underground shelter during the Nazi bombing of London, grow to care deeply for each other as they struggle against grave circumstances. Ultimately, they are separated by the English class system, but critics have admired the novel's lack of sentimentality and Paton Walsh's realistic depiction of the chaos and destruction of London during this period.

Among Paton Walsh's best-known works, *Goldengrove* and its sequel, *Unleaving,* are set in an isolated seaside landscape. In both novels she investigated the often painful experience of maturing from adolescence to adulthood. The titles are both taken from the opening of the poem "Spring and Fall: To a Young Child" by Gerard Manley Hopkins ("Margaret are you grieving / Over Goldengrove unleaving?"). The novels focus on a sensitive teenager, Margaret Fielding—called Madge—who spends her summer holidays at her grandmother's house on the Cornish coast. The tone of each work is bittersweet; the characters experience disillusionment as they lose the innocence of childhood, but they ultimately gain a greater appreciation for life. Reviewers of the books praised Paton Walsh's ability to evoke the beauty of the seaside setting and noted the influence of Virginia Woolf in Paton Walsh's style and themes.

Between *Goldengrove* and its sequel, Paton Walsh completed *The Emperor's Winding Sheet* (1974), a tale set during the fall of Constantinople. To ensure the authenticity of the novel she embarked on a research trip to Greece, an experience which also figured in the development of *Children of the Fox* (1977), a trilogy set during the Greek-Persian wars. Paton Walsh later visited a coal mine to accurately portray mining conditions in another historical novel, *A Chance Child* (1978). In the story Paton Walsh depicted the exploitation of child labor in Victorian England through the story of "Creep," an abused child of the twentieth century, who through a device of time travel begins a new life in Victorian England.

Set during the Great Plague of 1665, *A Parcel of Patterns* (1983) addresses themes of faith, courage, and the meaning of community. In the novel Paton Walsh dramatized the isolation of a village that has contracted the plague when infected dress patterns arrive from London. Based on the true story of the village of Eyam, the story portrays the heroism of ordinary people who voluntarily quarantined themselves in order not to spread the fatal disease to their neighbors. Walsh achieved a sense of authenticity in these works though her use of carefully researched facts and colloquial language. As she wrote in *SAAS,* "I am not interested in writing about great heroes, just ordinary people in difficult times."

Inspired by her move to a little cottage near Cambridge that she shares with author and critic John Rowe Townsend, Paton Walsh wrote *Gaffer Samson's Luck,* a story for primary graders about a young boy who has moved to a new village and befriends a dying man. Through his quest for the man's good luck charm the boy gains courage and the acceptance of his new acquaintances.

In the late 1980s and 1990s Paton Walsh moved in a new direction as a writer, focusing on picture books for young children. As she told Barbara James in *Magpies* "my own children have grown up. I feel quite detached from the teenage audience because I am not living with them . . . and not living their exact kind of life. On the other hand, my partner how has grandchildren, and there are very young children in my life again, so I still find it quite easy to write picture books and retell folktales." Among these works are the folktales *Birdy and the Ghosties* (1988) and *Matthew and the Sea Singer* (1992), and the picture books *When Grandma Came* (1992) and *When I Was Little Like You* (1997). The two folktales center on Birdy, a generous young girl gifted with second sight and the ability to communicate with ghosts and sea creatures. The picture books describe satisfying intergenerational relationships. In *When Grandma Came* Paton Walsh portrays a globe-trotting grandmother who greets her granddaughter with compliments that compare her favorably to the wondrous places she has visited and the amazing things she has seen. In *When I Was Little Like You,* a book that is set in Paton Walsh's beloved St. Ives, little Rosie and her Gran stroll through the seaside village remarking on the things they see.

AWARDS

Paton Walsh has received numerous honors beginning with the *Book World* Festival Award in 1970 for *Fireweed,* a work that was also selected as a Notable Book by the American Library Association (ALA). *Goldengrove* was designated a Notable Book by the *New York Times* in 1972, and in 1974 Paton Walsh shared a Whitbread Prize with Russell Hoban for *The Emperor's Winding Sheet. Unleaving* won the *Boston Globe-Horn Book* Award in 1976. Paton Walsh won the Universe Prize in 1984 and was a runner-up for the Smarties Award in 1983 for *A Parcel of Patterns,* which was also named an ALA Best Book for Young Adults. Paton Walsh won the prestigious Smarties Award Grand Prix in 1984 for *Gaffer Samson's Luck.* In 1992 *School Library Journal* named *Grace* (1991) a Best Book, and Paton Walsh was a runner-up for the Mother Goose Award for *When Grandma Came.* *A Chance Child* was also named an ALA Notable Book. Her adult novel *Knowledge of Angels* (1994) was shortlisted for the Booker Prize. In addition to these book awards, Paton Walsh received Arts Council Creative Writing Fellowships in 1976 and 1977. She was awarded a CBE for her body of work and was also named a fellow of the Royal Society of Literature.

AUTHOR COMMENTARY

Jill Paton Walsh

SOURCE: "Front Cover: *Babylon,*" in *Books for Your Children,* Vol. 17, No. 2, Summer, 1982, pp. 16-17.

'All my books start with a dream of action—a plot which moves me in some way. It makes no important difference to me whether this action comes from the past or the present, except that more athletic leaps of the imagination are required to write about the present. **Babylon** grew from the simple thought that a weed-flowering viaduct was like a hanging garden. Then I wondered who apart from me, would see it that way, and I remembered really little kids, friends of my kids, singing "by the rivers of Babylon". It is in no way intended to be a didactic book. I have often, perhaps always, started out from a place, and though my stories could often be shifted about from one period to another without changing much, they are all very specific to one place, or seem so to me. Another thing **Babylon** has in common with other books of mine is the immense pleasure and interest I have derived from the form of children's books. Because they must be short, lucid, tightly constructed, and swift on their feet in style, they are an endlessly interesting technical challenge. The text of **Babylon** had to give a foothold for a different picture each page. I have never done a picture book before, and I was deeply interested.'

Jill Paton Walsh interviewed by Barbara James

SOURCE: An interview in *Magpies,* Vol. 13, No. 4, September, 1998, pp. 14-16.

*Bearing in mind the dictum that self-descriptions are generally the most accurate, I was intrigued when I came across an article in which Jill Paton Walsh was quoted as saying she was "a pre-feminist bluestocking trying to reconcile a hunger for the life of the mind with the demands of women's traditional roles and personal happiness." As she was one of my favourite writers, I was eagerly looking forward to her visit to Adelaide in the Festival. A decade ago she was considered to be at the height of her powers as a children's novelist, with twenty books written over the same number of years. Many of them—**Gaffer Samson's Luck, Goldengrove, Unleaving, A Parcel of Patterns, Fireweed** and **The Emperor's Winding Sheet**—had taken out English children's literary awards. Then she turned to writing adult fiction as well. Soon **Knowledge of Angels** (rejected by 19 British publishers before she published it herself.*

One reason given for rejecting it was that "the phrases 'well-established children's writer' and 'novel of ideas' just don't go together!") was being shortlisted for the Booker Prize and now **Thrones, Dominations** *is currently in the British and Australian bestselling list. Her detective novels are also very popular. Recently she received a CBE for services to literature. And she is a Fellow of the Royal Society of Literature.*

So here I was, sitting in the Festival Playhouse along with three hundred school children waiting for her Meet the Author *Session to begin. I had few preconceptions of what she would be like. The biographical notes on the backs of her dustjackets are typically sketchy. In the end I looked up her entry in* Contemporary Authors, *which mentioned an English childhood during World War II, Oxford University in the late 50s (philological courses)—with Tolkien and C. S. Lewis as lecturers—followed by teaching, marriage and three children, but it still seemed rather remote.*

Now, she was up on the stage, chatting to the children about first impressions—the unfamiliar night sky, the different trees, and how unexpectedly gentle kangaroos were (thinking of the cartoons where they wear boxing gloves!). She was brimming with warmth, grace, humour and intelligence. That rather self-derogatory description wasn't far from the mark, after all, I reflected. Then she started to tell a story about a schoolyard bully from her own schooldays in wartime England and the children, already attentive, became as quiet as little mice . . . . Eventually I caught up with her. I asked her first about being both a children's and adults' writer, rather than progressing from younger to older readers as authors often do. In fact there had been a progression.

[Jill Paton Walsh]: I haven't written for teenage children since bringing out **Grace,** five years ago, and that is because my own children have grown-up. I feel quite detached from the teenage audience because I am not living with them . . . and not living their exact kind of life.

On the other hand, my partner now has grandchildren, and there are very young children in my life again so I still find it quite easy to write picture books and retell folktales. The teenage line has, so to speak, dried up, but I'm expecting it to resume when the grandchildren grow up!

People seem to think there is more difference between writing for adults and children than there really is. It depends on whether you are a self-expression author or a craft author and I'm a craft author. A self-expression author is burning to open to the world some inner message, which I do feel to some extent but such a person may only have one voice. There are a lot of classic writers who only have one voice and they don't shape what they do differently to different audiences. You need only to read a paragraph to immediately recognise their voices, like D. H. Lawrence. You couldn't mistake them for any other writer.

There is another way of being a writer, which is to be instead of worrying about expressing yourself, your own vision of the world, you are actually creating something, making a story, as though it were an object like a beautiful sculpture. Then you make it to suit, you make it with the audience for it in mind . . . You craft it this way if it's going to be for children and another way if it's going to be for adults, trying to be in control of the effect and not just opening yourself out.

If you get interested in the craft of writing you need to know the audience before you start working, and obviously you get interested in the limitations. Writing for children needs to be tight and it needs to be indirect. You really have to have some mastery of the craft of storytelling—to make the actual storyline do the moral work and carry the meaning. When I come to write for adults I don't approach it in a completely different way. It isn't harder, it's easier. You can say what you like, approach subjects directly. It's the opposite to what some people sometimes think. Children's books are actually harder. Each should be well made of its kind. Of all things, for example, the Japanese adore British children's books and translate many of our authors, including me, in large numbers, yet they have no particular interest in British adult books.

Very mysterious. I came to the conclusion that it's because they like the elegance of the indirect statement in children's literature. Their poetry, like their art, is craft-like, exquisite—and they have a liking for understatement. Therefore our children's books can cross the boundaries of culture. They must find our adult books very shapeless, jumping all over the place. Otherwise I can't make any sense of it at all. Very peculiar, you write for children in some dull north London suburb and you get snapped up in Tokyo. Very strange.

[Barbara James]: *At this point I asked her whether the strong storyline characteristic of her adult novels is a carryover from her children's writing.*

In an adult work of fiction, you can put the weight of meaning in a number of different places, in the characterisation, in the view of the world, or the landscape or in the storyline but a children's book can only be in narrative form; the serious part of the meaning must be in the story. It's a strictly narrative art.

I think that's very much like what I want to read myself and what I feel comfortable writing. I have never felt I had to squash my own tastes in any way in order to craft a story for children. I love to read books when *what happens* contains most of the meaning. I don't like the kind of drifting book where there's a character and nothing much happens. I like changes of fortune, pirates, shipwrecks rather more than I like landscapes with no shape.

My favourite Australian author is Ivan Southall, pre-eminently a writer who relies on a high-drive story. The book that lies closest to my heart is *Josh,* and I also like *Ash Road.* I wouldn't mind you mentioning Ivan in the article because I do admire him so much! Certain writers' work are an example to you when you're writing your own.

Four of her books, **Goldengrove,** *and its sequel,* **Unleaving, The Serpentine Cave** *and the picture book* **When I Was Little Like You** *are set in the Cornish fishing village of St Ives where she lived as a young child. I asked her whether her books are at all autobiographical.*

I have never put my autobiography into a children's book but I have done in an adult's book. My first adult novel *Lapsing* was autobiographical. One is enough, they say. It's not a sensible thing to do. You're in the wrong relationship to it, but many people, myself, included, find they can't write as an adult writer until they've written the shape of their young adult life. Over and over again people write their autobiographical one first.

From our house in Cornwall you could see a lighthouse—the same lighthouse that Virginia Woolf wrote about. She had lived only a hundred and fifty metres from our house. All my life that lighthouse has come into my dreams. Now I have bought my own place near there.

I had just finished reading **Torch,** *which is set sometime in the future when our civilisation has collapsed.*

The memory of the Olympic Games was all but extinguished when two children living among the Greek ruins are entrusted with the Torch by an old man as he dies. He has been its guardian for many years. The children's quest is to find the torch its rightful home and the book's journey takes them around the Mediterranean.

Torch is essentially a fable. I was disturbed by all the stories that were breaking in the newspapers about the fixing of races and doping of athletes and I thought what a noble idea it had been when it was new: the games that would interrupt war . . . such a fine idea. I was rather upset. I'm not a sporting person myself, but I can see what the ideal of sport should be. So I wrote this book which is about a magic torch. The torch goes out if the game is fixed or has some evil purpose—if the winner is going to be sacrificed to the Gods, for example. I am making a statement about the value of the things that you do for their own sake, completely disinterested—actually, I was never completely happy about this book. I was contracted to write it to a particular date, but I broke my arm and couldn't write for days and got delayed. I learned my lesson and have never written to a deadline since. I would have liked to have given it a more thorough workover. It was made into a BBC television series which was extremely successful. Some changes were made, different locations, but they kept to the idea. Actress Dame Judy Dench played one of the characters. I had to change the part for her, but I would have rewritten Hamlet to get her, I am such a great fan of hers!

All too soon it was time to head back to the marquees of the Writers' Festival. Opening the discussion—Sacred Sites—Jill entertained us with an idea from **Knowledge of Angels,** *that as readers we are all in a literary sense, angels. It was a notion that went down very well with the audience—mellowed by wine and the warm afternoon sun. Then at the very end, when everyone else had had their say, and given all their different opinions, it was Jill who advanced the idea not of sacred sites, but sacred moments, the times in our lives that we are completely happy, but are rarely aware of at the time and her personal resolve to try to be aware of those times when they occur. And it was on this happy note, summing up so perfectly the mood of the moment—for collectively we realised that we were indeed a sublimely satisfied and contented audience—that Writers' Week ended.*

TITLE COMMENTARY

📖 *THE HUFFLER* (1975)

Kirkus Reviews

SOURCE: A review of *The Huffler,* in *Kirkus Reviews,* Vol. XLIII, No. 22, November 15, 1975, p. 1289.

The huffler in question—the term refers to pick-up kid labor—is really an eleven-year-old "young lady" who impulsively runs away from her resented new home to join two youngsters taking coal to a paper mill in a pair of horse-drawn canal boats. While Ned and Bess push to get their laid-up older brother's boat to the mill on time, Harry (short for Harriet) struggles to make herself useful and hide her upper class identity. Harry tells her story seven years later to a younger cousin, cast as narrator, and to a very proper suitor who, though tolerant of her adventure, is obviously no match for the spunky Harry. It's an old-fashioned story, not only in its setting but in its heroine's democratic defense of her poor but worthy companions, but winningly so. And canal boating will be a whole new world not only for Harry but for today's readers too.

Jean Mercier

SOURCE: A review of *The Huffler,* in *Publishers Weekly,* Vol. 208, No. 21, November 24, 1975, p. 52.

The author made many friends with her novels, **Goldengrove** and **The Emperor's Winding Sheet,** among others. Now she brings us an exquisitely wrought pastoral about life in a long-gone England. Harry, at 11, is an independent girl who runs away from home to team up with Ned and his sister, Bess. They are guiding their boats—the *Mary* and the *Beatrice*—through the inland locks. Harry has caught sight of what she has never seen before: boats sailing apparently through a meadow, led by a horse on a towpath. Harry becomes a "huffler," a helper, to brother and sister. They think she's a servant who has run away from a cruel mistress. The adventures are many, culminating in the terror of the boat children's parents when they meet Harry and realize she's the girl believed drowned in the canals.

Leah Deland Stenson

SOURCE: A review of *The Huffler,* in *School Library Journal,* Vol. 22, No. 4, December, 1975.

Displeased with her sheltered, upper class life and unsympathetic parents, Harry (Harriet) is 11 when she runs off to become a huffler, an extra hand on a pair of canal boats carrying coal to a paper mill. Before returning home Harry learns what it is like to do dirty, hard work and comes to respect and sympathize with the working class. So now, years later, she refuses to settle into mundane married life with a class-conscious snob. There are many fine aspects to the story—e.g., the unusual slant from which it's told (the narrator is Harry's young, impressionable cousin Kate); the sharply etched descriptions of England during the Industrial Revolution (Harriet's "tall rose-red brick mansion" in the lush, wooded countryside versus the "mean, close-packed houses" in the grimy factory towns); the absence of melodrama and a happily-ever-after ending—but the characterization is far too thin to make readers really care about Harry or the other characters.

Barbara Elleman

SOURCE: A review of *The Huffler,* in *Booklist,* Vol. 72, No. 12, February 15, 1976, p. 858.

When Harry is 11, she runs away from her lonely, regimented home for the adventure of her lifetime. Moping over her family's move to a new house, she is sent to the garden and there, to her delight, discovers barge boats traveling a nearby canal. On impulse she strikes up a conversation with Ned and his sister Bess, who are in charge of one of the boats, and before she knows it, becomes their "huffler"—an extra hand on board. A month of hard work, unknown freedom, and growing friendship with her companions gives Harry an appreciation of a life—and an England—she never knew existed. The story is told in retrospect, and if the happenings surrounding Harry's rash flight and resulting experiences are a bit unbelievable, the escapade itself can be absorbed like a fantasy many dream of but few realize.

The Horn Book

SOURCE: A review of *The Huffler,* in *The Horn Book Magazine,* Vol. LII, No., April, 1976, p. 159.

Very different from the author's brilliant novel **The Emperor's Winding Sheet,** the story is a period piece describing the work of canal boats carrying coal through England's inland waterways. The author has invented a realistic story about a few days on board the *Mary* and the *Beatrice* carrying cargo to a paper mill. Harry (for Harriet) recounts what happened when, upset some years ago by her family's move to a new home near a canal, she jumped onto a passing barge. Harry joined a small boy and his older sister and became a useful "huffler," or worker, on this "butty boat," pulled—in tandem with the other barge—by a horse along the towpath. Harry was needed, for the other two children were substituting for their older brother who had broken his arm. Suspense is skillfully achieved, with the children straining to complete the run on time. The writing has clarity and force; one feels the mood of "globules of moonlight floated on the troubled surface." Action-filled drawings add to the reality.

Bulletin of the Center for Children's Books

SOURCE: A review of *The Huffler,* in *The Bulletin of the Center for Children's Books,* Vol. 29, May, 1976, p. 151.

Jill Paton Walsh's historical fiction has previously been more broad and sweeping, but here she shows her versatility by creating a cameo, for *The Huffler* is a Victorian adventure, the story of a properly beruffled English miss who escapes to pose as a servant so that she can better fit into the life of a canal boat family. Or, rather, part of a family, for young Bess and Ned Jebb are making a cargo delivery alone because of a family crisis. The characters and dialogue have vitality but it is the setting that especially delights: the lore of the canal, the intricacies of the locks, the conviviality of the canal travelers.

THE ISLAND SUNRISE: PREHISTORIC CULTURE IN THE BRITISH ISLES (1975)

Margery Fisher

SOURCE: A review of *The Island Sunrise,* in *Growing Point,* Vol. 11, No. 6, December, 1975, pp. 2768-69.

The Island Sunrise is concerned with prehistoric Britain. . . . Jill Paton Walsh's definition of culture as "the traditional knowledge and behaviour by which a people live and find their food; in short, their way of life", provides a central point from which her account of the Stone, Bronze and Iron Ages develops. She writes lucidly, choosing her examples to illustrate how one discovery or successful invention could lead to another, and how such discoveries and invention altered life. Of iron, for instance, she writes:

> . . . it is stronger than bronze, and the ore from which it is obtained is very plentiful and occurs very widely, unlike the scarce tin needed for

bronze. From the first, therefore, iron could be used for workaday objects, for saws, nails and ploughshares, as well as for weapons.

She is always careful to view cave drawings, drinking vessels and the like in perspective, not with the superior hindsight of some history-books. Two appendices, on radiocarbon dating and tree-ring calibration, and on the Indo-European languages, firmly point to some of the methods by which the past can be explored and assessed.

Kirkus Reviews

SOURCE: A review of *The Island Sunrise: Prehistoric Culture in the British Isles,* in *Kirkus Reviews,* Vol. XLIV, No. 3, February 1, 1976, p. 143.

Drawing on archaeological evidence and its interpretation by scholars, Walsh has put together a responsible, thorough "cultural history" of prehistoric Britain from the earliest Stone Age wanderers through the Bronze Age (which, it is now believed, developed independently in Britain), and up to the Roman invasion. The scope and unavoidable sketchiness of the data predisposes such a work to a certain monotony of tone; not until the historically documented Celts appear does life begin to stir—and that largely with the aid of quotes from contemporary descriptions. But this is no droning recapitulation. Walsh's reporting is interspersed with commentary, conclusions and speculation, and she communicates her own evident interest in her subject in a way that is both accessible to her YA audience and totally uncondescending.

Books for Your Children

SOURCE: A review of *Island Sunrise,* in *Books for Your Children,* Vol. 11, No. 2, Spring, 1976, p. 15.

A highly praised account of a book which conveys the culture of the vast period of time when man developed from a primitive, restless, ape-like creature to a dweller in settled communities. Most beautifully produced and illustrated with photographs includes a first-rate index and appendix on radio carbon dating, etc. Jill Paton Walsh is a distinguished historical novelist able to lift young readers into her own sphere of imaginative grasp of the lives of vanished men.

Bulletin of the Center for Children's Books

SOURCE: A review of *The Island Sunrise: Prehistoric Culture in the British Isles,* in *The Bulletin of the Center for Children's Books,* Vol. 29, June, 1976, p. 166.

A serious study of the wanderers and settlers of British prehistory covers the millennia from the earliest migrants of interglacial times to the end of the Iron Age and the coming of the Romans. The author smoothly integrates the ebb and flow of influences and cross-cultural diffusion in discussing the artifacts and art of the early peoples, the archeological evidence of their increased skill at making and using tools, the growing agricultural stability and diversification of labor that laid the groundwork for a civilization possible only because of a food surplus. A well organized, informative, and competently written book, this has a base of solid research.

The Horn Book

SOURCE: A review of *The Island Sunrise: Prehistoric Culture in the British Isles,* in *The Horn Book Magazine,* Vol. LII, June, 1976, p. 300.

Illustrated with photographs, maps, sketches. Intended as a cultural history of pre-Roman Britain, the narrative emphasizes the significance of man's transition from food gatherer to food producer, from independent scavenger to member of a tribal community. By tracing the progress of Britain's early inhabitants through an analysis of their increasing sophistication—in designing the necessary tools for survival, in banding together for common purposes, in embellishing their possessions, in developing rituals for worship and burial—the author effectively underscores their likenesses to twentieth-century people rather than the disparities between them and their earliest ancestors. Of particular interest are the sections dealing with revised theories of external influences on the development of culture in early Britain based on recent advances in radiocarbon dating and tree-ring calibration. Because of the rich store of material condensed into a relatively brief volume, the narrative is as demanding as it is fascinating. However, summaries at the end of each chapter highlight the accomplishments of these early peoples and indicate the influences on succeeding generations. Two appendixes clarify and extend the notions of cultural development and diffusion; a bibliography and an index are included. Unfortunately, no separate listing of the eight color plates is provided, and, as they are not always numbered sequentially, some of the textual references to illustrations present difficulty.

Sue Ann Jargstorf

SOURCE: A review of *The Island Sunrise: Prehistoric Culture in the British Isles,* in *School Library Journal,* Vol. 23, No. 1, September, 1976, p. 140.

Walsh covers the cultural history of the British Isles from prehistoric times until the arrival of the Romans in 55 B.C. She focuses much attention on the first settlers, the Ice Age Neanderthals, and their probable way of life including the making of the hand axe and flake tools. The second epoch of the Neolithics who practiced agriculture and animal husbandry is traced through remains found at Skara Brae and Grimes Graves. The Bronze Age accomplishments of the Beaker peoples—the building of Stonehenge, for example—are covered in detail while the fourth and final epoch, the Iron Age, is traced through the appearance of the Hallstat peoples and the Celts. Appendices on archeological procedure and origins of Indo-European languages plus an index, bibliography, and profuse black-and-white and color illustrations further clarify this well-written book. Although not as broad in scope as the Quennells' *Everyday Life in Prehistoric Times* (Putnam, 1959), this does acknowledge new dating techniques (radiocarbon dating, tree ring calibrating) and will interest students of the period.

UNLEAVING (1976)

Elaine Moss

SOURCE: A review of *Unleaving,* in *Times Literary Supplement,* April 2, 1976, p. 375.

> Márgarét, are you grieving
> Over Goldengrove unleaving . . .
> It is the blight man was born for,
> It is Margaret you mourn for.

I cannot help wishing that Jill Paton Walsh had quoted Gerard Manley Hopkins's "Spring and Fall" at the beginning of her sequel to **Goldengrove:** the poem is at the core of **Unleaving**—a title that unexplained means little, whereas the whole grand design of this extraordinary novel could have been suggested to the reader by placing the title in context.

For the reader here needs help. How soon will he realize that the novel is set in two periods—that seventeen-year-old Madge of the earlier time is the elderly Gran of the later, that young Madge's traumatic experiences at Goldengrove during that fateful summer explain to a large extent the older woman? Approaching death by the end of the book, Madge can say to her grandchildren, "Well, we all die, but first we all live. Don't worry about what's the point. Just take your share. Take it two-handed and in full measure. You have to clap your hands and sing." What shall we sing about, asks her grandson; and Madge-Gran's reply is the whole answer: "What shall we clap? The lifeboat in the storm. What shall we sing? The wonders of the world."

Perhaps the author meant the revelation that the young Madge of the main sequences is the old Gran of the interspersed passages to come as a surprise to the reader just six pages before the end—a sudden jerking of the kaleidoscope so that the pattern, a puzzling disintegrated set of vivid shapes jostling one another, would suddenly fix itself, all elements at last acquiring an enduring, interrelated sharp-focus design. My real fear is that because the two periods are (purposely?) timeless and undifferentiated—dialogue, for instance, could easily have been used to strike a contrast, but has deliberately been levelled—readers may give up trying to sort out the two superficially unrelated sets of characters and stop reading. (Madge-Gran is the unifying force, but one might not guess.) They would then be deprived of the poetic experience of life Jill Paton Walsh is offering them so generously and with such assurance.

For her theme is life itself, no less. She explores its meaning, or lack of meaning, through the juxtaposition of a group of philosophy students and dons on a reading party in Cornwall, and young Madge who has inherited Goldengrove (the house they rent). Madge is a girl who lives through instinct and emotion rather than cold reason; she is sympathetic and loving.

Madge is falling in love with Patrick Tregeagle who is also a feeling person, deeply attached to his little sister Molly who is a mongol. Patrick cannot stand the cerebral pronouncements of his father, the professor of philosophy in charge of the reading-party, and is thoroughly riled by the students' interminable discussions on Wittgenstein, on ends and means on the intellect as divorced from the body and soul—the intellect being deemed immortal, body and soul mortal. Little Molly has no intellect; is she then in her father's eyes totally mortal, whereas he and his philosophy students will live on in some form for ever? Molly, who can be taught by Patrick to say "Cogito ergo sum" (a stomach-turning moment, this) as easily as she can say "petrol pump" or "butter-knife", is the catalyst in the story—for walking on a cliff-top with Patrick she reaches out for a flower and falls to her death on the rocks below. Did Patrick want her death? Did he push her, or try to save her? Will Patrick survive his "great attempt at action, at manipulating the universe, at refusing to leave things be and blame God"?

Though we do not meet Patrick again we know, through Madge, that he did survive—for he is re-

membered by Madge-Gran as the grandfather of the small children who, forty years later, are experiencing Cornwall in the way young Madge had grown through Goldengrove—unleaving, unleaving—until she became old Gran: "What shall we sing? The wonders of the world."

Jill Paton Walsh sees the world as immutably beautiful: her skilfully counterpoised descriptions of the ever-changing sea provide memorable mood-music for the ebb and flow, calm and storm of the narrative. Life, she tells us, is something incomprehensible and wonderful that we must live to the full, acknowledging, meanwhile, its mysticism. For old Gran is still recognizably young Madge despite "so many and so great revolutions in matter".

This is the essence of *Unleaving*—that the sapling and the old beech tree have a spiritual oneness. I suspect that the author of *Unleaving* did purposely superimpose one period upon the other for this confusion—in the purely literary sense of the word—makes her main point, artistically. But because she plays her trump card-of-identity so late, it is only on a second reading of this short but complex novel that the intricacies of its construction, the full force of its intellectual argument and the comfort of its spiritual message—that feeling, experiencing, reacting emotionally to life is what matters—stand boldly forth, as challenging and beckoning as the symbolic Godrevy light.

Jean Mercier

SOURCE: A review of *Unleaving*, in *Publishers Weekly*, Vol. 209, No. 14, April 5, 1976, p.

The British author's gifts as a storyteller seem almost magical. Using the same setting, she has written a followup to *Goldengrove*, which won her honors in 1972. The seaside estate has been inherited by Madge Fielding; the narrative slips subtly from past to present, describing a critical summer in Madge's young life and its effects on her as a grandmother. She has let Goldengrove to professors and their students for a season and is drawn to Patrick Tregeagle, her own age, despite his sometimes sullen nature. He has a young sister, Molly, who is sadly retarded; Patrick hates himself for wishing the child dead. On a fateful day, Molly is killed. Madge and her brother witness the "accident"—Madge is tortured because she believes Patrick has pushed the girl from a cliff, though her brother swears Patrick was trying to save her. It is a lyrically told, provocative and inspiring tale.

Kirkus Reviews

SOURCE: A review of *Unleaving*, in *Kirkus Reviews*, Vol. XLIV, No. 10, May 15, 1976, p. 601.

The same sort of idyllic seaside family scenes that Madge and her brother Paul enjoyed with Gran at *Goldengrove* (1972) in Cornwall are interspersed here with the events of the summer when Madge, in her late teens, shares Goldengrove (which she has just inherited from her grandmother) with two philosophy professors, their families, and a "reading party" of undergraduates. The dry philosophical chatter drifts by—means and ends, body and soul, life and death—and, to Madge, Paul and Professor Tregeagle's brooding son Patrick, seem variously fascinating, nonsensical, and remote. But around Patrick's mongoloid little sister the issues emerge in action, to be met by each teenager in his own way while the now grotesque philosophers continue their bloodless disputes. What happens is that tormented, pitying Patrick pushes his sister over a cliff to her death, though only Madge sees how it happens. A would-be rescuer drowns; Patrick is swamped by guilt; and Madge, an open, giving, perceptive girl, drawn to him from the start, recognizes her future with Patrick. Though Madge's ruminations are riddled with resounding quotes (the last from Yeats) and some irritating echoes of Virginia Woolf, Walsh is a highly accomplished craftsman, and the aura of Goldengrove compelling. Unless you share her optimism it's a bit of a shock to realize that those lovely scenes with Gran ("a queen among teacups"), which seem always misted over by idealized remembrance and often designed to demonstrate what a groovy old lady she is, are really future shots of a serenely aged Madge. Still, Walsh's fusion of themes, events, and musings is impressive and her affirmative vision projected here with full and harmonious coherence.

Margaret Meek

SOURCE: A review of *Unleaving,* in *The School Librarian,* Vol. 24, No. 2, June, 1976, p. 152.

A sequel to *Goldengrove* in the same haunting tune. English teachers who are in on the secret of all the overtones of *To the Lighthouse* will recommend this book with fervour to the exclusive group of readers who enjoy the intellectual game of allusions and word play. There is a story tucked into the landscape, but 'What happens next?' is the least important way through this rather intense, self-indulgent fine writing. The young who read it with me were glad when the heroine told the university don (staying in her house with a 'reading party') just what she thought of him for his lack of insight into the feelings of his moody son and the affections of his retarded daughter. There are many things of beauty and terror; a private kind of book.

The Booklist

SOURCE: A review of *Unleaving,* in *Booklist,* Vol. 72, No. 19, June 1, 1976, p. 1401.

Alternating narratives unfold two widely separated summers at Goldengrove, the Cornish seaside house inherited by Madge Fielding on her grandmother's death. In one, Madge, almost ready for college, opens the house to an Oxford professor and a group of undergraduates who spend the summer in reading and in philosophical discussion. Madge gets to know her future husband, Patrick Tregeagle, a strange and angry young man with a small, retarded sister named Molly. When Molly, in Patrick's charge, falls from a cliff and drowns, Patrick is racked with guilt because of his ambivalent feelings about his sister. In the other narrative, Madge's daughter, son-in-law, and grandchildren are visiting Goldengrove during a summer that is a happy though introspective time for her. Although the narrative shifts are smooth, they are, at times, infused with a dreamlike quality that leaves the reader unsure as to which narrative is the here and now—each has its own immediacy. With the same setting and family as *Goldengrove* but for a slightly older audience, this is an affecting and compelling story that can provoke thought about life, death, and the cycle of generations.

Nancy Gail Reed

SOURCE: A review of *Unleaving,* in *The Christian Science Monitor,* Vol. 68, No. 152, July 1, 1976, p. 23.

Two separate story lines intertwine in this well-crafted and sometimes astonishingly beautiful novel from Jill Paton Walsh. The story which centers around young Madge Fielding (whom we have met before in Mrs. Walsh's *Goldengrove*) is replete with all the carings and sufferings and anti-intellectual wanderings of youth. A bit angry, this story, which stars loveless philosopher types as the ultimate villains, and a moody, rebellious-young-man type as the recipient of Madge's sunny, reasonable affection.

But winding its way around this central story, like a generations-old vine around the garden trellis of a shabby, well-loved family estate, is the ephemeral substance of someone else's story—Gran's. Who is she, this peaceful, silent, old lady who has the wisdom to think, in her growing-foggy manner (but *foggy* as light diffused through mist, *foggy* as rainbows seen through lashes) of ideas such as this: "An aged man is but a paltry thing . . . yet inside I feel no different . . though it isn't monuments of magnificence for me . . . it's more the brightness falls from the air, the eternally changing sea, and the view of Godrevy light . . And, do you know, in all the talk I ever heard about the immortal soul, I never recall the eternal youth of the inner self brought in evidence against us being all bodies . . . "

At some point, we must begin to wonder when Madge and Gran will meet. They appear to be in the same general geographical area, and even to share some of the same sagacity. The fusion, in the end, of these two stories, like parallel tracks that do, indeed, meet at the horizon, dispels all confusion and awkwardness.

In the book's lyrical, present-tense voice, singing of the sea, one hears whispers of Virginia Woolf, although Mrs. Walsh cannot sustain this vision and sometimes interrupts the beauty with ill-fitting fantasy that puts sentiment into inanimate objects, such as bottles that "spew out half their contents on being opened, expressing their disgust at the warm, shaken ride in the car."

For the most part, however, *Unleaving* is satisfyingly full of finely presented basic human questions, which, Mrs. Walsh (with Gran) insists, must be resolved not through scholarly wisdom, but through wise love.

The Horn Book

SOURCE: A review of *Unleaving*, in *The Horn Book Magazine*, Vol. LII, No., August, 1976, p. 408.

A sequel to *Goldengrove* shows a deeper portrayal of human relationships and raises profound questions about life, death, and love. Young Madge has rented her inherited house in Cornwall to an Oxford professor who is leading a group of students in a "reading party." The young philosophers have worked through days of investigation when the focus abruptly shifts from abstract principles to actuality. The summer colloquy is pictured from Madge's point of view in flashbacks skillfully, if somewhat obscurely, inserted as retrospective views from the future when Madge is a grandmother. On a picnic with the students she sees the professor's teenage son Patrick and his mongoloid little sister playing together on the edge of a seaside cliff. Did he raise his arm to try to catch her or to push her? Madge knows the awful truth, and she helps Patrick struggle through the bleak, dreadful days that follow. The author has dealt with the whole book brilliantly, deftly raising issues without overburdening her story. At a point where the philosophizing must seem too much for a young reader, she

introduces the climactic incident which involves the death of a valiant seaman trying to recover the body of Patrick's sister. Set against a background of Cornish custom and tragedy at sea, the story is filled with introspection and description, which are balanced by fine characterization and a picture of normal, everyday living.

Margery Fisher

SOURCE: A review of *Unleaving*, in *Growing Point*, Vol. 15, No. 3, September, 1976, p. 2942.

Jill Paton Walsh demands from her readers a constant alertness and emotional response. *Unleaving* is a more complex book in construction than *Goldengrove*, for it works on a double time-scheme. In the Cornish setting of the earlier book we see Madge as a schoolgirl waiting to go to university and also as a grandmother. Allusively, in fragmentary scenes experienced or remembered, the story is unfolded of her meeting with Patrick and his mongol sister Molly and the seesaw of feeling she experiences as she tries to identify and reconcile her feelings for each of them. A little apart from the younger people (as Gran is apart from her grandchildren) stands the philosopher, father of Patrick and Molly, who has rented the seaside house (left to Madge by her grandmother) for a vacation reading-party. With sharp effect the syllogistic conversations of Professor Tregeagle and his disciples interrupt or interweave with those of the children and, in moments of tension and tragedy, reason and feeling are weighted one against the other. In her flexible, allusive, Woolfian style the author lays bare the wilful, puzzled, arrogant or insensitive attitudes of the various characters. Like a piece of music, the book has to be heard, its themes identified and their repetition noted: the shape and sound of the narrative, its essential quality, unite in a considerable literary whole.

C. S. Hannabuss

SOURCE: A review of *Unleaving*, in *Children's Book Review*, Vol. VI, October, 1976, pp. 22-3.

Unleaving is a sequel to *Goldengrove*.

The house on the Cornish coast now belongs to Madge, since Gran is dead, and Madge agrees to let the house to Professor Tregeagle and his group of students, who talk philosophy throughout their stay. Madge stays on to watch and listen, and grows increasingly angry at the empty pretentiousness of the discussions, a reaction she will certainly hold in common with most readers. *Unleaving* is a book which implies a double standard, for in highly intellectualised way it seeks to establish the futility of being merely intellectual. Then, in trying to set up a degree of reality in the main characters (Madge and the Professor's son Patrick), it makes the common intellectual error of assuming that, when one is being intellectual oneself, it is not merely intellectualising but in fact based upon feeling and experience. By this token, the overtly 'meaningful' (almost didactic) conversations they have are tautly ratiocinative, allusive, epigrammatic, and unreal. On top of this comes a second phoney premiss: it is centred on a tragic cliff accident when Patrick's Mongol sister falls to her death. The author devises a special kind of situation in order to make the special kind of intellectualising in the book seem irrelevant and unreasonable, and this is special pleading of a very devious kind. In the unravelling of Patrick's grief, Madge plays a vague but obviously decisive part, although Literature and Feeling play a larger: the final assumption is the curative and ordering power of these two forces, one which will convince only those teenagers who love their Eng./Lit. set books and plan to proceed on to Murdoch and allied reading, and—of course—those adults who feel that this form of culture is a Good Thing. An adult book, an adult indulgence.

The Junior Bookshelf

SOURCE: A review of *Unleaving,* in *The Junior Bookshelf,* Vol. 40, No. 5, October, 1976, pp. 292-93.

Seven pages from the end of this long, lovely novel, Jill Paton Walsh releases the clue which enables each separate episode to drop into place. It is a masterly exercise in control, one which may for a few readers prove to be self-defeating, for not everyone is likely to wait so long for the resolution of so leisurely-paced a narrative. The impatient ones will be the losers; the others will, as I did, turn back to the beginning and read straight through again.

The central character, as in the earlier *Goldengrove,* is Madge, teenage heir to a house in Cornwall. She lets the house during one hot summer to an Oxford reading-party, where she learns a little philosophy, a lot about philosophers, and more about the complexities of growing up. By means of the author's clever narrative device we see the action simultaneously close at hand and in the perspective of time.

The book may be too quiet, its emotions too delicate, for wide popularity. Those readers—girls mostly—who respond to its quiet appeal will love it dearly

and long. It could be taken as a model by aspiring writers who will learn in it how to vary pace, convey atmosphere, build up piece by piece a scene and the actors in it, above all how to blend mood and thought and action into one exquisite whole.

Millicent Lenz

SOURCE: "Through Blight to Bliss: Thematic Motifs in Jill Paton Walsh's *Unleaving,*" in *Children's Literature Association Quarterly,* Vol. 13, No. 4, Winter, 1988, pp. 194-97.

Unleaving, Jill Paton Walsh's novel for young adults, is rich in its presentation of psychological and spiritual growth, as seen in the heroine's progress from sensitive child to wise, warm, life-embracing grandmother. Paton Walsh exhibits remarkable artistry in weaving together certain thematic motifs to highlight Madge's growth towards a holistic vision of life's beauty and joy set against its harsher realities. My concern will be to illuminate these motifs as they signify Madge's progress through the blights and limitations of the human condition towards a celebratory vision of life, of the sheer bliss of being.

The first blight in Madge's life is the fact of her family's being broken by divorce. As Paton Walsh's earlier book *Goldengrove* relates, Madge has been brought up by her mother and a stepfather; her "cousin" Paul—revealed to be in truth her brother—has been raised by their father and his second wife. Madge's deepest sense of family has come from her grandmother, who has bequeathed to Madge her home by the sea, Goldengrove. *Unleaving,* the sequel to *Goldengrove,* tells of the summer when Madge returns to bury her grandmother and is drawn into a tragedy and a romance that shape her subsequent life. During the summer of *Unleaving,* Madge discovers the meaning of love and commitment, experiences the loss of innocence, and—through flash-forwards to the time when she is herself a grandmother, gives expression to a mature vision of the value of life.

Unleaving is remarkable in a number of respects—its highly vivid, metaphorical language, its allusive quality, and the author's artful handling of time. The title alludes to Gerard Manley Hopkins's "Spring and Fall: To a Young Child," with its opening "Margaret are you grieving / Over Goldengrove unleaving?" and it sets the stage for the book's revelation of the paradoxical truth that we mourn our own mortality in our grief for the deaths of others: "It is the blight man was born for, / It is Margaret you mourn for."

The story encompasses Madge's life-span, reflecting back to the times when she came to Goldengrove as a baby, and flowing forward to the time when she is herself "Gran" to a beguiling set of youngsters.

The book relates the events of the particular summer when Madge returns to take possession of Goldengrove, which she has agreed to share with two philosophy professors, their families, and their students who are here for a "reading party." Through coming to know the Tregeagles, a troubled, star-crossed family, Madge becomes aware of the pains of human connectedness, the sometimes sorrowful inadequacies of human relationships. Through her dawning love of Patrick Tregeagle, she also becomes aware of the mixed joys and complexities of love. She is initiated, one might say, into the consciousness of what the Romans called the *lacrimae rerum,* the undercurrent of pathos present in all of life. The ultimate vision of life presented in the book, however, goes beyond this, as shall be seen.

The events of the novel may be briefly summarized. Madge quickly perceives Professor Tregeagle's lack of empathy for his four-year-old daughter Molly, a victim of Downs' syndrome. He values intellect above all else and cannot bear to face the emotions that hover around his severely retarded daughter, whom he perceives as an embarrassment and a burden. Patrick Tregeagle, Molly's brother and Madge's contemporary in age, feels a frustrated empathy for Molly mingled with fear for her future and shame over his father's lack of sensitivity to her feelings. The other children, with the cruelty of childhood, taunt Molly and exclude her from their play, to Patrick's torment. Madge shows kindness to Molly, and nurtures a bittersweet love for Patrick (against the warnings of her brother Paul, who fears Patrick will bring her no happiness). It is Madge who keeps Patrick from despair and possibly madness after he does or does not—his responsibility is left open to interpretation—bring about Molly's death in a fall from a cliff into the rugged sea below. Patrick must also live with guilt over the drowning of Jeremy—a retired sailor and life-long friend of Madge and her brother—when Jeremy falls from the lifeboat while attempting to retrieve Molly's body.

The fluidity of narrative time in the book, with flashes between the summer of Madge's grandmother's death and a summer years later when she herself is "Gran," has the effect of blurring the identities of the two Grans—Madge's grandmother and Madge herself. Only at the end of the book does the text confirm the Gran/Madge identity, which serves artistically to es-tablish continuity and a sense of family bonding that transcends time and death. Madge, whom we have known primarily as a teenager quivering on the brink of adulthood, is suddenly revealed to us as a wise and spirited grandmother. In her grandchildren, she sees tracings of her young self as well as echoes of her now-dead husband Patrick. Subtly, Paton Walsh establishes a kinship that transcends the intervening years and their losses, and makes it possible for Gran/Madge to speak from the perspective of a lifetime rich in experiences. Throughout the book Paton Walsh has woven into the narrative a keen sense of the interrelatedness of "now" and timelessness, as in the passage early in the text where Gran/Madge sees rain as "an element of eternity, showing in its brilliant light-catching instant of fall the eternal aspect of the momentary now." She meditates on the paradox of the "immortal brevity" sensed in privileged moments of our lives, recalling Traherne's image of "orient and immortal wheat, which knew no seed and yet no harvest time."

There is a quality to Madge's love for Patrick that partakes, at least superficially, of perhaps too much self-sacrifice. Madge's willingness to entwine her life with Patrick's, knowing full well (as clear-eyed Paul sees) that she offers him more in the way of emotional support than he will give her in return, is open to question. Patrick does nevertheless enrich her life experience by drawing her with him into what one might call, applying traditional religious terms, the dark night of the soul. Without such a descent to the spiritual depths, Madge would remain, in William Blake's paradigm, in a kind of spiritual infancy, the period of "single vision" that cannot see into the essence of things. Through her love for Patrick, Madge shares in his guilt. She reflects, after she lies to protect him, "Patrick is a murderer, and I am his next of kin" (116). The text leaves Patrick's culpability in Molly's death unresolved (even he is not sure whether he precipitated her fall or tried to prevent it). What can be established is Madge's ability to see Patrick ('murderer' or not) as lovable. She reflects back to him a vision of himself as loved; he gives to her a recognition of her own capacity to see into the beauty deep within things that may appear unlovely to a more superficial eye. Paton Walsh portrays this capacity to see the beauty in the seemingly unlovable as essential to self-forgetting love (e.g. Patrick's love for Molly, which sees beyond her "clumsy gait" and "dribble"). Ultimately the novel affirms this kind of beauty-perceiving vision as the basis for love of creation itself on a cosmic scale: this vision comes to Gran/Madge towards the end of her life.

As for loving human relationships within the context of family, Paton Walsh poses and answers these questions in the novel: (1) What is the nature of love and what does a loving relationship entail? (2) How can a person find meaning and joy in life, given the inevitability of pain and death? Madge's grandson Peter puts it more colorfully: "'Gran, you see, first we grow up and have a lot of worries. And then we die, and I don't see the point'." The answers lie to some extent in direct statements made by several characters, but several key thematic motifs carry much of the weight of the meanings Gran/Madge brings to expression. I will center my discussion on four basic images and thematic motifs that I find especially significant: first, the Lifeboat in the Storm; second, the Web; third, the Secret Self; and fourth, Singing. I shall relate these motifs to statements made through characters to arrive at a number of conclusions about Paton Walsh's views on love and life.

The Lifeboat is introduced early in the book, when the funeral procession for Madge's Gran is interrupted by the bell signalling seafarers in distress. A number of the pallbearers, members of the lifeboat rescue squad, set down the casket and rush to offer aid, leaving the others to see Gran's remains safely to the grave. The implications are evident: saving life takes priority over attending to the dead, and the endangered lives at sea can be saved only through risk of other lives. It is largely through Jeremy, the seasoned old sailor, that this theme is further developed; Jeremy, who fears drowning more than any other fate, cannot refuse help when the bell tolls. His fear foreshadows his eventual fate, for it is his life that the sea claims in exchange for giving up Molly's corpse. So it seems, at any rate, to Madge and Paul, for whom Jeremy has been a mentor and father figure.

Throughout the book the repeated images of the child lost to the sea or stolen by Merfolk have a dual function: they foreshadow Molly's fate, and they also show by contrast the pity and terror of being torn away from the human family. Jeremy prefaces his story of Matthew Trewhella with a warning to Madge not to sing near the sea, for the Merrymaid steals human children with sweet voices and forces them to sing "below the waves." While Madge combs through books of folklore to find the derivation of Patrick's last name, "Tregeagle," she encounters the story of the Lady with the Lantern, "looking all night among the wavewashed rocks for her shipwrecked child." In a flash-forward to the "present" of Gran/Madge, her son-in-law Tom reads the pathetic newspaper story of a child lost through a fall down a mine shaft. All of these lost-child images stand in contrast to the Lifeboat as an image of the interrelatedness of human lives.

Similarly, Patrick's ambivalent thoughts on the occupation of a lighthouse keeper underscore the tension between human apartness and connectedness. He knows lighthouse-keeping would be a lonely life, yet it would have purpose: "One would keep a light that other men find their way by." In direct contrast to Patrick's felt need for relatedness is the aloofness of Andrew, another student in the reading party. Andrew says at one point, "I prefer to climb alone . . . One can concentrate better. One has only oneself to worry about . . . you can stop when you feel like it." The barrenness of his "go-it-alone" approach to life is brought out late in the book when he reappears as a philosophy professor who cherishes the memory of one summer when life seemed to offer something more than chilly intellectual self-absorption. Andrew is cut from the same cloth as Professor Tregeagle.

The images and characters thus far described underscore the thematic contrast between life-sustaining relationship and life-threatening isolation. The Lifeboat is a primary image of human relatedness and interdependence.

The Web (or Net) relates closely to the Lifeboat, though it has certain more negative connotations. It enters the story as an important image when Patrick throws a torn fishing net over Madge, exclaiming, "I fish for survival. And I've got her tangled." The implications of the relationship he thus defines are, clearly, more positive for Patrick (his life will be saved by the Net) than for Madge (she is restrained by it). Yet the two seem fatefully to complement each other, as in Paton Walsh's description of their polar views on life: Patrick cannot see the glorious aspect of life, whereas Madge cannot (yet) see its misery. They successfully illuminate each other's blind spots, each supplying the vision the other lacks.

The Secret Self is another major motif, growing out of Patrick's recognition of a truth about his parents' relationship. As Patrick and Madge commiserate over the prospect of becoming adults and puzzle about how adult life could possibly be bearable, Patrick observes that there is a "secret consolation" in adult life: "The lucky ones have love for someone. And it makes a private world nobody else can see at all. Then they're all right." He believes his father, by loving his mother and seeing in her "a carefree pretty person"—not just a drudge whose life is ground down by the frustrations of caring for Molly—"makes her a kind of secret self, to be for him . . . whatever she may have to be for anybody else." This is Patrick's perception of the identity-affirming and transforming aspect of love. Madge elaborates on his idea, saying she believes real happiness means having "one's favorite self, the person one most likes to be, loved by someone." But Patrick corrects one's "favorite" self to one's "nearest self—the self one truly is." Further, he says, one cannot be loved by just "any" person; it takes "a special person" to value and bring to life this true Secret Self.

Madge realizes, with an astuteness beyond her years, that to be loved like this, by someone with the intensity of Patrick, is not all joy. She feels discomfort over Patrick's "churned-up" nature, his tendency to fuss about things: "everything matters too much to him. But then everything includes me—I feel that I matter too. He pays such searchlight attention to one." She decides such "searchlight attention" is nonetheless perferable to the chill engendered by Andrew—even though Andrew is better-looking! Better too intense an attention, she decides, than so much sang-froid.

The final motif of Singing brings together a complex of meanings from the entire book. It is interwoven with Gran/Madge's thoughts on immortality and the meaning of life, triggered by her grandson Peter's puzzlement about death, and his blunt question, will she "mind" dying? Unruffled, she replies, "I shouldn't think so, dear . . . It isn't our own death that troubles us. We have enough to do surviving other people's." A chain of associated memories arises before her mind's eye, and she remembers being twice unshakably convinced of the soul's immortality—both times in the presence of death, first during her vigil at the coffin of Gran, then seeing Patrick dead. "It's an odd thing, but it's not the romantic opinion about the departing soul that is shaken in the actual presence of death;" rather, "in the actual presence of death it is the rational belief in mortality that is shattered."

Yet it is not an intuition of immortality that gives life "point" in Gran/Madge's view. Rather, as she explains to Peter, life's meaning is found in "things on the way"—small experiences to be treasured, fragments to be shored against our ruin—such as her memory of Patrick asleep beside her "in rumpled sheets, every muscle in his body slack, and on his face that shining serenity that never came to him awake." Her intuition of the part she plays in his serenity is one of the "things on the way" that give "point" to her life. She does not try to explain this to Peter, who translates "things on the way" into terms

he can understand—"birthdays," times that to his youthful imagination correspond with his grandmother's exclamation: "What shall we clap? . . . The lifeboat in the storm. What shall we sing? The beauty of the world!" Gran/Madge, like William Butler Yeats, is sailing to her own city of Byzantium. The soul, however tattered its mortal dress, rejoices in its aliveness to the wonders of existence itself. This apprehension of the wonder and beauty of all creation becomes, finally, the basis for the connectedness of all humankind, and the underlying source of all love. *Unleaving* culminates in Gran/Madge's personal "Ode to Joy." Madge, like the tree that moves Hopkin's Margaret to tears, has gone though the process of unleaving—the process by which life pares one down to the essentials of being. Madge is fortunate to have the clarity of vision to see much to celebrate in life so simplified. She rejoices in what Hopkins would call "the dearest freshness deep down things," the "pied beauty" of things in their infinite variety.

CROSSING TO SALAMIS (1977)

Margery Fisher

SOURCE: A review of *Crossing to Salamis,* in *Growing Point,* Vol. 16, No. 5, November, 1977, pp. 3200-01.

A direct and capable use of detail puts *Crossing to Salamis* within the understanding of some readers as young as eight or nine. They will find here the background facts about the evacuation of Athens and the defeat of the Persians at Salamis through the strategy of Themistokles, neatly inserted into a narrative concerned with a single household. Aster herself, a girl coming up to marriageable age, describes the narrow life she leads with a widowed mother and loyal family servant and we see how anxiety for her brother at Marathon, her mother's fear for the family estate, the preoccupation with respectability, all become less important when they are forced to flee to the island of Salamis. The freedom Aster finds in an improvised tent on a hillside can be appreciated by any young reader of today, and so circumstantial is the story that we can even accept the author's boldness in actually involving the girl, albeit indirectly, with the trick played by the Greek leader on the Persian fleet. In the "Long Ago Children" series, this accurate, lively picture of the distant past should find many willing readers.

The Junior Bookshelf

SOURCE: A review of *Crossing to Salamis,* in *The Junior Bookshelf,* Vol. 41, No. 6, December, 1977, pp. 370-71.

When the Persians attack Athens, Aster and her mother seek refuge on the island of Salamis along with most of their fellow Athenians. The change from a protected, indoor existence, spinning and weaving and looking after her pets, to the harsher freedoms of Salamis is a welcome escape for Aster. She stumbles quite fortuitously on a plan of treachery; she solves her dilemma by a direct approach through the army camp to General Themistokles, an action which plunges her into disgrace with her orthodox mother until the truth can be revealed.

David Smee's apposite drawings, Grecian style, add impact to this unvarnished tale, narrated with controlled concern for the central problem that faces young Aster. The two worlds she lives in are contrasted simply but effectively; Aster herself grows in stature as she resolves the demands of duty and conventional behaviour.

R. Bradbury

SOURCE: A review of *Crossing to Salamis*, in *The School Librarian*, Vol. 26, No. 1, March, 1978, p. 62.

In this series dealing with life in different periods of world history here is a well written, exciting tale of ancient Athens. Its heroine is the daughter of a soldier slain at Marathon and she, with her family, flees to Salamis when Athens is invaded by the Persians. By chance she too finds a way to serve her country and also meets Themistokles. Highly commended for its portrayal of old Greek customs.

THE WALLS OF ATHENS (1978)

Margery Fisher

SOURCE: A review of *The Walls of Athens*, in *Growing Point*, Vol. 16, No. 8, March, 1978, p. 3266.

Documentation is paramount in *The Walls of Athens* but the details are suitably selected for this example of the "Long Ago Children" series so that readers as young as nine or ten may sense the atmosphere of the past without feeling they are being instructed. Like the heroine of an earlier story in the series, *Crossing to Salamis,* young Demeas has been evacuated from Athens during the Persian invasion and now, returned to the family farm and its shattered olive groves, he learns that Themistokles has ordered the rebuilding of the city walls, but secretly, against the embargo of their Spartan allies. By chance Demeas, already renowned as a runner, finds himself

carrying the vital message to Themistokles, on an embassy in Sparta, that the walls are finished: his reward, a gift of young olive trees from Pausanias. There is plenty of domestic detail here and a clear explanation of the political situation after the Greek triumph at Salamis, but the easy manner of the story and the congenial theme of a boy rising to a challenge make this a very pleasant history lesson.

CHILDREN OF THE FOX (1978)

Jean Mercier

SOURCE: A review of *Children of the Fox*, in *Publishers Weekly*, Vol. 213, No. 24, June 12, 1978, p. 82.

Walsh won the admiration of critics and readers with her lyrical *Goldengrove, Unleaving* and other splendid novels. With the three stories in her new collection, the author invests the ancient past with the keen interest that too many historical works lack. Not dry as old bones, but a complex, sympathetic man is encountered in the events authentically described. He is the Athenian hero, Themistokles, pounded by the wars between the Greeks and the Persians, 480 to 470 B.C. In each tale, a young boy or girl comes to the aid of Themistokles and helps him with a plan that gets him out of a tight hole. The finale describes how the warrior was forced to flee for asylum to the stronghold of his former enemy, the Great King of Persia, when the Spartans and the Athenians turned against him. An afterword gives the book's factual base.

Kirkus Reviews

SOURCE: A review of *Children of the Fox*, in *Kirkus Reviews*, Vol. XLVI, No. 13, July 1, 1978, p. 690.

The fox is Themistokles, the Fifth-Century Athenian who was the hero of Walsh's only adult novel, *Farewell Great King* (1972); here he is glimpsed through the eyes of three different children who, in three separate but sequential stories, become accidentally involved in large events and invariably rise to the occasion. First Aster, an Athenian refugee on Salamis waiting for Persian invasion, cuts her hair (a scandal) and sneaks to the leader's tent with news of a night message being sent off to the Persians; Themistokles takes her into his confidence—he had sent the message to lure the Persians into a trap—and later, after his ruse has paid off, he rewards her with a Spartan husband whose customs allow girls more freedom and exercise than the Athenians deem proper. Sparta is less favorably projected in the second story, wherein young Demeas replaces a wounded runner en route to inform Themistokles, now playing for time with officials in suspicious, authoritarian Sparta—where the rebuilding of the Athenian wall is opposed—that the project has been safely completed. The last story takes place after Themistokles has lost favor in both cities; he is found in a sort of play-house by a girl whose mother, in turn, lends her own baby to a scheme to win the former hero safe-conduct to Persia. Walsh doesn't go into the politics behind the incidents but she is conscientiously true to the history, which takes precedence here over originality in plotting and characterization. Still, her skill in integrating the larger story with the lesser (though not common) lives is impressive.

Ruth M. McConnell

SOURCE: A review of *Children of the Fox,* in *School Library Journal,* Vol. 25, No. 1, September, 1978, pp. 165-66.

Major events in the Persian wars against the Greeks are set in three well-imagined encounters of the shrewd Athenian leader, Themistocles, with various children. The three short stories convey the shock to the Athenians of the burning of their city and girdling of its olive orchards; the battle of Salamis; the plot to rebuild Athens' walls; and the exile and escape of Themistocles. The brief form makes treatment of the children's enterprises a bit neat if satisfactory, with promises of wider doors opening to each lot. And, in only a few pages, the author establishes the well-born woman's restricted place in Athenian society (until being evacuated to Salamis, the 14-year-old heroine of the first story had never seen the sea) and provides insight into a segment of Greek history that makes excellent supplementary reading.

Barbara Elleman

SOURCE: A review of *Children of the Fox,* in *Booklist,* Vol. 75, No. 1, September 1, 1978, p. 54.

Walsh has designed three imaginary stories in which a young person has an amazing contact with the great Athenian general Themistokles, an actual figure in the wars against Persia (480-470 B.C.). In *Crossing to Salamis,* Aster and her mother leave their secluded Athens home ahead of the invading Persians. While in the evacuation camp, Aster disguises herself as a boy to take a message to Themistokles and finds herself the holder of a guarded secret. Demeas, a young

Athenian boy in *The Walls of Athens,* carries a vital message to the general when the regular runner is incapacitated; and in *Persian Gold* Lala, the daughter of the Molossian king, uses her influence to save Themistokles when he is rejected by the Athenians and helps him escape to Persia. Well integrated, clear explanations of the historical events allow young readers to sense the atmosphere of the past, while the lively characterizations bring a contemporary ambience to the tales.

The Horn Book

SOURCE: A review of *Children of the Fox,* in *The Horn Book Magazine,* Vol. LV, No. , October, 1978, p. 520.

Three stories, published separately in England, are included in a single volume. In the ancient world of Athens, Sparta, and Persia, two young heroines and a hero tell stories which are historically linked, though the three protagonists never meet. Each one renders brave service to Themistokles, known as "The Fox." The first story tells of impoverished Aster—about to be evacuated from Athens to the island of Salamis after her father is killed at Marathon—who risks her reputation by visiting Themistokles's camp at night to warn him of supposed danger. In the second narrative the boy Demeas is rounding up flocks of goats and swine in the mountains when he is called upon to replace an injured runner carrying an imperative message to Themistokles in Sparta. And finally Lala, a young princess, manages by a clever move to make her father save Themistokles, who finds safety among the Persians. Thus, each tale follows its central story-telling character in a crucial and dangerous venture and explains significant relationships among Athens, Sparta, and Persia during the Persian Wars. The graphic human details evoke the events as clearly as ancient Byzantium and its crises were brought to life in *The Emperor's Winding Sheet.*

A CHANCE CHILD (1978)

Jean Mercier

SOURCE: A review of *A Chance Child,* in *Publishers Weekly,* Vol. 214, No. 24, December 11, 1978, p. 69.

The British author's singular gifts have won her honors at home and abroad for *Goldengrove, Unleaving* and other books of surpassing loveliness. But never has she written with such impact as she does in this fact-fantasy, dedicated to real victims of the infant Industrial Revolution. Creep, a child of today, escapes from the closet where his despicable mother has imprisoned him. No one except his half-brother, Christopher, searches for the missing boy. Creep drifts back to the 1800s and joins the band of small boys and girls who are starved, beaten and forced to work all day at dangerous jobs. Chapters alternate between past and present, with Christopher sensing where his brother has gone and Creep helping the child laborers to better their lives. Desperate for reassurance on the fate of the vanished boy, Christopher studies records of Parliament and finally comes upon a deposition by "a chance child," Nathaniel Creep. Not even Dickens portrayed abused children (of yesterday and today) as Walsh does here. She dedicates her book to actual persons whose testimony she uncovered during her research. It's a list of names almost too poignant to read.

Kirkus Reviews

SOURCE: A review of *A Chance Child,* in *Kirkus Reviews,* Vol. XLVI, No. 24, December 15, 1978, p. 1359.

His abusive mother called him creep and so that's the name he goes by. We meet him in a sort of dump, from which he takes off along the canal in an abandoned boat. His brother Chris, who has kept Creep alive by sneaking leftovers to his closet prison, searches frantically when he finds him missing. But Creep, as finally becomes clear to Chris and to readers, has somehow slipped back into the 19th century—and, accompanied by two ill-treated runaways from the earlier period, into the cruel, crippling world of child labor. Walsh draws on contemporary reformist reports about maimed and whip-driven children for her descriptions of the very young trio's bouts of employment; meanwhile Chris, at the library, seeks his brother in those same old documents—and finds him, in one Nathaniel Creep's own account of a long, harsh, but happily married life. The book is slow to start, detailing Creep's route along the canal for a considerable way before his situation becomes clear; but once into its quiet, British flow, you'll find those sudden turning points—when Chris comes up against the 150-year-old letters spelling CREEP carved into a bridge; when Creep, after a semi-ghostlike sojourn in the 19th-century past, suddenly breaks through in full flesh, consumed with hunger—that much more involving. Moving, too, without a trace of sentimentality, are Creep's relationships with his child companions. Combining bleakest reality with a highly

imaginative construct, *A Chance Child* emerges as an extraordinarily well-knit and atmospheric time fantasy.

Laura Geringer

SOURCE: A review of *A Chance Child,* in *School Library Journal,* Vol. 25, No. 5, January, 1979, p. 63.

Caged in a dark nook below the stairs by his mother who tries to starve him, Creep escapes, finds a boat and follows a black, winding canal back to the late 18th Century and the beginning of the Industrial Revolution in England. His journey first floats him into a coal mine where, visible only to children, he saves Tom, a scarred but sturdy lad, from daily beatings, and on to a chain link forge where he meets his future bride, Blackie, an 8-year-old angelic girl whose crooked face is half charred from having fallen asleep and toppled into the fire during an endless night of treading the bellows. The wanderings of the runaway trio provide Walsh with a fictional peg upon which to hang well-researched and blood chilling accounts of the blighting labor conditions youngsters withstood in the "bad old days." Detailed descriptions of the workings of giant machines, the dreary and crippling tasks required to keep them going, and the transformation of green lands into grim pits and slashes in the earth are raw, precise, and memorable. Clipped dialogue including dialect and period idioms is pungent and, despite some unusual vocabulary, will not be a problem to good readers. Although the markings of historical tract show through the sometimes thin veneer of novel, the dramatic tension is sustained throughout by the artful handling of the time travel theme and the deft juxtaposition in alternate chapters of a parallel plot: Creep's half brother searches for the missing boy, tracking him, finally, to a capsule farewell in an obscure volume of Parliamentary Papers. Cleverly wrought and highly charged.

Paul Heins

SOURCE: A review of *A Chance Child,* in *The Horn Book Magazine,* Vol. LV, No. 1, February, 1979, p. 64.

It is not often that grim reality is presented in the mode of fantasy, but the author of *Fireweed, The Emperor's Winding Sheet,* and *Goldengrove* (all Farrar) has told a twofold story in which past and present impinge upon each other. Creep, an unwanted half-starved illegitimate child confined in a nook below the stairs, escaped when wreckers came to the house next door and made a hole in the wall. Finding himself in a sordid dump, he discovered an abandoned canal boat on a stretch of black water and sought shelter in it. He followed the course of the waterway, which took him to the England of the early years of the industrial revolution. Creep, however, had a half-brother who cherished him and used to feed him as best he could; and when Creep disappeared, the older boy explored the local canal system in search of him. Unsuccessful, but following a hunch, Christopher discovered the Parliamentary Papers of the first half of the nineteenth century and read them in an attempt to learn the fate of his brother. Modern urban devastation and nineteenth-century industrial landscapes are juxtaposed, and a neglected, mistreated twentieth-century child becomes the companion of two abandoned children seeking work in mine, foundry, factory, or mill. Chapters alternating between Creep's story and Christopher's form a firmly intermeshed counter-point of implied historical commentary, focusing on Christopher's emotions and Creep's experiences. The author's vivid and terrifying word pictures of the satanic mills are never allowed to turn the story in the direction of melodrama, and the element of time fantasy never supersedes the understated but genuine humanity of the characterization.

Bulletin of the Center for Children's Books

SOURCE: A review of *A Chance Child*, in *The Bulletin of the Center for Children's Books*, Vol. 32, April, 1979, p. 147.

Creep is an odd wan, a thin and silent child whose identity remains a mystery until well after his story begins; he proves to be the half-brother of a contemporary child who searches for Creep while the latter is having a series of grim adventures (in which he is joined by two other children) in various enterprises employing child labor during the time of the Industrial Revolution. The writing style is smooth but at times heavy, and the story gets off to a slow start; while this is a dramatic exposé of the cruel practices in the factories and coal mines of the period, it doesn't quite mesh as a time-shift story.

The Junior Bookshelf

SOURCE: A review of *A Chance Child*, in *The Junior Bookshelf*, Vol. 43, No. 2, April, 1979, p. 120.

A new book by this author is always of interest. This one is a complex 'Travel in Time' story. A neglected and cruelly treated child, Creep, finds himself—he does not know how nor does the reader—150 years back in the time of the Industrial Revolution with its hapless child victims. There he stays and finds some security and content.

A straightforward narrative? Far from it for the reader only learns of Creep's story gradually in a narrative which alternates with the search by Christopher of the twentieth century for his lost half-brother. It is difficult also to equate the wraith, invisible to all but children, with the real person Creep becomes, a printer of the nineteenth century.

The author has used this device of bridging time to inform the reader in detail of the misery of children in mines, nail-making, the cotton mills and the potteries. The overall impression is of a didactic and depressing book which not only dwells on the exploitation of children long ago, but reminds the reader uncomfortably that even in our own times, children are victims of cruelty.

Betsy Hearne

SOURCE: A review of *A Chance Child*, in *Booklist*, Vol. 75, No. 15, April 1, 1979.

A boy raised in a locked closet chances out of his prison when it is knocked open by a wrecking ball. Accepting the only name he's heard, Creep wanders down a river, through a lock, and into the past, where he finds children of the English Industrial Revolution just as mistreated as he. Joining forces with two of them, he establishes a place for himself, grows up, and leaves a message to be discovered by his brother, the only person who ever fed or cared for him. The writing is elegantly styled, the characterization practiced, and the concept intriguing. Unfortunately the beginning is mystifying as to concrete facts, and there is also some confusion as to whether the boy is ghost-like before he turns into a real citizen of the nineteenth century. Practiced readers of fantasy who can suspend their disbelief over this will find much to absorb and enjoy.

Margery Fisher

SOURCE: A review of *A Chance Child*, in *Growing Point*, Vol. 18, No. 1, May, 1979, p. 3517.

A Chance Child . . . must be read with head as well as heart; the full effect of the book depends on responding completely to its atmosphere while being aware also of the correspondences and connections that give it structural unity as well as providing clues to its meaning. The interaction here is between a gritty, grimy city with a filthy canal in the present day and the same grimy neighbourhood during the early days of the Industrial Revolution, when the canal is still incomplete. This waterway, flowing from warehouse and foundry to green fields, is the link between times as well as places, and between the characters as well. It is by way of the canal that Creep, a battered illegitimate child of the present, finds the way to his *alter ego* in the past. As an old flatboat, moving by unknown agency, carries the boy along the murky water, it leads him to work—brutal, bitter work for a small boy—in coal-mine, chain-forge, ceramic workshops, foundry and cotton mill—and brings him two friends, Tom from the mine and Blackie from the forge, both of whom can see him, though to the grown-ups he is at most times an invisible presence. Almost like a conscience, or (as some think) a knocker or mine-spirit, Creep moves towards his identity, till at the moment when he laughs spontaneously he becomes visible and actual and begins a life which, recorded in a pamphlet, is found as evidence for that identity by his half-brother, who has tried to find him in the twentieth century before realising he must look in the records of a grim past. This is a harsh book, shot with the lurid light of night fires and dark with cruelty, but though the author has spared us none of the horror of the details recorded in nineteenth-century Commissions on child-employment, she has contained them properly within her story, and has, besides, drawn some unexpected conclusions. Thus, Creep in the present day, hidden in a cupboard by his bitter mother, gets no help from the Welfare officers who have missed the fact of his existence; it is his counterpart, the Nathaniel Creep who leaves his testament for his descendant, who escapes from oppression by his own efforts. The emaciated boy and his derelict craft in their cruise along the midland canal are at once images of a cruel past and present and the centre of an intricate story of an individual whose existence, whether intermittent or continued, is never in doubt.

Books for Your Children

SOURCE: A review of *A Chance Child*, in *Books for Your Children*, Vol. 14, No. 4, Autumn, 1979, p. 9.

Creep is a chance child, a Spirit of all those neglected children who slaved in mine, factory and mill throughout the days of child labour and exploitation. This is a story to be taken at several levels; as poetry, as a fantasy, as the story of a modern boy searching for a lost brother. It is most beautifully written as are all Jill Paton Walsh's books and is a story not to be missed by any book loving child from around 10.

THE GREEN BOOK (1982)

Margery Fisher

SOURCE: A review of *The Green Book*, in *Growing Point*, Vol. 20, No. 6, March, 1982, p. 4025.

Forecasts of the future can be minatory or philosophical or predictable developments of space technology can be used merely to provide new venues to refresh familiar adventure plots. *The Green Book* is in essence a Robinsonnade projected into an unspecified but not too distant future. A small group of selected families from Earth land from a small antiquated space-ship (Britain as an 'old and poorer country' came last in the share-out when Earth was evacuated) on a small planet of acceptable atmosphere but bleak appearance. Allowed one book apiece, several children have brought *Robinson Crusoe,* and the first actions of the settlers in looking for water and making shelters are so far traditional that the reader is lulled into almost cosy security. Even if technology must be forgotten and hand-skills recalled, there can be little danger here, with no detectable animals or aliens and a soil seemingly suitable for the precious seed-corn. Speaking to the middle years through her central characters, Pattie and Jason (youngest of the group apart from infants born on the long journey), the author skirts gracefully the dangers of the crystalline structures of plants and the abrasiveness of varied personalities. But this is not the simple tale it might appear. From its carefully selected Crusonian details it moves to deeper implications. In a hidden valley found by the children, exquisite butterfly-like beings emerge from inhospitable boulders; it is the children who find a way to communicate with the winged creatures, in dancing and chasing games all can share. And it is the children who point to the one unsuspected gap in the carefully thought out development of the colony. The family choice of book is illuminating. Father's 'Dictionary of Alternative Technology' quickly becomes a standard reference book, as useful as Sarah's 'Pony Club rides again' is useless. Pattie's choice exasperated her family: she had brought an elegantly bound commonplace book with gilded edges, 'creamy silk ribbon to mark the places, and pretty brown and white flowered endpapers. And it was quite empty.' Sharing their goods at the end of the first months with their fellow-colonists, Father (who has become the community's story-teller) orders Pattie to add her book to the scant store of usable paper. He finds the book 'full of writing, very large and round and shaky': Pattie has become the colony's historian. The point is neatly made, almost offhand and in a subtly moving way; it brings to a fine conclusion a book which takes one possible line, and an optimistic one, on man's speculative future.

Dorothy Nimmo

SOURCE: A review of *The Green Book,* in *The School Librarian,* Vol. 30, No. 1, March, 1982, p. 39.

A small group from the doomed Earth sets out in an obsolescent spacecraft for an unknown planet carrying with them the bare necessities, including one book each. Pattie, the youngest, takes a book of blank pages, the green book, which she fills with this story and as Father reads it aloud everyone gathers round 'ready to make the words huge with listening to them'. They have exhausted *Robinson Crusoe* and the *Dictionary of Intermediate Technology;* only their own story is going to help them. The settlers find a way to light their homes with jellyfish oil, the boulders in the valley hatch into giant butterflies which fly away, the wheat grows crystalline and they think it is inedible but no, they can make a new kind of bread. I can believe these to be myths for the beginning of a new world. It is a beautifully optimistic book.

The Junior Bookshelf

SOURCE: A review of *The Green Book,* in *The Junior Bookshelf,* Vol. 46, No. 3, June, 1982, pp. 97-8.

The Green Book, . . . [is] a very carefully shaped and beautifully written space story, delicately and imaginatively illustrated by Joanna Stubbs. The elements of the plot are not new—flight from an earth on the brink of destruction and the struggle for survival in a "desert" setting—but Jill Paton Walsh dresses these in details which make them accustomed and believable, not least the mystery over the child-narrator's identity, so charmingly resolved by the surprise ending. The planet on which the battered old space ship lands is a kindly one, with attractive landsape and seasons despite the difficulties caused by its metallic vegetation: Pattie, the youngest of the central family, names it "Shine." The explorers' projected social structure is in the actuality reserved, and as crops fail and the future looks black, the children's father, with his handbook of intermediate technology, becomes of more importance than the scientist—leader of the expedition. With their greater attention to detail, the children of the colony are the ones who find the only intelligent form of life and a means of future subsistence. There is wry comment on human nature, for instance the unsuitable "single book" chosen by most travellers: 4 copies of *Robinson Crusoe,* with its deceptively similar but much easier situation, Pattie's empty green album, and no Shakespeare. This is a book worth more than many such SF tales for younger readers, with a charm which masks an underlying depth of conception.

Kirkus Reviews

SOURCE: A review of *The Green Book,* in *Kirkus Reviews,* Vol. L, No. 12, June 15, 1982, pp. 678-79.

"Father said, 'We can take very little with us.'" So begins this tale of space-age pioneers, who then travel for four years to a distant planet where they will try to establish a colony. Others, in more sophisticated ships, are headed still further. (Walsh doesn't say why the earth is being abandoned, but the problem seems to be slow atmospheric change, not nuclear destruction.) Each passenger is allowed one book, and Father chooses a fat *Dictionary of Technology.* A plain mechanic on earth, he plans to be "the contriver," and thus an important person, at Shine, the new home. Daughter Sarah reprimands Father, reminding him that everyone here counts equally—a conversation that might seem to foreshadow a larger conflict, but doesn't. Father's skills and his book do prove useful, however, as the people build dwellings of split "trees" which aren't at all like wood. All the vegetation in fact turns out to be shiny and clear like glass, and the glassy grass kills the rabbits brought from earth. When vegetables from earth seeds fail, and then the wheat also grows hard and faceted, the colonists despair: once their imported rations are gone, there will be "only a box of pills that would be kinder than hunger." But then Sarah undertakes to grind and cook the glassy wheat; and when she and brother Joe and little sister Patti eat it and survive, the colony is saved. It will also have a history, for Patti's one book has been a blank one, and when Father opens it at the end he begins to read: "Father said, 'We can take very little with us.'" With descriptions of life on Shine, and with a fluttery passage wherein friendly giant moths hatch out and dance with the children before flying off, the book (Patti's and Walsh's) is written in the stately, solemn manner of an important chronicle. If you can accept this as such, it is expertly done; but readers seeking imaginative speculation, philosophic ideas, or glimpses of the future will be disappointed.

Katharyn F. Crabbe

SOURCE: A review of *The Green Book,* in *School Library Journal,* Vol. 29, No. 2, October, 1982, pp. 156-57.

The Green Book is a clever and beautifully shaped little combination of future fiction and metafiction. A first-person narrative, it is the record of the exodus of a group of Britons from a dying Earth to a new planet. These inhabitants of "an old and poorer country" have been given an old spaceship and told to limit their personal luggage severely. When Pattie, the youngest, is discovered to have brought an empty commonplace book, she is ridiculed. After years of travel, the company land and establish their settlement, Shine. The basic form of the new world is crystalline—trees and flowers shatter like glass, and the wheat (the only Earth crop that flourishes) yields "a pile of hexagonal yellow beads. . . . " In short, though beautiful, the planet does not seem to be hospitable to humans, and the adults despair. The naive courage of the children, who grind the wheat to make bread, saves the colony. Then, when the adults requisition the useless **Green Book** to record the distribution of the crop, they discover that it has become the most important of their supplies, for by then it has been filled with Pattie's story, at once the beginning of the history and literature of the new culture. Walsh is an excellent stylist who can create a mood in a single sentence: "Father said, 'We can take very little with us.'" The story is compelling and poetic, and the narrative strategy resembles E. Nesbit's in the way Pattie reveals herself throughout but is not revealed until the end.

The Horn Book

SOURCE: A review of *The Green Book,* in *The Horn Book Magazine,* Vol. LVIII, No. 6, December, 1982, pp. 651-52.

With Earth's destruction imminent, three children and their father join a hand-picked group which embarks on a long journey to a small—and they hope—life-supporting planet. Fascinated by the planet's glittery, sparkling quality, the youngest child names it Shine. Ironically, the same quality threatens the colonists when they discover that the plant life is crystalline. The glasslike grass presumably causes their rabbits' death; vegetable seeds fail to produce, and although wheat flourishes, its grains are hard and faceted. With the planet's fauna inedible (only green jellyfish, which the group burns for light, and giant ephemeral moths whose wing fibers they weave into cloth), the colony faces starvation. But Sarah, the middle child, gambles; secretly, she grinds the wheat grains into flour, cooks and eats it—and survives, thereby saving the colony. Moving quickly and credibly through the profusely illustrated pages, the story raises thought-provoking questions for an age group

for which there is little serious science fiction: Is survival possible on another planet? What might life be like? What would be necessary for survival? The characters, although minimally developed, seem real and are perceptively presented. Yet the somber tone and the emphasis on loss, boredom, and death are oppressive; despite the glitter of Shine, life there seems somewhat lackluster.

BABYLON (1982)

Margery Fisher

SOURCE: A review of *Babylon,* in *Growing Point,* Vol. 21, No. 2, July, 1982, p. 3916.

Picture-story books are required to tell a story, but not necessarily, or at least not primarily, in words. In a genre where the number of words is limited (in some degrees even in picture-story books for older children), it is for the illustrator to expand the text by suggesting emotion, setting and atmosphere, supplying descriptive or dramatic detail (and even, in a few cases, totally reversing the point of the text for satirical purposes). This is not to diminish the importance of the text; at its best, the alliance is one of equals, each working towards excellence within agreed limits. The story of **Babylon,** simple in itself, is turned into a mini-novel of character and circumstance as much by Jill Paton Walsh's scrupulously selected words as by Jennifer Northway's glowing pictures. Three West Indian children explore the soaring viaduct of a closed railway, looking down with interest on a rich variety of back-yards. For David and Lesley the adventure is fun and no more: Dulcie, christening the overgrown heights Babylon, is overcome with sadness, for she was born in England and can't remember their Babylon, Jamaica, as the others can. Back home, she complains to her mother that she has 'nothing to weep for'; her mother has an answer—'Don't matter where you been, or where you never been, you surely will have something to weep for, by and by'. Unerringly reflecting the child's point of view as she has done throughout her tale, the author assures us that the child is cheered by this statement, and the artist confirms this unerringly, as she has in every phase of the anecdote shown the glee, the occasional nervousness and the moments of reflection in the children. Add to that her addition of visual adjectives, with brilliant colour-wash suggesting an exotic, flower-filled secret place where the children, as their faces show, are for a time in command of the world below, and you have a sequence of pictures whose style exactly fits the case.

The Junior Bookshelf

SOURCE: A review of *Babylon,* in *The Junior Bookshelf,* Vol. 46, No. 4, August, 1982, p. 137.

A disused railway viaduct runs through the inner city. Its shadow blights Dulcie's backyard, but from David's window halfway up a tower block the children can see wildflowers growing atop the ancient brickwork. Eventually, with their friend Lesley, they manage to reach nature's garden in the sky. Walking along it their imaginations range from the hanging gardens of Babylon and on to Zion. For David and Lesley these thoughts recall memories of their own homeland, Jamaica. It saddens Dulcie that, having been born in England, she has no Zion to cry for.

Jill Paton Walsh enriches this slight story by sounding a faint echo of Caribbean speech rhythms in her text. Happiest feature of all is the collaboration of this experienced writer with a less familiar but extremely talented artist. Jennifer Northway's illustrations transform what is almost a slum into an environment as vivid and colourful as its West Indian inhabitants.

Publishers Weekly

SOURCE: A review of *Babylon,* in *Publishers Weekly,* Vol. 222, December 3, 1982, p. 60.

The hot, lovely colors in Northway's paintings convey the atmosphere of a London working-class area where a black child, Dulcie, goes exploring with her friends, David and Leslie. On top of a high, long-disused railway viaduct, the three walk in a profusion of wild flowers, a place Dulcie says is like the hanging gardens of Babylon. "Why they weep in that hymn about the waters of Babylon?" Leslie asks. Dulcie says that a bad king has brought the people there, out of Zion, and they are crying for their own country. The boys remember Africa, their Zion, but Dulcie is sad: "I always been here; I ain't got no Zion to weep for." Later, David's mother tells Dulcie she needn't worry: "You will surely have something to weep for, by and by." And Dulcie, cheered up, runs singing home. Adults, grasping the profound implications in Walsh's story, will be glad that children will enjoy it only as the exciting adventure it is on the surface. This stands as one of the award-winning British author's most impressive creations.

The Horn Book

SOURCE: A review of *Babylon,* in *The Horn Book Magazine,* Vol. LIX, No. 1, February, 1983, p. 39.

Children often transform biblical stories into their everyday play, and the author has sensitively dramatized such play. The actors are three black children of Jamaican ancestry who live in a crowded row of urban houses in England, overshadowed by an old railway viaduct. The Jamaican lilt of the children's speech is neatly phrased by the author; and this catch in rhythm is echoed in the subtle changes that pace the story as the children seek a way to the top of the disused viaduct. Their spoken cadence gives a tone of strangeness to the barren land in which the children live, and the reader senses the need for their climb. Once there, the three children find a world in bloom—a seemingly suspended garden of wild flowers. The setting reminds them of the song "'By the rivers of Babylon, where we sat down . . . Where we sat down, there we wept, When we remembered Zion.'" For the garden suggests the hanging gardens of Babylon, and the game becomes real. David and Lesley remember Jamaica as their Zion and can weep for their reminiscences of that land; Dulcie, however, was born in England and is saddened when she realizes she has no Zion to weep for. Rather than picture the drabness of the place, the lively illustrations capture the spirit of the children and their speech and pleasurably amplify the story. The boys feel the song of Zion deeply. Dulcie's ultimate joy, which David's mother tenderly offers her, is the climax of the quiet tale.

John W. Blos

SOURCE: A review of *Babylon,* in *School Library Journal,* Vol. 29, No. 9, May, 1983, p. 67.

Two Jamaican children in London, and Dulcie, who was born in London, climb to the railway viaduct which transects their neighborhood. Long unused and now overgrown, it seems to Dulcie a hanging garden. "We in Babylon," she exults. This book is lovely and daring; but it may attempt too much. While the deep-toned full-color illustrations on smooth and lustrous paper provide a rich effect, it is questionable how much will be understood by the intended audience. Many five to eight year olds will be more than puzzled by the protagonist's observation that, "Babylon ain't no fun without you got Zion to weep for." And how many will hear the harmonics of meaning in David's mumma's answering statement; "Don't matter where you been, or where you never been, you surely will have something to weep for, by and by"?

📖 *A PARCEL OF PATTERNS* (1983)

Jean Mercier

SOURCE: A review of *A Parcel of Patterns*, in *Publishers Weekly,* Vol. 224, No. 23, December 2, 1988, p. 89.

In the fall of 1665, a tailor in the Derbyshire village of Eyam received a parcel of cloth patterns from London, contaminated pieces that infected him with the plague. Before the fall of 1666, nearly 300 of the village's approximately 350 inhabitants died of the disease. When the people realized their helplessness, they agreed to cut themselves off to avoid spreading the plague to neighboring communities.

This history is the bedrock on which the British author builds a novel that draws readers into the account related by Mall Percival, a young woman betrothed to Thomas Torre, who lives outside the doomed village. Mall describes incidents of suffering, heroism and cowardice as well as her savage grief when she alone in her family survives. Determined to save Tom, she sends word that she is dead but the news she hopes will keep him away brings him to her side and they marry. Together, they care for the sick and Tom takes over the burial chores when the gravedigger dies.

The gravedigger is one of many real people whose records the author has studied and shares with the reader. A strapping, kind youth digs his own grave to save the small people in his family the need. Eyam's two parsons, divided by conflicting dogma, unite to console and support the survivors who voluntarily isolate themselves. A spiteful woman declares that only sinners are stricken; the "Godly" like herself will be saved. A few frightened people sneak out of the village. A compassionate nobleman sends the besieged inhabitants food and medicine daily.

The Unleaving and Walsh's other novels are honor winners in England and America, and this beautifully written, meaningful story should add to her laurels.

Margery Fisher

SOURCE: A review of *A Parcel of Patterns*, in *Growing Point,* Vol. 22, No. 5, January, 1984, pp. 4182-83.

Scholarship and novelistic skill consort well together in *A Parcel of Patterns.* With the familiar, well-documented story of the Derbyshire village of Eyam as her source, Jill Paton Walsh has had no room for invention as far as plot is concerned, but she has been free to develop the personalities of the actors in this sombre drama, lightly in the case of those who really lived (the parson Momphesson and his wife, for example) and more fully in those she has invented or expanded from recorded names, with Mall Percival the narrator and her sweetheart Thomas Torre central among them. She has also brilliantly extended the local map, picturing in detail the known contours of the parish, the village street and cottages, and using locality as one way of conveying the atmosphere of that small village, devastated by plague and finding a brave way to contain infection. The horrifying effect of plague on Eyam comes to us sometimes through direct statement, sometimes in dialogue, and often in this kind of reverberant, intuitive description:

> I walked down Eyam street like a stranger, as though I looked upon it as had seen it never before, and came to Sydall's house, of which the door stood wide, with coltsfoot growing free upon the threshold. I stepped within, staring all around. Grass grew up through each chink between the floor-flags; the pewter plates and pans were tarnished dark, the kettle flecked with rust, and in the garden windows spiders spun screens of web all thick with dust. The rain through the cold chimney had wet the hearth-stone, greening now with moss, and the linnet lay dead in its hanging wicker cage.

It is not only the precise domestic detail that touches the reader here but also, and above all, the rhythmic, singing prose which is unequalled in its flexibility, now offering neutral dialogue which still suggests the 1660's in sentence structure and syntax, now communicating through Mall's young, warm-hearted voice the appalling facts of the months after the canvas dress-patterns for pretty Catherine Momphesson's coveted London fashions had been delivered to a journeyman tailor lodging in the village. This is a fine example of the way imagination and craftsmanship can work on fact without distortion, without partiality, without romanticisation, and bring the past within our view.

The Junior Bookshelf

SOURCE: A review of *A Parcel of Patterns*, in *The Junior Bookshelf,* Vol. 48, No. 1, February, 1984, p. 37.

Jill Paton Walsh's liking for a strong historical background for her novels has certainly been put to good use in this her latest novel. The village of Eyam in

Derbyshire shut itself off from the rest of England in an attempt to contain the outbreak of Plague brought in by a parcel of patterns sent up from London to satisfy the vanity of fashion-conscious Catherine Momphesson, the parson's pretty young wife. The story is told by Mall Percival, a character of the author's invention. The others are supplied by the records of the ill-fated village that watched over so many deaths and burials before the plague passed away and our heroine sets out for America to start a new life with Francis Torre. It is a bitter-sweet ending since her heart had been given to Thomas the brother of Francis but her foolishness had lured Thomas into the plague-stricken village and to her eternal self-reproach he was smitten and died.

How skilfully Mrs. Walsh has captured the atmosphere of this isolated village with its medical ignorance and religious wisdom! The dead are buried so long as the living are able and the hand of God sought despairingly in explanation. Mall tells her story in a style and with a sentence structure which cleverly creates the atmosphere of those times so long ago and the skill with which it is maintained throughout contributes greatly to the authenticity of the milieu.

Young readers who stay with this stark theme and serious treatment will experience the rewards that a novel of this quality can bring.

Barbara Chatton

SOURCE: A review of *A Parcel of Patterns,* in *School Library Journal,* Vol. 30, No. 6, February, 1984, pp. 85-6.

Mall Percival is 16 when a parcel of patterns for new dresses brings the plague to her town of Eyam, England in 1665. Before the plague begins, Mall introduces readers to the people of her town and tells of her secret courtship with the shepherd, Thomas. Through her eyes readers watch the devastation of life and family ties and of the individual spirit as the disease, at first sporadic, gains strength and ravishes the town. When the villagers voluntarily cut themselves off from the world to prevent the spread of the plague, Mall terminates her relationship with Thomas with disastrous consequences. Readers enter a time period in which narrow-minded Puritan townspeople find it easy to believe that those who die must be sinners; a time when suspicion of a new liberal parson keeps many from practices which might prevent the spread of the plague. Walsh writes in the 17th-century speech patterns Mall Percival would have used; this language provides a formidable obstacle. While tena-

cious readers will find the language becoming more comprehensible as they become involved in the trials of the villagers, many readers may give up before the drama of the story can capture their interest. But those who persevere will be rewarded; this is a fine novel and Mall is an engaging heroine.

Rodie Sudbery

SOURCE: A review of *A Parcel of Patterns,* in *The School Librarian,* Vol. 32, No. 1, March, 1984, p. 73.

This is the story of the plague in Eyam, the Derbyshire village which enclosed itself to protect other people from infection; a compulsive account of heroism and suffering in which we see the bravery and endurance of the villagers and the growing fear both within Eyam and outside. The eventual decision to seal the village off separated an actual pair of lovers, Roland and Emmot; to them the author has added an imaginary pair, Thomas and Mall. Their fate has an unexpected pattern and a moving inevitability of its own. We experience the year through the record of Mall, who (unusually among her contemporaries) can read and write. I readily accepted this for the sake of descriptions like that of the tailor, sitting in concentration before his steaming, smelling pattern pieces from London 'so still that there was not stir enough in the room to fright the rats from creeping about the floor'; and the magnificent last sentence, in which Mall sums up the human plight in words that cannot be bettered.

The Horn Book

SOURCE: A review of *A Parcel of Patterns,* in *The Horn Book Magazine,* Vol. LX, No. 2, April, 1984, p. 203.

In the late seventeenth century a package of contaminated dress patterns was delivered to a tailor in the small Derbyshire village of Eyam, causing an outbreak of the plague, which destroyed nearly three quarters of its population. From actual records and histories the author has created an engrossing story of the disaster as experienced by a young girl, Mall Percival. To rid herself of her grief and her horror, Mall recorded her memories of that frightful time during which the plague ran its course. "Many of the smallest and some of the strangest details," the author tells us, are "from the history and traditions of Eyam." To contain the disease the town apparently did voluntarily isolate itself from neighboring villages and was provisioned by the generosity—and prudence—of the Duke of Chatsworth. Mall recounted the clash between the old puritanical minister, who believed that God would preserve the righteous, and his more worldly practical replacement. She recalled the petty meanness, the brief moments of humor, and the acts of great compassion and courage. In understated prose the horrors of the disease—the stench and the mounting deaths—come vividly to life. Yet amid the terror friendships endure and love grows between Mall and the young Thomas Torre, as the author skillfully re-creates the speech cadences and the beauties and homely details of rural seventeenth-century England.

Mary W. Sucher

SOURCE: A review of *A Parcel of Patterns,* in *Voice of Youth Advocates,* Vol. 7, No. 1, April, 1984, p. 36.

Based on the true story of Eyam's devastation by the plague, this is told in the first person by Mall, who was 16 when the new parson came to her Derbyshire village in the spring of 1665. The plague came to Eyam on the parcel of patterns sent from London at the request of the parson's wife. So many had died by the following June that the parson and the strong Puritan minister he had replaced both urged the villagers, for the good of the rest of the country, to swear not to leave their village. Compassion and cruelty, self-sacrifice and selfishness all color Mall's realistic chronicle, full of the nuance of the terror of the disease which is, nevertheless, met with the knowledge that life must go on. Along with this true story of the plague-torn village, the quiet beauty of Mall's time spent with her sheep and her love for the shepherd she had met when only eight add a bittersweet note to the account. The exceptionally beautiful and meaningful dust-jacket will encourage many teenagers to open the covers for a deeply affective reading experience. Interesting note: John Rowe Townsend first told the author Eyam's story.

Sylvia Oettle

SOURCE: A review of *A Parcel of Patterns,* in *ALAN Review,* Vol. 11, No. 3, Spring, 1994, p. 33.

In the year 1666, according to history and tradition, the village of Eyam in Derbyshire was struck by the Plague. The disease had arrived in a package sent from London to the journeyman tailor who was to fashion garments for the new parson's wife.

In Jill Paton Walsh's *A Parcel of Patterns,* Mall Percival relates the tragedies wrought by the deadly disease. Although the story is mainly hers, her percep-

tion guides her to chronicle the effects of the Plague on family, friends, and neighbors as well. It is Mall's hope that in recording the events, she will rid herself of their traumas.

The tale is told in the language of the times, a wholesome departure from the brazen tongue that pervades so many young adult novels today. The metaphors have an old world charm; and though much of the story deals with fear and hopelessness, the tone, paradoxically, is gentle. Drawn with particular sensitivity is the relationship between Mall and her beloved Thomas whom she hopes to marry.

Since the language and events in *A Parcel of Patterns* are not contemporary, the book may have limited appeal. It is recommended for supplementary reading, grades seven through ten.

GAFFER SAMSON'S LUCK (1984)

Bulletin of the Center for Children's Books

SOURCE: A review of *Gaffer Samson's Luck,* in *The Bulletin of the Center for Children's Books,* Vol. 38, No. 5, January, 1985, p. 97.

Here is a dependably fine writer at her best. Jill Paton Walsh writes with sentiment but without sentimentality, in a story with a vivid, evocative setting. Her characterization is rich and strong, with a seamless knitting of people and events, a touching story of friendship between a young boy and a very old man, Gaffer Samson. His "luck" is a lucky charm, long hidden, that young James hunts for, finds, and passes on to someone else. Among its other strengths, this is a trenchant story about a child's courage and adaptability, as James works to become accepted in the rigid clan structure of the children in the village, to which he has just moved, in the English Fens.

Ethel R. Twichell

SOURCE: A review of *Gaffer Samson's Luck,* in *The Horn Book Magazine,* Vol. LXI, No. 2, March-April, 1985, p. 181.

Employing a familiar theme—a child's struggle for acceptance in a new community—the author creates an unusual story of grace, thoughtfulness, and wit. James feels utterly displaced when he moves with his parents from the rugged landscape of Yorkshire to the English fen country—a vast flat watery terrain stretching away under an open sky. Living in an interesting old cottage, he is rejected as a stranger by his classmates—most belligerently by the tough, suspicious village children. In despair the boy realizes that his only friends are Angey, a faithful, ragged part-Gipsy girl ostracized at school, and old Gaffer Samson, his helplessly ill next-door neighbor. When "the Gaffer" begs James to hunt for a stone luck charm that has lain buried for seven years, the boy undertakes a fruitless search for it in the remains of the old man's former home. Then, after a week of heavy rain the land lies drowned—its normal contours submerged "under floodwater, for miles and miles. The river was nowhere: the river was everywhere. The air sky and the water sky fused seamlessly on the horizon. And the world shone above, below, and from edge to edge." In the dramatic climax James not only sees revealed the Gaffer's ruined cottage, but in the dark of that night he braves the ruthless water and triumphantly meets the dangerous challenge of the village gang. Descriptive, often metaphorical, images lend richness and vigor to the storytelling, but the book is no mere exercise in fine writing. Imbuing the narrative with a graphic, insistent sense of place, the author has also woven into it patterns of social custom, human behavior, and childhood feelings, giving the brief novel both sensibility and suspense.

LOST AND FOUND (1985)

Ron Morton

SOURCE: A review of *Lost and Found,* in *Books for Your Children,* Vol. 20, No. 1, Spring, 1985, p. 16.

Jill Paton Walsh has come up with an idea which is simple yet clever—and I only wish that I had thought of it first! The story consists of four similar yet interrelated incidents separated in time. Little Ag, a boy living in the Iron Age, is given the task of taking a much needed arrowhead to his grandfather. On the way he is distracted by something else which causes him to lose the arrowhead, thereby leaving him to continue his journey with his new find which he offers to his grandfather as compensation.

A couple of centuries later a child is given the task of delivering a jug of milk to her grandmother becomes distracted when she discovers an old arrowhead. Forgetting where she put the jug, she completes her journey making the offer of her find to her grandmother in place of the lost jug of milk. And so the pattern is repeated throughout the passage of time.

What I particularly like about the book is the game-story element similar to those round-the class

memory games that children are encouraged to play and which are thoroughly enjoyed. With *Lost and Found,* when read aloud to a class of children they soon got the gist of the story and quickly extended it beyond its historical settings and into other geographical and cultural surroundings. This is a good book for developing that aspect of reading involving anticipation and prediction, but it is ideally for the more accomplished reader, for the text is quite full whilst the competent illustrations serve the continuity. A useful book for the classroom.

Bulletin of the Center for Children's Books

SOURCE: A review of *Lost and Found,* in *The Bulletin of the Center for Children's Books,* September, 1985.

Although the patterned nature of the story strikes an artificial note (each child sent on an errand loses what he or she is carrying, but finds the article lost by the previous child) most children should delight in the concept of articles that become artifacts as the centuries progress. The first child is a prehistoric cavedweller who loses an arrowhead, the next is a child of medieval times who finds the arrowhead and presents it to her grandmother instead of the jug of cream she's mislaid, and so on to a contemporary child and her grandmother. Simply and effectively told, this has no breaks between incidents, but the clothes show a passage of time, as do the architectural details of a growing town and increasingly large and complex bridges crossed by the children. The authors have been careful to keep the language more or less consistent with the period.

TORCH (1988)

The Junior Bookshelf

SOURCE: A review of Torch, in *The Junior Bookshelf,* Vol. 52, February, 1988, p. 55.

Jill Paton Walsh has over the years collected most of the major awards but somehow the Carnegie Medal has eluded her. With this magnificent novel she must now be a very serious contender, the waywardness of some of the recent choices notwithstanding.

Torch is a story of the future. Don't be alarmed. This is not science-fiction but a novel of character and ideas. Cal and Dio are young people living in the tradition-ridden village of Olim. Theirs is to be a marriage of convenience which will unite not so much two people as two plots of land. Before the wedding they must go to the marble fields to seek the approval of the Guardian to the union. When they get there—both of them going reluctantly because they dislike the forced marriage—the Guardian is dying, and in his last hours he makes Dio his heir and gives him a sadly inadequate account of his duties. So begins a quest whose objective is unknown. Dio finds the ancient torch which is to be his charge and lights it from the reflected rays of the sun. So the young couple set out, with a few friends, and take to the mountains.

Gradually, as we read, we realize that all is not as strange as it seems. Dio and Cal and the others have truncated Greek names. Their village is Olympia, and they are carrying the last Olympic torch in search of games which after all these centuries still honour the Olympic ideal.

Their journey takes them to three Games, in Corfu, where the winner is sacrificed to the sea, North Africa, where the races are used as a method of cutting down the surplus population, and Provence, where the atheletes are as valuable and enslaved as racehorses. The sacred flame of the torch refuses to burn for such corruptions of the ideal. At last, the Nikathlon, a boy whom they have picked up on the way and who lives only to run and win, slashes his hamstrings, and they all make their weary way across the cold sea to Britain. There, in a shattered land dominated by the grass-grown swathes of the 'mowerways', the youngsters run for sheer joy of living on a sunset beach, and the torch, long dormant, sends up 'a sudden blaze of glorious, fiery light'.

It is difficult to explain the hypnotic power that this story exercises over the reader. Partly it is sheer brilliance of narrative; this is a writer who knows all about the art of story-telling. All the characters, major and minor, are drawn in depth. Above all, I think, it is the landscape-painting. There are marvellous pictures of the desert in all its heat and strange beauty. One shares too the bitterness of post-nuclear Europe. The story reaches its climax, not in one of the moments of high drama, but in one of the pauses of the children's Odyssey when, in Spain, they find an old scholar who can explain to them the background to their mission. Not even he can tell them the secret of the torch; only Cassie (who is Cassandra) knows this; the knowledge is no comfort to her, but she cannot speak of it. It is not only the scholar who weeps as the children—children no longer—tell their story. They have brought him, and us, a 'living spark' which is 'the impulse in you . . . that made you take

it up and carry it through the world, without understanding what you were doing.' We too may not altogether understand, yet still find inspiration in this powerful and moving story.

Kirkus Reviews

SOURCE: A review of *Torch,* in *Kirkus Reviews,* Vol. LVI, No. 5, March 1, 1988, p. 371.

In a splendid odyssey set a few generations forward—when technology and knowledge are much diminished—the noted British author (*Fireweed, A Parcel of Patterns*) takes a group of young Greeks on a quest for a worthy setting for the long-preserved Olympic flame.

Initially on the run because their vigil with the dying Guardian of the torch has set them outside the law, Dio, his former fiancée Cal (the narrator), and their friends seek a competition to match the legends of "Ago" and "Antiquity"; in so doing they traverse the Mediterranean world and some of history's moral pit falls. At a race on "Corfoo," the drugged winner, a local troublemaker, is tossed over a cliff in a profane fraud of a ritual. Deep in the desert, another winner is rewarded with rich prizes, but a second race is used to weed out the feebler children from an overlarge population. Champion Philip, one of an international group that has joined the travelers, is caught by slavers (unfortunately named Hassades) and sold to run while his rich owner gambles. Meanwhile, the group has grown in wisdom and loyalty, but—until a permanent home is found and a final race is run for pure joy—only Cassie understands the link between the flame and the moral climate that surrounds it.

A richly textured novel with a strong theme concerning the value to society—in any age—of cooperation and choices freely made, this will delight thoughtful readers with the evocative beauty of its language and its neatly interlocking allusions (Dio [genes] carries the lamp), as well as by being a rousing adventure that is especially timely in this Olympic year.

Publishers Weekly

SOURCE: A review of *Torch,* in *Publishers Weekly,* Vol. 233, March 18, 1988, p. 89.

In a time and place that might be in the future but feasibly could have been in the past, Walsh writes of two teenagers, Cal and Dio, who are put in charge of a torch when its old guardian dies. Dio is possessed by the idea of finding the torch's true resting place, and so they begin a journey, accompanied by some friends from their village and taking on others along the way. Some of the people they meet allude to the idea that this torch has come from the fires of the last Olympics; the teenagers are, rightfully or wrongfully, taken as the true torchbearers and find themselves involved with corrupt Games. The torch, they find, has mysterious ways—it only flares up when someone is doing something purely for the love of the act, not for glory. The conceptual landscape of Walsh's journey is powerfully drawn and full of provocative questions about the meaning of sports and sportsmanship. It is a gripping story, both as an adventure and as a timeless quest, with no foreseeable end or any easily inferred answers.

Ilene Cooper

SOURCE: A review of *Torch,* in *Booklist,* Vol. 84, No. 16, April 15, 1988, p. 1439.

Dio and Cal are to visit the old man who lives in the marble fields and receive his permission to marry, but when they reach the ancient ruins, the old man is dying. He appoints Dio the guardian of the torch, something from the Ago when men could fly in the air and carry boxes that gave forth music. Knowing that their futures are doomed because they have spent the night together without being married, Dio and Cal and several other village children run away with the torch, hoping they will find the Games where the flame belongs. So begins a perilous adventure that leads the band to various cultures, where the children are exposed to both good and evil. At times, readers may find the journey arduous as well—the story gets bogged down with too many characters and details. The explanation for the demise of Ago (apparently nuclear disarmament that allowed industrialized countries to be overrun) is not very well explained. Still, Walsh's major characters are well defined, and the basic premise that highlights the true meaning of the Olympic torch is involving.

Christine Behrmann

SOURCE: A review of *Torch,* in *School Library Journal,* Vol. 34, No. 8, May, 1988, p. 111.

Paton Walsh takes on competition, as metaphorically represented by a torch held in secret by a Guardian living in a primitive future society on a Greek island. When Dio and his fiancée, Cal, seek the Guardian for their required marital instruction, they discover that he is near death. He passes on his responsibility for the torch to Dio as they spend the night in his deathwatch. This action so compromises them that they

have no choice but to flee their village, and, joined by other young teens, they go on a quest to find the people who existed in a time called the Ago when games called the Olympiad were held—for this is the last Olympic torch. The journey itself reveals the many faces of the games, as different societies find ways to use contests for selfish and often cruel ends. When one of the teens is kidnapped to run for profit, his companions search for him and meet a scholar who, in the heart of the book, reveals the secret of the Ago. As the book closes, the children have found a home for the torch and themselves. This is not an entirely successful book. Paton Walsh has concentrated so much on the ideas behind her plot that she has left strings dangling, such as the universal use of English by most of the characters, despite their geographic isolation. Also, most of the characters are poorly defined, and some are stereotypes. The lack of attention to detail can mar readers' concentration on the larger ideas of Paton Walsh's narrative, which are indeed challenging and original. If her book is not entirely successful, it is a rewarding challenge to readers who will not emerge with answers but rather an added ability to ask some important questions— not a bad accomplishment for any novel.

Bulletin of the Center for Children's Books

SOURCE: A review of *Torch,* in *The Bulletin of the Center for Children's Books,* Vol. 41, May, 1988, p. 191.

Set, as are so many novels of the future, in a world that has lost its technological knowledge and reverted to a simpler society, this tells of a group of children from Greece who go on a quest. If the setting is familiar, the development is fresh in a story with nuance and suspense. Cal and Dio have agreed, in a deathbed promise to the old Guardian, to take on the quest of finding the "Games" for which he had been guarding the torch. Readers will recognize, as Dio and Cal and the other children move through a series of dangerous adventures, references to the Olympics or variants on names and terms from the past. There is one fantastic element, the torch that dims or lights again in response to their behavior as they search for the place and race that feels right. An intriguing adventure story is written with the author's usual flair, nicely knitting history, legend, and quest.

Carolyn Polese

SOURCE: A review of *Torch,* in *The Christian Science Monitor,* Vol. 80, No. 113, May 6, 1988, p. B6.

Jill Paton Walsh is known for the sensitivity, intelligence, and craftsmanship of her novels. In her latest book, **Torch** she takes young readers into the distant future to explore timeless themes.

When the Guardian entrusts the last Torch to Dio, the boy and his friends leave their isolated Greek village, Olim. Searching for a place to deliver the Torch, the children travel through a world of primitive city-states, the remnants of our own collapsed civilization.

The meaning of the Olympic torch has been lost, as has the written word. To the children, our time—the Ago—is the time of myth, of "mechos and singing boxes and flying cars." Ancient Greece and Rome have slipped beyond memory.

Skillfully, Walsh weaves elements of our own and past cultures into the ageless patterns of mythology to explore themes of freedom and faith. This odyssey is a fresh and personal narrative that will engage readers through the very humanness of its young heroes.

Jean S. Bolley

SOURCE: A review of *Torch,* in *Voice of Youth Advocates,* Vol. 11, No. 3, August, 1988, p. 139.

In a semi-primitive future that refers to our time as Ago, in a remote village in Greece, 13 year olds Cal and Dio are sent, on their wedding day, to get the old man's approval, as is the custom. The find the old man injured and, after appointing Dio Guardian of the Torch and telling him he must watch over it until someone comes to fetch it for the games, the old Guardian dies. Cal, Dio and some of their friends do find the treasure, the last of the torches to be used to light the Olympic flame, but Dio decides to seek out the games rather than wait for someone to come for it. They set out, traveling far, learning a little more about Ago and picking up companions along the way. Cal narrates the story and we learn more about her and the others even as they learn about the Torch, and about themselves. This is a well-written, moving story of special interest in this Olympic year, but not limited to that. Deserves Best Books consideration, highly recommended.

N. Thomas

SOURCE: A review of *Torch,* in *Books for Your Children,* Vol. 24, No. 3, Autumn-Winter, 1989, p. 29.

Set in a post-mechanical future when civilisation has dwindled to a primitive agricultural economy, this powerfully-written story concerns a group of teenage children living on the slopes of Mount Olympus who discover the only surviving Olympic torch and are charged with carrying the Olympic flame to the Games. Unfortunately, no one knows if the Games are still held, let alone where, and though the children journey to other lands the torch itself has the ability to tell them that the games they find are not the true ones. Apart from the sobering picture of the future and the implied indictment of the folly of our own times, the book is full of hope and suggests that the true Olympic spirit is never completely lost.

Adrian Jackson

SOURCE: A review of *Torch,* in *Books for Keeps,* No. 58, September, 1989, p. 12.

It's partly a game played with our expectations: the setting, for instance, reads like the classical past but is a future in which the achievements of the intervening centuries have almost been erased. We come to realise that the children of the story have found the Olympic torch and are responding to the historical quest to carry it to its home. Places and people reveal historical connections, fragments of the past. Where the torch should go is only one question among many—what happened to the science of 'Ago', what quality revives the torch's flame? It's a fascinating book despite an awkward ending and ought to be available to 2nd, 3rd and possible 4th years.

GRACE (1992)

Melody Lott

SOURCE: A review of *Grace,* in *Voice of Youth Advocates,* Vol. 15, No. 5, December, 1992, p. 284.

In October 1838, a violent storm rages off the Northumbrian coast of England. Grace Darling spies a shipwreck during her watch at the lighthouse. She awakens her father and they hurriedly decide to brave a rescue attempt. The sea is tumultuous and the weather foul but their rescue is successful. The are able to heroically save nine lives.

Grace Darling's orderly, quiet life at the lighthouse is totally disrupted by the fervor and pandemonium created after the rescue. Grace becomes an unwilling young heroine. She is showered with letters, gifts, and money. People come from near and far to gawk and worship Grace. She is not granted a moment's respite. Soon, the townspeople come to resent Grace. They accuse her of making the rescue for purely monetary gain and she comes to doubt her own motives. Throughout her ordeal, Grace's family, especially her father, remain steadfast and loyal.

The book is written in the English of the 1800s and younger readers may have difficulty understanding some of the terminology and colloquialisms of that era. However, Grace Darling's story is truly poignant and moving. At first I was not sure if this book was going to appeal to me. After a while, I found myself enjoying **Grace,** and reluctant to put it down.

Eileen Van Kirk

SOURCE: "Imagining the Past Through Historical Novels," in *School Library Journal,* Vol. 39, No. 8, August, 1993, pp. 50-51.

[A] writer who totally captures the era she writes about is Jill Paton Walsh. In **Grace,** she undertakes an even riskier task, because Grace Darling was a real person.

Walsh has kept her narrative as true to life as possible, working from letters, journals, and newspaper articles. (Grace became a national heroine when she assisted her father, a lighthouse keeper, in rescuing survivors of a tragic shipwreck). The author admits, however, to having imagined certain events and conversations. Nonetheless, and with admirable discipline, she keeps Grace's speech, thoughts, and behavior strictly within her own time. The novel is told in the first person, and it is Grace's voice throughout. One would be hard put to tell where facts end and imagination begins.

Also, although the deluge of publicity that followed this rescue was largely due to the fact that a mere girl had temporarily taken over a man's job, Walsh never turns her story into a feminist tract. In 19th-century England, as in America, there was a sharp division of labor among the sexes, and while Grace could stand her watch and tend the lamps in the lighthouse, she was also expected to cook, scrub, polish, mend, and sew. And these things she regarded as her duty.

WHEN GRANDMA CAME (1992)

The Junior Bookshelf

SOURCE: A review of *When Grandma Came,* in *The Junior Bookshelf,* Vol. 56, No. 4, August, 1992, p. 145.

There is plenty of subtlety in Jill Paton Walsh's exquisitely crafted rhythmic prose and in Sophy Williams' accompanying pictures, both dedicated to the beauty of the world and the enduring power of love. Grandma tells little Madeleine about the places she has visited around the world, making lovingly frank comparisons with the child beside her. She has seen Hippos in their mud-bath but 'never seen anything as messy as you!' This is a book for young mums at least as much as for their children, and one in which eternal truths shine out from the pages. There is a fine harmony between author and artist in an outstanding picture-book.

Sue Rogers

SOURCE: A review of *When Grandma Came,* in *The School Librarian,* Vol. 40, No. 4, November, 1992, p. 144.

A picture book which marries the talents of noted author Jill Paton Walsh and a new illustrator, published for the first time, Sophy Williams. It is a sophisticated book which shows a grandmother, returning from roaming around the wonders of the world, meeting her grand-daughter Madeleine for the first time. She tells the little girl that although she has seen some wonderful sights, 'she has never seen anything as "heaven-and-earthly as you!"' The flowing text beautifully portrays the contrast between the sheer scale of the countries of the world and the little girl's home, and Sophy Williams's colourful full-size illustrations have a misty, dreamlike quality to them which greatly enhances the story.

Stephanie Zvirin

SOURCE: A review of *When Grandma Came,* in *Booklist,* Vol. 89, No. 5, November 1, 1992, p. 523.

Double-page spreads summoning delicately edged memories of Grandma's adventurous life alternate with pictures of Grandma and her baby granddaughter as the girl grows into childhood. Walsh's pensive text sets the tone for the pictures, measuring Grandma's pride in her own extraordinary achievements in the Arctic, the desert, and other places "far away" against the wonders she observes as she watches her granddaughter. Underlined with tender humor—baby's wakeful, and messy, and loud, as well as a satisfaction beyond compare—this is an affectionate intergenerational picture book about growing up with someone you love and who loves you back. Its marvelous last portrait shows a confident child ready to embark on expeditions of her own—an obvious but still joyful metaphor for life.

Roger Sutton

SOURCE: A review of *When Grandma Came,* in *The Bulletin of the Center for Children's Books,* Vol. 46, No. 6, February, 1993, p. 196.

When this peripatetic Grandma comes around, she announces her presence with an extravagant comparison to say how happy she is to see her granddaughter: "I have been to Mount Desert Island, far away, and seen the shape of a great whale rolling in the deep . . . but I have never, no never, seen anything as tremendous as you!" Each return visit brings another flattering comparison ("Never, no never") and finds the granddaughter a little older; by the end, the girl is able to respond "I love you too, Grandma." Sweet, soft, gently rounded pastel paintings illustrate this soothing litany, which would make a perfect bedtime story . . . for Grandma. Kids, though, may find the story repetitive and the mood a little *too* cozy.

Books for Keeps

SOURCE: A review of *When Grandma Came,* in *Books for Keeps,* No. 85, March, 1994, p. 9.

A well-travelled and youthful grandmother arrives to live with her new grand-daughter. Grandma compares wonderful beasts from faraway places to the child's wakefulness, messiness, bounciness and so on. This book has a dreamlike quality and we swing from grandmother to child to arctic, jungle, desert or city. There's a delight and wonder throughout the pages and a sense of security as the attachment forms between grandmother and granddaughter. A most unusual and beautiful book recommended for 3-5s and their families.

📖 *MATTHEW AND THE SEA SINGER* (1993)

Emily Melton

SOURCE: A review of *Matthew and the Sea Singer,* in *Booklist,* Vol. 89, No. 16, April 15, 1993, p. 1518.

British author Walsh tells an unusual and strange tale in which a raggedy young orphan boy named Matthew is bought from the orphan master for a shilling by a girl called Birdy. Birdy soon discovers that Matthew has a lovely but untrained voice, so she takes him to the parson, who teaches Matthew to sing so beautifully that all who hear him are reminded of the happiest, most wonderful and comforting things in life. But one day, Matthew is taken deep down to the bottom of the sea by the seal-queen, whose own child can only make horrible screeching noises when it tries to sing. Birdy wants Matthew back, but the seal-queen won't surrender him unless the seal-child is taught to sing as beautifully as Matthew sings. Walsh tells a wonderfully imaginative, humorous, and thoroughly enchanting story, which sounds as if it were part legend, part myth, and part nonsense made up by white whiskered old men sitting in front of blazing fires.

Virginia Opocensky

SOURCE: A review of *Matthew and the Sea Singer,* in *School Library Journal,* Vol. 39, No. 5, May, 1995, p. 90.

Young Birdy pays the orphan master her birthday shilling to rescue a raggedy boy named Matthew. The next morning, she is amazed to hear the lad singing a song without words, too beautiful to be believed. The parson agrees to tutor him to sing Sunday music and soon his angelic voice is enchanting the village folk and all living creatures. When Matthew disappears, Birdy suspects that he has been stolen. She calls the seal-queen, a "half-and-half kind" of creature, up from the sea and strikes a hard bargain with her—the parson must teach one of her pups to sing in return for Matthew's release. It's a struggle transporting the reluctant student to the church and instructing him. When Pagan finally sings, his song conjures up all things dark and terrifying, but is nonetheless beautiful. Together Matthew and Pagan's voices produce a sound so wondrous that listeners can grasp the whole world in their minds. The lyrical text evokes the music of the sea, as do the half-page watercolor paintings in shades of aqua, blue, and shell tones alternating with fog gray. And, in the best folklore tradition, there is a satisfying happy ending to this lovely, quiet story.

Bulletin of the Center for Children's Books

SOURCE: A review of *Matthew and the Sea Singer,* in *The Bulletin of the Center for Children's Books,* Vol. 46, No. 9, May, 1993, pp. 297-98.

"Once there was a little girl called Birdy who paid a shilling for a living boy," saving him from a cruel orphan master on the ferryboat rowed by her father. Thus begins Walsh's companion to *Birdy and the Ghosties,* and the story continues with the compressed pace of a fairy tale, or rather a legend; for the unwanted orphan boy, Matthew, has a golden singing voice that leads to his kidnapping by sealfolk, whose pups sound "like old rocks rubbed together." It's Birdy who rescues Matthew again, refusing the treasure offered by the seal-queen and training a pup to sing (a comic sequence—it stays wet in the church font) as ransom for Matthew's return. The exchange is dramatic when Matthew finally matches his bright voice to the pup's dark one: "You could grasp the whole world in your mind." Like all fairy tales, this one ends happily, with the hint of Birdy's eventual marriage to Matthew, who might still be heard occasionally joining his voice with the seal's at the edge of the sea. Walsh is as effective in layering short stories with depth and style as she is elaborating complex novels. In spite of the text's easy reading level, it will prove less an exercise for practicing readers than an étude for their enjoyment, and Marks' watercolors have a bit of lightly mythic resonance about them, as well as an ambiance of Celtic coastline.

📖 *PEPI AND THE SECRET NAMES* (1994)

Philip Pullman

SOURCE: A review of *Pepi and the Secret Names,* in *Times Educational Supplement,* No. 4089, November 11, 1994, pp. 12.

Here [is a book that demonstrates] . . . the enduring decorative spell which Egypt, the most glamorous of ancient civilisations, has cast over modern Western design. Art Deco factories, Tutankhamun-inspired jewellery, lotus-blossom cocktail cabinets, and, of course, children's books: Egypt is part of us.

Jill Paton Walsh's *Pepi and the Secret Names* engages with the visual directly. Pepi is the son of a painter employed to decorate the tomb of Prince Dhutmose, and he persuades the lion, the crocodile and other fierce beasts to come and pose for his father by revealing that he knows their secret names. The names are shown to us in hieroglyphs, which we can decipher by means of a key at the back.

It's a delightful idea, though I'm not sure how Pepi manages to say them, because you can't speak in hieroglyph any more than you can in sans serif; I'd have been happier if he'd drawn them in the sand. However, the story is both serious and engaging. Art is about dangerous and important matters, as Jill Paton Walsh's work in other forms is showing us with increasing clarity and force, and at the same time it's a source of sensual delight. Fiona French's illustrations have an appropriately Pharaonic sumptuousness and elegance.

The Junior Bookshelf

SOURCE: A review of *Pepi and the Secret Names,* in *The Junior Bookshelf,* Vol. 58, No. 6, December, 1994, p. 200.

[Unity of style is echoed with great subtlety] in a remarkable collaboration between Jill Paton Walsh and Fiona French, each capturing the elegant formality of Ancient Egypt in her characteristic way. Pepi's father is painting the inside of Prince Dhutmose's tomb, he hopes to the satisfaction of the Prince, who is by no means dead. As he paints the god/animal figures Pepi is able to gain the animal's co-operation by his knowledge of the creature's 'secret name'. When the moment comes for the royal inspection the animal models are at hand to confirm their own approval. The secret names are printed in hieroglyphs devised by the author and explained in the final pages. Jill Paton Walsh's story, told with solemnity and quiet eloquence and at greater length than is usual in a picture-book, is complemented most brilliantly in Fiona French's richly coloured, strongly stylized designs which frame the letterpress on every page. It is a book which demands the reader's collaboration as well as his full attention. High intelligence is allied with æsthetic excellence in a rarely stimulating way.

Prue Goodwin

SOURCE: A review of *Pepi and the Secret Names,* in *The School Librarian,* Vol. 43, No. 1, February, 1995, p. 20.

With the combination of talent in its creators, *Pepi and the Secret Names* promised to be something special—and it didn't disappoint.

The book, set in ancient Egypt, tells the story of Pepi's father who is engaged in painting the walls of a tomb which is being prepared for Prince Dhutmose. Pepi realises that the pictures will be more successful if his father paints from live models. There is no problem providing a live goose, but what about a lion, a hawk and a crocodile? Pepi knows the power of 'secret names' and he has the wit to work out each creature's name and use it. One by one the wild creatures agree to sit for Pepi's father and, as a result, the tomb paintings are magnificent.

The 'secret names' are revealed to the reader only in hieroglyphics, but there are clues in the text and an 'alphabet' at the end of the book to help you interpret the symbols. The illustrations have the same impact on the eye as real ancient Egyptian relics, such as the bejewelled face of Tutankhamun. They encompass the written text with images and colours which enhance and develop the unfolding narrative. Both words and pictures remind us that it was the painters, not the princes, who created many of the lasting remains of that mighty civilisation.

This is a beautiful book which can be enjoyed and treasured whatever the age of the reader. It should be available in any collection of books intended to delight and inspire children but especially when they first become independent readers.

Publishers Weekly

SOURCE: A review of *Pepi and the Secret Names,* in *Publishers Weekly,* Vol. 242, No. 11, March 13, 1995, p. 69.

Pyramids, hieroglyphics, secret names, a lowly painter and an exacting pharaoh—the elements of this elegantly illustrated story are ripe with possibilities, but they never cohere. When Pepi's father descends into Prince Dhutmose's tomb to paint the animals that will accompany the prince to the Land of the Dead, Pepi bravely provides him with live models—a lion, hawk, crocodile and cobra for he has guessed their secret names (the point of a secret name, however, is never explained). In the text, the names are presented in hieroglyphics, thus bringing the story to a temporary halt; a code in the back of the book, though not linguistically accurate, allows readers to write English words in hieroglyphics "just for fun." Nor are similarly elaborate details fully integrated into the narrative. Greenaway Medalist French (Anancy and Mr. Dry Bone) combines crisply stylized tomb paintings with child-pleasing caricatures of animals, but the page design sometimes seems frenetic—pale, pastel designs oddly mingling with brightly colored Egyptian motifs. While the writer and the illustrator each-demonstrate individual strengths, text and pictures do little to enhance each other. Ages 6-up.

S. Bates

SOURCE: A review of *Pepi and the Secret Names,* in *Books for Your Children,* Vol. 30, No. 1, Spring, 1995, p. 15.

Pepi's father is employed by Prince Dhutmose to paint and carve animal pictures on the walls of the Great Tomb where eventually the Pharaoh will be buried. The problem is that father works best from real-life studies so Pepi embarks on a campaign to bring all the animals that his father will portray into the tomb. He learns their secret hieroglyphic names—and even manages to entice a lion, a cobra and a crocodile to pose. They weave in and out of doorways giving the impression of all the many chambers inside. A special creature arrives every day too, with Pepi, and she is depicted in every room which particularly pleases the Prince. Jill Paton Walsh's intricate tale of ancient Egypt is matched by stylish, period illustrations from Fiona French. Curious young readers will absorb a great deal of incidental information from this most unusual and attractive treasure-trove of story, illustrations, puzzles and pure entertainment.

Cathryn A. Camper

SOURCE: A review of *Pepi and the Secret Names,* in *School Library Journal,* Vol. 41, No. 4, April, 1995, pp. 119-20.

Pepi's father is an artist who has been commissioned by Egyptian Prince Dhutmose to decorate his royal tomb. To help the man accurately portray creatures like the Lions of the Horizon and Horus the Hawk, Pepi befriends the real-life animals, guesses their secret names, and convinces them to pose for his father. When all the work is completed, Prince Dhutmose is well pleased with the artwork, with Pepi's talent at name-guessing, and with the chance inclusion of the prince's well-loved cat in the many tomb paintings. Based on imagination and fact, this oversized book with its brilliant illustrations in lapis, sand, and crocodile tones will make a good addition to units on ancient Egypt. Kids might also get a kick out of deciphering the hieroglyphics using the key at the back of the book.

Kay Weisman

SOURCE: A review of *Pepi and the Secret Names,* in *Booklist,* Vol. 91, No. 16, April 15, 1995, p. 1501.

Pepi's father, who has been commissioned to decorate the tomb of Prince Dhutmose, likes to work with live models when creating carvings and paintings. The family goose is readily available, but lions, hawks, crocodiles, and cobras are more difficult to procure. Coming to his father's aid, Pepi persuades these wild creatures to pose by guessing each one's secret name (spelled out for readers in hieroglyphics). French's boldly colored illustrations mesh closely with the text and echo both the style and content of Egyptian funereal decorations. She includes representations of several Egyptian gods and symbols, as well as many traditional designs. Children will particularly enjoy searching for the little tabby cat (Prince Dhutmose's pet, Lady Tmiao), who works her way into each portion of the painting. The appended section explaining Egyptian picture writing will encourage young readers to create their own glyphs, making this a valuable addition to classroom units to ancient Egypt.

Kirkus Reviews

SOURCE: A review of *Pepi and the Secret Names,* in *Kirkus Reviews,* Vol. LXIII, No. 8, April 15, 1995, p. 560.

Paton Walsh (**Matthew and the Sea Singer,** 1993, etc.) skillfully synthesizes scary situations, comic twists, and the secret code in an exotic setting radiating from the past.

Pepi's father has been ordered to paint the necessary pictures on the walls of Prince Dhutmose's tomb. When it is time to paint a lion, Pepi, who knows that his father works best when painting from life, goes out to the desert and forces a lion to come to the tomb by guessing its secret name (the name is written in the text as hieroglyphics). By the same process, Pepi brings in other dangerous animals—a hawk, a crocodile, a snake. The story is constructed in the style of a folktale—the first day, second day, third day theme and variations—with elegant loops in the plot, all tied together at the end. An epilogue follows, explaining the principles of hieroglyphic writing and decoding the animals' names. The stylized illustrations are imitations of Egyptian tomb paintings; enclosed in elaborate decorative borders, they depict miniature people and enormous animals sprawled out across intricately detailed spreads.

THOMAS AND THE TINNERS (1995)

Audrey Laski

SOURCE: A review of *Thomas and the Tinners,* in *The School Librarian,* Vol. 43, No. 3, August, 1995, p. 110.

Thomas is an apprentice tin miner who, like all the miners, gets a new name with 'Jack' in it when he begins work. He also, like the other miners, gets a Cornish pasty from Birdy, the ferryman's daughter, who has already appeared in another story by Jill Paton Walsh. But he doesn't get to eat it; he, alone among the miners, can hear the Little People who are starving for want of mortal food, and though Birdy

gives him a bigger pasty every day, they always eat it up, leaving him only a bit of crust. But, as in all good fairy stories, his generosity is rewarded and indeed saves the mine; from 'Prentice Jack' he becomes 'Prospect Jack', and a prosperous man. Jill Paton Walsh tells a simple and satisfying story with clarity; she is not afraid to introduce dialect words in explanatory contexts, or to let detailed descriptions flow, even at the risk of temporarily holding up the story. Alan Marks's pen and wash illustrations, some coloured, some grey and white, admirably complement the telling.

CONNIE CAME TO PLAY (1996)

Stephanie Zvirin

SOURCE: A review of *Connie Came to Play,* in *Booklist,* Vol. 92, Nos. 9-10, January 1, 1996, p. 849.

The concept of sharing is at the heart of this story about two children, one of whom thinks only of himself. "When Connie came to play in Robert's house," Robert wouldn't share his toys. He didn't know how. But Connie really didn't mind; she knew how to play with Robert's toys by using her imagination; and being more generous than her playtime companion, she agreed to include him in her special game by telling him a story. Lambert's pictures convey as much story as the words, but young children may find them a trifle confusing at first, not understanding that the wordless double-spread ones depict Connie's imagination at work. Kids won't misunderstand the clearly expressed emotions on the children's faces, though, and there's a hazy, innocent quality about the art that has great child appeal. The pictures are perfectly attuned to the spare, subtle rendering of a familiar childhood situation.

Kathy Piehl

SOURCE: A review of *Connie Came to Play,* in *School Library Journal,* Vol. 42, No. 2, February, 1996, p. 90.

Walsh and Lambert effectively contrast the limitations of the concrete with the power of imagination. When Connie visits Robert's house, he is determined to keep all his toys to himself. Undaunted, the clever little girl embellishes each object in her mind to create a richer world of make-believe. At last, Robert decides to play with his friend, and Connie shares a story with him. The white backgrounds and simple toys depicted in Robert's portion of the narrative contrast with the lushly colored double-page spreads of Connie's fanciful musings. This juxtaposition recalls John Burningham's books about Shirley (HarperCollins), another girl who excelled at creating her own imagined worlds. Here, text and illustrations work harmoniously to carry viewers through the story. The book may also provide the opportunity to initiate conversations about sharing.

Jo Goodman

SOURCE: A review of *Connie Came to Play,* in *Magpies,* Vol. 11, No. 1, March, 1996, p. 26.

When all the elements in a picture book—text, layout, illustration—are just right the result is serendipitous, a delight to behold. The theme is a familiar one: when Connie visits him Robert does not want to share his toys, but Connie has a terrific imagination, and first the reader, and then Robert, become involved in her games. The illustrations, in clear bright colours with a minimum of detail, are warm and inviting, the moral is understated, the tone is joyful. A lovely book to share.

Roy Blatchford

SOURCE: A review of *Connie Came to Play,* in *Books for Keeps,* No. 106, September, 1997, p. 21.

When Connie comes to play in Robert's house Robert is endlessly possessive of his train, rope, bricks, trumpet, rocking horse and diving set. Connie's way of dealing with this is immediately to imagine herself into another setting where she is riding a *real* train or horse, diving into a *real* deep-sea or building a tower out of *real* bricks.

This intriguingly designed picture book alternates reality and fantasy worlds that are a delight to share with early readers. The expressions on the children's faces and the dreamlike escapism of the fantasy double spreads offer lots of scope for parent and child chat about what belongs to whom. Furthermore, the power of the imagination to take young and old alike into other landscapes is at the golden heart of this book. Composers often talk about the space between the notes; this collaboration of author and illustrator is worth reading both for its economy of narrative *and* the words left off the page!

📖 *WHEN I WAS LITTLE LIKE YOU* (1997)

Kirkus Reviews

SOURCE: A review of *When I Was Little Like You,* in *Kirkus Reviews,* Vol. LXV, No. 20, October 15, 1997, pp. 1585-86.

While on a seaside stroll with her grandmother, Rosie learns how things in her present-day environment compare with the olden days of Gran's time.

Beginning each passage with the refrain, "When I was little like you," Gran describes steam engines that "puffed round the point" and the ice cream that was peddled by a man on a bicycle. Fish was sold right from the dock while swimmers played catch-as-catch-can with the breakers. The simple then-and-now contrasts are ideal for sharing, inviting young listeners to ask questions of their own elders. One constant is the old lighthouse, which looks just the same on fine summer evenings past and present. Walsh provides a finale as sweet as the old-fashioned four-for-a-penny candy in glass jars, when Rosie asks Gran if she liked the world better back then. Gran replies, "The world is more fun by far now it has you in it!" Fuzzy-edged blocks of color form the shapes of uncluttered seascapes and cherubic, rosy-cheeked characters. Puffs of cottony clouds and ice cream, rounded hills, and gently pitched hat brims add to the amiable, pastoral feel of this saunter through summer memories.

Publishers Weekly

SOURCE: A review of *When I Was Little Like You,* in *Publishers Weekly,* Vol. 244, No. 47, November 17, 1997, p. 60.

In this quiet tale, a seaside stroll prompts young Rosie to point out various sights, which trigger a series of recollections by her grandmother. When Rosie sees a diesel train speeding through the valley ("Look Gran. Look at the train, Gran"), for example, Gran tells her, "When I was little like you, a steam engine pulled the cars. It made little homemade clouds as it puffed round the point." After a few more vignettes (the phrases, "Look Gran, look at [that], Gran" and "When I was little like you," recurs in each), Rosie understandably wonders whether "you like the world better, Gran, the way it was when you were little like me?" While Walsh (*Goldengrove*; *Unleaving*) has some lyrical descriptions (Gran remembers buying "a brace of bright mackerel for supper," right off the boat, "still fresh and shining"), her prosaic subject matter lacks the drama and drive to hold the target audience's interest—and the two characters' refrains quickly wear thin. Lambert (*Connie Came to Play*) renders the world in geometric shapes in citrus orange, spring green and blueberry colors, and his gauzy surfaces help to create the overall mood of reminiscence. Yet he offers no stylistic differences between the past and the present (even the clothing of the two eras looks the same), which makes it difficult to decipher any visual distinctions between the two time periods. Ages 2-6.

Beth Tegart

SOURCE: A review of *When I Was Little Like You,* in *School Library Journal,* Vol. 43, No. 12, December, 1997, pp. 102-03.

A delightful story about times past, grandparents, and change. As Rosie and Gran take a stroll through their seaside village, Rosie points out a train, an ice-cream van, boats, a fish shop, a candy store, and surfers. Gran reminisces about how each of those sights was different, "When I was little like you." When they reach the old lighthouse, Gran confides how it looks just the same as when she played there. The two cozily settle in the sand and then she adds, "The world is more fun by far now it has you in it." Lambert's softly muted pastel watercolors depict both modern Rosie and a young Gran delighting in the wonders of daily life as the story shifts from generation to generation. The subtle changes from the present to past are carried out beautifully in the three-quarter and double-page spreads. While curriculum connections are obvious, this title deserves a space in picture-book collections not for how it can be used, but for what it is—a warm, "read it again" story.

Janet Tayler

SOURCE: A review of *When I Was Little Like You,* in *The School Librarian,* Vol. 46, No. 1, Spring, 1998, p. 22.

Rosie and her gran spend the day at the coast together. Gran tells Rosie how it was when she was young, with steam trains, sail boats and an ice-cream man on a bicycle. But this is a comparison with no sense of it having been better in the past. Stephen Lambert's beautiful soft pastel illustrations take us effortlessly back and forth between the present and Gran's childhood. The text has a repetitive pattern which works well with young listeners; and words from a previous generation such as 'brace' and 'farthing' help to evoke a sense of the past.

This gentle story definitely deserves a place in your picture book collection.

Judith Sharman

SOURCE: A review of *When I Was Little Like You,* in *Books for Keeps,* No. 110, May, 1998, p. 21.

Paton Walsh's spare text with its repetition and soft lilting rhythms make gentle if somewhat idyllic, comparisons between Gran's childhood and Rosie's. It is complemented well with Lambert's soft pastel illustrations that reinforce the impression of a lazy afternoon in which Gran has all the time in the world for Rosie. The implicit message, especially important in these times of high tech communication, is that we must not neglect the tradition of passing information from one generation to the next, sharing the cultural changes as well as the things that stay the same, from the landmark lighthouse to the loving relationship between child and grandmother. *When I Was Little Like You* is an ideal gift from grandparents and should also have a special place in classroom collections.

Additional coverage of Paton Walsh's life and career is contained in the following sources published by the Gale Group: *Contemporary Authors New Revision Series,* **Vols. 38, 83;** *Junior Discovering Authors; Major Authors and Illustrators for Children and Young Adults; Something about the Author Autobiography Series,* **Vol. 3; and** *Something about the Author,* **Vols. 4, 72, 109.**

How to Use This Index

The main reference

> **Baum, L(yman) Frank**
> 1856-1919 .... **15**

lists all author entries in this and previous volumes of *Children's Literature Review*.

The cross-references

> See also CA 103; 108; DLB 22; JRDA;
> MAICYA; MTCW; SATA 18; TCLC 7

list all author entries in the following Gale biographical and literary sources:

AAYA = *Authors & Artists for Young Adults*
AITN = *Authors in the News*
BLC = *Black Literature Criticism*
BLCS = *Black Literature Criticism Supplement*
BW = *Black Writers*
CA = *Contemporary Authors*
CAAS = *Contemporary Authors Autobiography Series*
CABS = *Contemporary Authors Bibliographical Series*
CANR = *Contemporary Authors New Revision Series*
CAP = *Contemporary Authors Permanent Series*
CDALB = *Concise Dictionary of American Literary Biography*
CDBLB = *Concise Dictionary of British Literary Biography*
CLC = *Contemporary Literary Criticism*
CMLC = *Classical and Medieval Literature Criticism*
DA = *DISCovering Authors*
DAB = *DISCovering Authors: British*
DAC = *DISCovering Authors: Canadian*
DAM = *DISCovering Authors: Modules*
    DRAM: Dramatists Module; MST: Most-Studied Authors Module;
    MULT: Multicultural Authors Module; NOV: Novelists Module;
    POET: Poets Module; POP: Popular Fiction and Genre Authors Module
DC = *Drama Criticism*
DLB = *Dictionary of Literary Biography*
DLBD = *Dictionary of Literary Biography Documentary Series*
DLBY = *Dictionary of Literary Biography Yearbook*
HLC = *Hispanic Literature Criticism*
HLCS = *Hispanic Literature Criticism Supplement*
HW = *Hispanic Writers*
JRDA = *Junior DISCovering Authors*
LC = *Literature Criticism from 1400 to 1800*
MAICYA = *Major Authors and Illustrators for Children and Young Adults*
MTCW = *Major 20th-Century Writers*
NCLC = *Nineteenth-Century Literature Criticism*
NNAL = *Native North American Literature*
PC = *Poetry Criticism*
SAAS = *Something about the Author Autobiography Series*
SATA = *Something about the Author*
SSC = *Short Story Criticism*
TCLC = *Twentieth-Century Literary Criticism*
WLC = *World Literature Criticism, 1500 to the Present*
WLCS = *World Literature Criticism Supplement*
YABC = *Yesterday's Authors of Books for Children*

CLR Cumulative Author Index

Aardema, Verna 1911- **17**
See also Vugteveen, Verna Aardema
See also MAICYA; SAAS 8; SATA 4, 68, 107

Aaseng, Nate
See Aaseng, Nathan

Aaseng, Nathan 1953- **54**
See also AAYA 27; CA 106; CANR 36; JRDA; MAICYA; SAAS 12; SATA 51, 88; SATA-Brief 38

Abbott, Sarah
See Zolotow, Charlotte S(hapiro)

Achebe, (Albert) Chinua(lumogu) 1930- . **20**
See also AAYA 15; BLC 1; BW 2, 3; CA 1-4R; CANR 6, 26, 47; CLC 1, 3, 5, 7, 11, 26, 51, 75, 127; DA; DAB; DAC; DAM MST, MULT, NOV; DA3; DLB 117; MAICYA; MTCW 1, 2; SATA 38, 40; SATA-Brief 38; WLC

Ada, Alma Flor 1938- **62**
See also CA 123; CANR 87; SATA 43, 84

Adams, Richard (George) 1920- **20**
See also AAYA 16; AITN 1, 2; CA 49-52; CANR 3, 35; CLC 4, 5, 18; DAM NOV; JRDA; MAICYA; MTCW 1, 2; SATA 7, 69

Adelberg, Doris
See Orgel, Doris

Adkins, Jan 1944- **7**
See also CA 33-36R; MAICYA; SAAS 19; SATA 8, 69

Adler, Irving 1913- **27**
See also CA 5-8R; CANR 2, 47; MAICYA; SAAS 15; SATA 1, 29

Adoff, Arnold 1935- **7**
See also AAYA 3; AITN 1; CA 41-44R; CANR 20, 37, 67; JRDA; MAICYA; SAAS 15; SATA 5, 57, 96

Aesop 620(?)B.C.-(?)B.C. **14**
See also CMLC 24; MAICYA; SATA 64

Affabee, Eric
See Stine, R(obert) L(awrence)

Aghill, Gordon
See Silverberg, Robert

Ahlberg, Allan 1938- **18**
See also CA 111; 114; CANR 38, 70; MAICYA; SATA 68; SATA-Brief 35

Ahlberg, Janet 1944-1994 .... **18**
See also CA 111; 114; 147; CANR 79; MAICYA; SATA 68; SATA-Brief 32; SATA-Obit 83

Aiken, Joan (Delano) 1924- **1, 19**
See also AAYA 1, 25; CA 9-12R; 182; CAAE 182; CANR 4, 23, 34, 64; CLC 35; DLB 161; JRDA; MAICYA; MTCW 1; SAAS 1; SATA 2, 30, 73; SATA-Essay 109

Akers, Floyd
See Baum, L(yman) Frank

Alcock, Vivien 1924- **26**
See also AAYA 8; CA 110; CANR 41; JRDA; MAICYA; SATA 45, 76; SATA-Brief 38

Alcott, Louisa May 1832-1888 .... **1, 38**
See also AAYA 20; CDALB 1865-1917; DA; DAB; DAC; DAM MST, NOV; DA3; DLB 1, 42, 79; DLBD 14; JRDA; MAICYA; NCLC 6, 58, 83; SATA 100; SSC 27; WLC; YABC 1

Aldon, Adair
See Meigs, Cornelia Lynde

Alexander, Lloyd (Chudley) 1924- **1, 5, 48**
See also AAYA 1, 27; CA 1-4R; CANR 1, 24, 38, 55; CLC 35; DLB 52; JRDA; MAICYA; MTCW 1; SAAS 19; SATA 3, 49, 81

Aliki **9**
See also Brandenberg, Aliki (Liacouras)

Allan, Mabel Esther 1915-1998 .... **43**
See also CA 5-8R; 167; CANR 2, 18, 47; MAICYA; SAAS 11; SATA 5, 32, 75

Allen, Adam
See Epstein, Beryl (M. Williams); Epstein, Samuel

Allen, Alex B.
See Heide, Florence Parry

Allen, Pamela 1934- **44**
See also CA 126; CANR 53; SATA 50, 81

Andersen, Hans Christian 1805-1875 ..... **6**
See also DA; DAB; DAC; DAM MST, POP; DA3; MAICYA; NCLC 7, 79; SATA 100; SSC 6; WLC; YABC 1

Anderson, Poul (William) 1926- **58**
See also AAYA 5, 34; CA 1-4R; 181; CAAE 181; CAAS 2; CANR 2, 15, 34, 64; CLC 15; DLB 8; INT CANR-15; MTCW 1, 2; SATA 90; SATA-Brief 39; SATA-Essay 106

Angeli, Marguerite (Lofft) de
See de Angeli, Marguerite (Lofft)

Angell, Judie
See Gaberman, Judie Angell

Angelou, Maya 1928- **53**
See also AAYA 7, 20; BLC 1; BW 2, 3; CA 65-68; CANR 19, 42, 65; CDALBS; CLC 12, 35, 64, 77; DA; DAB; DAC; DAM MST, MULT, POET, POP; DA3; DLB 38; MTCW 1, 2; SATA 49; WLCS

Anglund, Joan Walsh 1926- **1**
See also CA 5-8R; CANR 15; SATA 2

Anno, Mitsumasa 1926- **2, 14**
See also CA 49-52; CANR 4, 44; MAICYA; SATA 5, 38, 77

Anthony, John
See Ciardi, John (Anthony)

Ardizzone, Edward (Jeffrey Irving) 1900-1979 .... **3**
See also CA 5-8R; 89-92; CANR 8, 78; DLB 160; MAICYA; SATA 1, 28; SATA-Obit 21

Armstrong, William H(oward) 1914-1999 . **1**
See also AAYA 18; AITN 1; CA 17-20R; 177; CANR 9, 69; JRDA; MAICYA; SAAS 7; SATA 4; SATA-Obit 111

Arnette, Robert
See Silverberg, Robert

Arnold, Caroline 1944- **61**
See also CA 107; CANR 24; SAAS 23; SATA 36, 85; SATA-Brief 34

Arnold, Emily 1939-
See McCully, Emily Arnold
See also CA 109, 180; MAICYA; SATA 50, 76

Arnosky, James Edward 1946- **15**
See also Arnosky, Jim
See also CA 69-72; CANR 12, 32; SATA 22

Arnosky, Jim
See Arnosky, James Edward
See also MAICYA; SATA 70

Arrick, Fran
See Gaberman, Judie Angell
See also CLC 30

Aruego, Jose (Espiritu) 1932- **5**
See also CA 37-40R; CANR 42; MAICYA; SATA 6, 68

Arundel, Honor (Morfydd) 1919-1973 ..... **35**
See also CA 21-22; 41-44R; CAP 2; CLC 17; SATA 4; SATA-Obit 24

Ashabranner, Brent (Kenneth) 1921- **28**
See also AAYA 6; CA 5-8R; CANR 10, 27, 57; JRDA; MAICYA; SAAS 14; SATA 1, 67

Asheron, Sara
See Moore, Lilian

Ashey, Bella
See Breinburg, Petronella

Ashley, Bernard 1935- **4**
See also CA 93-96; CANR 25, 44; MAICYA; SATA 47, 79; SATA-Brief 39

Asimov, Isaac 1920-1992 .... **12**
See also AAYA 13; BEST 90:2; CA 1-4R; 137; CANR 2, 19, 36, 60; CLC 1, 3, 9, 19, 26, 76, 92; DAM POP; DA3; DLB 8; DLBY 92; INT CANR-19; JRDA; MAICYA; MTCW 1, 2; SATA 1, 26, 74

Atwater, Florence (Hasseltine Carroll) 1896-1979 .... **19**
See also CA 135; MAICYA; SATA 16, 66

Atwater, Richard (Tupper) 1892-1948 ..... **19**
See also CA 111; 135; MAICYA; SATA 54, 66; SATA-Brief 27

Avi **24**
See also Wortis, Avi
See also AAYA 10; SATA 71, 108

Awdry, Wilbert Vere 1911-1997 .... **23**
See also CA 103; 157; DLB 160; SATA 94

Aylesworth, Thomas G(ibbons) 1927-1995 .... **6**
See also CA 25-28R; 149; CANR 10, 26; SAAS 17; SATA 4, 88

Author Index

Disch, Thomas M(ichael) 1940- **18**
  See also AAYA 17; CA 21-24R; CAAS 4;
  CANR 17, 36, 54, 89; CLC 7, 36; DA3;
  DLB 8; MAICYA; MTCW 1, 2; SAAS
  15; SATA 92
Disch, Tom
  See Disch, Thomas M(ichael)
Dixon, Franklin W. **61**
  See also CA 17-20R; CANR 27; MAICYA;
  SATA 1, 67, 100
Dixon, Paige
  See Corcoran, Barbara
Doctor X
  See Nourse, Alan E(dward)
Dodd, Lynley (Stuart) 1941- **62**
  See also CA 107; CANR 25, 51; SATA 35,
  86
Dodge, Mary (Elizabeth) Mapes
  1831(?)-1905 .... **62**
  See also CA 109; 137; DLB 42, 79; DLBD
  13; MAICYA; SATA 21, 100
Dodgson, Charles Lutwidge 1832-1898 ..... **2**
  See also Carroll, Lewis
  See also DA; DAB; DAC; DAM MST,
  NOV, POET; DA3; MAICYA; SATA 100;
  YABC 2
Dogyear, Drew
  See Gorey, Edward (St. John)
Doherty, Berlie 1943- **21**
  See also AAYA 18; CA 131; JRDA; MAI-
  CYA; SAAS 16; SATA 72, 111
Domanska, Janina 1913(?)-1995 .... **40**
  See also AITN 1; CA 17-20R; 147; CANR
  11, 45; MAICYA; SAAS 18; SATA 6, 68;
  SATA-Obit 84
Donovan, John 1928-1992 .... **3**
  See also AAYA 20; CA 97-100; 137; CLC
  35; MAICYA; SATA 72; SATA-Brief 29
Dorris, Michael (Anthony) 1945-1997 ..... **58**
  See also AAYA 20; BEST 90:1; CA 102;
  157; CANR 19, 46, 75; CLC 109; DAM
  MULT, NOV; DA3; DLB 175; MTCW 2;
  NNAL; SATA 75; SATA-Obit 94
Dorris, Michael A.
  See Dorris, Michael (Anthony)
Dorritt, Susan
  See Schlein, Miriam
Dorros, Arthur (M.) 1950- **42**
  See also CA 146; SAAS 20; SATA 78
Dowdy, Mrs. Regera
  See Gorey, Edward (St. John)
Doyle, Brian 1935- **22**
  See also AAYA 16; CA 135; CANR 55;
  JRDA; MAICYA; SAAS 16; SATA 67,
  104
Dr. A
  See Asimov, Isaac; Silverstein, Alvin
Dr. Seuss **1, 9, 53**
  See also Geisel, Theodor Seuss; LeSieg,
  Theo.; Seuss, Dr.; Stone, Rosetta
Draper, Sharon M(ills) 1952- **57**
  See also AAYA 28; CA 170; SATA 98
Drapier, M. B.
  See Swift, Jonathan
Drescher, Henrik 1955- **20**
  See also CA 135; MAICYA; SATA 67, 105
Driving Hawk, Virginia
  See Sneve, Virginia Driving Hawk
Drummond, Walter
  See Silverberg, Robert
Dryden, Pamela
  See St. John, Nicole
Duder, Tessa 1940- **43**
  See also CA 147; SAAS 23; SATA 80, 117
Duke, Kate 1956- **51**
  See also SATA 90

Duncan, Lois 1934- **29**
  See also AAYA 4, 34; CA 1-4R; CANR 2,
  23, 36; CLC 26; JRDA; MAICYA; SAAS
  2; SATA 1, 36, 75
Dunne, Marie
  See Clark, Ann Nolan
Duvoisin, Roger Antoine 1904-1980 .... **23**
  See also CA 13-16R; 101; CANR 11; DLB
  61; MAICYA; SATA 2, 30; SATA-Obit 23
Eager, Edward McMaken 1911-1964 .... **43**
  See also CA 73-76; CANR 87; DLB 22;
  MAICYA; SATA 17
Eckert, Horst 1931-
  See Janosch
  See also CA 37-40R; CANR 38; MAICYA;
  SATA 8, 72
Edgy, Wardore
  See Gorey, Edward (St. John)
Edmund, Sean
  See Pringle, Laurence (Patrick)
Edwards, Al
  See Nourse, Alan E(dward)
Ehlert, Lois (Jane) 1934- **28**
  See also CA 137; MAICYA; SATA 35, 69
Eliot, Dan
  See Silverberg, Robert
Ellen, Jaye
  See Nixon, Joan Lowery
Elliot, Don
  See Silverberg, Robert
Elliott, Don
  See Silverberg, Robert
Ellis, Sarah 1952- **42**
  See also CA 123; CANR 50, 84; JRDA;
  SATA 68
Emberley, Barbara A(nne) 1932- **5**
  See also CA 5-8R; CANR 5; MAICYA;
  SATA 8, 70
Emberley, Ed(ward Randolph) 1931- **5**
  See also CA 5-8R; CANR 5, 36, 82; MAI-
  CYA; SATA 8, 70
Ende, Michael (Andreas Helmuth)
  1929-1995 .... **14**
  See also CA 118; 124; 149; CANR 36; CLC
  31; DLB 75; MAICYA; SATA 61; SATA-
  Brief 42; SATA-Obit 86
Engdahl, Sylvia Louise 1933- **2**
  See also CA 29-32R; CANR 14, 85; JRDA;
  MAICYA; SAAS 5; SATA 4
Enright, Elizabeth 1909-1968 .... **4**
  See also CA 61-64; 25-28R; CANR 83;
  DLB 22; MAICYA; SATA 9
Epstein, Beryl (M. Williams) 1910- **26**
  See also CA 5-8R; CANR 2, 18, 39; SAAS
  17; SATA 1, 31
Epstein, Samuel 1909- **26**
  See also CA 9-12R; CANR 4, 18, 39; SAAS
  17; SATA 1, 31
Estes, Eleanor (Ruth) 1906-1988 .... **2**
  See also CA 1-4R; 126; CANR 5, 20, 84;
  DLB 22; JRDA; MAICYA; SATA 7, 91;
  SATA-Obit 56
Estoril, Jean
  See Allan, Mabel Esther
Ets, Marie Hall 1893-1984 .... **33**
  See also CA 1-4R; CANR 4, 83; DLB 22;
  MAICYA; SATA 2
Farjeon, Eleanor 1881-1965 .... **34**
  See also CA 11-12; CAP 1; DLB 160; MAI-
  CYA; SATA 2
Farmer, Penelope (Jane) 1939- **8**
  See also CA 13-16R; CANR 9, 37, 84; DLB
  161; JRDA; MAICYA; SAAS 22; SATA
  40, 105; SATA-Brief 39
Feelings, Muriel (Grey) 1938- **5**
  See also BW 1; CA 93-96; MAICYA;
  SAAS 8; SATA 16

Feelings, Thomas 1933-
  See Feelings, Tom
  See also BW 1; CA 49-52; CANR 25; MAI-
  CYA; SATA 8
Feelings, Tom **5, 58**
  See also Feelings, Thomas
  See also AAYA 25; SAAS 19; SATA 69
Ferry, Charles 1927- **34**
  See also AAYA 29; CA 97-100; CANR 16,
  57; SAAS 20; SATA 43, 92
Field, Rachel (Lyman) 1894-1942 .... **21**
  See also CA 109; 137; CANR 79; DLB 9,
  22; MAICYA; SATA 15
Fine, Anne 1947- **25**
  See also AAYA 20; CA 105; CANR 38, 83;
  JRDA; MAICYA; SAAS 15; SATA 29,
  72, 111
Fisher, Aileen (Lucia) 1906- **49**
  See also CA 5-8R; CANR 2, 17, 37, 84;
  MAICYA; SATA 1, 25, 73
Fisher, Leonard Everett 1924- **18**
  See also CA 1-4R; CANR 2, 37, 77; DLB
  61; MAICYA; SAAS 1; SATA 4, 34, 73
Fisher, Suzanne
  See Staples, Suzanne Fisher
Fitch, John IV
  See Cormier, Robert (Edmund)
Fitzgerald, Captain Hugh
  See Baum, L(yman) Frank
Fitzgerald, John D(ennis) 1907(?)-1988 ..... **1**
  See also CA 93-96; 126; CANR 84; MAI-
  CYA; SATA 20; SATA-Obit 56
Fitzhardinge, Joan Margaret 1912-
  See Phipson, Joan
  See also CA 13-16R; CANR 6, 23, 36;
  MAICYA; SATA 2, 73
Fitzhugh, Louise 1928-1974 .... **1**
  See also AAYA 18; CA 29-32; 53-56;
  CANR 34, 84; CAP 2; DLB 52; JRDA;
  MAICYA; SATA 1, 45; SATA-Obit 24
Flack, Marjorie 1897-1958 .... **28**
  See also CA 112; 136; CANR 84; MAI-
  CYA; SATA 100; YABC 2
Fleischman, Paul 1952- **20**
  See also AAYA 11; CA 113; CANR 37, 84;
  JRDA; MAICYA; SAAS 20; SATA 39,
  72, 110; SATA-Brief 32
Fleischman, (Albert) Sid(ney) 1920- **1, 15**
  See also CA 1-4R; CANR 5, 37, 67; JRDA;
  MAICYA; SATA 8, 59, 96
Forbes, Esther 1891-1967 .... **27**
  See also AAYA 17; CA 13-14; 25-28R; CAP
  1; CLC 12; DLB 22; JRDA; MAICYA;
  SATA 2, 100
Foreman, Michael 1938- **32**
  See also CA 21-24R; CANR 10, 38, 68;
  MAICYA; SAAS 21; SATA 2, 73
Foster, Genevieve Stump 1893-1979 .... **7**
  See also CA 5-8R; 89-92; CANR 4; DLB
  61; MAICYA; SATA 2; SATA-Obit 23
Fox, J. N.
  See Janeczko, Paul B(ryan)
Fox, Mem **23**
  See also Fox, Merrion Frances
  See also MAICYA; SATA 103
Fox, Merrion Frances 1946-
  See Fox, Mem
  See also CA 127; CANR 84; SATA 51
Fox, Paula 1923- **1, 44**
  See also AAYA 3; CA 73-76; CANR 20,
  36, 62; CLC 2, 8, 121; DLB 52; JRDA;
  MAICYA; MTCW 1, 60
Freedman, Russell (Bruce) 1929- **20**
  See also AAYA 4, 24; CA 17-20R; CANR
  7, 23, 46, 81; JRDA; MAICYA; SATA 16,
  71
Freeman, Don 1908-1978 .... **30**
  See also CA 77-80; CANR 44; MAICYA;
  SATA 17

Hamley, Dennis 1935- **47**
　　See also CA 57-60; CANR 11, 26; SAAS
　　22; SATA 39, 69
Handford, Martin (John) 1956- **22**
　　See also CA 137; MAICYA; SATA 64
Hanel, Wolfram
　　See Haenel, Wolfram
Hansen, Joyce (Viola) 1942- **21**
　　See also BW 2; CA 105; CANR 43, 87;
　　JRDA; MAICYA; SAAS 15; SATA 46,
　　101; SATA-Brief 39
Hargrave, Leonie
　　See Disch, Thomas M(ichael)
Harris, Christie (Lucy) Irwin 1907- **47**
　　See also CA 5-8R; CANR 6, 83; CLC 12;
　　DLB 88; JRDA; MAICYA; SAAS 10;
　　SATA 6, 74; SATA-Essay 116
Harris, Joel Chandler 1848-1908 .... **49**
　　See also CA 104; 137; CANR 80; DLB 11,
　　23, 42, 78, 91; MAICYA; SATA 100; SSC
　　19; TCLC 2; YABC 1
Harris, Lavinia
　　See St. John, Nicole
Harris, Rosemary (Jeanne) **30**
　　See also CA 33-36R; CANR 13, 30, 84;
　　SAAS 7; SATA 4, 82
Hartling, Peter **29**
　　See also Haertling, Peter
　　See also DLB 75
Haskins, James S. 1941- **3, 39**
　　See also Haskins, Jim
　　See also AAYA 14; BW 2, 3; CA 33-36R;
　　CANR 25, 48, 79; JRDA; MAICYA;
　　SATA 9, 69, 105
Haskins, Jim
　　See Haskins, James S.
　　See also SAAS 4
Haugaard, Erik Christian 1923- **11**
　　See also CA 5-8R; CANR 3, 38; JRDA;
　　MAICYA; SAAS 12; SATA 4, 68
Hautzig, Esther Rudomin 1930- **22**
　　See also CA 1-4R; CANR 5, 20, 46, 85;
　　JRDA; MAICYA; SAAS 15; SATA 4, 68
Hay, Timothy
　　See Brown, Margaret Wise
Hays, Wilma Pitchford 1909- **59**
　　See also CA 1-4R; CANR 5, 45; MAICYA;
　　SAAS 3; SATA 1, 28
Haywood, Carolyn 1898-1990 .... **22**
　　See also CA 5-8R; 130; CANR 5, 20, 83;
　　MAICYA; SATA 1, 29, 75; SATA-Obit 64
Heide, Florence Parry 1919- **60**
　　See also CA 93-96; CANR 84; JRDA; MAI-
　　CYA; SAAS 6; SATA 32, 69
Heine, Helme 1941- **18**
　　See also CA 135; MAICYA; SATA 67
Henkes, Kevin 1960- **23**
　　See also CA 114; CANR 38; MAICYA;
　　SATA 43, 76, 108
Henry, Marguerite 1902-1997 .... **4**
　　See also CA 17-20R; 162; CANR 9; DLB
　　22; JRDA; MAICYA; SAAS 7; SATA
　　100; SATA-Obit 99
Hentoff, Nat(han Irving) 1925- **1, 52**
　　See also AAYA 4; CA 1-4R; CAAS 6;
　　CANR 5, 25, 77; CLC 26; INT CANR-
　　25; JRDA; MAICYA; SATA 42, 69;
　　SATA-Brief 27
Herge **6**
　　See also Remi, Georges
Hesse, Karen 1952- **54**
　　See also AAYA 27; CA 168; SAAS 25;
　　SATA 74, 103; SATA-Essay 113
Highwater, Jamake (Mamake) 1942(?)- .. **17**
　　See also AAYA 7; CA 65-68; CAAS 7;
　　CANR 10, 34, 84; CLC 12; DLB 52;
　　DLBY 85; JRDA; MAICYA; SATA 32,
　　69; SATA-Brief 30

Hill, Eric 1927- **13**
　　See also CA 134; MAICYA; SATA 66;
　　SATA-Brief 53
Hilton, Margaret Lynette 1946-
　　See Hilton, Nette
　　See also CA 136; SATA 68, 105
Hilton, Nette **25**
　　See also Hilton, Margaret Lynette
　　See also SAAS 21
Hinton, S(usan) E(loise) 1950- **3, 23**
　　See also AAYA 2, 33; CA 81-84; CANR
　　32, 62; CDALBS; CLC 30, 111; DA;
　　DAB; DAC; DAM MST, NOV; DA3;
　　JRDA; MAICYA; MTCW 1, 2; SATA 19,
　　58, 115
Hitz, Demi 1942- **58**
　　See also CA 61-64; CANR 8, 35; MAICYA;
　　SATA 11, 66, 102
Ho, Minfong 1951- **28**
　　See also AAYA 29; CA 77-80; CANR 67;
　　SATA 15, 94
Hoban, Russell (Conwell) 1925- **3**
　　See also CA 5-8R; CANR 23, 37, 66; CLC
　　7, 25; DAM NOV; DLB 52; MAICYA;
　　MTCW 1, 2; SATA 1, 40, 78
Hoban, Tana **13**
　　See also CA 93-96; CANR 23; MAICYA;
　　SAAS 12; SATA 22, 70, 104
Hobbs, Will 1947- **59**
　　See also AAYA 14; SATA 72, 110
Hoberman, Mary Ann 1930- **22**
　　See also CA 41-44R; MAICYA; SAAS 18;
　　SATA 5, 72, 111
Hogrogian, Nonny 1932- **2**
　　See also CA 45-48; CANR 2, 49; MAICYA;
　　SAAS 1; SATA 7, 74
Holland, Isabelle 1920- **57**
　　See also AAYA 11; CA 21-24R, 181; CAAE
　　181; CANR 10, 25, 47; CLC 21; JRDA;
　　MAICYA; SATA 8, 70; SATA-Essay 103
Hollander, Paul
　　See Silverberg, Robert
Holling, Holling C(lancy) 1900-1973 .... **50**
　　See also CA 106; MAICYA; SATA 15;
　　SATA-Obit 26
Holton, Leonard
　　See Wibberley, Leonard (Patrick O'Connor)
Hopkins, Lee Bennett 1938- **44**
　　See also AAYA 18; CA 25-28R; CANR 29,
　　55; JRDA; MAICYA; SAAS 4; SATA 3,
　　68
Houston, James A(rchibald) 1921- **3**
　　See also AAYA 18; CA 65-68; CANR 38,
　　60; DAC; DAM MST; JRDA; MAICYA;
　　SAAS 17; SATA 13, 74
Howe, James 1946- **9**
　　See also CA 105; CANR 22, 46, 71; JRDA;
　　MAICYA; SATA 29, 71, 111
Howker, Janni 1957- **14**
　　See also AAYA 9; CA 137; JRDA; MAI-
　　CYA; SAAS 13; SATA 72; SATA-Brief
　　46
Hudson, Jan 1954-1990 .... **40**
　　See also AAYA 22; CA 136; JRDA; SATA
　　77
Hughes, Edward James
　　See Hughes, Ted
　　See also DAM MST, POET; DA3
Hughes, (James) Langston 1902-1967 ...... **17**
　　See also AAYA 12; BLC 2; BW 1, 3; CA
　　1-4R; 25-28R; CANR 1, 34, 82; CDALB
　　1929-1941; CLC 1, 5, 10, 15, 35, 44, 108;
　　DA; DAB; DAC; DAM DRAM, MST,
　　MULT, POET; DA3; DC 3; DLB 4, 7, 48,
　　51, 86; JRDA; MAICYA; MTCW 1, 2;
　　PC 1; SATA 4, 33; SSC 6; WLC

Hughes, Monica (Ince) 1925- **9, 60**
　　See also AAYA 19; CA 77-80; CANR 23,
　　46; JRDA; MAICYA; SAAS 11; SATA
　　15, 70
Hughes, Shirley 1927- **15**
　　See also CA 85-88; CANR 24, 47; MAI-
　　CYA; SATA 16, 70, 110
Hughes, Ted 1930-1998 .... **3**
　　See also Hughes, Edward James
　　See also CA 1-4R; 171; CANR 1, 33, 66;
　　CLC 2, 4, 9, 14, 37, 119; DAB; DAC;
　　DLB 40, 161; MAICYA; MTCW 1, 2; PC
　　7; SATA 49; SATA-Brief 27; SATA-Obit
　　107
Hungerford, Pixie
　　See Brinsmead, H(esba) F(ay)
Hunt, Francesca
　　See Holland, Isabelle
Hunt, Irene 1907- **1**
　　See also AAYA 18; CA 17-20R; CANR 8,
　　57; DLB 52; JRDA; MAICYA; SATA 2,
　　91
Hunter, Kristin (Eggleston) 1931- **3**
　　See also AITN 1; BW 1; CA 13-16R;
　　CANR 13; CLC 35; DLB 33; INT CANR-
　　13; MAICYA; SAAS 10; SATA 12
Hunter, Mollie 1922- **25**
　　See also McIlwraith, Maureen Mollie
　　Hunter
　　See also AAYA 13; CANR 37, 78; CLC 21;
　　DLB 161; JRDA; MAICYA; SAAS 7;
　　SATA 54, 106
Hurd, Clement (G.) 1908-1988 .... **49**
　　See also CA 29-32R; 124; CANR 9, 24;
　　MAICYA; SATA 2, 64; SATA-Obit 54
Hurd, Edith (Thacher) 1910-1997 .... **49**
　　See also CA 13-16R; 156; CANR 9, 24;
　　MAICYA; SAAS 13; SATA 2, 64; SATA-
　　Obit 95
Hurmence, Belinda 1921- **25**
　　See also AAYA 17; CA 145; JRDA; SAAS
　　20; SATA 77
Hutchins, Pat 1942- **20**
　　See also CA 81-84; CANR 15, 32, 64; MAI-
　　CYA; SAAS 16; SATA 15, 70, 111
Hyde, Margaret O(ldroyd) 1917- **23**
　　See also CA 1-4R; CANR 1, 36; CLC 21;
　　JRDA; MAICYA; SAAS 8; SATA 1, 42,
　　76
Hyman, Trina Schart 1939- **50**
　　See also CA 49-52; CANR 2, 36, 70; DLB
　　61; MAICYA; SATA 7, 46, 95
Ichikawa, Satomi 1949- **62**
　　See also CA 116; 126; SATA 47, 78; SATA-
　　Brief 36
Innocenti, Roberto 1940- **56**
　　See also SATA 96
Irving, Robert
　　See Adler, Irving
Irwin, Ann(abelle Bowen) 1915-1998 .... **40**
　　See also Irwin, Hadley
　　See also CA 101; 170; CANR 19, 36; MAI-
　　CYA; SATA 44, 89; SATA-Brief 38;
　　SATA-Obit 106
Irwin, Hadley **40**
　　See also Hadley, Lee; Irwin, Ann(abelle
　　Bowen)
　　See also AAYA 13; SAAS 14
Isadora, Rachel 1953(?)- **7**
　　See also CA 111; 137; MAICYA; SATA 54,
　　79; SATA-Brief 32
Iwamatsu, Jun Atsushi 1908-1994
　　See Yashima, Taro
　　See also CA 73-76; 146; CANR 45; MAI-
　　CYA; SATA 14, 81

CLR Cumulative Nationality Index

AMERICAN

Aardema, Verna **17**
Aaseng, Nathan **54**
Adkins, Jan **7**
Adler, Irving **27**
Adoff, Arnold **7**
Alcott, Louisa May **1, 38**
Alexander, Lloyd (Chudley) **1, 5, 48**
Aliki **9**
Anderson, Poul (William) **58**
Angelou, Maya **53**
Anglund, Joan Walsh **1**
Armstrong, William H(oward) **1**
Arnold, Caroline **61**
Arnosky, James Edward **15**
Aruego, Jose (Espiritu) **5**
Ashabranner, Brent (Kenneth) **28**
Asimov, Isaac **12**
Atwater, Florence (Hasseltine Carroll) **19**
Atwater, Richard (Tupper) **19**
Avi **24**
Aylesworth, Thomas G(ibbons) **6**
Babbitt, Natalie (Zane Moore) **2, 53**
Bacon, Martha Sherman **3**
Ballard, Robert D(uane) **60**
Bang, Molly Garrett **8**
Baum, L(yman) Frank **15**
Baylor, Byrd **3**
Bellairs, John (A.) **37**
Bemelmans, Ludwig **6**
Benary-Isbert, Margot **12**
Bendick, Jeanne **5**
Berenstain, Jan(ice) **19**
Berenstain, Stan(ley) **19**
Berger, Melvin H. **32**
Bess, Clayton **39**
Bethancourt, T. Ernesto **3**
Block, Francesca Lia **33**
Blos, Joan W(insor) **18**
Blumberg, Rhoda **21**
Blume, Judy (Sussman) **2, 15**
Bogart, Jo Ellen **59**
Bond, Nancy (Barbara) **11**
Bontemps, Arna(ud Wendell) **6**
Bova, Ben(jamin William) **3**
Boyd, Candy Dawson **50**
Brancato, Robin F(idler) **32**
Branley, Franklyn M(ansfield) **13**
Brett, Jan (Churchill) **27**
Bridgers, Sue Ellen **18**
Brink, Carol Ryrie **30**
Brooks, Bruce **25**
Brooks, Gwendolyn **27**
Brown, Marcia **12**
Brown, Marc (Tolon) **29**
Brown, Margaret Wise **10**
Bruchac, Joseph III **46**
Bryan, Ashley F. **18**
Bunting, Eve **28, 56**
Burch, Robert J(oseph) **63**
Burnett, Frances (Eliza) Hodgson **24**
Burton, Virginia Lee **11**

Butler, Octavia E(stelle) **65**
Byars, Betsy (Cromer) **1, 16**
Caines, Jeannette (Franklin) **24**
Calhoun, Mary **42**
Cameron, Eleanor (Frances) **1**
Carle, Eric **10**
Carter, Alden R(ichardson) **22**
Cassedy, Sylvia **26**
Charlip, Remy **8**
Childress, Alice **14**
Choi, Sook Nyul **53**
Christopher, Matt(hew Frederick) **33**
Ciardi, John (Anthony) **19**
Clark, Ann Nolan **16**
Cleary, Beverly (Atlee Bunn) **2, 8**
Cleaver, Bill **6**
Cleaver, Vera (Allen) **6**
Clifton, (Thelma) Lucille **5**
Coatsworth, Elizabeth (Jane) **2**
Cobb, Vicki **2**
Cohen, Daniel (E.) **3, 43**
Cole, Brock **18**
Cole, Joanna **5, 40**
Collier, James L(incoln) **3**
Colum, Padraic **36**
Conford, Ellen **10**
Conrad, Pam **18**
Cooney, Barbara **23**
Cooper, Floyd **60**
Corbett, Scott **1**
Corcoran, Barbara **50**
Cormier, Robert (Edmund) **12, 55**
Cox, Palmer **24**
Creech, Sharon **42**
Crews, Donald **7**
Crutcher, Chris(topher C.) **28**
Cummings, Pat (Marie) **48**
Curry, Jane L(ouise) **31**
Cushman, Karen **55**
Dalgliesh, Alice **62**
Danziger, Paula **20**
d'Aulaire, Edgar Parin **21**
d'Aulaire, Ingri (Mortenson Parin) **21**
Davis, Ossie **56**
Day, Alexandra **22**
de Angeli, Marguerite (Lofft) **1**
DeClements, Barthe **23**
DeJong, Meindert **1**
Denslow, W(illiam) W(allace) **15**
dePaola, Tomie **4, 24**
Diaz, David **65**
Dillon, Diane (Claire) **44**
Dillon, Leo **44**
Disch, Thomas M(ichael) **18**
Dixon, Franklin W. **61**
Dodge, Mary (Elizabeth) Mapes **62**
Domanska, Janina **40**
Donovan, John **3**
Dorris, Michael (Anthony) **58**
Dorros, Arthur (M.) **42**
Draper, Sharon M(ills) **57**
Dr. Seuss **1, 9, 53**
Duke, Kate **51**

Duncan, Lois **29**
Duvoisin, Roger Antoine **23**
Eager, Edward McMaken **43**
Ehlert, Lois (Jane) **28**
Emberley, Barbara A(nne) **5**
Emberley, Ed(ward Randolph) **5**
Engdahl, Sylvia Louise **2**
L'Engle, Madeleine (Camp Franklin) **1, 14, 57**
Enright, Elizabeth **4**
Epstein, Beryl (M. Williams) **26**
Epstein, Samuel **26**
Estes, Eleanor (Ruth) **2**
Ets, Marie Hall **33**
Feelings, Muriel (Grey) **5**
Feelings, Tom **5, 58**
Ferry, Charles **34**
Field, Rachel (Lyman) **21**
Fisher, Aileen (Lucia) **49**
Fisher, Leonard Everett **18**
Fitzgerald, John D(ennis) **1**
Fitzhugh, Louise **1**
Flack, Marjorie **28**
Fleischman, (Albert) Sid(ney) **1, 15**
Fleischman, Paul **20**
Forbes, Esther **27**
Foster, Genevieve Stump **7**
Fox, Paula **1, 44**
Freedman, Russell (Bruce) **20**
Freeman, Don **30**
Fritz, Jean (Guttery) **2, 14**
Fujikawa, Gyo **25**
Gaberman, Judie Angell **33**
Gag, Wanda (Hazel) **4**
Gaines, Ernest J(ames) **62**
Galdone, Paul **16**
Gallant, Roy A(rthur) **30**
Gantos, Jack **18**
Garden, Nancy **51**
Gauch, Patricia Lee **56**
Geisel, Theodor Seuss **53**
George, Jean Craighead **1**
Gibbons, Gail **8**
Giblin, James Cross **29**
Giovanni, Nikki **6**
Glenn, Mel **51**
Glubok, Shirley (Astor) **1**
Goble, Paul **21**
Goffstein, (Marilyn) Brooke **3**
Gordon, Sheila **27**
Gorey, Edward (St. John) **36**
Graham, Lorenz (Bell) **10**
Gramatky, Hardie **22**
Greene, Bette **2**
Greene, Constance C(larke) **62**
Greenfield, Eloise **4, 38**
Grifalconi, Ann **35**
Grimes, Nikki **42**
Gruelle, Johnny **34**
Guy, Rosa (Cuthbert) **13**
Hadley, Lee **40**
Haley, Gail E(inhart) **21**
Hamilton, Virginia **1, 11, 40**

Nationality Index

CLR Cumulative Title Index

Title Index

Title Index

Title Index

Title Index

Title Index

Title Index

Title Index

Title Index

Title Index

Title Index

Title Index

Title Index

ISBN 0-7876-4571-0

90000